OXFORD MONOGRAPHS IN
INTERNATIONAL LAW

General Editors

PROFESSOR VAUGHAN LOWE QC
*Chichele Professor of Public International Law in the University of Oxford and
Fellow of All Souls College, Oxford*

PROFESSOR DAN SAROOSHI
*Professor of Public International Law in the University of Oxford and
Fellow of The Queen's College, Oxford*

PROFESSOR STEFAN TALMON
*Professor of Public International Law in the University of Oxford and
Fellow of St. Anne's College, Oxford*

Disobeying the Security Council

OXFORD MONOGRAPHS IN INTERNATIONAL LAW

The aim of this series is to publish important and original pieces of research on all aspects of international law. Topics that are given particular prominence are those which, while of interest to the academic lawyer, also have important bearing on issues which touch the actual conduct of international relations. Nonetheless, the series is wide in scope and includes monographs on the history and philosophical foundations of international law.

Disobeying the Security Council

Countermeasures against Wrongful Sanctions

ANTONIOS TZANAKOPOULOS

OXFORD

UNIVERSITY PRESS

OXFORD
UNIVERSITY PRESS

Great Clarendon Street, Oxford OX2 6DP

Oxford University Press is a department of the University of Oxford.
It furthers the University's objective of excellence in research, scholarship,
and education by publishing worldwide in

Oxford New York

Auckland Cape Town Dar es Salaam Hong Kong Karachi
Kuala Lumpur Madrid Melbourne Mexico City Nairobi
New Delhi Shanghai Taipei Toronto

With offices in

Argentina Austria Brazil Chile Czech Republic France Greece
Guatemala Hungary Italy Japan Poland Portugal Singapore
South Korea Switzerland Thailand Turkey Ukraine Vietnam

Oxford is a registered trade mark of Oxford University Press
in the UK and in certain other countries

Published in the United States
by Oxford University Press Inc., New York

© Antonios Tzanakopoulos, 2011

British Library Cataloguing-in-Publication Data
Data available

Library of Congress Cataloging in Publication Data
Data available

Typeset by Newgen Imaging Systems (P) Ltd., Chennai, India
Printed and bound by
CPI Group (UK) Ltd,
Croydon, CR0 4YY

ISBN 978–0–19–960076–2

5 7 9 10 8 6 4

General Editors' Preface

Multilateralism and the United Nations are, in the liberal canon, regarded as good things. But there is an increasing realization that there is an associated danger arising from the propensity of States to deflect legal challenges to their actions by claiming that they were only obeying orders—the orders of the Security Council. What may begin as a socially- and politically-responsible desire to act collectively in the face of international threats may result in the shifting of responsibility onto the shoulders of a body that is, for practical purposes, beyond legal and political accountability to the individuals whose lives it touches.

Few would seek to argue against the proposition that the United Nations must itself be subject to at least some legal constraints upon its powers; but the implementation of that view is a matter of considerable complexity and difficulty. This incisive study by Dr Tzanakopoulos is a very significant contribution to the debate, combining intellectual acuity with a clear-eyed perception that—as the final clause of the Greek Constitution bravely insists—the ultimate guarantee of the maintenance of the Rule of Law lies in the hands of the citizen and in the right and duty to resist its subversion.

AVL

Oxford, 29 October 2010

Preface and Acknowledgements

The measures taken and the obligations imposed by the United Nations Security Council on Member States of the organization under Article 41 of the UN Charter are one of the few, but increasingly significant, instances where an international organization may exercise 'sovereign' or 'governmental' powers. Reading about it as a graduate student, I could not help but notice the amount of attention paid in scholarly writings to the 'limits' of the powers exercised by the Security Council or to the power of 'judicial review' of the International Court of Justice over Security Council decisions. Still there was no comprehensive debate of what happens if the Security Council goes beyond the alleged limits to its powers, or of who can actually find the Council to have gone beyond those limits if—as is to be expected—the International Court does not become involved. In that realization I had found an interesting—if challenging—project.

This book, which is an updated version of the DPhil thesis I defended at the University of Oxford in October 2009, aims to tackle the imposition of non-forcible measures under Article 41 of the UN Charter in a comprehensive manner, approaching the issue from the perspective of international responsibility. It thus deals not only with how the imposition of 'sanctions' may engage the responsibility of the UN (Part I), but also with how—and by whom—this engagement is determined to have taken place (Part II). Most importantly, however, it discusses at length the possibilities for implementation of the UN's international responsibility for wrongful sanctions. It argues that the *ultima ratio*—the right of 'last resort'—of disobedience to the Security Council's order is a response provided for by law, and can be qualified as a countermeasure taken against the international organization (Part III). I have sought to bring the manuscript up to date with the cut-off set at 1 June 2010.

In the long process of completing my DPhil thesis and the manuscript for this book, I have incurred many debts. Acknowledging all the people and institutions whose help has proved invaluable over the last five years would make for a much longer note. Still, there are some whose help was absolutely crucial, a *sine qua non*, for this project to come to fruition.

My doctoral research at the University of Oxford was supervised by Professor Stefan Talmon. To Professor Talmon I owe enormous gratitude—his guidance is much more than any graduate student could ever wish for; his friendship more than what one could hope for. He was there in good and bad times, pushing me to my limits but also supporting me and encouraging me when I needed a helping hand. I only wish that I will be as good a supervisor to my students as Stefan was to me. Thank you.

Professor Vaughan Lowe QC, the Chichele Professor of International Law at the University of Oxford, is so much more than a sharp lawyer. He is a true teacher and a fascinating thinker. I hope that I will continue to live up to his expectations. His (and Sally's) hospitality, and the company of Meg and Triggs, provided me with some of the most relaxing and refreshing moments during my time in Oxford, and afterwards.

At the University of Oxford I should also like to thank Professor Dan Sarooshi, Professor Guy Goodwin-Gill, and Dapo Akande. Their input—at different times and on different issues—was extremely helpful and I feel my work is better for it. My teachers at the University of Athens, my *alma mater*, merit special mention. In particular I wish to thank Professors Emmanuel Roucounas, Angelos Yiokaris, Antonios Bredimas, Linos-Alexander Sicilianos, Photini Pazartzis, Lena Divani, Maria Gavouneli, Lina Kouskouna, and Achilles Skordas (now at the University of Bristol), as well as Aspasia Zirou and the team at the International Studies Department of the School of Law.

At the NYU School of Law, where the idea for this project was born while I was reading towards an LLM degree, I am indebted to the late Professor Tom Franck who taught me 'Constitutional Law of the UN', together with Professor Simon Chesterman, who also supervised my LLM thesis on an early version of the subject that was to become this book; but also to Professors Joseph Weiler, Benedict Kingsbury, and Philip Alston. Many thanks are due to Professor Giorgio Gaja, whose assistant I was during the 2005 session of the International Law Commission, an internship that was made possible by NYU's generous funding.

Professors Erika de Wet and August Reinisch helped in different but equally important ways, and for this I thank them. Professor Christian J Tams at the University of Glasgow was a great help and a great friend during the last stages of preparation of the manuscript, as were Drs Akbar Rasulov and James Sloan. Everyone should be so lucky to work among such a talented and friendly team of colleagues.

The DPhil thesis that has become this book could not have been completed without the generous support of IKY, the Hellenic State Scholarship Foundation, which granted me a scholarship for doctoral studies between 2006 and 2009. The Arts and Humanities Research Council in the UK complemented this support through a fees-only grant for doctoral studies. My College, St Anne's, and the University of Oxford have provided me with various small grants, as well as with many opportunities for research. To all of them, many thanks are due. I should also thank Ruth Bird and the staff at the Bodleian Law Library, which was my second—if not my first—home during my years in Oxford, as well as the porters of the St Cross Building who shared the occasional smoke and chatted with me during breaks.

Special thanks are of course due to Oxford University Press and its Delegates, as well as personally to John Louth, Merel Alstein, Lucy Page, and Joy Ruskin-Tompkins for their careful work and their help and support in turning the manuscript into a book.

My friends in Oxford, New York, Athens, and elsewhere, helped me in various ways. I will take the liberty of singling out Gleider Hernández, Markos Karavias, Mehmet Karlı, Mārtiņš Paparinskis, James Upcher, Lema Uyar, Farid Ahmadov, Omer Bekerman, and Keren Michaeli, as well as Loukas and Christina Moutsiana,

Abigael Baldoumas, Samir Bhatt, Nabil and Rachel Hamdi, Eugenia Balamoti, and Stella Sarma.

Last but certainly not least, I would like to thank my family, and in particular my dad Moschos, my siblings Dimitris and Maria, and aunt Tassia, for their unwavering love and support throughout the years; as well as Lily, who has endured much of the burden that I was during the various phases of completing my doctorate. This book is dedicated to them, and to the loving memory of my mom Lopa.

AT
University of Glasgow
June 2010

Contents

III THE CONSEQUENCES OF RESPONSIBILITY

Table of Cases

INTERNATIONAL COURTS AND TRIBUNALS

International Tribunal for the Law of the Sea

World Trade Organization Dispute Settlement Body

Table of Other Primary Authorities

List of Abbreviations

AB	Appellate Body (WTO)
ACP	African, Caribbean and Pacific Group of States
AFDI	Annuaire français de droit international
A-G	Advocate-General (ECJ)
AIDI	Annuaire de l'Institut de droit international
AJIL	American Journal of International Law
AO(s)	Advisory Opinion(s)
APSR	American Political Science Review
ARSIWA	Articles on the Responsibility of States for
(and Commentary)	Internationally Wrongful Acts in UN Doc A/56/10 (2001); (2001) II(2) YILC 26 (and Commentary ibid 31)
ARSP	Archiv für Rechts- und Sozialphilosophie
ASILProc	Proceedings of the Annual Meeting of the American Society of International Law
ATCA	Alien Tort Claims Act (US)
AVR	Archiv des Völkerrechts
AYIL	Australian Year Book of International Law
BDGVR	Berichte der Deutschen Gesellschaft für Völkerrecht
BIICL	British Institute of International and Comparative Law
BVerfG	Bundesverfassungsgericht (Federal Constitutional Court—Federal Republic of Germany)
BVerfGE	Entscheidungen des Bundesverfassungsgerichts
BYIL	British Year Book of International Law
CESCR	Committee on Economic, Social and Cultural Rights (ICESCR)
CFI	Court of First Instance of the European Communities
CFSP	Common Foreign and Security Policy (EU)
Charte Commentaire	J-P Cot and A Pellet (eds), *La Charte des Nations Unies—Commentaire article par article* (Economica, Paris 1985)
Charte Commentaire (2005)	J-P Cot, A Pellet, and M Forteau (eds), *La Charte des Nations Unies—Commentaire article par article* (3rd edn, Economica, Paris 2005)
Charter Commentary	B Simma (ed), *The UN Charter: A Commentary* (2nd edn, OUP, Oxford 2002)
ChicJIL	Chicago Journal of International Law
CJIL	Chinese Journal of International Law
CJTL	Columbia Journal of Transnational Law
CLP	Current Legal Problems
CMLRev	Common Market Law Review
CPA	Coalition Provisional Authority (Iraq)
CYIL	Canadian Yearbook of International Law/Annuaire canadien de droit international

DARIO   Draft Articles on the Responsibility of International Organizations
                adopted on first reading and reproduced in UN Doc A/64/10
                (2009) 19
DC   Drafting Committee (International Law Commission)
diss op   dissenting opinion
DPRK   Democratic People's Republic of Korea
DR   Decisions and Reports (European Commission of
                Human Rights)
DSB   Dispute Settlement Body (WTO)
DSU   Dispute Settlement Understanding (WTO)
Dutchbat   Dutch Battalion (UNPROFOR Srebrenica)

EC   European Community/European Communities
ECCC   Extraordinary Chambers in the Courts of Cambodia
ECHR   European Convention of Human Rights and
                Fundamental Freedoms
ECJ   Court of Justice of the European Communities
ECOMOG   ECOWAS Monitoring Group
ECOSOC   Economic and Social Council (UN)
ECOWAS   Economic Community of West African States
ECtHR   European Court of Human Rights (ECHR)
ed(s)   editor(s)
EJIL   European Journal of International Law
EJIL: Talk!   Blog of the European Journal of International law
                <http://www.ejiltalk.org>
EPIL   R Bernhardt (ed), *Encyclopedia of Public International Law*, vols 1–4
                (Elsevier, Amsterdam 1992–2000)
EU   European Union
EuConst   European Constitutional Law Review

FAO   Food and Agriculture Organization of the United Nations
FILJ   Fordham International Law Journal
FSIA   Foreign Sovereign Immunities Act (US)
FYIL   Finnish Yearbook of International Law

GA or Assembly General Assembly (UN)
GAR(s)   General Assembly Resolution(s) (UN)
GC   Grand Chamber (ECtHR)
GST   Transactions of the Grotius Society
GVICL   Griffin's View on International and Comparative Law
GWILR   The George Washington International Law Review
GYIL   German Yearbook of International Law

HICLR   Hastings International and Comparative Law Review
HILJ   Harvard International Law Journal
HRLR   Human Rights Law Review

ICAO   International Civil Aviation Organization
ICC   International Criminal Court

ICCPR	International Covenant on Civil and Political Rights
ICESCR	International Covenant on Economic, Social and Cultural Rights
ICJ	International Court of Justice
ICJ Pleadings	International Court of Justice—Pleadings, Oral Arguments, Documents
ICJ Rep	International Court of Justice—Reports of Judgments, Advisory Opinions and Orders
ICLQ	International and Comparative Law Quarterly
ICTR	International Criminal Tribunal for Rwanda
ICTY	International Criminal Tribunal for the former Yugoslavia
IDI	Institut de droit international
IHL	International Humanitarian Law
IJGLS	Indiana Journal of Global Legal Studies
IJHR	International Journal of Human Rights
IJIL	Indian Journal of International Law
ILA	International Law Association
ILA Report	International Law Association, 'Final Report on the Accountability of International Organisations' in *Report of the Seventy-first Conference—Berlin* (London, 2004) 164
ILC	International Law Commission
ILDC	International Law in Domestic Courts (OUP) <http://www.oxfordlawreports.com>
ILF	International Law Forum/Forum de droit international
ILM	International Legal Materials
ILO	International Labour Organization
ILOAT	Administrative Tribunal of the International Labour Organization
ILR	International Law Reports
IMCO	International Maritime Consultative Organization (now IMO)
IMO	International Maritime Organization
indiv op	individual opinion
IO(s)	International Organization(s)
IOLR	International Organizations Law Review
IowaLR	Iowa Law Review
ISSJ	International Social Science Journal
ITLOS	International Tribunal for the Law of the Sea
ITO	International Trade Organization (never established)
IYIL	Italian Yearbook of International Law
JDI	Journal du droit international (Clunet)
JIA	Journal of International Affairs
JICJ	Journal of International Criminal Justice
JJIL	Japanese Journal of International Law
JZ	JuristenZeitung
KFOR	Kosovo Force (NATO)
LJIL	Leiden Journal of International Law
LPICT	The Law and Practice of International Courts and Tribunals

MichJIL	Michigan Journal of International Law
MichLR	Michigan Law Review
MONUC	United Nations Mission in the Democratic Republic of the Congo
MPEPIL	R Wolfrum (ed), *Max Planck Encyclopedia of Public International Law* (OUP) <http://www.mpepil.com>
MPUNYB	Max Planck Yearbook of United Nations Law
MS	Member State(s)
NATO	North Atlantic Treaty Organization
NILR	Netherlands International Law Review
NJ	Neue Justiz
NJIL	Nordic Journal of International Law
NYIL	Netherlands Yearbook of International Law
NYUJILP	New York University Journal of International Law and Politics
NYULR	New York University Law Review
OAU	Organization of African Unity (now African Union)
OFF	United Nations Oil-for-Food Programme (Iraq)
OIC	Organization of the Islamic Conference
OJ	Official Journal of the European Communities
OJLS	Oxford Journal of Legal Studies
OMPI	Organisation des Modjahedines du Peuple d'Iran
ONUC	United Nations Operation in the Congo
ÖZöR	Österreichische Zeitschrift für öffentliches Recht
PCIJ	Permanent Court of International Justice
PKO(s)	Peacekeeping Operation(s)
PYIL	Polish Yearbook of International Law
RADIC	Revue africaine de droit international et comparé/African Journal of International and Comparative Law
RBDI	Revue belge de droit international
RdC	Recueil des cours de l'Académie de droit international de La Haye
RDI	Revue de droit international
RDIDC	Revue de droit international et de droit comparé
RDISDP	Revue de droit international, de sciences diplomatiques et politiques
Repertoire	*Repertoire of the Practice of the Security Council* (UN, New York 1954–)
Repertory	*Repertory of Practice of United Nations Organs* (UN, New York 1955–)
REDI	Revue égyptienne de droit international
RGDIP	Revue générale de droit international public
RHDI	Revue hellénique de droit international
RIAA	Reports of International Arbitral Awards
RivistaDI	Rivista di diritto internazionale
RiW	Recht der internationalen Wirtschaft
RSDIE	Revue suisse de droit international et européen/Schweizerische Zeitschrift für internationales und europäisches Recht
RTDP	Rivista trimestrale di diritto pubblico
RYDI	Jugoslovenska revija za medunarodno pravo (= Revue yougoslave de droit international)

SC or Council	Security Council (UN)
SCR(s)	Security Council Resolution(s) (UN)
SCSL	Special Court for Sierra Leone
sep op	separate opinion
S-G	Secretary-General (UN)
SFRY	Socialist Federal Republic of Yugoslavia
SoCalLR	Southern California Law Review
SR	Special Rapporteur
STL	Special Tribunal for Lebanon
TEC	Treaty Establishing the European Community (as amended)
UDHR	Universal Declaration of Human Rights
UN	United Nations
UNAT	United Nations Administrative Tribunal
UNC or Charter	Charter of the United Nations
UNCIO	*Documents of the United Nations Conference on International Organization* (United Nations Information Organizations, London/New York 1945)
UNCLOS	United Nations Convention on the Law of the Sea
UNEF	United Nations Emergency Force (Egypt-Israel)
UNEP	United Nations Environmental Programme
UNICEF	United Nations Children's Fund
UNITA	União Nacional para a Independência Total de Angola (National Union for the Total Independence of Angola)
UNJY	United Nations Juridical Yearbook
UNMIK	United Nations Mission in Kosovo
UNOSOM	United Nations Operation in Somalia
UNPROFOR	United Nations Protection Force (former Yugoslavia)
UNTS	United Nations Treaty Series
USC	United States Code
VaJIL	Virginia Journal of International Law
VCCR	Vienna Convention on Consular Relations
VCLT	Vienna Convention on the Law of Treaties
Vienne Commentaire	O Corten and P Klein (eds), *Les Conventions de Vienne sur le droit des traités—Commentaire article par article* (Bruylant, Bruxelles 2006)
VJTL	Vanderbilt Journal of Transnational Law
WEU	Western European Union
WFP	World Food Programme
WHO	World Health Organization
WTO	World Trade Organization
YECHR	Yearbook of the European Convention on Human Rights
YILC	Yearbook of the International Law Commission
YIPO	Yearbook of International Peace Operations
YJIL	Yale Journal of International Law
ZaöRV	Zeitschrift für ausländisches öffentliches Recht und Völkerrecht

Note on Citation

Citation in this text follows a modified OSCOLA convention. Books are cited using a short title and the year of publication. Articles are cited without giving the title, but merely the journal reference. Chapters in books are cited without giving the title, but merely the book reference (using the short title and year). Numbers in brackets indicate paragraphs or marginal notes; they supplement pinpoint citations to pages or are given without page references when no such page references are available. Only the numbers (not the titles) of UN and other international organizations' documents are given. Following the entry into force of the Lisbon Treaty, references to the EC should be considered as references to the EU; it was decided not to change the references to the EC, to its organs, or to treaty provisions in the text.

1

Responsibility as a Form of Accountability and the UN Legal Order

It is by now almost banal to state that there has been a proliferation of international organizations in the last 60 years, a proliferation, no less, which has arguably led to 'the gradual emergence of a kind of superstructure over and above the society of States'.[1] It is also commonplace to concede the fact that these organizations are constantly expanding the scope of their operations and consequently their impact on international life and on international law.[2] One would not be exaggerating in admitting that certain international organizations, among which the WTO, the Bretton Woods Institutions, the EC, and the UN, have to a limited but significant extent replaced States with respect to decisions that have pervasive socioeconomic, political, and legal impact.[3] Some have even coined the term 'functional state-hood' as an appropriate description of these organizations.[4] States have conferred on them some of their sovereign powers, which, whereas subject—when exercised at the national level—to a number of constraints, both political and legal,[5] seem prima facie to be beyond control when exercised by an international organization. Congruent with the admission of the fact that international organizations are today in possession of significant sovereign powers is the augmentation of calls for the exercise of control over their use of these powers. The far-reaching (governmental) power of certain IOs is today indisputable and in fact by and large undisputed, to the extent that they have been called 'a fourth branch of government'.[6] This 'power entails accountability, that is the duty to account for its exercise', as the ILA pointed out in its study on the Accountability of IOs.[7]

The United Nations, the seminal international organization, has the power, through its Security Council acting under its Chapter VII mandate, not only

---

[1] H Mosler (1974) 140 RdC 189.

[2] eg K Wellens (1999) 1 ILF 107; T Broude and Y Shany in eidem (eds), *The Shifting Allocation of Authority in International Law* (2008) 4. Significantly also already S Bastid in *Festschrift Spiropoulos* (1957) 35.

[3] G Hafner in RSJ Macdonald and DM Johnston (eds), *Towards World Constitutionalism* (2005) 593. See generally the contributions in A von Bogandy et al (eds), *The Exercise of Public Authority by International Institutions* (2010); and D Sarooshi, *IOs and their Exercise of Sovereign Powers* (2005) with respect to the degree of such 'replacement', depending on the nature of the conferral of powers that has taken place. On the effect of globalization in removing public responsibilities from traditional governments see S Chesterman (2008) 14 Global Governance 39.

[4] 'Funktionelle Staatlichkeit' according to A Reinisch (2007) 42 BDGVR 82.

[5] See Sarooshi (n 3) 14.   [6] E-U Petersmann (1997) 10 LJIL 442.

[7] ILA Report 168.

to impose binding sanctions on States and non-State entities,[8] but also, as it has increasingly done lately, to impose other non-forcible binding measures, such as the establishment of ad hoc international criminal tribunals,[9] as well as a number of international obligations on Member States with respect to the financing of terrorism and the non-proliferation of weapons of mass destruction.[10] These broad powers of the Council were first allowed to be exercised and reveal their potential impact after the end of the Cold War and the resolution of an almost 45-year-long deadlock due to the use of the veto. The problem with respect to the operation of the Council was thus recast from one dealing with the abdication of power to one concerned with the potential abuse of power.[11] It has been noted, significantly, that recent interest in the accountability of international organizations is 'owed primarily' to this extensive activity of the Security Council.[12]

Before one discusses the 'accountability' of the Council—and of the Organization of which it is an organ—for its exercise of powers, one should first attempt to define this rather vague term. Its indeterminacy notwithstanding, 'accountability' has come, as of late, to be used extensively, without, however, always being assigned the same (or, sometimes, any) meaning.[13] Accordingly the term will be analysed (Section I), before the specific form(s) of accountability applicable to the Council in light of the nature of its function under Chapter VII and specifically under Article 41 UNC is discussed (Section II).

I. Forms of Accountability and the Significance of (Legal) Responsibility

1. Substance of the notion of accountability

The term 'accountability' has been characterized as 'vague',[14] as 'broad and flexible',[15] as 'escaping *prima facie* any clear definition',[16] as 'multifaceted',[17] and so forth. As Brierly put it more than 80 years ago—admittedly in another

---

[8] Art 41 UNC. See eg SCRs 232 (1966) [Southern Rhodesia]; 418 (1977) [South Africa]; 661 (1990) [Iraq]; 713 (1991) [SFRY]; 733 (1992) [Somalia]; 748 (1992) [Libya]; 788 (1992) [Liberia]; 841 (1993) [Haiti]; 864 (1993) [UNITA]; 918 (1994) [Rwanda]; 1054 (1996) [Sudan]; 1132 (1997) [Sierra Leone]; 1267 (1999) [Taliban]; 1298 (2000) [Eritrea and Ethiopia]; 1572 (2004) [Côte d'Ivoire]; 1718 (2006) and 1874 (2009) [DPRK]; 1737 (2006) and 1929 (2010) [Iran].

[9] SCRs 808 and 827 (1993) [ICTY], and 955 (1994) [ICTR]. See briefly for Chapter VII measures related to international and internationalized criminal courts A Tzanakopoulos in A Cassese (ed), *The Oxford Companion to International Criminal Justice* (2009) 260–1.

[10] SCRs 1373 (2001); 1540 (2004).

[11] cf R Higgins, *Problems and Process* (1994) 184–5.

[12] A Reinisch (2001) 44 GYIL 275; see also R Hofmann (2007) 42 BDGVR 13.

[13] Reinisch (n 12) 273.   [14] Ibid.

[15] A Gowlland Gualtieri (2001) 72 BYIL 214. Similarly D Curtin and A Nollkaemper (2005) 36 NYIL 4.

[16] Hafner (n 3) 586. cf also idem (2003) 97 ASILProc 236. Similarly J Brunnée (2005) 36 NYIL 22.

[17] ILA Report 168.

context—'an adequate definition of terms is the *result* of an inquiry and *not its starting point*'.[18] There is thus no point in striving to provide 'adequate definition' of the term accountability at this juncture, especially given the rather problematic nature of the term. 'Yet', Brierly continues, 'some preliminary understanding of the meaning in which a term is used is necessary at the outset'.[19] It is questionable, however, if even such a 'preliminary understanding' of the term 'accountability' is possible, given particularly that there are many different understandings and uses of the term in very diverse settings with only marginal convergence.[20] Indeed, the term 'accountability' has been used to signify the duty of an *international organization* to account for the impairment of the rights and interests of individuals (but presumably not of States);[21] the process of holding *individuals* personally responsible for human rights abuses they have committed;[22] one of the several ways in which power can be constrained;[23] whereas in some cases the term is not defined at all and simply treated as self-explanatory.[24] In many instances the term is used (or understood) as tantamount to (and interchangeable with) State responsibility, or international responsibility in general,[25] while some practitioners seem to find no justifiable use for it in legal discourse, precisely for this reason.[26] Others still distinguish accountability of international organizations from the concept of legal remedies in general and from the concepts of liability under domestic law and responsibility under international law in particular,[27] while only generally defining the notion as 'answerability for the performance of an office, a charge, or a duty'.[28]

This is a difficulty that stems from the fact that 'accountability' is used differently in different fields, such as social studies and international relations theory, international law, domestic constitutional and administrative law, and so on.[29] Within each such discipline, there may be some convergence on what the term is supposed to mean.[30] However, the 'interdisciplinarity' of the notion of

---

[18] JL Brierly in H Lauterpacht and CHM Waldock (eds), *The Basis of Obligation in International Law* (1958) 2 [emphasis in original].

[19] Ibid.   [20] cf Hafner (n 16) 236–7.   [21] Reinisch (n 12) 271.

[22] SR Ratner in GH Fox and BR Roth (eds), *Democratic Governance and International Law* (2000) 449. Also K Ambos (2000) 6 International Peacekeeping 67.

[23] RW Grant and RO Keohane (2005) 99 APSR 29.

[24] eg M Pallis (2005) 37 NYUJILP 869.

[25] eg M Scheinin in H-O Sano and G Alfredsson (eds), *Human Rights and Good Governance* (2002) 31 and *passim*; H-O Sano in ibid 137, 141; K Wellens (2004) 25 MichJIL 1161; M Zwanenburg, *Accountability of Peace Support Operations* (2005) *passim*; S Chesterman, *Who Needs Rules?* (2005) 5 <http://www.iilj.org/research/documents/panel_2_report.pdf>. Significantly, Higgins (n 11) 147 has used the term 'accountability' to describe international responsibility as 'accountability for violations of international law'.

[26] eg LD Johnson in NM Blokker and HG Schermers (eds), *Proliferation of IOs* (2001) 471.

[27] S Schlemmer-Schulte (1999) 45 RiW 180.

[28] Eadem in Blokker and Schermers (n 26) 508 at n 90. Curtin and Nollkaemper (n 15) 4 define the core of the notion as 'the process of being called "to account" to some authority for one's actions'.

[29] Significantly, the ILA Report 168 seems to be treating the notion as an 'autonomous' one, to borrow the phraseology used in the context of the ECHR by the ECtHR: the term is not considered as corresponding to homonymous terms in use in particular domestic or regional legal systems. For a critique of the ILA's approach in general see Hafner (n 3) 599–601.

[30] eg in Keohane's treatment of the concept there is an implicit acceptance that there exists a standard definition of accountability as being dependent on two conditions: availability of information to accountability-holders, and their ability to sanction power-wielders: (2003) 24 MichJIL 1123.

accountability, combined with the stunning observation that 'it is not an *entirely* legal concept',[31] creates problems with respect to understanding how this term can be employed in international law, especially when dealing with the limitations and control of Security Council action under Chapter VII of the Charter, and in particular with binding non-forcible action under Article 41.

A standard starting point would be to fall back to 'an essentially commonsense understanding of "accountability", meaning that those who exercise power on behalf of others can be held accountable if that power is misused or abused'.[32] However, besides being open to the objection that common sense is not always *that* common, this definition (and other similar definitions, such as the one by the ILA in its Report or that by Schlemmer-Schulte)[33] leaves much to be desired. It does not answer who should be accountable to whom, through what modalities, for compliance with what rules, and so forth. Furthermore, it disregards a feature of this term that is often overlooked in Anglo-Saxon literature, and that is that it finds no corresponding term in other major languages.[34]

Be that as it may, one could perhaps accept the term as an 'umbrella term',[35] which simply stipulates that an organ exercising power must account, that is, be subjected to control, for the exercise of that power. An attempt to look into the different forms of accountability may help to clarify the issue.

2. Forms of accountability

The very vague notion of accountability is usually broken down into several different 'forms'. These distinctions may correspond to the differing nature of commitments which lie at the basis of the various forms,[36] to the different modalities of holding power to account or the sanctions involved,[37] to different accountability-holders or beneficiaries,[38] etc. The standard (and most meaningful) distinction is between political and legal accountability, as the two extreme points of a spectrum, with several other possible forms posited along that spectrum and designated here as 'others':[39] these include financial accountability, administrative accountability, hierarchical accountability, market accountability, (public)

He also notes that there is 'wide agreement' on how to define accountability, ibid. Despite this 'wide agreement', the author goes on to provide no less than four different definitions, ibid 1124. cf also Grant and Keohane (n 23) 30.

[31] Schlemmer-Schulte (n 27) 180 and fn 39; eadem (n 28) 508 at fn 90. Others have characterized it as an 'intrinsically non-legal concept': Curtin and Nollkaemper (n 15) 16.

[32] A-M Slaughter (2001) 8 IJGLS 349; cf N Woods (2001) 77 International Affairs 83.

[33] See nn 7 and 28 and corresponding text.

[34] ILA Report 168; Hafner (n 3) 516; C Harlow, *Accountability in the EU* (2002) 14 seq, 23. See by way of example the use of the term in G della Cananea (2003) 53 RTDP 731, where the author notes that the first problem with respect to 'accountability' is the lack of a corresponding term in Italian (738). cf also in this respect J Kokott (2004) 64 ZaöRV 528.

[35] cf Slaughter (n 32) 350.   [36] Hafner (n 3) 588.

[37] Keohane (n 30) 1130 seq.   [38] cf ibid 1124.

[39] cf A Tomkins in P Craig and A Tomkins (eds), *The Executive and Public Law* (2006) 37; Chesterman (n 3) 44.

reputational accountability, and so forth.[40] One could further proceed to break down accountability into different distinctions and sub-distinctions *ad nauseam*, for example distinguishing political accountability into parliamentary account-ability, democratic accountability, electoral and non-electoral forms of democratic accountability, and so forth.[41]

The concept of 'political accountability' may be subject to many sub-distinctions, as apparent immediately before, but it is effectively distinguished from 'legal accountability' in that it can be entirely or relatively arbitrary.[42] At least in its electoral forms, voters are not required to give any reasons for their decision,[43] whereas in its non-electoral forms control will in general be politically motivated.[44] In the last instance, the political challenges mounted will be on policy, on which reasonable people may reasonably disagree, and in that challenges based on political preferences or positions will be *quasi*-arbitrary. Legal accountability on the other hand demands that the decision-maker have an objectively convincing reason for the decision made, usually compliance with a legal rule.[45] Upon closer examination, political accountability refers to evaluating the *personnel* of the organ exercising power (to this correspond democratic and electoral forms of political accountability) and the *policies* put forward by that organ (to which correspond forms of parliamentary accountability), whereas legal accountability refers to reviewing the legality of the organ's *action* (or *inaction*).[46]

It is common that legal accountability be equated with judicial review within the context of both municipal,[47] and international law.[48] It is, however, submitted that, with respect to international law, responsibility for internationally wrongful acts (within the meaning of the work of the International Law Commission)[49] is what should be understood under the term 'legal accountability',[50] although the latter concept is broader in some respects. Responsibility is an *in rem ex post facto* control mechanism. This means that subjects are held accountable for specific actions or omissions (in short: acts, or: conduct)[51] after these have occurred, and which constitute violations of international law. The law of responsibility

---

[40] For a typology see Grant and Keohane (n 23) 35 seq; Keohane (n 30) 1130 seq. The ILA Report 168–9 distinguishes between political, legal, financial, and administrative accountability, without, however, any elaboration; throughout the Report it rather refers to the three 'levels' of accountability, the first one of which relates to 'monitoring and scrutiny', whereas the other two are concerned with legal liability and responsibility. cf also Reinisch (n 12) 274.

[41] cf T Macdonald and K Macdonald (2006) 17 EJIL 90 seq. cf also Curtin and Nollkaemper (n 15) 11–12.

[42] Chesterman (n 3) 44.   [43] Idem (n 25) 6.

[44] Harlow (n 34) 8.   [45] Chesterman (n 3) 44; idem (n 25) 6.

[46] cf P Craig and A Tomkins in eidem (n 39) 1 [emphasis added].

[47] Ibid; Harlow (n 34) 146.

[48] Chesterman (n 25) 7. Franck notes that judicial review of Council actions for 'gross abuse of discretion' would assure the UN membership that these latter remain *accountable*: TM Franck in C Tomuschat (ed), *The UN at Age Fifty* (1995) 37 [emphasis added].

[49] See ARSIWA Commentary 32 [1]; UN Doc A/58/10 (2003) 35 [4]–[5].

[50] cf E Suzuki and S Nanwani (2006) 27 MichJIL 178, 180.

[51] cf ARSIWA Commentary 35 [4].

is traditionally thought of as a 'tough' branch of international law[52]—even 'the heart and lungs' of international law one might venture to say—not least because, in the words of Ian Brownlie, it 'put[s] a harder edge on legal rights and duties'.[53] In international law, responsibility is implemented in the first instance by those subjects of the law to which the international obligation breached is owed.[54] As such, it does not require a court, although a finding of responsibility by a disinterested third party will in most cases be the ideal circumstance. Thus 'legal accountability' of international organizations can be said to correspond to their responsibility for internationally wrongful acts. A lot of water has flowed under the bridge since the ILC pointed out that 'it must not be forgotten that, by their very nature, International Organizations normally behave in such a manner as not to commit internationally wrongful acts':[55] the Commission has now adopted on first reading a set of draft Articles on the Responsibility of International Organizations.[56]

In the quest to determine whether 'accountability' is a *terminus technicus* 'with a semblance of fixed meaning' or just a catch-all or umbrella term, many have come out on the side of generality.[57] Given the haphazard way in which the concept is sometimes used, its open-ended definition and its multifaceted nature, it is hard for one to disagree with the following statement by Hafner:

It is . . . suggested to put aside the claims raised under the heading of accountability, which purport to subject the performance of IOs to standards which are neither rooted in hard law nor can be generalized, and to start the further discussion from the original objectives of the claims of accountability, namely to limit activities of IOs by the applicable law and to hold them answerable for violations of this law . . . What remains under this heading of accountability is that IOs are bound to comply with applicable rules of international law in the widest sense, and that they are answerable for their activities by assuming international responsibility. But so understood, no separate label such as 'accountability' would be required, since both aspects, the duty of compliance and responsibility, are traditional concepts of international law. IOs in their quality as subjects of international law would automatically become subject to these concepts.[58]

Before finally subscribing to this view and exploring its consequences, it is useful to review possible 'forms' of accountability that may be applicable in the specific case of the United Nations Security Council imposing non-forcible measures under Chapter VII of the UN Charter.

---

[52] C Brölmann (2001) 70 NJIL 331.

[53] I Brownlie, *State Responsibility—Part I* (1983) 87.

[54] Accountability is a 'relational term', in that someone must always be accountable 'to someone else'. See Keohane (n 30) 1124. In this sense, the accountability-holders in the case of international responsibility are fairly easily identifiable in that they are the entities to which the international obligation is owed.

[55] (1975) II YILC 87 [3].

[56] (2000) II(2) YILC 131 [729]; UN Doc A/57/10 (2002) 228 [461]; UN Doc A/64/10 (2009) 13 [31] seq; 19 [50].

[57] See Harlow (n 34) 8, 23; cf Slaughter (n 32) 350.   [58] Hafner (n 3) 601.

II. Accountability for the Exercise of Non-Forcible Powers by the Security Council

1. The nature of Council powers under Chapter VII of the Charter

It has been contended that accountability for the exercise of public power is best served when several forms of it (political, financial, administrative, legal, and so forth) are put in operation simultaneously.[59] However, in order to identify the most appropriate forms of accountability in a realistic manner, one must first attempt to determine the nature of the functions and powers of the organ one seeks to hold to account. In this respect, the Security Council presents a particular problem, especially when acting under Chapter VII UNC. This is because, according to some, it hardly makes sense to attempt to draw meaningful parallels between the Council and domestic institutions exercising legislative, judicial, or executive power.[60] The Council hardly ever distinguishes between these three heads of power when it is acting, not less so because, as the Appeals Chamber stated in *Tadić*,

> the legislative, executive and judicial division of powers which is largely followed in municipal systems does not apply to the international setting nor, more specifically, to the setting of an international organization such as the United Nations.[61]

There is indeed no clear separation of powers in the United Nations, but rather 'distribution' of powers among the organs.[62] UN organs thus cannot be qualified as 'executive' or 'legislative', notwithstanding the fact that the ICJ is the 'principal judicial organ' of the Organization,[63] and that the Council has been called the '*de facto* executive organ' of the UN.[64] Furthermore, it must not be forgotten that the Organization was 'neither designed nor equipped' to accommodate any legislative function and thus does not feature any corresponding organ.[65] This has led some scholars to argue in favour of a 'functional' separation of powers for the Council,

---

[59] ILA Report 168; also Keohane (n 30) 1134.

[60] S Chesterman and DA Jordan, *The SC as World Executive?* (2006) 2 <http://www.iilj.org/research/documents/panel_4_report.pdf>. Thus, scholars have referred to the 'sovereign' powers conferred by States to IOs, including the full range of executive, legislative, and judicial powers: see Sarooshi (n 3) 1, 10.

[61] *Tadić* (Appeal on Jurisdiction) IT-94-1-AR72 (2 October 1995) [43]; (1996) 35 ILM 46.

[62] *Lockerbie* [1992] ICJ Rep 138 (sep op Lachs), 165 (sep op Weeramantry); *Nicaragua* [1984] ICJ Rep 433 [92]. cf D Sarooshi (1996) 47 BYIL 463 and fn 227; S Lamb in *Honour Brownlie* (1999) 365; D Schweigman, *The Authority of the SC* (2001) 381. However, as M Koskenniemi (1995) 6 EJIL 337 notes, the Charter 'was meant to be based on a separation of functions', which, it is submitted, should be understood as largely tantamount to a separation of powers. See generally on the lack of separation of powers in international organizations WE Holder (2003) 97 ASILProc 235. But see also TM Franck in *Festschrift Eitel* (2003) 99.

[63] *Tadić* (n 61) 47 [43].

[64] Sarooshi (n 62) 463; Wellens (n 25) 1179. Some have even called it the 'megaphone' of executives: Schweigman (n 62) 381. cf also T Sato in J-M Coicaud and V Heiskanen (eds), *The Legitimacy of IOs* (2001) 312. Koskenniemi (n 62) 338–9 terms the Council 'policeman', in an analysis assimilating it to an executive and juxtaposing it to the 'Temple of Justice'.

[65] A Bianchi (2006) 17 EJIL 911.

according to which each Council action or decision shall be determined as falling within the scope of one of the three powers and evaluated accordingly.[66] What is customarily overlooked, however, is the extreme difficulty in defining 'executive' power. While legislative and judicial power are relatively easier to define, even national constitutions usually fail to provide an adequate and formal definition of executive power.[67]

The UN Charter does not include any reference to executive or legislative functions. Much like in the case of the European Communities, or any other international organization for that matter, there are only provisions in the constituent instrument that deal with the organs of the UN and their competences. Thus there is nothing in the Charter that can help define 'executive power' and identify the organ(s) that exercise it. However, a core set of tasks undertaken by the executive branch of national governments can and has been identified, and this can prove useful in the discussion: the executive usually sets the overall priorities and the agenda for legislation, has the responsibility for the effective implementation of the legislation, and has a significant role in the structure and allocation of the budget.[68]

Within the UN framework, it seems obvious that what might be called 'the agenda for legislation and the overall priorities' may be set by both the GA and the SC, in different ways: whereas the Assembly can call upon States to hold a diplomatic conference with a view to negotiating an international convention, or adopt an international convention in the course of its operation, the Council may impose on States, in the face of a threat to international peace and security, certain general measures, without a limitation in time, which correspond to general international legal obligations, as it has done with Resolutions 1373 (2001) and 1540 (2004). The responsibility for the effective implementation of the law can be seen to fall upon the Council, to the extent that it has the power to respond to threats to the peace, which can be created, among other things, by non-compliance with certain fundamental obligations under international law and the Charter. Finally, the approval of the budget of the Organization falls squarely within the powers of the Assembly under Article 17 UNC.[69]

From this discussion it is evident that—in general terms—executive power within the UN framework is both *de jure* and *de facto* shared between at least the Assembly and the Council.[70] In the same way, it could be said that 'legislative' power is also shared, in that the Assembly may 'legislate' by adopting resolutions and declarations by consensus—which may subsequently evolve to become customary norms of international law.[71] The Assembly also has a mandate, under Article 13(1)(a) of the Charter, to 'encourag[e] the progressive development of international law and its codification'.[72] The Council, on the other hand, may impose non-forcible measures, acting under Chapter VII, of such generality so as

---

[66] Sato (n 64) 329–30.   [67] Craig and Tomkins (n 46) 4.
[68] P Craig in idem and Tomkins (n 39) 317–18.   [69] See also *Expenses* [1962] ICJ Rep 162.
[70] cf Craig (n 68) 317 with respect to the EC.
[71] cf J Alvarez, *IOs as Law-makers* (2005) 159.   [72] cf B Elberling (2005) 2 IOLR 343.

to qualify as 'legislative' measures.[73] This conclusion does nothing but reiterate the assertion that the Council acts under all three heads of power without distinction[74] (including the judicial power, as it did for example already in Resolution 95 (1951) where the Council determined the existence of a violation of the Armistice Agreement between Egypt and Israel,[75] or as it does when it makes findings such as the one with respect to the delimitation of the boundary between Iraq and Kuwait being governed by the 1963 agreement[76]), and thus presents 'an accountability problem'.[77] Such an approach, however, does little to advance the discussion, while at the same time disregarding the fact that, in most States, the executive power always tends to undertake both legislative and judicial functions to some extent, the limits of which are anything but clear.[78]

A closer look into the nature of Council Chapter VII powers reveals that these are very close to the powers of the executive branch in domestic jurisdictions. In order for Chapter VII to come into play, the Council has to find, in accordance with Article 39 of the Charter, that there exists at least a threat to the peace, or a breach of the peace or act of aggression.[79] Once such a finding has been made, the Council can then impose far-reaching binding measures on the membership of the Organization under Article 41 UNC. This type of determination that certain findings of fact respond to a notion used in the law (here the Charter) to allow for the exercise of power is highly reminiscent of the classical way in which municipal laws will provide for the exercise of power by the executive to be contingent on the finding that a certain heading of jurisdiction exists.[80] The problem that arises in this respect is that the notions used in laws to provide for a heading of jurisdiction of the executive are usually (if not always) *'vague to a great extent*, because of their prognostic or valuing content'.[81] This is most certainly the case with respect to the notion of a 'threat to the peace', which triggers Council Chapter VII powers, a fact which is reiterated by the telling example employed by Schmidt-Aßmann and Möllers to demonstrate such a 'greatly vague notion', namely the finding by the

---

[73]　See generally among others S Talmon (2005) 99 AJIL 175; C Denis, *Le pouvoir normatif* (2004) 19. The latter, despite rejecting the transposition of any sort of doctrine of separation of powers in international law (at 2), employs both the term 'legislative' and the term 'judicial power' with respect to actions of the Council. See finally J Alvarez in E de Wet and A Nollkaemper (eds), *Review of the SC by MS* (2003) 121 who finds that in instances such as the adoption of SCR 1373 (2001) the Council has acted 'in ways that are hard to distinguish from the law-making actions [by] domestic executive branches pursuant to delegated legislative authority'.

[74]　Elberling (n 72) 337–8; cf Alvarez (n 73) 122.

[75]　In SCR 95 (1951) the Council 'finds' that certain practice constitutes a violation of the Armistice Agreement between Egypt and Israel (at [1]), 'further finds' that the said practice cannot be justified as necessary for self-defence (at [3]), and finally 'calls upon' Egypt to terminate that practice (at [4]).

[76]　See Sarooshi (n 62) 466–8. Also I Brownlie in *Honour Wang Tieya* (1994) 97; cf Denis (n 73) 19.

[77]　Chesterman and Jordan (n 60) 2.

[78]　See generally Craig and Tomkins (n 46) 5 and the chapters to which they refer. cf also G della Cananea in Craig and Tomkins (n 39) 250, according to whom 'enacting rules', for example, is included in the powers of the executive.

[79]　See in more detail Chapter 3.I.1 below.

[80]　cf E Schmidt-Aßmann and C Möllers in Craig and Tomkins (n 39) 286.

[81]　Ibid; similarly with respect to Britain Tomkins (n 39) 43.

(German) executive that a situation constitutes a 'danger to public security and order'.[82]

Within municipal legal orders, this type of executive power is primarily held to account through legal means, in particular through judicial review.[83] It is useful, however, to determine what other forms of accountability may be operable, appropriate, and effective with respect to controlling the actions of the Council under Article 41—and Chapter VII in general—of the UN Charter.

2. Appropriate and effective forms of accountability for Council action

In the first instance, one must go through the several sub-forms of political accountability, in order to determine whether any of them may operate with respect to Council action under Chapter VII. 'Democratic' accountability, especially in its electoral forms, refers to personnel,[84] or to replacing the holders of office through elections.[85] Such methods of political control do exist in international organizations, and they include for example the exercise of voting rights in such a way as to prevent reappointment of officials, as was the case with US opposition to the re-election of Secretary-General Boutros Boutros-Ghali.[86] With particular reference to the Council, however, it is crucial that, while ten of its members stand to be voted for or against, the prohibition on re-election already significantly limits the meaningful applicability of such a form of accountability,[87] a form by default fatally weakened by the assignment of five permanent seats in the Council. Furthermore, any such form of accountability does not relate specifically to the exercise of Chapter VII powers by the Council, and, like most forms of political accountability, does not require any objective—or even substantive—justification.[88] Finally, it is hardly worthy of the designation 'democratic', as it actually simply constitutes a form of internal electoral political accountability, in the sense that MS of the Organization may express their discontent with the Council through the exercise of their voting rights—but not to any avail, given the permanent seats and the prohibition on re-election.

---

[82] Schmidt-Aßmann and Möllers (n 80) 286. 'Open-ended legal concepts' such as 'good morals' or 'threat to the peace' are common and necessary in any legal order that seeks to provide the requisite flexibility that allows for legal interpretation to follow social developments: cf J Pauwelyn, *Conflict of Norms in Public International Law* (2003) 12 and 267; A Orakhelashvili, *Peremptory Norms in International Law* (2006) 15. For such an 'open-ended legal concept' to be operational, however, it needs to be concretized and qualified as applicable on specific sets of facts. Often, the organ empowered—subject to limits—to make that concretization is an executive organ.

[83] See eg Schmidt-Aßmann and Möllers (n 80) 286; Harlow (n 34) 165. On the availability of judicial review with respect to Council action see Chapter 4.III below.

[84] See n 46 and corresponding text.   [85] Harlow (n 34) 8.

[86] Reinisch (n 12) 286 and fn 73.   [87] Chesterman (n 3) 45.

[88] See nn 42–4 and corresponding text. With respect to the inadequacy of elections in general as a means of securing accountability (in the case of national elections) see N Woods and A Narlikar (2001) 53 ISSJ 574.

Parliamentary sub-forms of political accountability refer to policy.[89] However, since in the UN there is no 'governmental' organ that is responsible to an 'elected' organ, accounting for the exercise of power in terms of any sort of 'parliamentary' accountability does not appear possible.[90] The fact is that the GA could be seen as having been given a general power under the Charter to control the Council with respect to its policy choices:[91] Article 24(3) stipulates that the Council 'shall submit annual and, when necessary, special reports to the General Assembly for its consideration'.[92] Indeed, even the Appeals Chamber in *Tadić* hinted to this provision as envisaging some sort of control on Council powers, given that it mentioned it in passing while discussing the limits on Council power imposed by the UNC.[93] The submission of periodic reports by a non-plenary to a plenary can serve as a useful accountability tool,[94] but in the specific case the reports are not qualitative and receive no substantive consideration; they have rather taken the form of a 'documentary compendium'.[95] In any event, the Council's 'terms of reference' under Chapter VII in particular are far too broad to allow for any meaningful control by another political organ. Vested with primary responsibility to maintain or restore international peace and security,[96] the Council has admittedly very extensive discretion in this respect.[97]

A limited financial or, more broadly, political accountability mechanism relates to the exclusive power of the Assembly to approve the budget of the Organization. While it is true that it is the Council that creates mandates, it is the Fifth Committee of the Assembly that allocates the resources for their implementation, and this has been characterized as a 'key restraint' on Council powers, since MS are using it as a mechanism of exerting influence on the implementation of Council decisions.[98] It is generally accepted that the approval of the budget by one organ of an international organization can serve as an internal accountability mechanism, in the sense of exercising some control over the actions of another organ.[99] This has also been conceded specifically with respect to the Assembly exerting some control over other principal organs of the UN, particularly the Council.[100] However, neither non-forcible 'legislative' or 'atypical' measures, nor any other measures (sanctions) under Article 41 do usually require any sort of funding: approval of the budget does not come into play. This mechanism of accountability could only prove effective, or at least operational, with respect to such 'atypical' Article 41 measures as the establishment of ad hoc international criminal tribunals or other subsidiary organs.[101]

---

[89] See n 46 and corresponding text.
[90] cf della Cananea (n 34) 739 with respect to the WTO.
[91] See R Monaco in *Festschrift Schätzel* (1960) 332; N Elaraby in *Festschrift Eitel* (2003) 59–60.
[92] cf also Art 15 UNC.   [93] *Tadić* (n 61) 42 [28].
[94] K Wellens in Blokker and Schermers (n 26) 450.
[95] Ibid 451; cf also E Suy in H Fox (ed), *The Changing Constitution of the UN* (1997) 68. But see idem in (2007) 42 BDGVR 115–16.
[96] Art 24(1) UNC.   [97] See in more detail Chapter 3.1.1 below.
[98] Chesterman and Jordan (n 60) 3–4.   [99] cf Wellens (n 94) 448.
[100] Sarooshi (n 62) 474–6.   [101] See ibid 473–7.

All these sub-forms of political accountability of the Council are only available to the other organs of the Organization, and thus to the MS constituted as these (plenary) organs. The MS constituted as a plenary organ (the GA) are the only actors nominally able to hold the Council to account in this respect, the apparent lack of effectiveness notwithstanding. In that, these forms of accountability are internal in nature.[102] In discussing the potential of any other form of political or democratic accountability of the Organization and the Council to the public at large, we need to keep in mind that there is a lack of a distinct polity in world politics and thus also in international law.[103] This lack of *demos*, in the words of Joseph Weiler,[104] necessarily means there can be neither democracy nor any sort of democratic or political accountability in that sense. Public reputational accountability could serve as an external control and compensate to some extent (or even disprove) the lack of a *demos*. However, the Security Council rarely gets its 15 minutes of fame, mainstream media reporting being usually limited to domestic executive action (even though this may be mandated by the Council), or generally uncritical. Consequently, public reaction to Council action has also been limited, while the Council does not seem to be particularly concerned with its reputation with the public. Notwithstanding publicity moves,[105] when it comes to Article 41 measures the Council will not easily relent. The Lockerbie incident furnishes a striking example. Certain media grew increasingly doubtful of whether Libya had any involvement with the bombing of the airliner over Lockerbie in Scotland—and more than twenty years after the incident significant doubts persist.[106] However, the Council sanctions on Libya remained in place, and were only suspended when the (then) OAU decided on mass disobedience of the sanctions.[107]

If the SC is by definition undemocratic, this does not mean that it is necessarily unaccountable at the same time.[108] Lack of accountability as a result of the existence of a democratic deficit is a deterministic concession imposed by a participatory conception of accountability, according to which the accountability-holder is the public at large, that is, the individuals affected by the exercise of power by the Council.[109] Rather, when accepting the predominance, in the case of an undemocratic organ with extensive discretion, of a delegation-based conception of accountability, according to which the accountability-holder is the one who has delegated certain powers to the acting organ for a specific purpose, and which is most prominently served by international (legal) responsibility in the given case, it

---

[102] See eg Holder (n 62) 233.

[103] Grant and Keohane (n 23) 33–4; Keohane (n 30) 1122.

[104] JHH Weiler (2004) 64 ZaöRV 560.

[105] Such as holding the occasional public debate: eg on 'Women and Peace and Security' S/PV.5556 (2006); 'Protection of Civilians in Armed Conflict' S/PV.6066 (2009).

[106] See for an overview P Foot in J Pilger (ed), *Tell Me No Lies* (2005) 216–54; B Frederking, *The US and the SC* (2007) 73–6; and cf BBC News, 'Lockerbie Evidence Not Disclosed', 28 August 2008 <http://news.bbc.co.uk/1/hi/scotland/south_of_scotland/7573244.stm>. See also J Pilger, 'Megrahi was Framed', *New Statesman*, 7 September 2009, 14.

[107] On which see Chapters 5 and 7 below.   [108] cf Keohane (n 30) 1122, 1136 seq.

[109] cf N Krisch (2006) 17 EJIL 250; Pallis (n 24) 870.

appears clear that the democratic deficit does not block accountability to the entity (or entities, in this case States) empowering the organ.[110]

In this connection, the following statement by Zimbabwe in the Council is instructive:

this 15-member Council acts on behalf of a total of 175 States Members of the United Nations. This means that 160 States have placed their security, and possibly their very survival, in the hands of the 15.... It is therefore of crucial importance that every decision taken by the Security Council be able to withstand the careful scrutiny of the 160 Member States on whose behalf the Council is expected to act. This is only possible if the Council insists on *being guided in its decisions and actions by the Charter and other international conventions*.[111]

This passage reveals two important aspects: first of all that the predominant accountability-holder in the case of the SC acting under Chapter VII is neither the membership of the Organization constituted as a plenary organ, nor the public at large or the individuals affected by its exercise of power, but rather each and every MS of the Organization which has placed its 'security...in the hands of the [Council]'. Furthermore, the quote highlights the predominance of the Council's legal accountability to the States, or its international responsibility.

Indeed, legal accountability—or more specifically in this case international responsibility—is the only form of accountability that refers specifically to action (and not to personnel or policy).[112] Council action under Chapter VII to maintain international peace and security is the only meaningful object of any type of control. The control of such action's legality thus presents itself as a meaningful bar to this oligarchic organ's broad powers. Furthermore, over and above accountability, which in its 'commonsensical' definition deals with control over power exercised *on behalf of* someone else,[113] that is, over power that has been conferred, international responsibility also allows third States (non-members of the Organization) to challenge the Council for breaches of international law.

There are a number of complex issues that arise with respect to the control of legality of Council action under Chapter VII UNC and the subsequent engagement of the international responsibility of the United Nations. First of all, there are the preliminary questions regarding the possibility of engagement of UN responsibility under international law through Council non-forcible action, namely the issues of attribution and breach of an international obligation, dealt with in Part I of this work. Then there is the issue of the possibility of (authoritative) determination that the international responsibility of the Organization has been engaged by a competent court or tribunal, or in a decentralized manner. This question is dealt with in Part II. Finally, there is the question over the content and, most importantly, the implementation of UN responsibility for wrongful SC non-forcible action, which is the subject of Part III.

---

[110] cf Grant and Keohane (n 23) 33.

[111] S/PV.3063 (1992) 54–5 [emphasis added].

[112] See n 46 and corresponding text.

[113] See n 32 and corresponding text.

PART I

THE ENGAGEMENT OF RESPONSIBILITY

Every internationally wrongful act of the United Nations entails the Organization's international responsibility.[1] For the UN to perpetrate an internationally wrongful act the relevant conduct must be, first of all, attributable to the Organization, and it must also constitute a breach of the Organization's international obligations.[2] Although there may be 'nothing exotic about holding [international] organizations responsible',[3] the necessary preliminary step is to discuss the conditions under which the international responsibility of the United Nations for Security Council non-forcible measures under Chapter VII UNC can be engaged.

The following chapters will first establish which conduct on the part of the Council, as well as the Organization's Member States, is susceptible of engaging UN international responsibility and how this conduct may be attributable to the Organization through the Council (Chapter 2), before discussing whether such conduct may constitute a breach of an international obligation incumbent upon the UN (Chapter 3).

---

[1] Art 3 DARIO; UN Doc A/51/389 (1996) 4 [6].
[2] Art 4 DARIO; UN Doc A/51/389 (1996) 4 [6].
[3] J Klabbers, *An Introduction to International Institutional Law* (2nd edn, 2009) 279. Almost 50 years earlier, J-P Ritter was noting that 'there is nothing extraordinary' in a State resorting to the classical institution of diplomatic protection against an IO seeking reparation, when the latter has perpetrated a wrongful act causing damage to one of its citizens: (1962) 8 AFDI 428.

2

Attribution of Conduct to the United Nations

'Attribution' is the operation of attaching a 'given action or omission' (conduct) to a State or an international organization.[1] The attribution of conduct to an actor capable of bearing responsibility under international law is 'essential', according to the ILC, for an internationally wrongful act to occur.[2] Attribution of conduct either to an international organization or to its Member States (or some of them) constitutes one of the thorniest issues in the field of responsibility of international organizations. This fact has been registered by the ILC already at the very outset of its work on the responsibility of international organizations, as early as 2002.[3] To contend, then, that 'attribution of a wrongful act to an international organization may be a difficult affair'[4] sounds almost like an understatement.

An identifiable problem with respect to attribution of conduct to international organizations in general and the UN in particular is that conduct always originates in individuals, that is to say natural persons, rather than in fictional (legal) entities, such as a State or an IO.[5] Thus, the 'normative' or intellectual operation

---

[1] ARSIWA Commentary 36 [12]; cf UN Doc A/58/10 (2003) 46 [4]. Also P Klein, *La responsabilité des organisations internationales* (1998) 375. R Ago (1971) II(1) YILC 214 [50] notes that attribution 'indicate[s] the simple fact of attaching to the State a given action or omission', which is a 'legal connecting operation' (ibid 218 [58]). That this is not only limited to States is evident when, in discussing attribution in his Hague lectures, Ago postulated that for attribution to be possible, there must be a subject capable of having conduct attributed to it, thus any subject of international law, however defined: R Ago (1939) 68 RdC 450 seq (hereinafter: Ago RdC). cf H Kelsen, *Reine Rechtslehre* (1934) 119–21. See *contra* G Arangio-Ruiz in *Honour Virally* (1991) 32, who questions the legal quality of the connecting operation, characterizing it rather a factual connection—in an analysis, however, that does seem to be limited to States.

[2] UN Doc A/58/10 (2003) 46 [4]. Writing in 1938, JG Starke commented that imputability is 'not practically essential in the law as to international delinquencies' only to retract the statement two pages later by finding that 'a precise notion of imputability is...essential, not merely scientifically but practically...': (1938) 19 BYIL 104, 106 respectively.

[3] UN Doc A/CN.4/L.622 (2002) 5 [15].

[4] J Klabbers, *An Introduction to International Institutional Law* (2nd edn, 2009) 280.

[5] The fact that a State cannot act of itself, but only through its agents and representatives, already stated by the PCIJ in *German Settlers in Poland* [1923] PCIJ Ser B No 6 at 22, is characterized as 'elementary' by the ILC in ARSIWA Commentary 35 [5]. See also Ago RdC (n 1) 459 seq, making the general point that no legal person has an actual physical existence; idem (n 1) 217–18 [57] and fns 75–6. cf Kelsen (n 1) 120; generally: idem *General Theory of Law and State* (1961) 97–9. This 'elementary fact' is equally true for international organizations: see S Talmon in *Memory Schachter* (2005) 409–10; Klein (n 1) 375–6; M Hirsch, *The Responsibility of IOs Toward Third Parties* (1995) 61; J-P Ritter (1962) 8 AFDI 441. cf finally A Malintoppi in *Hommage Guggenheim* (1968) 826.

of attribution is necessary to bridge the gap between the acting individual and the subject of (international) law.[6] This problem also appears, of course, with respect to attribution of conduct to States, albeit in a less complex form. In that latter case, individuals must be linked to the State through an institutional (or 'organic') link in the first instance in order for their conduct to be attributable to the State—they must be or make up organs of the State.[7] Exceptionally, in the absence of an institutional or organic link, the conduct of natural persons may be attributable to a State on the basis of a control link, that is to say when the State directs or controls their conduct,[8] or, even more rarely, when the State has adopted the relevant conduct as its own.[9]

In IOs attribution is also based on the existence of an institutional or organic link between the organization and the acting individual(s).[10] However, there is an 'additional layer' which causes complications. The 'individual' in the case of international organizations is the MS, which then will act through the natural persons making it up. Thus the natural person or group of natural persons acting in the case of IOs will be connected through an institutional or a control link both to the organization and to their home State.[11] The implications of this 'dual allegiance', or *dédoublement fonctionnel*,[12] are evident in a number of instances: the persons occupying seats in the Security Council make up an organ of the UN, but are also 'persons delegated by their respective Governments, from whom they receive instructions and *whose responsibility they engage*'.[13] A soldier belonging to a national military contingent participating in a UN PKO acts in this context as a subsidiary organ or an agent of the UN,[14] but at the same time she is an organ of her respective State.[15] In instances such as these, where conduct is susceptible of being attributed to two or more distinct subjects of international law, the problem is more than obvious: in a rather simplistic but still telling description, IOs, unlike States, are not directly made up by individuals but rather by States, which in turn are made up by individuals. Thus an IO, a subject of international law in all but few cases, is made up by other subjects of international law, namely sovereign States and/or other IOs.[16] This additional 'layer' perplexes the attribution of conduct to

---

[6] ARSIWA Commentary 35 [6]; cf Starke (n 2) 105. 'Legal operation' of attaching the activity of an individual to the collective entity is what Ago (n 1) 216 [53] characterizes it. But see also Arangio-Ruiz (n 1) for a different view.

[7] Art 4 ARSIWA.   [8] Art 8 ARSIWA.   [9] Art 11 ARSIWA.

[10] Art 4(1) DARIO. Also Klein (n 1) 376 and references; M Pérez Gonzalez (1988) 92 RGDIP 81.

[11] cf M Hirsch (2005) 6(2) GVICL 9; R Higgins (1995) 66-I AIDI 260; Ritter (n 5) 442; Klein (n 1) 382.

[12] cf H Kelsen, *Allgemeine Staatslehre* (1925) 174–5; G Scelle, *Précis de droit des gens*, vol 1 (1932) 43.

[13] *Interpretation of Article 3 para 2 of the Treaty of Lausanne* [1925] PCIJ Ser B No 12 at 29 [emphasis added]. See also *German Settlers in Poland* (n 5) 22. cf ILA Report 202–4; J-P Jaqué in *Colloque de Strasbourg* (1988) 8; Klein (n 1) 383. But see also Higgins (n 11) 260–1.

[14] See UN Doc A/51/389 (1996) 6 [17]–[19].

[15] See Art 4(2) ARSIWA, according to which 'an organ includes *any person* or entity' [emphasis added]; cf B Amrallah (1976) 32 REDI 57; Ritter (n 5) 442–4. For another example see Klabbers (n 4) 279–80.

[16] cf C Brölmann (2001) 70 NJIL 322: 'The component elements of international organizations are eminent legal persons in their own right'; Hirsch (n 5) 96. See also S Talmon in P Shiner and

an international organization to some extent,[17] and creates problems with respect to the attribution of conduct to the UN through the Council acting under Chapter VII UNC.

The present chapter will deal successively with direct attribution of Council conduct to the UN (Section I), with attribution of conduct of other actors to the UN by virtue of their quality as an agent of the Organization or because of the control exercised over their conduct by the SC (Section II), and with the issue of UN responsibility for conduct attributable to another actor but connected to SC action (derivative responsibility) (Section III).

I. Attribution of Security Council Conduct to the United Nations

In the first instance, the international responsibility of the UN can be engaged by its own conduct, meaning the conduct of its organs or agents. According to the general rule of attribution reflected in Article 5(1) DARIO as adopted by the ILC on first reading,

[t]he conduct of an organ or agent of an international organization in the performance of functions of that organ or agent shall be considered as an act of that organization under international law whatever position the organ or agent holds in respect of the organization.[18]

The basic principle that international organizations are responsible for the acts of their organs or agents finds support in practice,[19] in the jurisprudence of

---

A Williams (eds), *The Iraq War and International Law* (2008) 223. Saying that the Organization is 'made up' of States who are 'made up' of individuals, however, is just a figure of speech, as an organization is not made up of anything—it 'is' simply its constitutive instrument, understood as a set of legal norms: Kelsen (n 5) 98–9.

[17] cf (1975) II YILC 87 [3], where the Commission notes that

it is not always sure that the action of an organ of an international organization...will always be purely and simply attributed to the international organization as such rather than, in appropriate circumstances, to the States members of the organization, if it is a collective organ, or otherwise to the State of nationality of the person or persons constituting the organ in question.

[18] cf ILA Report 179–80.

[19] The UN paid lump sums as compensation, when it accepted responsibility for the wrongful acts of ONUC in the Congo: see eg [1965] UNJY 39–40. There were a number of agreements to that effect with several States. See generally JJA Salmon (1965) 11 AFDI 468. Payments by the UN for damages caused by acts of its agents, such as the ones under the Spaak—U Thant agreements, can be seen as recognition by the UN of its international responsibility. This is because, despite the fact that the nationality of contingents that caused damages was known, neither the claimant State nor the UN referred to the contingents' sending States as responsible: cf P de Visscher (1971) 54-I AIDI 54–5. Furthermore, the S-G explicitly stated in response to protests for such payments that '[i]t has always been the policy of the United Nations...to compensate individuals who have suffered damages for which the Organization was legally liable': [1965] UNJY 41. But see de Visscher (this note) 52, Amrallah (n 15) 73 for cases where *ex gratia* payments are coupled with explicit denial of legal responsibility and/or wrongdoing.

international courts,[20] and in the relevant literature.[21] There is a similar, well-founded,[22] general rule of attribution of conduct to States, reflected in Article 4(1) ARSIWA: 'The conduct of any State organ shall be considered an act of that State under international law...'. A common objection to the analogous treatment of international responsibility with respect to both States and IOs focuses on the perceived differences between the two subjects, namely the lack of territory in the case of IOs,[23] their diversity in terms of competences (due to the principle of specialty in contrast to States' *plenitude des pouvoirs*), and their less comprehensive structure in comparison to States.[24] The general rules of attribution show, however, that the elements of territory and people, otherwise constitutive elements of the notion of the State, are not to be placed conceptually at the same level as the State's 'organization' when viewed from the perspective of international responsibility.[25] IOs do not have either territory or a permanent population, but this does not, in the final analysis, appear to be so important a difference;[26] it is the 'organic apparatus' that lies in the centre of both notions.[27]

This chapter deals with the seemingly straightforward issue of attributing the conduct of an organ of the Organization, namely the SC, to the Organization.[28] The particular focus will be on conduct of the Security Council in the imposition of non-forcible measures under Article 41 of Chapter VII.

1. Security Council conduct *proper*: identification and direct attribution

The Security Council is of course an organ of the UN (and a principal organ at that),[29] and accordingly its conduct is attributable to the Organization. The critical question, however, is what constitutes Council conduct. The first step, thus, in the

[20] *Immunity from Legal Process* [1999] ICJ Rep 88–9 [66]; *Behrami* (ECtHR GC) App Nos 71412/01 and 78166/01 (2007) [143].
[21] See among many others FV García-Amador (1956) 34 RDISDP 151; F Seyersted (1961) 37 BYIL 404–5; Ritter (n 5) 441; Salmon (n 19) 482; Amrallah (n 15) 73–4; Pérez Gonzalez (n 10) 64; Hirsch (n 5) 62; Higgins (n 11) 283.
[22] See *Bosnia Genocide* [2007] ICJ Rep [385].
[23] cf C Eagleton (1950) 76 RdC 385–6; Pérez Gonzalez (n 10) 68.
[24] cf Brölmann (n 16) 322.   [25] L Condorelli (1984) 189 RdC 114–15.
[26] But see Eagleton (n 23) 385–6, 399. Also F Morgenstern, *Legal Problems IOs* (1986) 4 points out that the lack of territorial jurisdiction makes the application of key concepts of responsibility, such as the exhaustion of local remedies, impossible. However, as noted by C Tomuschat in E Cannizzaro (ed), *The EU as an Actor in International Relations* (2002) 178, despite the fact that IOs lack 'flesh and blood' [read: territory and nationals], in some sectors 'their status is exactly the same as that of States', and 'the rules of international responsibility pertain to that class of rules'.
[27] Accordingly, the ILC noted that IOs lack territory, but limited the repercussions of this fact with respect to the rules of attribution in the non-inclusion in the DARIO of provisions similar to those in Arts 9 and 10 ARSIWA, which presuppose that the relevant entity exercises control over territory. See UN Doc A/59/10 (2004) 102–3 [6]; G Gaja (2004) UN Doc A/CN.4/541 at 29 [67]. cf also Brölmann (n 16) 323. As for the general proposition that conduct is defined simply as 'action or omission' see Ago (n 1) 201 [10].
[28] Talmon (n 16) 222 states that the question of attribution of SC conduct to the Organization 'can be disposed of quickly'; that much is true by all accounts. The focus in the upcoming chapter, however, is rather the *identification* of conduct that can be qualified as Council conduct *proper*.
[29] Art 7(1) UNC.

process of establishing whether and how the UN may perpetrate an internationally wrongful act through the Council is to identify conduct that is susceptible of engaging the international responsibility of the UN within the framework of Chapter VII coercive non-forcible measures.[30] In this respect, a preliminary enquiry would be to define the term.

'Conduct' has been defined as

one of the classical unilateral acts such as notification, protest, recognition, or promise, or one of the legal or obligatory acts such as the fulfillment of an international obligation, or even those acts that take place in the context of formation of international rules.[31]

While States regularly undertake all these acts, and IOs occasionally undertake some of them (eg notification, acts in fulfilment of international obligations, and the like), a wider definition of conduct as any given 'act[ion] or omission' is what the ILC appears to condone,[32] and it is in this sense that the term is used in this context. The notion of 'conduct' is central with respect to the engagement of international responsibility.[33]

Since IOs do not exercise jurisdiction over territory, their international personality is defined in functional rather than territorial terms.[34] Given this functional character of the international personality of IOs, the acts, or rather the conduct, which may potentially engage their international responsibility (*les faits générateurs de responsabilité*) will in most cases be normative in character.[35] Thus it will be primarily the promulgation of normative acts (*Rechtsakte*), namely of decisions *lato sensu*, that is susceptible of engaging the international responsibility of an IO and much less so operational activities,[36] such as PKOs. The latter are usually undertaken by organs of MS rather than by organs of the Organization. This brings to the forefront an array of other problems that needs to be dealt with.

Security Council conduct can be seen as being limited in the promulgation of decisions, of which the ones that are binding under Chapter VII UNC form the focus of the enquiry here.[37] The Council's conduct is quite multifaceted in this respect, despite the seemingly simple opening statement in this paragraph, which

---

[30] For both the term and the need to identify such 'susceptible' conduct see Ago (n 1) 216 [55]. It is the suspicion that certain conduct may constitute a breach and thus engage international responsibility that allows one to identify concrete conduct that needs to be attributed to a subject of international law. This is not meant to confuse the two separate elements of attribution and breach in any way: even though certain conduct may be attributable to the Council, it may turn out that it does not constitute a breach or does not finally engage UN responsibility due to the operation of a circumstance precluding wrongfulness: cf text at n 64 below.

[31] Condorelli (n 25) 38.   [32] ARSIWA Commentary 35 [6].

[33] cf ibid 34 [1]; UN Doc A/58/10 (2003) 45–6 [2].

[34] The ICJ made this clear in *Reparation* [1949] ICJ Rep 178. cf Brölmann (n 16) 323.

[35] Pérez Gonzalez (n 10) 67–8.

[36] Ibid; also W Wengler (1952) 44-I AIDI 278–9; M Virally in *Mélanges Rousseau* (1974) 286–8; A Reinisch (2007) 42 BDGVR 43. Significantly, in conceding implicitly that the EU, an IO, has achieved such high degree of integration to be placed on a par with national governments in respect of their institutional similarities, D Kennedy, *Of War and Law* (2006) 18 submits that the Union, having no significant 'military lever' [read: operational capacity] has to rely solely on law and regulation.

[37] B Conforti (1996) 43 RYDI 123 seq also notes that the Council's activities under Chapter VII are *normative* rather than *operational*.

appears to exhaust Council conduct in the 'promulgation of decisions'. The Council may (i) make (legal) determinations, such as those referring to the existence of a threat to the peace under Article 39,[38] to the international responsibility of a State in a given case,[39] to the validity of an international treaty,[40] to the legality of the creation of a State under international law,[41] or even to the legality of certain actions under international law;[42] (ii) impose binding non-forcible measures under Article 41;[43] (iii) delegate some of its powers under Chapter VII to one or more States or IOs;[44] (iv) create subsidiary organs in order to maintain or restore international peace and security.[45] This list of course does not purport to be exhaustive, but it highlights multifaceted Council conduct *proper* that may be, prima facie, susceptible of engaging UN responsibility.

i. Actions

A number of concrete examples of problematic Council conduct may be offered to elaborate on the general statement made above. One such example would be the adoption of a resolution under Chapter VII without determining the existence of a threat to the peace under Article 39, or where the determination is not at least readily inferred from the text of the relevant resolution, or even where the determination that there exists a threat to the peace is questionable. There have been some instances where MS—along with scholarly opinion—have actively questioned the existence of a threat to the peace despite the determination of the Council.[46]

Another example of problematic (cf 'susceptible') Council conduct would be a case where the Council passes (or keeps in force) a binding resolution under Chapter VII which is, say, contrary to the international prohibition of torture. As the ICTY held in *Furundžija*, 'the mere fact of keeping in force or passing legislation contrary to the international prohibition of torture' constitutes an internationally wrongful act.[47] Notwithstanding the many objections that may be voiced over whether a binding resolution of the Council under Chapter VII may be termed 'legislation' or be equated to State legislation in any way,[48] the fact remains that it is a binding normative act. It prescribes certain conduct on the part of States, and if the content of the binding normative act is contrary to (potential) international obligations

---

[38] See Chapter 3.I.1 below.   [39] eg SCR 687 (1991) [16].
[40] eg ibid [2]. See MH Mendelson and SC Hulton (1993) 64 BYIL 144–50; D Sarooshi (1996) 67 BYIL 466–8.
[41] S Talmon, *Kollektive Nichtanerkennung illegaler Staaten* (2006) 308–15, 320–5.
[42] See C Denis, *Le pouvoir normatif du Conseil de sécurité* (2004) 53–4.
[43] eg SCRs 687 (1991); 1267 (1999); 1373 (2001); 1822 (2008); 1929 (2010) and countless others.
[44] See D Sarooshi, *The UN and the Development of Collective Security* (1999) 11–13, 142 seq, 165. This includes authorizations under Chapter VII.
[45] See generally Sarooshi (n 40) 413 seq.   [46] See eg text at n 93 in Chapter 3.I.1 below.
[47] (Trial Chamber Judgment) IT-95-17/1 (10 December 1998) [150].
[48] In this respect, however, it may be useful to note that, in any case, resolutions combine elements of an inter-state agreement with elements of 'statutory' or regulatory administrative acts at the very least: A Orakhelashvili (2007) 11 MPUNYB 160. For an opinion implicitly but persuasively questioning the label of 'legislation' given by many commentators to SCR 1373 (2001) see G Abi-Saab in A Bianchi (ed), *Enforcing International Law Norms Against Terrorism* (2004) xix.

that prohibit torture and that are incumbent upon the UN, then the conduct of the Council (which is directly attributable to the Organization) in passing and keeping in force that act[49] is susceptible of constituting an internationally wrongful act which engages the Organization's responsibility.

The keeping in force of a sanctions regime that results in inhuman or degrading treatment of the population of the target State or of certain individuals may, by direct analogy, be deemed conduct susceptible of engaging UN responsibility. Similarly, it can be argued that obligations to freeze funds of individuals under Chapter VII resolutions, if maintained for a very long period of time, will cease to be 'temporary measures' and will result in affecting 'the very substance of the right of the persons concerned to property', thereby constituting 'arbitrary deprivation'. In such a case the relevant resolution could be found in violation of the right of property as guaranteed by Article 17 of the 1948 Universal Declaration of Human Rights, which might, according to the CFI at least, amount to the violation of a norm of *jus cogens*.[50] Further, the imposition of restrictive measures on individuals or legal entities without any possibility of a challenge to these measures being brought before a court or tribunal may be in breach of the internationally guaranteed right to a fair trial, which includes the right of access to a court and the right to an effective remedy.[51]

It is important to stress that reference is made to the *content* of the normative act as being in violation of international law, despite references to the potential results of conduct prescribed. The content of a normative act may constitute a violation of international law in and of itself, even if no application of the conduct prescribed has taken place in fact.[52] Whether this will be the case ultimately depends on the content of the primary rule.[53]

The promulgation of a decision delegating certain Chapter VII powers to MS or other IOs in a manner that is in violation of the UN Charter also constitutes conduct that could potentially engage the Organization's international responsibility. Significant attention has been devoted to the requirements established by the Charter, both explicitly and implicitly, for the lawful delegation of such powers,[54] which include establishing defined limits to delegations so as to remain in conformity with the Charter.[55] Suffice it here to note that one can find a number of examples of relevant conduct by the Council in its recent practice, examples which have been qualified as action under Article 41.[56] Such would be the adoption of Resolution 1373 (2001), by which the Council delegates to MS the discretionary

---

[49] Significantly, SCRs remain in force until formally revoked by the Council: see eg Talmon (n 16) 225 and cf E de Wet, *The Chapter VII Powers of the UN SC* (2004) 251–2 (on the 'parallelism of competence' and the 'parallelism of forms'). See also the GA reaction to the unilateral termination of sanctions against Southern Rhodesia in GAR 34/192 of 18 December 1979, UN Doc A/RES/34/192 at [9] and cf the formal termination in SCR 460 (1979) [2]–[3].

[50] cf T-315/01 *Kadi* [2005] ECR II-3649 [242]; see also [248], [289].

[51] See Arts 14 ICCPR and 6 ECHR and cf the case law presented and the arguments made in A Tzanakopoulos in A Reinisch (ed), *Challenging Acts of IOs before National Courts* (2010) 49 seq; in particular 73–4.

[52] eg *Modinos* (ECtHR) App No 15070/89 (1993) [23]–[26].

[53] ARSIWA Commentary 57 [12].   [54] eg Sarooshi (n 44) 18 seq; de Wet (n 49) 19.

[55] *Behrami* (n 20) [132]; cf [134]. See n 54.   [56] See eg de Wet (n 54) 316.

authority to designate persons to be included in 'blacklists'—as opposed to the regime established under Resolution 1267 (1999), according to which the relevant Sanctions Committee (a subsidiary organ of the Council) is the entity competent to devise the lists of persons and entities to be subjected to sanctions.[57] As Sarooshi has noted, it is the delegation of actual discretionary decision-making power which denotes a 'delegation of power' as opposed to a 'delegation of function', the latter only involving the delegation of implementation of a decision already taken.[58] In this context it is important to stress that the delegation of Chapter VII powers without adequate provision for exercise of effective control over the actual exercise of the powers by the delegatee constitutes conduct of the Council *proper*, which could amount to the breach of an obligation incumbent upon the Organization.[59]

The creation of subsidiary organs as measures to maintain or restore international peace and security, such as the establishment of the ICTY and ICTR, also constitutes conduct *proper* of the Council. The legality of such action can and has in fact been challenged.[60] Indeed, the creation by the Council of subsidiary organs may be in violation of the UN Charter, if the Charter's requirements for the lawful establishment of subsidiary organs have not been complied with.[61] It can also be in violation of general international law, if for example it is not in conformity with the principle *nullum crimen nulla poena sine lege*, a general principle of law in the sense of Article 38(1)(c) of the ICJ Statute. This susceptible conduct has been qualified as 'fall[ing] squarely within the powers of the Council under Article 41'.[62] Further, the Council may of course combine the creation of subsidiary organs with delegation of Chapter VII powers to these organs, as it did for example with Resolution 1244 (1999), whereby it established UNMIK and delegated Chapter VII powers to it.[63]

The instances of Council conduct described in the preceding paragraphs are bound to, and indeed have raised questions as to the legality of its action under the Charter and general international law.[64] The point at this juncture, however, is not to stress that Council conduct may be illegal, but rather that there exists conduct on the part of the Council, which is thus attributable directly to the Organization. It is simply more convenient to choose instances of Council conduct the legality of which has been questioned, to demonstrate how the Council's conduct *proper*

---

[57] See SCRs 1267 (1999); 1333 (2000); 1390 (2002) and so forth; the most recent relevant SCRs are 1822 (2008) and 1904 (2009). For the importance of the distinction between the '1267 regime' and the '1373 regime' with respect to the concept of 'normative control' see this chapter at Section II.2 below.

[58] Sarooshi (n 44) 11. cf *Kadi* (n 50) with T-228/02 *OMPI* [2006] ECR II-4665 [100]–[102]; JA Frowein in *Festschrift Eitel* (2003) 129.

[59] See Sarooshi (n 44) 41, 164; cf Talmon (n 16) 226–7.

[60] See eg discussion in C Tomuschat (1994) 49 Europa Archiv 64. cf also, on the establishment of subsidiary organs under Art 41 UNC, *Behrami* (n 20) [142].

[61] See generally Sarooshi (n 40); also *Behrami* (n 20) [132].

[62] *Tadić* (Appeal on Jurisdiction) IT-94-1-AR72 (2 October 1995) [36 *in fine*].

[63] SCR 1244 (1999) [5], [10]–[11]. See also *Behrami* (n 20) [142]. But see M Milanović and T Papić (2009) 58 ICLQ 278–9.

[64] See eg the criticism on the *vires* of SCRs in TM Franck (1992) 86 AJIL 519; P-M Dupuy (1993) 97 RGDIP 625–6; B Graefrath (1993) 47 NJ 435; idem (1993) 4 EJIL 184. See further Chapter 3.I below. For questions raised as to compliance with general international law see further Chapter 3.II.

is actually exhausted, as far as actions are concerned, in the promulgation of normative acts.

ii. Omissions

Conduct, however, is not limited to actions, but also includes omissions,[65] and this is prima facie applicable to the UN just as it is with respect to any other subject of international law.[66] As much has been admitted by the SR on the responsibility of IOs;[67] an admission which prompted rather heated exchanges in the ILC. Statements by the S-G to the effect that '[i]n 1994 ... the UN ... *failed to honour th[e] obligation* [to prevent genocide]' also point to such an admission.[68] Judge Elaraby, no less, writing in his capacity as a commentator, has alluded to omissions on the part of the Council ('benign neglect of breaches of the peace or acts of aggression') as being susceptible of constituting wrongful conduct.[69] Admittedly, the issue will turn on whether there is an obligation incumbent upon the Organization and the Council to act in such cases,[70] or whether it is simply a case of discretionary power to act. This is because both States and IOs (and individuals for that matter) *omit* to do things all the time;[71] there is thus no way to single out an omission—at least a *legally significant* omission—except in connection with a positive duty to act.[72] A parallel can be drawn here to the practice and *opinio juris* required for the establishment of a *prohibitive* customary rule. Because practice with respect to such a rule would consist in doing nothing, it is the element of *opinio juris* that assumes greater significance in the instance, because this is the one that will point to a duty to act or to refrain from acting, thus setting apart legally significant omissions

---

[65] As Ago notes (n 1) 216 [55], the cases in which the responsibility of a State has been invoked on the basis of omissions are perhaps more numerous than those based on action.

[66] eg in *Behrami* (n 20) [143], the ECtHR found no difficulty in attributing an omission to the UN through its subsidiary organ, the UNMIK.

[67] G Gaja (2005) UN Doc A/CN.4/553 at 3 [8] seq, and especially 4 [10].

[68] UN Doc SG/SM/7263 (1999) 1 [emphasis added]. The S-G went on implicitly to blame the Council in finding that the UN force in the country 'was neither mandated nor equipped' for the sort of action needed to prevent or halt the genocide (ibid).

[69] N Elaraby in *Festschrift Eitel* (2003) 56.

[70] This is what Elaraby seems to be claiming when he refers to the Council as being 'duty-bound' to adopt urgent measures to maintain international peace and security, ibid 63. This is also true for the S-G's statement with respect to the Rwandan genocide (n 68). Similarly C Tomuschat (1995) 33 AVR 12–13, who notes that the Council *must* act in cases where there's a threat to the peace [emphasis added]; as well as M Bedjaoui in *Colloque de Rennes* (1995) 301–2. cf also Klein (n 1) 387; K Hailbronner (1992) 30 AVR 11. cf finally C Amorim in *Festschrift Eitel* (2003) 12, who states that the Council is 'legally responsible' for the maintenance of international peace and security. But see H Kelsen, *Law of the UN* (1950) 285.

[71] cf AV Lowe *International Law* (2007) 41: 'States often do nothing, and for a wide range of reasons'.

[72] Ago RdC (n 1) 500 seq; cf also 441, 459: it is implied in the fact that conduct must be 'verifiable' in the 'real' world that there must be some reference to the conduct required by the primary rule in order to distinguish legally significant conduct. This is true for actions as well as omissions, but whereas one could simply attribute any action to a subject and then determine the establishment of responsibility at the stage of examination of the second essential element, the breach of an obligation, the attribution of any omission seems like a rather uneconomic thing to do.

from cases of simply 'doing nothing'.[73] Accordingly, it is necessary, in order to identify omissions, to make some preliminary reference to primary rules and the obligations these impose.

It is useful to draw a contradistinction to the law of State responsibility at this juncture. It has been noted that any act by an individual, group of individuals, or legal entity, or any incident which takes place in the territory of a State can be also construed as an omission on the part of the State to thwart the commission of the act by those actors, or to prevent the incident from occurring.[74] This act or incident has been termed *élément* (or *fait*) *catalyseur*.[75] Thus, whereas the conduct of the said actors will not be, in the first instance, attributable to the State, there will be in fact an act of State in the State's omission to prevent or possibly punish or otherwise react to that conduct or event.[76] Three remarks are pertinent in this respect. First of all, this statement demonstrates that it may sometimes be easier to identify potentially legally significant omissive conduct on the part of States when a certain incident occurs that is in some way connected to their territory—this is because of the principle of territorial jurisdiction.

The second point is that the above statement says in effect nothing about the potential engagement of the responsibility of the State in the instance; all we know is that there is omissive conduct attributable to the State. The existence of an internationally wrongful act will further depend on whether it can be established that the State is under an international obligation to prevent or punish the conduct of the individual or entity, or prevent the event from occurring.[77] If so established, as for instance with respect to the responsibility of Iran for not preventing the intrusion by a group of individuals in the US Embassy in Tehran, that is, for omitting to protect the Embassy as it was under an international obligation to do,[78] then the State becomes responsible for its *own* omissive conduct and not for the active conduct of the individual or entity.

The final point relates to the fact that IOs do not have territory or *plenitude des pouvoirs*, and thus in their case one cannot readily identify an omission by reference to an event occurring in connection with their territory. Still, conduct taken by an entity that is not an organ or agent of the organization can signify an omission of the organization to prevent it—it is just that reference will have to be made, in such cases, not to territory, but to the organization's areas of (exclusive) competence. This again relates to the functional rather than territorial nature of the legal personality of IOs.[79]

Notwithstanding the lack of territory in the case of IOs, it can be argued that MS conduct in an IO's area of competence constitutes at the same time an omission of the organization to prevent that conduct, if the organization has been conferred

---

[73] cf *'Lotus'* [1927] PCIJ Ser A No 10 at 28; Lowe (n 71) 41, 50–3. See also generally MH Mendelson in *Mélanges Virally* (1991) 373 seq.

[74] cf García-Amador (n 21) 148.

[75] See L Condorelli and H Dipla in *Honneur Ago* (1987) 71–3.

[76] García-Amador (n 21) 148.

[77] cf Condorelli and Dipla (n 75) 75; Milanović and Papić (n 63) 272–3.

[78] *Hostages* [1980] ICJ Rep 31 [61].   [79] See text at n 34.

the power to make relevant decisions which are binding on its MS. Examples of this can be drawn from the practice of the EC: as the SR notes in his Second Report, certain powers may have been conferred (or more specifically transferred) to an IO.[80] That organization may then proceed to conclude an agreement with third States, as for instance the EC may do in an area of exclusive EC competence. The implementation of the agreement is necessarily left to EC MS, however it is the organization that is responsible in case of an infringement of the obligations under the agreement.[81] The SR uses this as an example in order to demonstrate that responsibility of an IO does not necessarily rest on attribution—because the act of the organs of MS are not attributable to the organization, but to the MS under the basic rule of attribution in Article 4 ARSIWA.[82] Notwithstanding the fact that this is hardly reconcilable with the attribution of conduct being characterized as an 'essential element' for the engagement of international responsibility both with respect to States and IOs,[83] it can be argued that there *is* in fact conduct that is attributable to the IO in the case at hand: the omissive conduct of not preventing the act by the MS which results in the breach of the IO's obligations under the agreement. The assumption of an obligation to prevent breaches when these occur because of MS conduct can be understood as being implicit in the organization concluding the relevant agreement.[84] This is further supported by the fact that the organization (specifically here the EC) has the power to prevent breaches through the imposition of binding measures on the MS.

Another relevant example, again used by the SR (only to demonstrate that there can be attribution of responsibility without attribution of conduct, as above) is that of Annex IX of UNCLOS on the participation of IOs in the Convention.[85] According to Article 6, 'parties who have competence under Article 5 of Annex [IX] [ie IOs] shall have responsibility *for failure to comply* with obligations or for any other violation of this Convention.'[86] This can be seen effectively as the imposition of an obligation of result. Essentially the provision establishes a rebuttable presumption in favour of attribution of conduct to the participating IO in any case: if not for its action, then for its omission to prevent the breach by a MS in its area of competence.[87] Even more illuminating in this respect is the example

---

[80] The term 'transfer' here denoting the lack of ability of MS to exercise that power concurrently. See D Sarooshi, *IOs and their Exercise of Sovereign Powers* (2005) 28 seq, 65 seq. It is this terminology that is consistently used in the text.

[81] Gaja (n 27) 5 [10].

[82] Ibid 6 [11]. But see further idem (n 67) 5–6 [13]–[15].

[83] See Talmon (n 5) 409. See for another critique of this position, also on further grounds, E Paasivirta and PJ Kuijper (2005) 36 NYIL 214.

[84] cf Klein (n 1) 387. The SR (n 67) 5–6 [13]–[15] makes a similar point, likening the situation of the organization to that of Albania in *Corfu Channel* and discussing the possibility of obligations of result being incumbent upon IOs. Finally, Hirsch (n 5) 37 finds that there is an ancillary obligation of the organization to ensure compliance with its principal obligation by an entity that has the necessary means to comply.

[85] See Gaja (n 27) 6 [12].   [86] Emphasis added.

[87] cf J Heliskoski, *Mixed Agreements* (2001) 165, according to whom 'Articles 5 and 6 of Annex IX essentially create a procedural framework within which doubts as to questions of attribution can be addressed'. The SR (n 27) 6 [12] at fn 16 comments on this quote that '[it] should be understood as

of the request submitted by Chile and the EC to an ITLOS Special Chamber. The Court was asked to ascertain

whether the [EC] has complied with its obligations under the Convention, especially [A]rticles 116 to 119 thereof, to *ensure* conservation of swordfish, in the fishing activities undertaken by vessels flying the flag of any of its member States...[88]

These provisions are interpreted by Chile to impose on the Community an obligation of result;[89] what is attributable to the EC is not the acts of the vessels flying the flag of its MS, but rather its omission to *ensure* that these vessels do not undertake any operation that may lead to a breach of its obligations under the Convention.[90] How the Community will ensure such compliance is not pertinent in any case.

Turning to an example related to the UN, in the *Behrami* case, the ECtHR found that an omission to de-mine a certain area on the part of UNMIK, a UN subsidiary organ, was attributable to the UN.[91] In order to reach this conclusion, the Court needed to determine at the same time whether there was an obligation on (the UN and thus on) UNMIK to de-mine the area, and it did so on the basis of the organ's mandate under SCR 1244.[92] This does not necessarily prejudge the decision whether the omission will in fact have breached the obligation—there may be other reasons why UNMIK failed to de-mine the specific area, as the UN claimed in *Behrami*,[93] while a final decision on the issue would also depend on the precise content of the obligation. It is sufficient for the purposes of attribution that prima facie there was an obligation on the UN and thus on UNMIK to take certain action with respect to de-mining, which in the instance UNMIK omitted to do. Of course, the very same case can be seen from the vantage point of an incident occurring within the Organization's (and its subsidiary organ's, UNMIK) area of competence (which in this case is almost comparable to a State's territorial jurisdiction),[94] which the Organization had an obligation to but failed to prevent.

referring to attribution of responsibility, not of conduct', without providing any reason why it should be so.

[88] *Swordfish* (Order) Case No 7 (20 December 2000) [2(3)(a)] [emphasis added].

[89] The verb 'to ensure' has been noted as establishing an obligation of result rather than an obligation of conduct, in particular within the framework of UNCLOS: see Condorelli and Dipla (n 75) 86–7. An obligation of result is an obligation to succeed in bringing about the required result whatever the circumstances: see *Bosnia Genocide* (n 22) [430]. However, it is questionable whether Arts 116–19 UNCLOS do in fact impose obligations of result, Chile's interpretation notwithstanding.

[90] Significantly, in *Hostages* (n 78) 31 [61] the Court stated that 'Iran was placed under the most categorical obligations...to take appropriate steps to *ensure* the protection of the United States Embassy...' [emphasis added]. cf also Klein (n 1) 387. Gaja (n 27) 7 [12], on the other hand, seems to suggest that there is no conduct here attributable to the Community, as the alleged omission to *ensure* conservation would include omissions on the part of the national States of the ships concerned to adopt relevant measures. However, the Community has the power to impose on MS measures to be taken in their national legal orders—if it failed to do so or if it was ineffective in its attempt to regulate the matter, then it has *failed to ensure* the conservation, and this omission is certainly attributable to the EC.

[91] *Behrami* (n 20) [142]–[143].   [92] Ibid [125]–[127], [142]–[143].

[93] Ibid [119].

[94] See eg the legal opinion of the Secretariat, according to which UNOSOM II is 'the effective authority in Somalia'—however, the opinion considers that the UN is not responsible for breaches

The explosion of a mine signifies the omission of UNMIK to de-mine the area, something that fell within its mandate. Both considerations (ie a prima facie reflection on the primary rule *and* a consideration of territorial jurisdiction or area of competence) are pertinent when attempting to establish the existence of a legally significant omission.

To conclude on this point, it becomes apparent that certain acts of individuals or MS or even simple incidents can in fact signify an omission by an IO to prevent or suppress them. This omission, and not the act of the individual or MS, will be directly attributable to the organization. Whether it will also constitute a breach of an international obligation so as to engage the responsibility of the organization is another matter altogether (although it has been incidentally discussed above). Further, the identification of legally significant omissions will require some venture into primary rules, in order to ascertain a prima facie duty to act. Accordingly, it is conceivable that an omission by the SC is an omission attributable to the UN, and could engage the latter's responsibility if it also amounts to the breach of an international obligation incumbent upon the UN by virtue of its constitutive instrument or general international law.

Of course the Council's conduct will not always be either an action or an omission, but rather it may constitute a web of intersecting actions and omissions, thus being complex in nature. The transfer of Iraqi OFF funds to the CPA in Iraq serves as yet another example of problematic conduct, but it also allows multiple legal bases for holding the UN—through the Council—responsible. In passing Resolution 1483 (2003) under Chapter VII UNC, and presumably under Article 41 (the Council, as per its 'custom' does not specify under which provision of the relevant Chapter it is acting), the Council provided for the transfer of OFF funds to the CPA.[95] These funds were administered up to that point by the UN itself.[96] The funds in any case were the property of the Iraqi people, if not the Iraqi State. Their transfer to the CPA (ie the US and UK) by the Council without putting in place any measures of vigilance or any sort of oversight mechanism—in short accompanied by a carte blanche for the CPA to act as it wills—could be deemed as contrary to the Council's obligation to act in good faith as the trustee of the Iraqi money.[97] This constitutes complex conduct involving both actions and omissions on the part of the Organization. At the same time, the transfer of funds can (or even must) be seen as accompanied by a delegation by the Council of its Chapter VII—Article 41 power for the use of that money.[98] The legality of such a delegation under the Charter is questionable in view of the lack of oversight

---

of the Convention on International Trade in Endangered Species of Wild Fauna and Flora committed by servicemen of UNOSOM II, because it is not bound by the treaty: [1994] UNJY 450 [4].

[95] At [17]. Note that there have been some recent SCRs where the Council explicitly states that it is acting under Art 41: eg 1929 (2010); 1928 (2010); 1847 (2009); however, the trend of generically referring to Chapter VII without specifying a provision still holds strong: cf eg 1925 (2010); 1906 (2009); 1904 (2009); 1872 (2009).

[96] See SCR 986 (1995) [7]–[8] and UN Doc S/1996/356 (1996).

[97] See Talmon (n 16) 223–8 for full consideration of this case.   [98] See ibid 221–2.

mechanisms and on the basis of the relevant requirements alluded to by the Charter and elaborated on in the literature.[99]

To conclude this section, the following observations should be offered as a summary: what can be termed the 'normative conduct' of the SC will always be directly attributable to the Organization as conduct undertaken by one of its organs. Similarly, the conduct of other organs of the UN, be it principal or subsidiary organs, to which Chapter VII powers have been delegated, will also be attributable to the Organization by virtue of the quality of the aforementioned entities as organs of the UN. Before, however, one moves on to discussing the attribution of acts of other actors to the UN, predominantly individuals with no organic or institutional link to the Organization and MS, the issue of attribution to the UN of potentially *ultra vires* acts of the Council must be dispensed with.

2. The question of attribution of *ultra vires* conduct

Much discussion has been devoted to whether SC conduct *proper*, such as the promulgation of legislative resolutions,[100] or the establishment of ad hoc judicial organs,[101] or legal determinations and decisions,[102] is *ultra vires* (ie in violation of the Charter).[103] From this, a discussion of the validity of the attacked (or defended) resolution ensues. It is to be expected that a discussion of the *vires* of a resolution will be followed by one referring to the legal consequences of the relevant finding; the resolution may then be deemed voidable, void, invalid, non-existent, and so forth.[104] These discussions are either not concerned with attribution, or rather presuppose that the *ultra vires* conduct of the Council will be attributable to the Organization.

In discussing attribution of conduct to States, Condorelli put the issue with respect to *ultra vires* acts in the clearest of terms. He distinguished between the question of attribution of an act to a subject and the question of the act's international validity, by holding that the problem of attribution refers to all acts that may produce international legal effect, while the problem of validity necessarily presupposes that the issue of attribution has been resolved in a manner that attributes the relevant conduct to the specific subject.[105] The issue of *ultra vires* thus—logically—only arises *after* it has been determined that the act in question is attributable to the subject.

---

[99] See Sarooshi (n 44) 18–19 on the general point that for a delegation to be lawful it must not exceed the limitations upon the general or specific competence of the delegating organ (the Council in particular) to delegate the relevant power. See also n 61 above and accompanying text on the obligation to exercise effective control over the exercise of the delegated power by the delegatee.

[100] eg B Elberling (2005) 2 IOLR 337; M Fremuth and J Griebel (2007) 76 NJIL 339; M Happold (2003) 16 LJIL 593. See also n 63.

[101] eg K Zemanek in *Honour Bedjaoui* (1999) 630–1, 637 seq; E de Wet in R Wolfrum and V Röben (eds), *Developments of International Law in Treaty Making* (2005) 183. See also n 63.

[102] eg de Wet (n 101) 183. See also n 64.

[103] This accords with the general tendency to make claims that an IO acts *ultra vires*: see E Osieke (1976–7) 48 BYIL 262.

[104] See generally RY Jennings in *Honour McNair* (1965) 64 seq; E Lauterpacht in ibid 88 seq; Zemanek (n 101) 642. See further Chapter 7.II.2.ii below.

[105] Condorelli (n 25) 39.

While Condorelli's analysis is made with reference to States, there is no reason why it is not applicable to IOs.[106] In fact, it seems even more pertinent with respect to IOs, given especially that their acts only lay claim to *international* validity (as for IOs internal and international validity are one and the same thing), and so by logical necessity this is an examination that should *follow* attribution. The examination of an act's *vires* is in essence a determination as to whether the act is in conformity with the provisions of the organization's constitutive instrument and possibly other rules of the organization. The rules of the organization, in turn, give rise to international obligations binding on the organization itself—as a creation of States that endowed it with specific powers, the Organization must act in accordance with these powers.[107]

One could delve into a discussion as to what is the ultimate justification for attributing the *ultra vires* acts of State organs to the State, and whether this ultimate justification is equally applicable to IOs. Along these lines, it has been argued that, since the State has the right of auto-organization, that is, the right to organize itself and assign the exercise of governmental functions to different entities, it is an aspect of the principle of good faith that it cannot then contradict itself by claiming that the entities it elected to act through in order to exercise governmental authority have overstepped their competence.[108] This may not seem readily transferable in the field of IOs. However, an analogy does qualify as pertinent:[109] even if IOs do not auto-organize in the first instance, their organization is provided for by the States that confer powers on them. They are accordingly bound not to transgress their obligations to act in accordance with their constitutions. They should then not be able to deny the attribution of an *ultra vires* act, which constitutes at the same time the breach of an international obligation, as this would in effect mean that no act in violation of international law by an organ would ever be attributable to them: any violation of international law, stemming either from the constitutive instrument or from general international law (with which it could be assumed that the constituent instrument will require compliance, unless there is evidence to the contrary) could be claimed to be *ultra vires* the organ and the organization,[110] leading to non-attribution and to an *absurdum*. Also, IOs do auto-organize, in the same manner as States, except not in the first instance. Beyond the organization provided for in their constitutions, IOs then establish subsidiary organs and employ agents in order to exercise their functions,[111] and thus it would be a violation of the

---

[106] cf UN Doc A/59/10 (2004) 117 [5]: 'Article 6 only concerns attribution of conduct and does not prejudice whether an *ultra vires* act is valid or not under the rules of the organization'. See also Higgins (n 11) 278.

[107] Acts overstepping these powers are unlawful acts too, reminds Lauterpacht (n 104) 89. See n 110 below and for detailed discussion Chapter 3.

[108] Condorelli (n 25) 40, 54.

[109] The development of the law is, in the final analysis, 'a never-ending battle for control of the analogy' says AV Lowe in M Koskenniemi (ed), *International Law Aspects of the EU* (1998) 166.

[110] cf Condorelli (n 25) 81 with respect to States. This is the 'old temptation of regarding wrongs as *per se ultra vires*' as Jennings (n 104) 82 states. 'The question is rather', he continues, 'whether an *ultra vires* exercise of jurisdictions is *per se* a wrong'. This is a discussion for another chapter: 3.I.

[111] cf in this respect Sarooshi (n 40) 447 seq on the subordinate nature of subsidiary organs. cf also Virally (n 36) 293 on the qualification of such powers of IOs to supplement their organic apparatus as 'power of auto-organization'.

principle of good faith to subsequently claim that the *ultra vires* act of the entity they selected to act through is not attributable to them. This discussion serves to buttress the decision to apply similar rules to States and IOs in this respect. The Commission itself has noted that solutions analogous to the law of State responsibility must indeed be justified.[112]

As a matter of fact, the conclusion that if the *ultra vires* acts of State organs are attributable to the State, then also *ultra vires* acts of IO organs and agents must be attributable to the organization, was also reached by Gaja, the SR on responsibility of IOs. In his Second Report, Gaja found no reason to elaborate a different rule than the one in Article 7 ARSIWA, save for certain minor changes predominantly of stylistic character.[113] According to the SR, the ICJ has accepted that *ultra vires* acts of IOs are attributable to them when it stated in *Expenses* that 'both national and international law contemplate cases in which the body corporate or politic may be bound, as to third parties, by an *ultra vires* act of an agent'.[114] This statement needs to be treated with extreme care, as there is no direct link between organs whose conduct is attributable to an entity and organs that may bind an entity in international law.[115] The effect of this holding of the Court is solely that if an entity is to be bound by an *ultra vires* act of an organ or agent, then that act is definitely attributable—but this does not say much about *ultra vires* acts' attribution in general. It is the statement of the Court in *Immunity from Legal Process* that actually points to the direction of attribution of all *ultra vires* acts of organs and agents to an IO. The Court found that 'all agents of the United Nations, in whatever official capacity they act, must take care not to exceed the scope of their functions, and should so comport themselves *as to avoid claims against the United Nations*'.[116] It is apparent from this statement that the Court considers that *ultra vires* conduct by UN agents may lead to claims against the UN, and thus, by logical necessity, must also be attributable to the UN.[117]

The Commission agreed with the application to IOs of the same rule that is applicable to States in adopting Article 7 DARIO.[118] Accordingly, Council conduct *proper*, namely the Council's normative actions that consist in the promulgation of resolutions, are attributable to the UN irrespective of their *vires*, and notwithstanding any evaluation as to their validity, invalidity, binding force, and so forth. For the purposes of attribution of conduct, such considerations are not pertinent.

Passing (binding) resolutions is in effect the only thing that the Council (and thus the UN through the Council) can really 'do', at least under Chapter VII; it

---

[112] UN Doc A/57/10 (2002) 232 [475].   [113] Gaja (n 27) 26–7 [57]–[58].

[114] [1962] ICJ Rep 168. cf Gaja (n 27) 23–4 [52].

[115] In *Nottebohm* [1955] ICJ Rep 17–18, the ICJ held that Guatemala was not bound by acts of certain Guatemalan officials (despite the fact that these acts would be attributable to Guatemala for purposes of determination of State responsibility): see Lowe (n 109) 159–60.

[116] *Immunity* (n 20) 89 [66 *in fine*].

[117] cf Gaja (n 27) 25 [54], where the SR, however, focuses on the fact that this statement covers agents as well as organs of the Organization. But see also Amrallah (n 15) 62 and 71, who specifically finds this to mean that the Organization bears responsibility for *ultra vires* acts of its agents.

[118] cf UN Doc A/59/10 (2004) 100 [71]. This also appears to conform to the opinions of publicists: see eg Hirsch (n 5) 88 seq; T Ueki in *Honour Oda*, vol 1 (2002) 243.

cannot and does not undertake any operational activities, since coercive measures under Article 41 are not to be implemented by the Council itself (something that the Council would not be able to do anyway in view of the lack of any operational capacity whatsoever),[119] whereas military enforcement measures under Article 42 cannot practically be implemented by the Council in view of the lack of any Article 43 agreements to date.[120] The application and enforcement of the relevant resolutions rests with the MS,[121] or with the addressees of the resolutions in general. This brings up the question whether the responsibility that the UN incurs through the SC is limited to conduct of the Council per se, that is, to the promulgation of a decision that constitutes a breach of an international obligation incumbent upon the UN, or whether it may also extend to responsibility for the conduct of other entities or subjects of international law, acting on the basis of a SCR.

II. Attribution of Member State Conduct to the United Nations

It is not only the conduct of its organs—in particular the SC—that are attributable to the UN. By virtue of Article 5(1) DARIO, which must be seen as reflecting both customary law and the predominant view in literature,[122] it is also the conduct of agents that is attributable to the Organization. The term 'agent' is to be understood 'in the most liberal sense' in accordance with the jurisprudence of the ICJ,[123] and this is how the term is also to be understood for purposes of attribution of conduct of 'agents' to an IO.[124] There is no requirement for an official or institutional link, but rather an agent is any natural or legal person 'through whom [the Organization] acts'.[125] Whereas the distinction between organs and agents is not relevant, according to the ILC, for the purposes of attribution of conduct to an international organization, in the sense that the conduct of both its organs and its agents is attributable to it,[126] given the lack of operational capacity of the Council itself, the question arises under which circumstances States (or State organs) implementing binding resolutions under Article 41 can be considered as 'agents' of the Organization and thus have their conduct attributed to the UN. A further distinction can be drawn, which brings the notion of an 'agent' of an IO to

[119] The words of Wellens are telling in this respect:

> Even the most powerful executive organ on this planet—ie, the UN Security Council—has largely to rely on national administrations and courts for the implementation of its policies and decisions. ([2004] 25 MichJIL 1179)

[120] See eg Sarooshi (n 44) 142 seq; L-A Sicilianos (2002) 106 RGDIP 6; C Économidès (2005) 58 RHDI 327.

[121] See Art 25 UNC and cf Art 48.   [122] See nn 18–21 and accompanying text.

[123] *Reparation* (n 34) 177.

[124] *Immunity* (n 20) 88–9 [66]; Art 2(c) DARIO; UN Doc A/59/10 (2004) 106 [4]–[6]. Also S Yee in *Memory Schachter* (2005) 440; Talmon (n 5) 412–13; Klein (n 1) 377–8; Ritter (n 5) 441.

[125] *Reparation* (n 34) 177; UN Doc A/59/10 (2004) 106 [6]. cf G Gaja (2009) UN Doc A/CN.4/610 at 8–9 [23]; DC Report in UN Doc A/CN.4/L.743 (2009). In any event, this very wide definition of an agent applies to the UN as the definition accepted in UN practice, and thus under the rules of the Organization.

[126] UN Doc A/59/10 (2004) 106 [5].

the forefront: it has been noted that when the organization has a *volonté distincte*, which the UN certainly does,[127] the 'role of [MS] *qua* organs should be regarded as neutral', presumably also for purposes of attribution, because an organization is an integral whole.[128] The role of MS or their organs as potential agents, however, which may rest on a simple control link and thus not be part of the organization's 'integral whole', does require further examination.

1. State organs as UN(SC) agents

One of the more problematic issues identified with respect to attribution of conduct to IOs in general is the case where the conduct of a State organ not fully seconded to the organization (thus clearly constituting, if anything, its 'agent' and not its organ) is mandated by the organization (or takes place in an area that falls within the organization's exclusive competence).[129] The question thus arises as to whether (and in what circumstances) States and their organs may be considered as 'agents' of the UN when implementing binding SCRs under Chapter VII.

Given the liberal interpretation of the term 'agent', a State organ not fully seconded to an IO, but rather 'lent' to it (or 'employed' by it) in the sense of implementing a binding decision of the organization, which the latter lacks the operational capacity to implement itself, could be qualified as an 'agent' of the organization—in the final analysis, the organization 'acts through' that State organ in the specific instance.[130] Accordingly, State organs implementing binding SCRs imposing non-forcible enforcement measures under Article 41 could be considered agents of the Organization, and thus have their conduct directly (or 'automatically') attributed to it.

A similar issue presents itself with respect to the implementation of EC international obligations or secondary EC law (*droit dérivé*) by organs of EC MS; it may be cited here to provide some guidance. The EC has argued that in circumstances such as those described above, EC MS organs act as de facto organs (or, one could say more correctly, 'agents') of the Community.[131] WTO Panels have accepted this view,[132] which also finds some support in legal literature.[133] By

---

[127]   cf *Reparation* (n 34) 180; *Expenses* (n 114) 168.

[128]   See Higgins (n 11) 261.   [129]   See UN Doc A/CN.4/L.622 (2002) 6 [16].

[130]   In the implementation of Art 41 sanctions for example, MS act on account of (*compte*) the Organization: L-A Sicilianos in idem and LP Forlati (eds), *Les sanctions économiques en droit interna-tional* (2004) 17. It may also be significant (on the level of semantics if not otherwise) that MS have been called 'agents of execution' in this respect: ibid 68. See also idem *Les réactions décentralisées* (1990) 3.

[131]   See UN Doc A/CN.4/545 (2004) 19–20.

[132]   *EC—Trademarks* [2005] WT/DS174/R [7.98]; cf *EC—LAN* [1998] WT/DS62/R; WT/DS67/R; WT/DS68/R [8.16].

[133]   PJ Kuijper and E Paasivirta (2004) 1 IOLR 126–7; eidem (n 83) 215–16; Talmon (n 5) 412–13. Klein (n 1) 385 questions whether this can be accepted on the basis that the EC will lack sufficient control over the actions of the MS in most cases. However, it is crucial that attribution on the basis of an 'organic' link (as opposed to a 'control' link) is *automatic*: conduct of organs is auto-matically attributed to the State or IO, without any consideration of the control the latter exercises over the organ. This is also the justification for the attribution of acts of domestic courts to the State (as the State will not be able to 'control' its courts in any way, these normally enjoying independence

analogy, it could be claimed that MS organs implementing binding decisions of the SC act as agents of the UN.[134]

However, this somewhat simple solution is obfuscated by the existence of Article 4 ARSIWA. This general rule of attribution of conduct to States clearly demands that the conduct of an organ of a State be, at least in the first instance, attributable to that State,[135] and allows very few exceptions to that general rule—that is, when a State organ has been 'placed at the disposal' of another State.[136] Because of this general rule of attribution of conduct to States, one would not be free to qualify conduct by State organs as attributable to an IO on the basis of the former acting as agents of the latter: the ILC purports to attribute the conduct of State organs to an IO by virtue of Article 5 DARIO only when these State organs are fully seconded to the organization,[137] which is hardly the case when a State organ is implementing a binding decision of the SC or of the EC.[138] The EC thus asked for special rules to that effect with respect to itself (and 'other potentially similar organizations') when it came to the drafting of the relevant articles on attribution of conduct to IOs.[139] The ILC decided against adopting any sort of special rules with respect to specific organizations (or to specific types of organizations, such as 'organizations of integration').[140] While this may be justified in an attempt to hold back the fragmentation of international law, or for other reasons, the solution propounded

from the executive) as well as for the attribution of *ultra vires* acts. In the case of IOs, if agents are treated in the same manner as organs, then attribution of acts of agents should be automatic, irrespective of the 'control' that the IO exercises over them—if they act beyond their mandate or are difficult to control or contain, that is the organization's problem for selecting to act through the particular agent, but it does not eschew the attribution of the agent's acts to the organization. cf A Tzanakopoulos [2009] EJIL: Talk!, 10 March; n 161 below.

[134] Talmon (n 5) 414 states that this situation (of a MS performing the functions of an agent) 'seems to be limited to the particular structure of "supranational" organizations such as the EC'. However, there is no immediately obvious reason why the same should not apply to MS implementing binding obligations imposed by Chapter VII resolutions: in the final analysis, States are simply performing functions under the rules of the organization: Arts 24(1), 25, 39, and 41 UNC read in conjunction confirm this. In no other circumstances would the Organization be able to perform its function for the maintenance of peace—the performance of this function essentially depends on the MS performing part of the function by complying with and implementing Chapter VII SCRs. Hirsch (n 5) 82 seems to accept this argument when he considers that MS implementing an EC Regulation or an SC-imposed aerial blockade are in the same position with respect to being employed by the respective organizations in the fulfilment of their functions. There is an argument to be made that States implementing binding SCRs are fulfilling their *own* obligations under the Charter (in particular Art 25), as opposed to EC MS, which are acting in fulfilment of EC obligations. However, EC obligations are *channelled* to the MS, and thus imposed on them through legal instruments, so as to constitute MS obligations as well. Further, it could be argued that UN MS act in fulfilment of UN obligations (imposed on the Organization by virtue of its constituent instrument, say for the maintenance of peace and security) when implementing SC decisions. In any case, when the focus is on the functions of the organization, it becomes clear that both the EC and the UN *utilize* their MS and 'act through them' in order to exercise the functions that have been conferred on the IO.

[135] See G Gaja in *Festschrift Tomuschat* (2006) 519.

[136] See Art 6 ARSIWA and Commentary 43–5.

[137] UN Doc A/59/10 (2004) 110 [1]. This probably means that they are under the *exclusive* authority of the Organization as stated by Ritter (n 5) 444 and UN Doc A/51/389 (1996) 6 [17].

[138] cf Gaja (n 27) 6 [11], 7–8 [13].   [139] See UN Doc A/C.6/59/SR.21 (2004) 5 [18].

[140] Or 'regional economic integration organizations'. On the term see Paasivirta and Kuijper (n 83) 204 seq, especially 211. For another critique of the decision see R Hofmann (2007) 42 BDGVR 33–4.

by the EC may not really require *special* rules:[141] it could in fact be of general application. Be that as it may, in the present state of affairs the general rule of attribution of conduct to States in Article 4 ARSIWA seems to block the immediate qualification of State organs that are not fully seconded to an IO as 'agents' of that IO and, subsequently, any direct attribution under Article 5 DARIO.

It is not immediately obvious why this should be the case—if a State organ can be qualified as acting as an agent of an IO in certain circumstances, as it has been suggested above, then Articles 4 ARSIWA and 5 DARIO could apply simultaneously, thus leading to dual or concurrent attribution of the conduct in question, both to the State and the IO. The ILC and the SR both have accepted the possibility of such dual attribution,[142] which in any case does not *necessarily* lead to concurrent responsibility: what may be a breach for the organization may not be a breach when it comes to the State and vice versa.[143] What seems to be the logic behind the argument that Article 4 ARSIWA blocks the application of Article 5 DARIO to State organs is that the latter are not private bodies or individuals, but rather part of the machinery of a State, a subject of international law in its own right.[144]

ECtHR jurisprudence confirms that conduct of MS organs in compliance with a binding IO decision is attributable to the State. The Court has consistently found that an action or omission by the organ of a State party to the ECHR is always attributable to that State, irrespective of whether that action or omission was necessary for the State to comply with an international obligation.[145] The ECtHR will then usually go on to determine whether the conduct in question also constitutes a breach of the State's obligations under the ECHR, where a number of other considerations come into play.[146] However, it is important to note that this discussion refers to whether the conduct is in breach of obligations under the ECHR—the question of attribution of the conduct to the State is readily resolved with an application, in essence although not explicitly, of Article 4 ARSIWA. The question of attribution to the IO becomes irrelevant for the Court once the conduct has been attributed to the ECHR State party.

The same (implicit) acceptance of the application of Article 4 ARSIWA to the acts of State organs, even when these are taken in implementation of Security Council resolutions, can be seen in the practice of the EC and domestic courts.[147] These have proceeded to review domestic implementing measures, not finding that the conduct complained of was exclusively attributable to the UN, even though the

---

[141]   See generally Talmon (n 5).

[142]   UN Doc A/CN.4/L.622 (2002) 5 [15]; A/59/10 (2004) 101 [4]; Gaja (n 27) 3 [6]; idem (n 125) 9 [25].

[143]   cf Talmon (n 5) 410. On the possible need and faculty of avoiding such dual attribution see further 413–14.

[144]   cf Talmon (n 16) 223.

[145]   See *M & Co* (1990) 64 DR 144; *Bosphorus* (GC) App No 45036/98 (2005) [153].

[146]   See this chapter at Section II.2.

[147]   The CFI goes in this direction, judging by its statement in *Kadi* (n 50) [209]; see also infra n 198 and accompanying text for the ECJ and cf the Canadian Federal Court in *Abdelrazik* 2009 FC 580 (4 June 2009) [3], [44], [147]–[148], [156]. See further the cases mentioned in Chapter 5.II.3.ii and cf A Tzanakopoulos (2010) 8 JICJ 256–7.

domestic authorities were acting in implementation of UN obligations and thus conceivably as 'agents' of the UN. This of course does not disprove that domestic authorities *were* acting as UN agents in the instance. Domestic courts were not concerned with parallel attribution to the UN: they are satisfied with attribution to the State, which then allows them to review State conduct.

Where the implementing State act is not considered to be attributable to the State, but to an IO, the ECtHR has explicitly stated this: in *Behrami*, the first case where the Court found conduct to be attributable to an IO, it held that 'in the present cases, the impugned acts cannot be attributed to the respondent States'.[148] The ECtHR did not shed any light as to why it considered attribution to the UN to be exclusive in the instance.[149]

Be that as it may, it is a fact that most IOs will act through State organs for lack of operational capacity in most cases,[150] and this is particularly true of the SC acting under Chapter VII UNC. In this context, the Appeals Chamber in *Tadić* put the issue very eloquently when it stated that '[i]t is only for want of . . . resources that the United Nations has to act through its Members'.[151] If these are not to be considered at least as 'agents' of the UN when acting in the implementation of Chapter VII binding resolutions, then there can be no simple (read: automatic) attribution of their acts to the Organization on the basis of Article 5 DARIO, and the inevitable question emerges as to whether their conduct is then in any other way attributable to the Organization.

2. Effective control, including *normative* control

i. *Effective control as factual control*

If State organ conduct in the implementation of Chapter VII measures cannot be considered as the conduct of an agent under Article 5 DARIO, maybe then it can be argued that it is attributable to the Organization as conduct of an organ 'placed at the disposal' of the IO. Under Article 6 DARIO,

The conduct of an organ of a State or an organ or agent of an international organization that is placed at the disposal of another international organization shall be considered under international law as an act of the latter organization *if the organization exercises effective control over that conduct.*[152]

---

[148] *Behrami* (n 20) [151]. This line has been followed by the ECtHR in a number of subsequent cases: see eg App Nos 31446/02; 363507/04; 6974/05. Similarly in *HN v The Netherlands* (NL 2008) ILDC 1092 [4.15] The Hague District Court attributes the conduct of Dutchbat (UNPROFOR) in Srebrenica to the UN, excluding any concurrent attribution to the Netherlands. In that it applies *Behrami*: [4.12.3].

[149] See also A Sari (2008) 8 HRLR 159; F Messineo (2009) 56 NILR 41. Given that attribution to the UN in *Behrami* was found to have been prescribed by Art 6 DARIO, it is further discussed in the immediately following section.

[150] See Gaja (n 27) 14 [29]; Hofmann (n 140) 28.

[151] (n 62) 45 [36]. The Appeals Chamber goes on to characterize action by MS on behalf of the Organization as a 'poor substitute *faute de mieux*, or a "second best" for want of the first'.

[152] Emphasis added.

This provision could encompass all State organs 'not fully seconded to the international organization' in the sense that these operate under a 'dual allegiance', namely both as organs of the organization and as organs of their home State *at the same time*.[153] The provision seems to refer, however, almost exclusively to national military contingents put at the disposal of the UN for peacekeeping operations, as well as to similar arrangements such as KFOR,[154] or NATO forces participating in *Operation Allied Force*.[155] In fact this is how both the SR and the ILC perceive it.[156] These contingents are under the operational command and control of the UN, but their sending States retain criminal jurisdiction and disciplinary power over them (for lack of a UN jurisdictional mechanism to that effect, among other things).[157] A wealth of material has been forthcoming on the issue of attribution of acts of 'UN forces' to the UN and the relevant responsibility of the Organization;[158] this is one of the first instances that sparked the debate on the responsibility of IOs and one of the very few instances that have produced a significant amount of practice.

It has long been accepted that responsibility derives from control in one way or another.[159] States are responsible for the acts of their organs because they have control over the way they set up their organic apparatus,[160] even if they do not in fact exercise control over all their organs (all the time).[161] The same goes for IOs with respect to their organs.[162] In this case the control link can be seen as subsumed

---

[153] This, it is submitted, is not precisely the same as *dédoublement fonctionnel*. The latter term implies that the organ may act either for the State or for the IO, but it can be determined for which entity it is acting at any given point in time.

[154] In *Behrami* (n 20) [135]–[141], the ECtHR found that the actions of KFOR were attributable to the UN, based on the chain of command established by SCR 1244 (1999). In rough lines, the Council retained overall control over the force, which was under the effective operational control of NATO, and which was constituted by national contingents volunteered by States. Even though the Court purported to be applying (then Art 5 but now) Art 6 DARIO, it did not really do so: it attributed on the basis of *overall* rather than *effective* control. See Milanović and Papić (n 63) 281–9 and n 170 below.

[155] T Stein in C Tomuschat (ed), *Kosovo and the International Community* (2002) 189–90 has argued that the national contingents' actions during the operation are to be attributed to NATO, because the latter exercised effective control over them.

[156] UN Doc A/59/10 (2004) 110 [1]–[2], 111–15 [5]–[9]; Gaja (n 27) 15–23 [32]–[49]. But see Gaja (n 125) 9 [25 *in fine*].

[157] See the legal opinion of the UN Secretariat [1972] UNJY 153–4. The same applies to NATO forces: Stein (n 155) 190. It is of some importance, however, that the UN considers such forces as subsidiary organs and characterized their personnel as 'international personnel *under the authority* of the United Nations': see the legal opinion of the Secretariat [1996] UNJY 450.

[158] eg Seyersted (n 21) 351; DW Bowett, *UN Forces* (1964); Salmon (n 19) 468; Amrallah (n 15) 57.

[159] Eagleton (n 23) 385.   [160] Condorelli (n 25) 26–30.

[161] eg the US Federal Government cannot in fact exercise control over certain official acts of the Governor of Arizona; however, these acts are still attributable to the US: *LaGrand* [2001] ICJ Rep 44–6 [111]–[113], [115]. Furthermore, States do not exercise control over their national courts and judiciary, but judicial acts are still attributable to them: C Eustathiadès, *La responsabilité internationale de l'État pour les actes des organes judiciaires*, vol 1 (1936) 25; *LaGrand* (this note) 46 [114]–[115]; ARSIWA Commentary 40–1 [6]. Finally, States may not be in fact exercising control over the actions of State organs acting *ultra vires*, but these *ultra vires* acts are still attributable to the relevant State: ARSIWA Commentary 45–7. With respect to de facto organs see Talmon (2009) 58 ICLQ 501.

[162] cf K Ginther, *Die völkerrechtliche Verantwortlichkeit internationaler Organisationen gegenüber Drittstaaten* (1969) 106; G Gaja in HG Schermers et al (eds), *Non-Contractual Liability of the EC* (1988) 172.

in the organic or institutional link. States and IOs may also be responsible for the acts of individuals if they exercise control over them—in the case of IOs these individuals being qualified as 'agents' given the broad relevant definition. Significantly, in this latter case it is the institutional or organic link that seems to be subsumed in the control link, at least as far as IOs are concerned.[163] This is because of the lax definition of the term 'agent'.

For the conduct of State organs 'not fully seconded to the Organization' to be attributed to the UN, the ILC demands, by virtue of Article 6, that the Organization exercise 'effective control' over them with respect to the specific conduct.[164] It is this question of who exercises effective control over the conduct of this organ 'in limbo' that will finally determine whether the former is attributable to the IO or the sending (or 'lending') State. The requirement would still allow for the attribution of conduct of State organs to the UN in the implementation of a Chapter VII resolution, if it were to be understood as encompassing *normative* control.[165] For there is an argument to be made that such binding resolutions may exercise effective normative control over the relevant State organs.[166] This is because they do not allow for any room for manoeuvre on the part of the implementing State. The obligation of States to impose—through their competent organs—sanctions on the persons and entities blacklisted by virtue of Resolutions 1267 (1999) seq, or their obligations stemming from Resolutions 827 (1993) and 955 (1994) establishing the ICTY and ICTR, can serve as pertinent examples of decisions that leave States hardly any leeway in their implementation.[167]

---

[163] cf Klein (n 1) 378–9.

[164] This provision has been applied (or at least cited) both by the ECtHR in *Behrami* (n 20) and by the House of Lords in *Al-Jedda* [2008] UKHL 58. At the time it had been provisionally adopted as Art 5.

[165] In fact, a relevant argument was made during the ILC discussion on the matter, without, however, carrying the day. See also Stein (n 155) 189–90, who maintains that the decision made by NATO on targeting during *Operation Allied Force* constituted effective control over the acts of the national contingents, even despite the fact that 'national commanders in theater' could overrule the decision.

[166] cf A Pellet in Tomuschat (n 155) 197, according to whom NATO controls the MS when these act in accordance with NATO decisions.

[167] cf the claims by the applicant, and the concession by the Council and the CFI that the Community had no discretion in implementing measures under SCR 1267: *Kadi* (n 50) [150], [174], [214], [231]. See also Elberling (n 100) 354. There are of course resolutions, eg imposing sanctions under Art 41, which allow States a wide margin of appreciation, in that they set general objectives and rely on general notions which need to be concretized at the point of implementation. See eg SCR 687 (1991) [24]. In such cases MS action should not be attributable to the Organization, and this is also in fact the position of the UN: a legal opinion of the Secretariat states that

> responsibility for carrying out embargoes imposed by the [SC] rests with [MS], which are accordingly responsible for meeting the costs of *any particular action they deem necessary* for ensuring compliance with the embargo. ([1995] UNJY 465 [emphasis added])

Similarly, SCR 1373 allows discretion to MS to designate individuals and legal entities that will be targeted by asset freezes, in sharp contradistinction to the regime established under SCR 1267, which identifies the specific individuals and entities to be sanctioned: the distinction is drawn clearly by the CFI in *OMPI* (n 58) [100]–[102]; as well as by the UK Supreme Court in *HM Treasury v Mohammed Jabar Ahmed and Others (FC); HM Treasury v Mohammed al-Ghabra (FC); R (Hani El Sayed Sabaei Youssef) v HM Treasury* [2010] UKSC 2 [148] (Lord Phillips); [168] (Lord Rodger); [196] seq (Lord Brown). cf also the Swiss Federal Tribunal in *Nada g SECO, Staatssekretariat für Wirtschaft* (CH 2007) ILDC 461 [8.1].

However, according to the Commission, the criterion for attribution in this case is *factual* control, namely whether it is the sending State or the receiving organization that exercises effective factual control over the conduct in question.[168] This factual control is to be understood, as the Commission insinuates,[169] in the same manner as the notions of 'instructions' and 'direction or control' are to be construed in Articles 6 and 8 ARSIWA.[170] Presumably this means that it must be established that the Organization was *in fact* exercising effective control over the susceptible conduct of a State organ in the specific instance—mere control by virtue of law (ie of a normative act) not being sufficient.[171] Of course on such a basis it is extremely hard to attribute the acts of MS in the implementation of binding Chapter VII resolutions to the Organization—the factual control exercised by the Organization over the MS in such a case is limited at best;[172] in most cases it will be non-existent.

ii. Normative control as effective control

On the other hand, it must be of some importance that whereas States have no normative power they can exercise over organs of another State (in Article 6 ARSIWA), international organizations basically function by exercising normative powers over their MS—at least the IOs that have been conferred the power to make decisions that are binding on their MS in certain areas of competence.[173] The SR himself has conceded—in earlier writing—that MS conduct may be *determined* by the IO in the implementation of the latter's binding decision.[174]

It seems pertinent at this point to attempt to define the notion of 'normative control'.[175] It is submitted that MS of an IO are under the effective normative control of the latter when they have no discretion or no 'margin of appreciation' in the implementation of a binding normative act of the organization.[176] Whether this is the case or not can admittedly only be determined in the specific instance;

---

[168] UN Doc A/59/10 (2004) 111 [3], 113 [7]. cf also Gaja (n 162) 171; Klein (n 1) 378–82.

[169] UN Doc A/59/10 (2004) 111 [3]–[4].

[170] ARSIWA Commentary 44 [2], 47 [1]. But this is not how the ECtHR understood the provision, as is apparent in *Behrami* (n 20), which adopts a much more lax standard of 'overall authority and control'. For this the decision was rightly criticized, including by the SR on the Responsibility of International Organizations: Gaja (n 125) 9–10 [26]. cf Messineo (n 149) 41 seq; Sari (n 149) 162 seq; Milanović and Papić (n 63) 281–9.

[171] This is so notwithstanding the fact that the ILC has accepted that such normative control could be considered to amount to *actual* control (as different from *factual*, one cannot help but wonder?), or 'control of an operative kind' within the meaning of Art 17 ARSIWA, when commenting on the notion of direction and control under Art 14 (then 13) DARIO: see UN Doc A/60/10 (2005) 98 [3]. See further text at n 228 below.

[172] cf Klein (n 1) 385–6. Also Hirsch (n 5) 83–5; Ritter (n 5) 441; Gaja (n 162) 171. The House of Lords in *Al-Jedda* was not particularly helpful with the determination of the notion of effective command and control, but did make a positive contribution by stating that 'it is one thing to receive reports, another to exercise effective command and control': (n 164) 46 [24] (Lord Bingham). In any case, it is extremely difficult to attribute conduct on the basis of the factual effective control test in general: cf Tzanakopoulos (n 133) with further references; Talmon (n 161) 503 and *passim*.

[173] cf the statement by Kennedy (n 36) 18.   [174] Gaja (n 162) 172.

[175] Which has also been called 'legal' control—denoting, however, the very same notion: Hirsch (n 5) 87.

[176] Gaja (n 162) 172; see also text at nn 57–60 and n 167.

however, there are numerous examples where MS have absolutely no freedom as to the measures they will take in compliance with a Chapter VII resolution of the Council, some of which have already been alluded to.[177] It is instructive in this respect that, in a relevant legal opinion, the Secretariat seems to indicate that a State may be obliged to make full use of the extraterritorial reach of its prescriptive jurisdiction to cover conduct by corporations (registered in that State) in the territory of another State, which is targeted by Article 41 measures, so as to prevent any circumvention of the sanctions regime, and in order to remain in compliance with the obligations imposed by the Council.[178] The legal opinion suggests how this may be in conformity with the general international law on the differing reach of prescriptive and enforcement jurisdiction.[179] Conversely, when faced with a claim that a particular action by a State, allegedly in compliance with SC-mandated measures against Libya under SCR 748 (1992), had caused damage to an airline company, the Secretariat pointed out that the relevant resolution did not prescribe the conduct complained of.[180] Belgium considered, when implementing SC sanctions ordering the freezing of funds in the Libyan case, that it was not bound by the relevant SCR to also freeze payments necessary for the functioning of embassies.[181] The Hague District Court found that SCR 1737 (2006) did not strictly impose on Dutch authorities the introduction of a particular limitation to individual rights, and thus that limitation should be able to withstand scrutiny under the ECHR and other human rights instruments applicable in the Netherlands.[182] The UK Supreme Court drew a distinction between the obligations imposed by SCRs 1267 (1999) and 1373 (2001), finding the latter to allow certain latitude in its implementation, unlike the former.[183] The same distinction had earlier been drawn by the CFI,[184] but was completely obfuscated by the ECJ in *Kadi*.[185]

---

[177] See text at nn 57–60 and n 167.   [178] [1973] UNJY 148 [4]–[6].

[179] Ibid. A possible interpretation of the Secretariat's opinion is that, if the action is prescribed by the relevant decisions of the Council, then the State is under normative control, thus its action is attributable to the Organization. However, by remaining within the contours of general international law, the action is not susceptible of constituting an internationally wrongful act.

[180] See [1993] UNJY 353.

[181] See N Angelet (1999) 32 RBDI 174–5, where the author also notes that this practice has not been criticized by the Sanctions Committees.

[182] *A and Others v The Netherlands* (NL 2010) ILDC 1463; LJN: BL1862/334949 [4.6].

[183] *HM Treasury v Mohammed Jabar Ahmed and Others* (n 167) [148] (Lord Phillips); [168] (Lord Rodger); [196] seq (Lord Brown).

[184] *OMPI* (n 58) [100]–[102].

[185] C-402/05 P *Kadi* [2008] ECR I-6351 [280], [286]–[288], [296]–[297], and especially [298], where the ECJ finds that, while the EC must give effect to the obligations under the SCR 1267 sanctions regime, it is not limited in the way it will elect to do so. But when the obligation is to freeze the assets of a specific person (in the instance Mr Kadi), it is hard to imagine how the EC could comply with it in any other way but through the freezing of the assets of that person: the obligation imposed by the Council requires a particular result to be achieved, and anything short of achieving that result would constitute a breach of the obligation. This strategy of 'disengaging' the domestic implementing measure from the international measure that conditions it and strictly imposes it (ie the non-acceptance of normative control) is what allows domestic courts to then review these domestic implementing measures for compliance with domestic law: see Tzanakopoulos (n 51) 58 seq; and cf idem (n 147) 256–8.

Be that as it may, the SR will not even consider the possibility that State organs implementing binding decisions of an IO, and in particular SCRs under Chapter VII UNC, be considered as organs 'lent'—even though not 'fully seconded'—to the Organization, so that their conduct may be directly attributed to the UN in case the latter exercises effective normative control over it in the specific instance.[186] The ILC reserves such an approach solely, it seems, and except for few other conceivable circumstances, for military contingents participating in UN PKOs. Instead, it deals with the issue of State organ conduct in the implementation of binding decisions within the context of *derivative* responsibility of an IO, by adopting a special provision.[187]

The existence and operation of the concept of normative control can be detected in the jurisprudence of the ECtHR. As briefly discussed earlier, the ECtHR attributes almost all acts by State organs to the relevant State, in compliance with Article 4 ARSIWA.[188] If the Court finds that the act is attributable to the State, as it usually does, it then goes on to review the compatibility of impugned conduct with ECHR obligations. But the Court distinguishes between different possibilities, which entail differing standards of substantive review of the compatibility of the conduct with Convention obligations. Either the conduct (i) is taken in compliance with a *strict* international legal obligation flowing from the State's membership of an international organization,[189] or (ii) it is not, in the sense that the State has some margin of appreciation or discretion with respect to the concrete or specific measures to be taken in order to comply with a general (thus not *strict*) international obligation, or (iii) the conduct is freely taken by the State, without any constraints flowing from membership of an IO.[190] In the latter two cases the Court proceeds substantively to review the conduct,[191] but in the former case it satisfies itself on the compatibility of the conduct with Convention obligations on the basis of a presumption. More specifically, the ECtHR examines whether the organization that (strictly) imposed the impugned conduct offers protection of human rights 'at least equivalent' to ECHR standards, and once it so finds, it presumes that the conduct is thus in conformity with obligations under the Convention.[192] The presumption can be rebutted only if it is shown that in the particular case the protection of Convention rights was 'manifestly deficient'.[193]

In staging its approach in this way, the Court accepts attribution to the State under Article 4 ARSIWA, and then determines the compatibility of the conduct with 'what is required' by a State under the ECHR,[194] simply using a different standard of review in sufficiently different situations. So far, so good; however,

---

[186] See Gaja (n 125) 12 [31]–[33].   [187] On which see this chapter at Section III.

[188] Except when it finds that the act of the State organ is attributable to an IO because it took place under the (factual) control of that organization, as it did in the problematic *Behrami* case (n 20) [30]–[33] and [128] seq and those that follow the *Behrami* reasoning: see further nn 145–8 and accompanying text.

[189] That the international obligation complied with must be strict is evident when one compares [155] with the first sentence of [157] in *Bosphorus* (n 145).

[190] Ibid [157].   [191] Ibid [157] seq.

[192] *M & Co* (n 145) 145; *Bosphorus* (n 145) [155]–[156]; *Behrami* (n 20) [145].

[193] Ibid.   [194] cf Arts 1, 12 ARSIWA.

what the Court further does is to concede that it cannot really review conduct (i) attributable to an IO that is not party to the ECHR, which raises no doctrinal (if it does raise other) problems; and (ii) attributable to a State (because of Article 4 ARSIWA), but taken in conformity with a strict obligation imposed by an IO. In the latter case, the concession is made through establishing a presumption of compatibility of the conduct with the ECHR, simply because the organization happens (in general!) to offer 'equivalent protection' of rights guaranteed under the Convention.[195] Rebuttable as the presumption may be, it seems doubtful that the Court would be willing to entertain any sort of plea that the protection offered by an organization such as the EC (implementing SC obligations, but still the EC) displayed 'manifest deficiency' in protecting human rights. Effectively, what the Court does is to acknowledge that the MS is under the *normative* control of an IO, given that it has no discretion in the application of the imposed measure—and because reviewing the implementing act would amount to review of the decision of the organization, the ECtHR invents a different standard of review (a very lax one at that) to avoid ever having to go into the issue.[196]

The CFI adopted a somewhat comparable approach in *Kadi*. The Court seems to apply Articles 4 ARSIWA and 5 DARIO when it states that 'neither [the EC MS] nor its institutions [read: organs] can avoid a review of the question whether *their acts* are in conformity with the basic constitutional Charter, the Treaty'.[197] This would necessarily mean, however, (i) that the acts which were imposed by the terms of SCR 1267—by the CFI's own admission leaving no margin of discretion to the States or the EC[198]—are attributable to the MS and the EC (depending on which entity took which impugned conduct), and thus the CFI has jurisdiction; and (ii) that the CFI can accordingly review these acts for conformity with the TEC. The Court, of course, realized that this would mean an indirect review of the SCR strictly imposing these measures, thus necessitating the acts on the part of the EC and its MS, for conformity with the TEC, which would make for a prima facie absurd outcome.[199] Instead of finding that the acts were not attributable to the Community or the MS, because they were under the effective normative control of the SC, the CFI rather accepted that it *had* jurisdiction to review the contested act, and thus indirectly the SCR imposing it, but not with respect to

---

[195] This is in fact an application of the 'doctrine of equivalence' (in part an 'avoidance technique' or 'evasive tactic') elaborated by the BVerfG in *Solange II* (BVerfGE 73, 339 at 378). For the impact of the '*Solange* argument' in the relationship between States and IOs see generally A Tzanakopoulos in OK Fauchald and A Nollkaemper (eds), *Unity or Fragmentation* (forthcoming 2011).

[196] cf Gaja (n 135) 526 who seems to admit this implicitly in stating that there were 'policy considerations that may have led to exonerating [MS] for acts attributed to them *but which were in fact attributable to another entity*' [emphasis added]. A similar line is taken by some domestic courts: see Tzanakopoulos (n 51) 61–3.

[197] *Kadi* (n 50) [209] [emphasis added]. cf also *Kadi* (n 185) [281], [314] distinguishing *Behrami*.

[198] *Kadi* (n 50) [214], [231]. Also text at n 167.

[199] This in fact is done by the ECJ on appeal in *Kadi* (n 185): it implicitly attributes the acts in implementation of SCRs to the EC and goes on to test the EC acts for conformity with the TEC, finding them lacking and annulling them. The attribution issue is as straightforward as in the CFI's *Kadi*; but for other issues raised by the ECJ decision see Chapters 5 and 7 below and n 185 above.

their conformity with the TEC: rather, with respect to their conformity with *jus cogens*,[200] making the outcome only slightly less doctrinally absurd than it would have been originally.[201] Here the Court calls to its aid 'structural limits to judicial review' imposed by general international law or the TEC,[202] to justify resorting to a very lax standard of review of compatibility with *jus cogens*—thus in effect avoiding review of the SCR.[203]

The preceding two paragraphs are not necessarily meant to dispute that the two Courts referred to should not have avoided directly or indirectly reviewing the legality of the acts of an IO;[204] however, if they wished to adopt this course of action, a more solid basis would have been that the acts complained of were attributable to that organization, over which they can legally exercise no jurisdiction. This would have been more doctrinally coherent (even if undesirable, one could argue) than accepting to review and then in effect *not* reviewing, thus lending legitimacy to the decision having successfully withstood (even incidental) judicial review. In any event, the problematic justifications of the two Courts' actions in these cases highlight the doctrinal problems inherent in not admitting the notion of effective normative control.

The ILC has thus excluded the *direct* attribution of conduct of MS organs not seconded to the UN to the Organization. Neither Article 5 nor Article 6 DARIO apply to MS organs implementing binding decisions of the SC under Chapter VII UNC, notwithstanding the fact that the obligations stemming from the resolutions may be *strict*, in the sense of allowing no margin of discretion or room for manoeuvre, thus exerting effective normative control over the conduct of the MS. This, however, is not the end of the discussion with respect to direct attribution of MS conduct to the UN. The possibility still exists that the Organization, potentially through the SC, will act in such a manner as to acknowledge the conduct of the MS and adopt it as its own, as provided for in Article 8 DARIO, which closely mirrors Article 11 ARSIWA.[205]

This would allow for direct attribution of the conduct of the MS (as well as an individual or group of individuals) to the Organization, although it would again *not* preclude the concurrent attribution of the very same conduct to the MS. Accordingly, the UN could, through the Council, acknowledge and adopt conduct of MS in the implementation of Council measures, and thus have their actions directly attributed to it. Indeed, it could be claimed that, by means of a resolution endorsing certain conduct, the SC may adopt it as its own.[206] However,

---

[200] *Kadi* (n 50) [225], [282]–[283].

[201] See further Tzanakopoulos (n 51) 61–5; idem (n 147) 257–60.

[202] *Kadi* (n 50) [212] seq.

[203] But see also with respect to standard of review Orakhelashvili (n 48) 175.

[204] There are other ways in which a decision by the courts to perform incidental review could be framed (cf eg L Gradoni in WJM van Genugten et al (eds), *Criminal Jurisdiction* (2009) 149–52, and E Savarese (2005) 15 IYIL 127–30). These are discussed in detail in Chapters 4, 5, and 7 below.

[205] See UN Doc A/59/10 (2004) 120 [2].

[206] eg it could be claimed that the series of resolutions in which the Council commends and urges cooperation with ECOWAS and ECOMOG for the intervention in Sierra Leone, while excepting them from the sanctions regime, could amount to such adoption and acknowledgement; see SCRs

it would be the odd case if this were to happen without a specific intention on the part of the Council to have conduct attributed to it. This is evident from the actual conduct of the EC, which has a stated intention of having MS conduct attributed to it for purposes of determination of responsibility,[207] as is also evident from its statements in pleadings before WTO panels,[208] also cited by the SR.[209] The Council has not, to date, shown any such intention, and the UN in general is keen to avoid claims being brought against it.[210] In any case, the possibility of actually using this provision to effect what could otherwise not be effected through Articles 5 and 6 DARIO has been evaluated as 'a second-best' alternative, in view of the inability to attribute MS conduct directly to an IO.[211]

The conclusion to be drawn from this discussion is that, if one does not accept the concept of normative control, and except for the odd case of adoption of the conduct of a MS in the implementation of a Chapter VII SCR, there would be no other way of attributing such conduct to the UN, and thus the examination as to whether the Organization's international responsibility has been engaged would have to cease at this early stage. There may be cases, however, where the Organization may incur responsibility for conduct that is clearly attributable to another subject of international law, that is, a State or another IO, but which falls within the limited number of instances where there is derivative or ancillary responsibility (*responsabilité dérivée*) in accordance with Chapter IV of Part One of ARSIWA, virtually mirrored in DARIO.[212]

III. Derivative Responsibility of the UN for Internationally Wrongful Acts of Member States—Attribution of Responsibility rather than Conduct

There are some special cases in which the responsibility arising from an internationally wrongful act attaches not to the act's author, but to another actor. Thus, a subject may be found responsible for conduct that is attributable to another subject of international law:[213] this is when a subject of international law aids or assists, directs and controls, or coerces another subject of international law

---

1162 (1998) [2]; 1171 (1998) [3]; 1181 (1998) [5]; 1260 (1999) [3]. This instance, of course, does not relate to the implementation of Art 41 measures, but demonstrates how the Council may adopt or acknowledge conduct by another actor. Furthermore, it has been claimed that the Council's actions with respect to Kosovo could be interpreted as an implicit authorization *ex post facto* of NATO's *Operation Allied Force*: see Stein (n 155) 181. If it is accepted that there is such a thing as *ex post facto* authorization, then this could also amount to adoption and acknowledgement.

[207] See n 131, n 139 and accompanying text.
[208] *EC—Trademarks* (n 132) [7.98]; *EC—LAN* (n 132) [3.3], [4.11]; cf *EC—Biotech Products* [2006] WT/DS291/R; WT/DS292/R; WT/DS293/R [7.101].
[209] (n 27) 27 [61]; (n 125) 12 [32].   [210] cf *Immunity* (n 20) 89 [66 *in fine*].
[211] Paasivirta and Kuijper (n 83) 217.
[212] See ARSIWA Commentary 65 [7]; UN Doc A/60/10 (2005) 92–3 [1].
[213] ARSIWA Commentary 64 [5].

in the commission of an internationally wrongful act.[214] As Ago stated in 1971, this is the case when the act's author 'is not free to determine its conduct in the sphere in which the wrongful act was committed'.[215] Then responsibility should attach to the subject of international law that was 'in a position to control' the action of the author and to 'restrict its freedom',[216] and for this there is a need for a special rule.

1. Derivative responsibility and the ambit of primary rules

In cases of derivative responsibility one finds oneself outside the ambit of attribution of conduct, strictly speaking—it is actually attribution (or: allocation) of responsibility which is taking place,[217] in the sense that conduct (and thus the internationally wrongful act) is attributable to one actor, but the responsibility which this act engages is (also) allocated to another.[218] The issue, of course, is not that simple—one could easily make the point that there *is* in fact attribution of conduct to the actor that is ultimately to bear responsibility in such cases: the conduct depriving the other actor of its freedom to determine its own conduct is certainly attributable; so is the conduct of providing aid or assistance.[219] The next issue is whether such conduct will also be found to be in breach of an international obligation incumbent upon the first actor, and that is far more problematic. The provisions of Chapter IV of Part One ARSIWA may definitely create the impression that they are in fact prohibiting (even if by implication) such inter-ference with another actor's conduct as aid or assistance or direction and control (conceding that coercion is prohibited in any case by general international law),[220] thus establishing new primary rules.[221] However, it is stressed that responsibility in such cases is *derivative*, in the sense that it does not attach to the actor's conduct per se,[222] but rather it is dependent upon the commission of an internationally wrongful act by another actor.[223]

---

[214] cf Arts 16–18 ARSIWA with Arts 12–14 DARIO.

[215] Ago (n 1) 213 [47]. The then SR did not use the term 'derivative' responsibility for such cases, but rather the terms 'indirect' responsibility or 'responsibility for the acts of others'. But the term 'indirect' responsibility has also been used to refer to the difference between responsibility for action and omission: see H Fox in *Honour Oda*, vol 1 (2002) 148 seq, who, however, is justified in dis-approving such use in ibid, 152 seq.

[216] cf Ago (n 1) 213 [47]. This is in accordance with the principle that responsibility derives from control: see text at n 159.

[217] cf R Ago (1979) II(1) YILC 5 [3].

[218] cf Ago (n 1) 213 [47]; see also ARSIWA Commentary 65 [8].

[219] cf AV Lowe (2002) 101 JJIL 4–5.   [220] See Arts 2(4) UNC; 51–2 VCLT.

[221] The Commission is aware of such an eventuality as is apparent from its comment in ARSIWA Commentary 65 [7].

[222] With the exception of coercion in the perpetration of an internationally wrongful act, which, however, constitutes a breach of the international obligation of non-intervention under general inter-national law: ibid 65 [8]; the beneficiary of the obligation of non-intervention is, *in casu*, the coerced State, which is thus injured. All the same, responsibility is still derivative under Art 18 ARSIWA, as long as it refers to the relationship between the coercing State and the State that was injured from the wrongful act procured by coercion: ibid 69 [1].

[223] Ago (n 217) 24 [42].

As the SR on the responsibility of IOs has noted, there is little reason for departing from ARSIWA with respect to the derivative responsibility of an IO.[224] An IO may thus be held derivatively responsible for an internationally wrongful act committed by a State or another IO under the same conditions as a State,[225] with the concomitant (theoretical) problems that this creates.[226] Furthermore, it is not unfathomable that an IO, and specifically the UN through the SC acting under Chapter VII, may, for example, aid or assist States in the perpetration of internationally wrongful acts. In fact, it has been convincingly argued that the UN assisted the occupying powers in Iraq in their internationally wrongful misappropriation of Iraqi State funds by continuously transferring such Iraqi State funds to them, even after the first reports of squandering had been made publicly available.[227]

As far as direction and control is concerned, the Commission's Commentary to Article 14 DARIO seems to envisage that the requirement of actual control 'of an operative kind' required by sister Article 17 ARSIWA may be satisfied by the operation of a binding decision, thus accepting to some degree the notion of normative control that it summarily rejected with respect to Article 6 DARIO.[228] What prompts this change of heart is at any rate not explained.

The exceptional nature of derivative responsibility is stressed—by the Commission as much as by anyone else,[229] and must have some bearing in the relevant considerations. What is particularly perplexing is that, while the ILC has accepted the exceptional nature of derivative responsibility, in practice it went on to transform this exceptional feature into a general rule with respect to IOs, making it the only case under which an IO can be made responsible for the acts of State organs implementing the organization's binding decisions. IOs act almost exclusively through their MS, while States rarely ever act 'through' other States. As such, one will have to rely continuously on the supposedly exceptional feature of derivative responsibility. While the SR and the ILC saw little reason to depart from the provision made with respect to the derivative responsibility of States,[230] it is submitted that the aforementioned difference in the operation of IOs as opposed to States should have been reason enough.

The ILC indeed considered that a special provision was needed to cover the case where certain conduct is taken by State organs in the implementation of a decision of

---

[224] Gaja (n 67) 11 [27].
[225] UN Doc A/58/10 (2003) 35 [4]; UN Doc A/60/10 (2005) 92–3 [1].
[226] Derivative responsibility is far from deprived of theoretical ambiguity, especially with respect to aid and assistance, or 'complicity' as it is also sometimes called: see Lowe (n 219) 4 seq. See also Ago (n 217) 4 [1], who distinguishes between the concept of complicity and the derivative responsibility for the wrongful act of another. See finally, for an example of the theoretical difficulties of the concept of complicity described by Lowe (this note), Amrallah (n 15) 69, who finds that in case a host State is complicit in the internationally wrongful act of an IO it becomes responsible for its *own* conduct in aiding and assisting.
[227] See Talmon (n 16) 228–9. For further examples see Gaja (n 67) 11–12 [28].
[228] UN Doc A/60/10 (2005) 98 [3]; but cf the somewhat different opinion of the SR (n 67) 15–16 [35].
[229] ARSIWA Commentary 65 [8]; also Ago (n 1) 213 [47]; idem (n 217) 5 [4].
[230] See nn 224–5 above.

an IO,[231] despite possible overlaps, especially with Article 14 DARIO.[232] Thus far, such conduct would *solely* be attributable to the State, as Articles 5 and 6 DARIO would not permit even concurrent attribution to the IO.[233] The Commission focuses on the notion of 'circumvention' of an organization's obligations through the 'outsourcing' of its MS.[234]

Article 16(1) DARIO deals with binding decisions by an IO, which thus includes Chapter VII SCRs. According to the provision

An international organization incurs international responsibility if it adopts a decision binding a member State or international organization to commit an act that would be internationally wrongful if committed by the former organization and would circumvent an international obligation of the former organization.

The provision does not require the act to be committed in fact—mere stipulation in the binding decision suffices for the engagement of responsibility, because 'compliance by members with a binding decision is to be expected', and thus 'the likelihood of a third party being injured would then be high'.[235]

This amounts by all accounts to a *curiosum*: as argued above,[236] a (binding) decision is a normative act. As such, it is always attributable to the organization. At the same time, it may amount to the breach of an international obligation in and of itself, that is, when it violates the organization's constitutive instrument, or when it violates general international law, such as the prohibition of torture. Similarly, it is accepted that the adoption of legislation by a State may amount to the breach of an international obligation, even if no action has been taken under the legislation in its implementation. Whether and to what extent a normative act will amount to a breach of an international obligation will depend on the content of the primary rule. Why this should be any different with respect to IOs, so as to require—in lieu of the normal operation of the rules for the engagement of responsibility—a special provision, is not entirely clear.

Unlike the situation described above, certain primary rules will require that an implementing act or conduct be taken for the obligation to be breached: as the ICJ stated in *LaGrand*, in some cases 'a distinction must be drawn between [the] rule [of domestic law] and its specific application in [a given] case'.[237] In the instance, the rule per se does not violate the obligation—it is rather its application in the specific case that may have this result.[238] More specifically, this will be because the rule leaves it open for the subject of international law to comply with its international obligation, that is, the rule does not amount to a breach in and of itself because it *does not necessitate* the breach of an international

---

[231] UN Doc A/60/10 (2005) 93 [3].
[232] Ibid 99 [4].   [233] See this chapter at Section II.
[234] UN Doc A/60/10 (2005) 101 [1] seq. Incidentally, it may be noted that, given that the 'outsourcing' by the MS of the organization was also so far not averted, the Commission adopted a relevant provision (provisionally Art 28, on first reading Art 60 DARIO) to make MS of an IO responsible for the circumvention of obligations through the provision of competence to the organization: see UN Doc A/61/10 (2006) 262 [90], 283 seq.
[235] UN Doc A/60/10 (2005) 102 [5].   [236] See nn 34–6, n 48 and accompanying text.
[237] *LaGrand* (n 161) 496 [90].   [238] cf ARSIWA Commentary 57 [12].

obligation when implemented.²³⁹ Thus, it will be this implementing act or conduct which will engage international responsibility and not the adoption of the rule per se.

In its Article 16(1) DARIO, the Commission actually follows this exact same logic:²⁴⁰ the 'binding decision' referred to in the provision is 'assumed to necessarily entail circumvention' (read: breach) by the organization of one of its international obligations,²⁴¹ in that it does not allow for any discretion on the part of the implementing State. If this is not the case, and there is room for discretion, then the 'binding decision' is downgraded to mere recommendation or authorization, and it is paragraph 2 of the same Article which should apply.²⁴² This provision in turn requires that an implementing act actually occur for responsibility to be engaged. Admittedly, the problem in this case is that the actor that promulgates the normative act is not the same as the one that implements it: in the case of States it is the State that promulgates a rule, which may in and of itself be found to amount to a breach of an obligation; and, if this is not the case, it is still the State that may implement the rule in such a way in a given case, so as to bring about the breach of its obligation. In the case of IOs, the first postulate holds true as well; but the second does not: if the decision does not amount to a violation per se, it will be a different subject of international law implementing the decision—the conduct of its organs will be attributable to that latter subject of the law and not the organization which is the source of the problematic decision.

However, this does not necessitate resort to derivative responsibility. It is submitted that (i) in the first case, where the rule per se amounts to a violation, the normative conduct of promulgating the rule is (a) attributable to the organization, and (b) (as assumed) contrary to the organization's international obligations.²⁴³ (ii) If the rule does not per se amount to a violation, but its implementation necessarily entails the breach (by whatever implementing actor) of the organization's obligations, it can either be said that this is tantamount to the rule per se breaching the obligation, in which case what was stated under (i) still holds, or that the implementing conduct of the actor is (or should be) attributable to the organization, even if that actor is a State organ, by virtue of the notion of normative control. (iii) Finally, if the binding decision does in fact allow for MS discretion in its implementation, then any conduct by a MS is attributable to that State, and will engage its responsibility if it also amounts to a breach. It is only in this instance that the need for a special rule on circumvention arises, to cover the possibility that the organization is bound by an obligation which is not incumbent on the MS as well.

Article 16(1) DARIO is further problematic in that it does not require the conduct of the subject from which the IO derives its responsibility to be unlawful,²⁴⁴ even in the first instance, that is, before the consideration of applicability of a circumstance

---

²³⁹ Ibid.   ²⁴⁰ UN Doc A/60/10 (2005) 102–3 [6]–[7].
²⁴¹ Ibid 103 [7].   ²⁴² Ibid.
²⁴³ See also Chapter 3 on obligations incumbent on the UN with respect to Council non-forcible Chapter VII measures. A rule that per se amounts to a violation, without implementing action even being contemplated, would be a rule in violation of the organization's constituent instrument.
²⁴⁴ UN Doc A/60/10 (2005) 104–5 [13].

precluding wrongfulness. As such, it breaks from its companions in the same Chapter and creates doctrinal incoherence: derivative responsibility is supposed to be engaged as a consequence of the *wrongful* act of another actor.[245] Even more problematically, the provision does not in fact require any conduct at all except for the promulgation of a binding decision—how this can lead to 'responsibility for the *act* of another' is baffling. Article 16(1) is a special provision that does not *necessarily* 'channel' to the organization the responsibility of another actor. Rather, what it does is to create a primary rule that establishes the prohibition of recommending or authorizing conduct that is in violation of the organization's obligations.[246] As far as binding decisions are concerned, the provision is unnecessary, in that conduct of MS in the implementation of binding decisions which do not allow for discretion would either be attributable to the organization under Article 6 DARIO, if one were to accept the notion of normative control, or it would engage the derivative responsibility of the organization under Article 14 DARIO, since the Commission seems in this case to accept the notion of normative control.

In the final analysis, however, and notwithstanding doctrinal difficulties with DARIO, the fact remains that MS conduct in the implementation of binding SCRs under Chapter VII, while attributable to the State, seems not directly attributable to the Organization under the current interpretation of the DARIO. It is submitted that a more coherent interpretation would allow for direct attribution of MS conduct to the Organization in such situations, based on the notion of normative control, without necessarily blocking concurrent attribution to the MS. As things stand, though, the Organization's responsibility may only be engaged derivatively, under the special requirements of Article 14 or 16(1) DARIO. But engaged it may be, and this necessitates further investigation with respect to the breach of international obligations incumbent upon the UN when the Council is acting under Chapter VII. That is, after one final comment on attribution and related problems.

2. The problem of 'double evasion'

The attribution of conduct to a subject of international law is the first hurdle that needs to be overcome in the long quest of establishing the engagement of that subject's international responsibility—which is then just a prologue to the even longer quest of the implementation of that responsibility. The attribution of conduct to IOs, and to the UN in particular, in connection with SC action under Article 41 of Chapter VII UNC, is riddled with even more problems than the attribution of conduct to States. Most tellingly, for example, a SCR under Chapter VII may be implemented in the EU/EC by means of a Common Position (under the CFSP) and an EC Regulation and then further implemented in the domestic legal orders of MS by State organs, which in this case are acting under the authority of both an EC normative act and the UN normative act which the former is implementing.

---

[245] cf Lowe (n 219) 3.
[246] Thereby also creating concerns with respect to the concept of privity (*res inter alios acta*).

It may be that international law is 'poorly equipped', as Lowe states, 'to deal with circumstances where causes or effects, or both, of injurious activities are widely dispersed', as in the case described immediately above, '*no one actor having major standing in this respect*'.[247]

The cumbersome rules of attribution need to be interpreted in a doctrinally coherent manner. As has been shown in this chapter, they are adequate to some degree to deal with the case of SC non-forcible action, and potentially with any kind of action by or through IOs. However, a rigid interpretation of these cumbersome rules is bound to stop the process of establishing the responsibility of the IO, or even of any subject of international law in connection with conduct by an IO, dead in its tracks. This is because of the emerging problem of 'double evasion'.

It is a well-established principle that a State cannot evade its international obligations by conferring (either delegating or transferring) powers to another entity, most significantly an IO.[248] At the same time, an IO, a separate entity and a subject of international law in its own right, necessarily exercises either delegated or transferred powers,[249] the responsibility for the exercise of which it cannot evade by delegating these powers back to the States.[250] It is evident that both types of entities, the MS *and* the IO must bear some degree of responsibility for the exercise of these powers. This creates a vicious circle, and a corresponding problem of 'double evasion'.

In the example of the SC acting under Article 41, the Council exercises delegated powers of imposing measures aimed at inducing compliance with international obligations: these are powers that the MS can exercise concurrently to some degree, but which they also have delegated to the Council through the UNC, in an attempt to partially centralize their exercise.[251] In the exercise of these delegated powers, the Council must rely on implementation of its binding measures by the MS,[252] which now can claim, however, that they are bound to implement the measures under the UNC. Or, alternatively, the Council may re-delegate the powers to MS, as it arguably did in the case of the CPA. This chain of delegation has the effect of weakening attribution links: a State can claim, as it so often does,[253] that responsibility rests with the IO, while the organization can

---

[247] AV Lowe in M Byers (ed), *The Role of Law in International Politics* (2000) 209 [emphasis added].

[248] *Matthews* (ECtHR GC) App No 24833/94 (1999) [32]. See also I Brownlie in *Festschrift Zemanek* (1994) 300–1; Sarooshi (n 44) 164; Stein (n 155) 182.

[249] Generally Sarooshi (n 80).   [250] Sarooshi (n 44) 164 and fn 85.

[251] eg States may still engage in countermeasures against another State if they consider it responsible for the breach of an obligation owed to them, while at the same time the SC may impose mandatory measures under Chapter VII against that same State on the basis of the same facts: see further text at nn 45–7 in Chapter 3; R Uerpmann (1995) 33 AVR 111.

[252] cf T Gazzini in Forlati and Sicilianos (n 130) 281, 289; Fremuth and Griebel (n 100) 359. The point can be made of course more generally with respect to all IOs, which are created by voluntary action and thus depend on 'voluntary' action: Hirsch (n 5) 4–5. Or even more generally with respect to the system of international law, which depends on the 'willingness' of States to comply: Fremuth and Griebel (n 100) 359, or, in other words, in the decentralized nature of the system: Uerpmann (n 251) 107–8.

[253] See eg the arguments by responding and intervening States in *Behrami* (n 20) [82] seq; *Bosphorus* (n 145) [110]; *M & Co* (n 145) 144; the defence raised by the Dutch Government,

hide behind the fact that the conduct of State organs will usually be attributable solely to the State.[254]

This problem is not peculiar to attribution. It pervades the subject of international responsibility for conduct of or through IOs, and in particular the UN SC. It is important to stress it at the stage of attribution, however, to make the point that the rules of attribution provide the requisite foundation for attributing conduct concurrently to States and IOs, thus pointing to a partial solution.[255] At the same time, there is the possibility of attributing certain conduct to the organization, while other *related* conduct may be attributable to the MS, such as, for example, their failure to ensure that a certain result would ensue or not ensue, as per their primary obligations.[256] A large part of this chapter was devoted to showing that conduct of State organs in the implementation of binding IO decisions could be attributed to the IO, without *necessarily* negating concurrent attribution to the State.[257] Whether the organization (and the State involved) will end up bearing international responsibility, and the extent to which this may be invoked and implemented, is an issue that will be finally resolved *after* attribution. At this stage, however, it is important to interpret the relevant rules so as to allow for further consideration of the engagement of responsibility.

IV. Interim Conclusion

The normative acts of the Security Council are clearly attributable to the UN, as they constitute acts of one of the Organization's organs. When the conduct that is to be attributed ceases to be purely juridical or normative, but rather constitutes action 'on the ground', the question emerges whether acts of State organs—which will be the ones usually acting on the ground—may be attributable to the Council. One way to broach the question is to distinguish clearly between actions by State organs 'lent' to the UN and those that are simply acting in the implementation of a binding decision. In the first case, the organs are under the factual control of the Organization, they are its agents, and their conduct is attributable to the Organization. In the second case, they are not, their acts thus being attributable to their home State. Institutional operations and collective operations are clearly

---

successfully in *HN v The Netherlands* (n 148) [4.15] but unsuccessfully in *A and Others* (n 182) [4.6]; the defence raised by Canada in *Abdelrazik* (n 147); the defence raised by HM Treasury in *A, K, M, Q and G v HM Treasury* [2008] EWHC 869 (Admin) [19 *in fine*]; the arguments of the EC and intervening States in *Kadi*, both before the CFI (n 50) [153] seq, and particularly [162]–[164], and before the ECJ (n 185) [262], [269], [271]; and see also Tzanakopoulos (n 51) 256.

[254] cf thus C Wickremasinghe and G Verdirame in C Scott (ed), *Torture as Tort* (2001) 474. Also Stein (n 155) 191.

[255] See Hofmann (n 140) 29.

[256] See *Matthews* (n 248) [34]. See also Pellet (n 166) 200–1.

[257] cf also the comments by I Seidl-Hohenveldern in *Colloque de Strasbourg* (1988) 226. But see Pellet (n 166) 200–1.

distinguishable in principle—in the first instance the Organization is acting through its agents on the ground, while in the second it is the States who are acting, the Organization's conduct remaining 'purely juridical'.[258] However, in practice the oscillation between the two is quite progressive and thus one may come to question the sustainability of the distinction,[259] particularly with respect to the consequences for purposes of attribution. Whether through factual or through normative control, it is the Organization 'acting through' MS.

---

[258] See Virally (n 36) 286–8.
[259] cf ibid 288.

3

The Element of Breach: Sources of Obligations Incumbent upon the United Nations

Every internationally wrongful act of the United Nations entails the Organization's international responsibility.[1] For the UN to perpetrate an internationally wrongful act through the Security Council, the susceptible conduct, shown to be attributable to the Organization, must also constitute a breach of the Organization's international obligations.[2] In discussing the breach of an international obligation as an element of the internationally wrongful act, it is imperative first to determine the obligations incumbent upon the relevant subject, in this case the UN.[3] This chapter focuses on the sources of international obligations of the UN, and thus the SC when acting under Article 41 UNC.

There are, of course, those who have claimed that the Council is *legibus solutus*, namely that there are no legal limits to its powers under Chapter VII UNC.[4] It is true that at San Francisco, the possibility of expressly allowing the ICJ to exercise compulsory jurisdiction over the legality of acts of the political organs of the UN, and specifically the Council, whereas popular with smaller and medium-sized States,[5] met with significant opposition by the Great Powers, allegedly for fear of impeding the effective operation of the Council, and the relevant attempts were finally dropped.[6] In domestic law it is conceivable that if judicial review is refused, governmental action remains uncontrolled, regardless of its legality, and continues to bind the subjects.[7] Domestic legal orders can in fact function without judicial review mechanisms, although this is not usually the case.[8] Notwithstanding the fact that the SC is not a world government, as has been

---

[1] Art 3 DARIO. See C Eagleton (1950) 76 RdC 385 seq; P de Visscher (1963) 40 RDIDC 167; R Zacklin in *Colloque du Mans* (1991) 91–2.

[2] Art 4 DARIO. Also E Butkiewicz (1981–2) 11 PYIL 118 seq; M Pérez Gonzalez (1988) 92 RGDIP 78; M Hirsch, *The Responsibility of IOs Toward Third Parties* (1995) 12 seq; K Ginther, *Die völkerrechtliche Verantwortlichkeit internationaler Organisationen gegenüber Drittstaaten* (1969) 174.

[3] cf Eagleton (n 1) 385.   [4] eg GH Oosthuizen (1999) 12 LJIL 549.

[5] UNCIO XIII 633–4, 645.

[6] H Steinberger in *Judicial Settlement of International Disputes* (1974) 198; JA Frowein and N Krisch in *Charter Commentary* (2002) 703.

[7] K Doehring (1997) 1 MPUNYB 94.

[8] eg Swiss federal legislation is not judicially reviewed for constitutionality: L Caflisch in N Al-Nauimi and R Meese (eds), *International Legal Issues* (1995) 637. See further Chapter 4 below.

stressed only too often,[9] the issue of whether there are international obligations incumbent upon the Organization which constitute legal limits to Council action should be distinguished from whether judicial control can be exercised over the latter's acts—the absence of judicial control in international law does not preclude the possibility of being bound by the law.[10] Further attempts to restrict the powers of the Council, for example by making the proviso requiring conformity with the principles of justice and international law in Article 1(1) UNC directly applicable to any action taken with respect to the maintenance or restoration of peace, were also defeated.[11] Thus, based on the preparatory works, one could maintain that the Council is unbound by law.[12]

There are a number of reasons, however, why significance of the *travaux préparatoires* in the interpretation of the UNC is secondary at best. First of all, recourse to preparatory works is simply a supplementary means of interpretation under the VCLT.[13] Also, one cannot but always keep in mind that the Charter was being drafted while the Second World War was still raging: 'any settlement was better than war',[14] and thus the main principles of the Charter were accepted at San Francisco practically without dissent.[15] Counsel for the UK during the oral pleadings in *Corfu Channel* also questioned the advisability and permissibility of recourse to the *travaux* of the Charter, presenting an analysis which is in almost total consonance with the—then not yet existent—VCLT.[16] He went on to state that

when what is in question is a multilateral treaty, covering forty or more different States taking part in the negotiations, and when it is a treaty of a constitutional and law-making kind, in which . . . not all the eventual parties were parties to the preparatory work, the preparatory work is . . . a very unsafe and uncertain guide.[17]

Indeed, the Charter can be seen as a 'living instrument',[18] and its 'constitutional' nature must be conceded,[19] in the sense at least that it is not simply a contract between States, but rather an instrument establishing an IO.[20]

---

[9] D Akande (1997) 46 ICLQ 315. cf *Reparation* [1949] ICJ Rep 179.

[10] cf *Effect of Awards* [1954] ICJ Rep 65 (indiv op Winiarski); S Talmon (2005) 99 AJIL 178; M Payandeh (2006) 66 ZaöRV 48–9; E Lauterpacht in L Boisson de Chazournes and P Sands (eds), *International Law, the ICJ and Nuclear Weapons* (1999) 94; J Crawford in H Fox (ed), *The Changing Constitution of the UN* (1997) 13; M Bedjaoui in *Hommage Rigaux* (1993) 93.

[11] UNCIO VI 23, 34.   [12] cf Oosthuizen (n 4) 552–3.   [13] cf Arts 31–3.

[14] M Koskenniemi (1995) 6 EJIL 335, quoting FH Hinsley, *Power and the Pursuit of Peace* (1963) 338.

[15] Koskenniemi (n 14) 335–6. According to N Schrijver (2006) 10 MPUNYB 4, the draft Charter was accepted without too many changes, despite the fact that no fewer than 1,500 amendments were submitted. cf B Conforti, *The Law and Practice of the UN* (3rd edn, 2005) 4–5, who characterizes the Charter as a 'constitution granted (*octroyée*)', noting that at San Francisco no substantial changes to the Dumbarton Oaks proposals were possible; J Spiropoulos (1948) 1 RHDI 263, reiterating.

[16] *Corfu Channel* [1950] ICJ Pleadings III 73.   [17] Ibid 74.

[18] See O Schachter, *International Law in Theory and Practice* (1991) 118–19; B Fassbender, *UN SC Reform* (1998) 130–1; Schrijver (n 15) 34. cf *Nuclear Weapons in Armed Conflict* [1996] ICJ Rep 75 [19] (on IO constitutions in general); but also *Lockerbie* [1998] ICJ Rep 80, 171 (diss op Schwebel).

[19] K Skubiszewski in *Festschrift Mosler* (1983) 895; G Ress in *Charter Commentary* (2002) 19; generally JE Alvarez, *IOs as Law-makers* (2005) 95–7.

[20] cf *Nuclear Weapons* (n 18) 75 [19]; *Conditions of Admission* [1948] ICJ Rep 68 (indiv op Alvarez). See further Chapter 7.II.1.ii below.

It is 'almost inconceivable' that there might be no legal limits to the power of the SC.[21] Indeed, the ICTY has found that 'neither the text nor the spirit of the Charter conceives the Security Council as *legibus solutus*'.[22] What is of importance then is to locate the *lex lata* that binds the Organization with respect to Council action. Accordingly, one will be able to discern the obligations that are incumbent upon the UN and the Council, the breach of which will engage the Organization's responsibility.

***

The source of an international obligation is of no significance when it comes to determining the existence of a breach for the purposes of determining the engagement of the responsibility of a State or an IO. Thus, international obligations may have their origin in customary international law, treaty, general principle, unilateral act, or any other valid source.[23] However, contrary to the common perception that internal (domestic) rules are irrelevant for international law purposes,[24] the 'internal' law of IOs gives rise to international obligations. According to the ILC,

for an international organization, most obligations are likely to arise from the rules of the organization, which are defined...as meaning 'in particular: the constituent instruments...'.[25]

In its DARIO, thus, the Commission has adopted Article 9, which states that

(1) There is a breach of an international obligation by an international organization when an act of that international organization is not in conformity with what is required of it by that obligation, regardless of its origin and character.

(2) Paragraph 1 includes the *breach of an international obligation that may arise under the rules of the organization*.[26]

As reiterated by the ICJ, one of the main sources of international obligations for an IO will be its constituent instrument, as well as any other secondary law (*droit dérivé*).[27]

---

[21] Akande (n 9) 314.

[22] *Tadić* (Appeal on Jurisdiction) IT-94-1-AR72 (2 October 1995) [28].

[23] ARSIWA Commentary 55 [3]. Also P Klein, *La responsabilité des organisations internationales* (1998) 311 seq.

[24] See Arts 3, 32 ARSIWA; 27 VCLT. cf PJ Kuijper and E Paasivirta (2004) 1 IOLR 116; G Gaja (1987) 58 BYIL 260–3.

[25] UN Doc A/60/10 (2005) 88 [4].

[26] As 'restructured' in UN Doc A/CN.4/L.743 (2009) and adopted on first reading [emphasis added]. cf C Dominicé in *Memory Schachter* (2005) 365; T Ueki in *Honour Oda*, vol 1 (2002) 240.

[27] See *Interpretation of Agreement* [1980] ICJ Rep 89–90 [37]. That the Organization is bound by its secondary law is also confirmed in a legal opinion by the Secretariat, where it is stated that

the policies and restraints in the resolutions [concerning South Africa] constitute direct- ives with which those who act under the authority of the...principal organs of the United Nations are bound to comply. For whether or not such resolutions are considered legally binding by States, UN organs are bound to apply such resolutions to their own actions. ([1973] UNJY 145)

Still, as subjects of international law, IOs are also bound by general international law.[28] It is thus prima facie conceivable that the SC may, when acting under Article 41 UNC, breach obligations incumbent upon the Organization not under the Charter, but under general international law.[29] IOs are constituted on the basis of inter-State agreements, and thus the latter may constitute *lex specialis* with respect to general international law.[30] However, the maxim *lex specialis derogat legi generali* applies only in the case of a normative conflict.[31] Absent such conflict (or: in the silence of the special norm),[32] the general norm applies. Importantly, furthermore, not all general international law can be abrogated through inter-State agreement. Stated in another way, the Council must act within the ambit of the powers that have been conferred to it by the Charter (*lex specialis*), but in the exercise of these powers it must respect international law (*lex generalis*).[33] As such one must examine the obligations incumbent upon the UN, and thus the Council, by virtue of the rules of the Organization (Section I) and by virtue of general international law (Section II).

I. Charter Law: The *Lex Specialis*

It has been said that the UNC is far from being a 'model of flawless drafting'.[34] Be that as it may, it is the foundation of the Council's existence, posing absolute limits to the latter's action.[35] The Council thus enjoys powers only insofar as they

cf also AJP Tammes (1958) 94 RdC 267, 269; S Talmon in P Shiner and A Williams (eds), *The Iraq War and International Law* (2008) 225; G Gaja, 'Seventh Report' (2009) UN Doc A/CN.4/610 at 7 [19].

[28] *Interpretation of Agreement* (n 27) 89–90 [37]. Also S Talmon (2004) 75 BYIL 161; cf *Namibia* [1971] ICJ Rep 294 [115] (diss op Fitzmaurice).

[29] *Contra* H Kelsen, *The Law of the UN* (1950) 294–5; Talmon (n 10) 184.

[30] cf A Orakhelashvili (2005) 16 EJIL 60; K Zemanek in *Honour Bedjaoui* (1999) 642.

[31] cf (with particular reference to the 'fragmentation' of international law and self-contained regimes) B Conforti (2007) 111 RGDIP 8–9. The principle of *lex specialis*, a corollary of the nature of most of general international law as *jus dispositivum*, is an element of 'occasional hierarchy'. Conversely, 'structural hierarchy' is established by the acceptance of certain norms as *jus cogens*: see E Roucounas (1987) 206 RdC 60 seq, particularly 62. The fact that a rule is given priority through the application of the principles of *lex specialis* or *lex posterior* does not denote any substantive superiority of the particular rule, which may again yield to a more special or later rule. By contrast, rules of *jus cogens* always (and not only occasionally) take priority, because they are 'higher law'. cf Report of the Study Group of the International Law Commission, 'Fragmentation of International Law: Difficulties Arising from the Diversification and Expansion of International Law' (2006) UN Doc A/CN.4/L.682 at 16 [18]. For differing definitions of 'conflict' between norms cf CW Jenks (1953) 30 BYIL 426 (adopting the strict approach, according to which there is a conflict of norms when two norms impose mutually exclusive obligations) with J Pauwelyn, *Conflict of Norms in Public International Law* (2003) 169–75 (adopting a broader approach which considers that two norms come in conflict when one prohibits conduct that the other allows).

[32] On the existence of a general presumption against conflict see Jenks (n 31) 427–9; Pauwelyn (n 31) 240–1; ILC Study Group on Fragmentation (n 31) 25–6 [37]–[38]; M Akehurst (1974–5) 47 BYIL 275–6; see further this chapter at Section II.2.

[33] cf C Dominicé (1996) 43 RYDI 198.   [34] Skubiszewski (n 19) 891.

[35] A Pellet in *Colloque de Rennes* (1995) 233; E de Wet (2006) 55 ICLQ 53.

are conferred on it explicitly or implicitly in the Charter,[36] and must exercise these powers in accordance with the Charter.[37] The ICJ early on stated that

The political character of an organ cannot release it from the observance of the treaty provisions established by the Charter when they constitute limitations on its powers or criteria for its judgment. To ascertain whether an organ has freedom of choice for its decision, reference must be made to the terms of its constitution.[38]

This is also exemplified in Article 25 UNC, a key article,[39] according to which the members of the UN undertake to carry out the decisions of the Council 'in accordance with the ... Charter'. Whereas there has been some controversy as to whether this latter phrase should be read as referring to the way in which MS must carry out the decisions of the Council,[40] or as simply reiterating that certain Council decisions are binding,[41] the preponderant view seems to be that the Members are obliged to carry out all resolutions 'which the Security Council *is authorized by the Charter to issue* with the intention to bind the members at whom they are directed'.[42] Thus, it is argued that only decisions taken in accordance with the Charter (ie *intra vires* decisions) acquire binding force.[43] This interpretation is supported by the fact that Council resolutions are part of the secondary law, which is subjected to the Charter.[44]

It is important, however, to differentiate between the types of conferrals of powers on the UN with respect to the Council. Whereas the power of an IO to make binding decisions generally signifies a *transfer* of powers to it by the MS,[45] it must be held that Article 41 powers have been *delegated* to the UN and thus the Council. This is because MS have clearly retained their power to impose unilateral non-forcible measures to induce compliance with an international obligation notwithstanding the exercise of the Council's powers under Article 41;[46] for example Japan imposed unilateral non-forcible measures against the DPRK shortly before the Council imposed Article 41 measures against the same State, and while the Council was considering (and finally took) such action; similarly, the US and other States customarily impose measures before the SC has adopted an Article 41 resolution or go beyond the measures imposed by the Council.[47]

---

[36] Talmon (n 10) 182. cf D Sarooshi, *IOs and their Exercise of Sovereign Powers* (2005) 22.
[37] SR Ratner in DM Malone (ed), *The UN SC* (2004) 593.
[38] *Conditions of Admission* (n 20) 64.
[39] E Suy in *Charte Commentaire* (1985) 475. cf idem and N Angelet in *Charte Commentaire* (2005) 909.
[40] See N Angelet in *Honour Suy* (1998) 278 (commenting on the French version of the article); LM Goodrich et al, *UNC* (1969) 208.
[41] See JE Alvarez in E de Wet and A Nollkaemper (eds), *Review of the SC by MS* (2003) 124–5.
[42] Kelsen (n 29) 95 [emphasis added]. cf *Namibia* (n 28) 54 [116]; DW Bowett in Fox (n 10) 79; Counsel for the UK in *Corfu Channel* (n 16) 77. cf finally Art 2(5) UNC.
[43] This can be seen as implied in the Court's statements in *Namibia* (n 28) 53–4 [115]–[116], where it finds that decisions adopted 'in conformity with the Purposes and Principles of the Charter' are binding on all MS of the UN. See for a reiteration *Repertory*, vol II (1955) 41–2, 48. Also B Simma (1994) 250 RdC 264. See, however, Chapter 7.II.2.i below.
[44] cf Orakhelashvili (n 30) 79.   [45] Sarooshi (n 36) 59.
[46] See C Leben (1982) 28 AFDI 66–7.
[47] M Turner et al, 'Japan Approves N Korea Sanctions', *Financial Times*, London, 12 October 2006 <http://www.ft.com/cms/s/a9676dbc-5a15-11db-8f16-0000779e2340,i_rssPage=abb716b0 -2f7a-11da-8b51-00000e2511c8.html>. Art 41 sanctions were imposed by SCR 1718 (2006) and

Conversely, for instance, Article 42 measures can *only* be imposed by the Council and signify a *transfer* of powers, since Article 2(4) forbids States unilaterally to resort to forcible measures, with the exception of self-defence and only until such time as the Council has taken measures to address the situation.[48] In view of the above, the conferral of powers by the States to the Organization under Article 41 can be characterized as a *sui generis* delegation, in that it grants the Organization the power to bind States internationally, but at the same time allows for concurrent exercise of the sanctioning power—thus moving the conferral along the spectrum of conferrals of powers somewhat away from delegation and closer to transfer.[49] Notwithstanding the bearing this distinction may have both on issues of attribution of conduct and on issues of implementation of an organization's responsibility,[50] it also serves to underline the obligation of the Organization to exercise the powers which have been delegated to it, and which it exercises with binding force for the MS, in accordance with its constituent instrument.

The Council, in the exercise of its powers, interprets international law, and in particular the Charter—and its obligations under it.[51] However, given that the Council does not have the power authoritatively to interpret its constituent instrument,[52] its interpretations are open both to objections—by States and by theory—and, potentially, to judicial review.[53] The obligations which stem from the Charter and which bind the UN and the Council acting under Article 41 must thus be determined.

reiterated in SCR 1874 (2009). States have generally considered the (discussion on) imposition of UN sanctions as a general grant of authority to impose unilateral countermeasures, presumably because they regard the discussion in the Council as revolving around a breach of international law, even if not as grave as to constitute a threat to the peace. cf GL Burci, *Legal Aspects of UN Economic Sanctions* (2000) 3–4 <http://www.lcil.cam.ac.uk/Media/lectures/doc/Burci.doc>; G Guillaume (2004) 53 ICLQ 544.

[48] Art 51 UNC.

[49] For the spectrum of power conferrals and relevant discussion see Sarooshi (n 36) 28–32 and *passim*.

[50] See generally Chapters 2 above and 7 below, respectively.

[51] When the SC takes action under a specific heading of the Charter, it implicitly interprets the action to fall under the said heading of competence, and the relevant purposes of the Organization: *Repertory*, vol I (1955) 8. Eg SCR 1696 (2006). States support this interpretation when they contend that the former 'has rejected the lawfulness' under the Charter of a type of retaliatory action: *Repertory*, supp 3 vol IV (1973) 209. Council practice reiterated the aforementioned statement in the specific case with the adoption of SCR 188 (1964). More recently, see the statement by Tanzania in S/PV.5474 (2006) 21. cf I Johnstone (2003) 14 EJIL 452; MP de Brichambaut in M Byers (ed), *The Role of Law in International Politics* (2000) 275; MC Wood (1998) 2 MPUNYB 77; R Higgins, *The Development of International Law through the Political Organs of the UN* (1963) 5.

[52] *Expenses* [1962] ICJ Rep 168. Also UNCIO XIII 668–9, 687–8, 709–10, 831–2. Finally M Bedjaoui, *The New World Order and the SC* (1994) 10–11.

[53] cf *Tadić* (n 22). The Council's establishment of ad hoc criminal tribunals has also been challenged before national courts: see *In re surrender of Ntakirutimana* 1998 US Dist LEXIS 22173 (SD Texas) 100–2; see further Chapter 4 below. Numerous decisions taken by the Council have been indirectly challenged, through a challenge to the domestic implementing measures, before national courts: see generally A Tzanakopoulos in A Reinisch (ed), *Challenging Acts of IOs before National Courts* (2010) 49; further Chapter 5.II.3.ii below.

1. The obligation to determine the existence of a 'threat to the peace'

According to Article 39 UNC, the Council 'shall determine the existence of any threat to the peace, breach of the peace, or act of aggression'[54] in order to exercise its powers under Chapter VII, thus discharging its 'primary responsibility for the maintenance of international peace and security'.[55] This systematic interpretation is based on the position of Article 39 in the general structure of the Charter, at the beginning of Chapter VII. The provision effectively enunciates the precondition for action under the relevant Chapter;[56] indeed, a number of States, including permanent members of the Council, have supported this interpretation.[57] Further, international courts have treated the determination as 'necessary' for the Council to act under Chapter VII.[58] Even if the Council has sometimes purported to adopt resolutions under Chapter VII without expressly determining the existence of a threat, such as 1160 (1998) and 1422 (2002), its consistency in making the determination in all other cases, along with the criticism of the aforementioned resolutions, even within the Council, for lack of the Article 39 determination,[59] denote the Council's understanding that the making of an Article 39 determination is a prerequisite for resort to Chapter VII measures.[60] Be that as it may, the important question is whether the Council is absolutely free in determining that there exist the prerequisites for such action.

A 'threat to the peace' is admittedly a very vague and elastic notion,[61] and it can be contended that the obligation to determine the existence of such a situation is an empty letter. Attempts at San Francisco[62] to concretize the prerequisites for the Council to resort to Chapter VII action failed, although specifically because

[the Council's obligations to act in accordance with the Purposes and Principles of the Organization and the provisions of the Charter] were already stated in Chapter [VI, rendering it] unnecessary to make special mention of them in ... Chapter [VII].[63]

---

[54] The notions 'breach of peace' and 'act of aggression' have hardly ever been used in Council practice; see, however, SCRs 82 (1950) and 660 (1990). cf Frowein and Krisch in *Charter Commentary* (2002) 722.

[55] Art 24(1) UNC.

[56] D Sarooshi, *The UN and the Development of Collective Security* (1999) 9–10, 33; idem (2000) 53 CLP 625, 636; idem in D McGoldrick et al (eds), *The Permanent ICC* (2004) 100; TD Gill (1995) 26 NYIL 45.

[57] Statements by US in S/PV.5500 (2006) 3; France in S/PV.3453 (1994) 3; Russia, Mexico in S/PV.5474 (2006) 17, 30; UK in *Repertoire 1946–1951* (1954) 424. Also *Repertory*, vol II (1955) 368–9, 384 and supp 3 vol II (1971) 199–201, 228.

[58] See the ECtHR in *Behrami* (GC) App Nos 71412/01 and 78166/01 (2007) [128].

[59] See statements at n 57.

[60] According to FL Kirgis (1995) 89 AJIL 512, the practice of the Council to make determinations under Article 39 'now amounts to an authoritative interpretation ... to the effect that an Article 39 determination must be made in advance of, or at the time of, enforcement action.' Even in the case of SCR 1160 (1998) the Council proceeded to make a specific Art 39 determination with a subsequent resolution, namely SCR 1199 (1998). With respect to reactions on SCR 1422 (2002) see text at n 93. See also the legal opinion of the Secretariat in [1994] UNJY 502–3.

[61] B Conforti in R-J Dupuy (ed), *Le développement du rôle du Conseil de sécurité* (1993) 53. According to O Schachter in CC Joyner (ed), *The UN and International Law* (1997) 12, elasticity and abstract principles are general features of the Charter.

[62] UNCIO XII 334 seq, 379–81.   [63] Ibid 505.

In any case, the current wording of Article 39 was adopted with the stated objective to allow the Council to decide freely on a case-by-case basis.[64] At the same time, the fears of arbitrary determinations of the notion of 'threat to the peace' were thwarted by the invocation of the requirement for the concurring vote of all five permanent members.[65]

A part of theory adheres thus to the approach that a 'threat to the peace' is whatever the Council decides to call a threat to the peace. Such a position, which is epitomized in Combacau's circular definition,[66] releases the Council from any constraint in the interpretation of the notion, effectively negating the Article 39 prerequisite's status as an obligation incumbent upon the Council. It is accordingly maintained that the Council has full discretion in making the relevant determination,[67] which is not challengeable on legal grounds.[68]

A measure of discretion is always involved in evaluating the facts of a situation, especially in view of the vague terms which Article 39 employs.[69] However, 'a discretion can only exist within the law'.[70] It is exactly this kind of broad discretionary power that runs the danger of being exercised arbitrarily.[71] The Council is thus not unfettered in interpreting the notion of 'threat to the peace', although it may have wide discretion.[72] The obligation of establishing the existence of such a situation is a substantial one.

The interpretation of the Council cannot but conform to the well-established rules (the ordinary meaning to be given to the terms in the light of the Charter's object and purpose),[73] whereas it cannot amount to a denial of the content of the notion—in other words, the notion cannot be interpreted *contra legem*: the Council cannot term anything and everything a 'threat to the peace', subject only to

---

[64] Ibid 502–5.   [65] G Gaja (1993) 97 RGDIP 299.

[66] J Combacau, *Le pouvoir de sanction de l'ONU* (1974) 100:

une menace pour la paix au sens de l'article 39 est une situation dont l'organe compétent pour déclencher une action de sanctions déclare qu'elle menace effectivement la paix.

[67] Kelsen (n 29) 727; WM Reisman (1993) 18 YJIL 418.

[68] See Schachter (n 61) 12. cf R Degni-Segui in *Charte Commentaire* (1985) 464–5.

[69] Goodrich et al (n 40) 293. cf generally nn 80–2 and accompanying text in Chapter 1.II.1 above.

[70] I Brownlie in *Honour Tieya* (1994) 95. cf *Lockerbie* (n 18) 110 (diss op Jennings).

[71] Doehring (n 7) 105. cf A Watts (1993) 36 GYIL 34, who states that while *in principle* the line to be drawn between 'discretion' and 'arbitrariness' is 'clear enough', the borderline can *in practice* become very blurred, particularly when the discretion is 'wide' (see also next note and accompanying text). Still, one should not shy away from the difficult questions.

[72] Although *Tadić* (n 22) 42 [28] suggests that there are limits to the SC's discretion under Art 39, this discretion is still described as broad. But the outer limits are sketched by Judges Gros and Fitzmaurice in their dissents in *Namibia* (n 28) 340 [34], and 293 [112], 294 [116] respectively. The Council itself, through its practice, has demonstrated that it does not conceive its powers as being entirely unlimited: L Oette (2002) 13 EJIL 98.

[73] Art 31(1) VCLT. See to this effect the arguments on the interpretation of the notion advanced in a number of cases before the Council, which are couched in legal terms: *Repertory*, vol II (1955) 346–56 and supp 3 vol II (1971) 205. Significantly also the construction by France with respect to the differentiation between Arts 34 and 39 in *Repertoire 1946–1951* (1954) 425, as well as further arguments with respect to the correct interpretation of the notion in ibid 426. cf also Dominicé (n 33) 202; generally on interpretation by political organs H Lauterpacht (1950) 43-I AIDI 375–6.

reaching political consensus,[74] otherwise the prerequisite of such a determination in Article 39 would be devoid of any meaning.[75] As such, the Council has discretionary power to select any of the possible alternative meanings of the term 'threat to peace', as long as these *remain*, but do not *exceed*, the interpretative radius of the provision.[76]

Indeed, the Council is competent to order binding enforcement measures *only* when the prerequisites of Article 39 are present.[77] It must *ascertain* the existence of these prerequisites in a resolution,[78] or perhaps also in a presidential statement.[79] In the context of the *Spanish Question* the Council decided to 'make...studies' as to the existence of a threat to the peace,[80] since a number of representatives stated that no evidence to this effect had been adduced.[81] It thus established a Sub-Committee which, after considering the 'juridical meaning' of Article 39,[82] found that the Council could not, on the available evidence, make the relevant determination.[83]

The determination that there exists a threat to the peace is a legal determination, because it constitutes a qualification (or characterization) of a factual situation,[84] which then draws (albeit at the discretion of the Council) certain legal consequences,[85] namely sanctions or other enforcement action under Article 41 or 42. Chapter VII action has been challenged as devoid of any legal basis for the lack of existence (or rather misinterpretation) of a threat to the peace.[86] If the latter were simply a factual (or political) determination, it would deprive the point of actually requiring such a determination as a prerequisite to Chapter VII action. There would be no need for the permanent five and another four members of the Council to reach consensus on the existence of a threat.[87] Their reaching consensus as to the imposition of binding measures would have

---

[74] Zemanek (n 30) 629–30 could not help but note that this is indeed the impression that some of the Council's decisions convey.

[75] cf *Conditions of Admission* (n 20); *Namibia* (n 28) 294 [116] (diss op Fitzmaurice); cf Amerasinghe, *Principles of the Institutional Law of IOs* (2nd edn, 2005) 55, 59–60.

[76] The interpretative radius of a provision signifies the range of possible meanings attributable to it. Even the widest interpretative range must permit a determination of whether a specified meaning is covered or not. The authority of an organ to apply the provision extends necessarily to the selection of any of the possible meanings *within* the interpretative range. See EP Hexner in *Honor Kelsen* (1964) 123. This selection between the meanings (interpretations) allowed is an unchallengeable political decision: cf Kelsen (n 29) xvi.

[77] A Verdross and B Simma, *Universelles Völkerrecht* (1984) 145.

[78] Ibid [emphasis added].

[79] On the legal nature of presidential statements see S Talmon (2003) 2 CJIL 447 seq.

[80] SCR 4 (1946).   [81] *Repertory*, vol I (1955) 107.

[82] *Repertoire 1946–1951* (1954) 425.   [83] *Repertory*, vol I (1955) 40.

[84] cf ibid vol II (1955) 355. Also J-M Sorel in *Colloque de Rennes* (1995) 52; B Graefrath in *Honour Suy* (1998) 242; cf AV Lowe in Byers (n 51) 213. France stated in S/PV.710 (1956) that the appreciation of the facts led it to avoid an Art 39 determination by a 'very slight margin': *Repertoire*, supp 1956–58 (1959) 170. A legal determination (*qualification juridique*) is the inverse of interpretation, in the sense that it is an inductive process: G Abi-Saab in *Festschrift Bernhardt* (1995) 9–10.

[85] cf G Abi-Saab in *Colloque de Rennes* (1995) 304–5; *Lockerbie* [1992] ICJ Rep 33 (diss op Shahabuddeen); the US stated in S/PV.172 (1947) that the invocation of Art 39 'raises very complex and serious questions of *law*' [emphasis added].

[86] S/PV.5500 (2006) 9 (Iran). See further Chapter 7.II.3.ii below.

[87] cf E de Wet, *The Chapter VII Powers* (2004) 136–7.

been sufficient. Such an approach would make the provision of Article 39 redundant,[88] which in turn would be contrary to the well-established principle that if two interpretations of a provision are possible, but one of them would have as a result the redundancy of the provision, the other interpretation is to be preferred.[89]

To paraphrase Lauterpacht in another context, it is not to be lightly assumed that a legal document contains terms devoid of legal significance.[90] This is particularly so with regard to a notion that effectively circumscribes the scope of application of the entire Chapter VII;[91] only under such an interpretation can the provision of Article 2(7), namely the protection of the *domaine réservé* of domestic jurisdiction and thus sovereignty, have any ascertainable meaning.[92]

Before the adoption of Resolution 1422 (2002), a number of States questioned the latter's *vires* on the basis that it was to be adopted under Chapter VII in the absence of a threat to the peace: the jurisdiction of the ICC over peacekeeping forces could not be logically (and thus legally) determined to constitute such a threat.[93] With respect to the other triggers of Chapter VII action in Article 39, it has been noted that the fierce controversies over the linkage of 'aggression' in Article 5 of the ICC Statute with the relevant authority of the Council to determine the existence of such a situation under Article 39 exemplifies the lack of willingness on the part of those States 'controlling' the Council to condone any type of review of the Council's 'quasi-judicial determinations'.[94] If anything, this is just another corroboration that determinations under Article 39 are legal determinations through and through.

It is not the object of this study to determine the exact content of the notion of 'threat to the peace'.[95] It is, however, important to stress that the determination of the Council is a legal qualification and constitutes an obligation under the Charter. While it is true that the Security Council is not a judicial organ,[96] but rather a political one, the power of making legal determinations is not a monopoly

---

[88] cf T Schilling (1995) 33 AVR 79–80.

[89] *Ut res magis valeat quam pereat.* cf (1966) II YILC 219 [6]; Ress (n 19) 31; Amerasinghe (n 75) 45. See also G Fitzmaurice, *The Law and Procedure of the ICJ* (1986) 345; H Thirlway (1991) 62 BYIL 44–8.

[90] H Lauterpacht, *The Development of International Law by the International Court* (1958) 112–13.

[91] M Bothe in Dupuy (n 61) 71–2. cf generally CHM Waldock (1962) 106 RdC 176.

[92] TM Franck in Dupuy (n 61) 84. Also Schilling (n 88) 84–5; A Verdross in *Mélanges Rousseau* (1974) 268. cf S/PV.5685 (2007) 3 (Indonesia). The UK acknowledges the point when it defends a measure by claiming that 'it is not a *capricious intervention or interference* in the domestic political affairs of a sovereign State', ibid 6 [emphasis added].

[93] Statements by Canada, Jordan, Liechtenstein, Mexico, Venezuela, Samoa, Germany in S/PV.4568 (2002) 3, 16, 20, 26–7, 30, (Resumption 1) 7, 9; somewhat more guarded the UK at 16. cf B Elberling (2005) 2 IOLR 339; C Fritsche in *Festschrift Eitel* (2003) 113–15; A Zimmermann in ibid 262–6 for similar assessments. A number of States also questioned the existence of a real threat to the peace with respect to the situation in Haiti: see S/PV.3413 (1994). For the OAU reaction to the Libyan sanctions see Chapters 5 and 7 below.

[94] A Reinisch (2007) 42 BDGVR 64.

[95] For an overview of attempts at definition see de Wet (n 87) 138 seq.

[96] *Tadić* (n 22) 45 [37]; O Schachter (1964) 58 AJIL 959 seq; Wood (n 51) 78.

of judicial organs; in fact many political organs make legal determinations in order to establish their competence to act under a certain heading.[97]

2. The obligation to take proportional action

i. *The concept of proportionality* (stricto *and* lato sensu)

The Security Council also enjoys discretion with respect to selecting the measures to be taken to counter the threat.[98] At the outset, it could be claimed that, if discretion can only exist within the law, then such 'margins of appreciation' always find their outer limits in the principle of proportionality (in part—in another part the margin of appreciation ends at the limits of the 'interpretative radius' of a provision). Indeed, in the case at hand, the Council's discretionary power must be exercised 'in a manner that is *conducive* to the maintenance of international peace and security',[99] because of the 'functional connection' between Articles 39 and 41:[100] Article 41 measures are taken to respond to an Article 39 threat to the peace, and must be appropriate to bring about their intended objective. This is apparent when members of the Council attempt to justify the imposition of a measure as one that will help protect and restore the peace,[101] question the *vires* of a measure which, according to them, cannot counter the threat,[102] or request the imposition of new measures 'sufficiently adequate' to remove the threat.[103] Accordingly, measures adopted by the Council under Article 41, be they specific (sanctions) or general (atypical or 'legislative', which in any case can only be based on Articles 39 and 41 of the Charter)[104] must be genuinely linked to the maintenance of international peace and security.[105] The ICTY implicitly accepted as much when it engaged with the language of proportionality in *Tadić*, even though the Appeals Chamber denied to review whether the enforcement measures in question did in fact contribute to the maintenance or restoration of peace in a specific case.[106]

---

[97] This is called a 'jurisdictional condition': see P Craig in idem and A Tomkins (eds), *The Executive and Public Law* (2006) 337. cf also G Nolte in Byers (n 51) 323; and nn 80–2 and accompanying text in Chapter 1.II.1 above. In *Tadić* (n 22) 45 [37] the Appeals Chamber concedes that the Council may exercise incidentally a quasi-judicial function when 'effecting determinations or findings'. Otherwise, one may add, it would not be able to operate. cf generally Lauterpacht (n 73) 375–6.

[98] Sarooshi, *Development* (n 56) 4; G Arangio-Ruiz in *Honour Cassese* (2003) 54.

[99] cf Talmon (n 10) 182 [emphasis added]; Arangio-Ruiz (n 98) 55.

[100] JD Aston (2002) 62 ZaöRV 269.

[101] France concludes with respect to the ICTR that it should 'in its own way contribute to restoring civil peace' in S/PV.3453 (1994) 3; similarly it finds the rejection of impunity through the establishment of a STL to be an 'essential guarantee of peace' in S/PV.5685 (2007) 6.

[102] S/PV.3453 (1994) 4 (Brazil); cf S/PV.5685 (2007) 4 (South Africa, China).

[103] Ethiopia in S/PV.1399 (1968); *Repertoire*, supp 1966–68 (1971) 208–9.

[104] Talmon (n 10) 179; E Rosand (2005) 28 FILJ 554–5; R Lavalle (2004) 51 NILR 419–20.

[105] Talmon (n 10) 183. Also LF Damrosch (1997) 269 RdC 105; Rosand (n 104) 557. cf finally UN Doc S/25704 in (1993) 32 ILM 1169 [26].

[106] *Tadić* (n 22) 45 [39]. The Appeals Chamber referred to the 'appropriateness' of the establishment of an international tribunal as a measure for the restoration of international peace, but did not launch into a full discussion, partly relying on the unfortunate formulation of the appellant's relevant argument, which was linked directly to the fact that the situation in the former Yugoslavia was no

Even more importantly, the ICJ in *Expenses* has found that action taken by the Organization, which is '*appropriate* for the fulfillment of one of [its] stated purposes', is presumed to be *intra vires*.[107] This language, which requires Article 41 measures to be *conducive* or *appropriate* to a certain end, is reminiscent of one aspect of the principle of proportionality *lato sensu*.[108] The latter can be further distinguished into the *conduciveness* of a measure towards a certain end (or its *appropriateness*), its *necessity*; and the *means–ends* (or *stricto sensu*) proportionality.[109]

The obligation of the Council to take measures conducive to the restoration or maintenance of international peace is but an aspect of its obligation to take proportional action under Article 41 UNC. The principle of proportionality has been said to constitute positive Charter law,[110] since the Charter indicates a desire to minimize the impact of enforcement measures without compromising their effectiveness.[111] As far as the other two aspects of *lato sensu* proportionality are concerned, it is important to note that while Article 42 explicitly refers to '*necessary* measures involving the use of armed force', neither Article 39 nor 41 make any reference to that aspect of the notion of proportionality.[112] However, members of the Council have relied on the necessity of an Article 41 measure in order to justify it,[113] and scholarly opinion seems to accept that action under Article 41 must be necessary to counter or remove the threat.[114] With respect to means–ends

---

better in 1995 than it was in 1993. However, the States have themselves made the argument for the need for measures to be appropriate: see nn 101–3 above and accompanying text.

[107] (n 52) 168 [emphasis added].

[108] C-189/01 *Jippes* [2001] ECR I-5689 [81]; C-110/03 *Belgium v Commission* [2005] ECR I-2801 [61]; and case law cited therein.

[109] Ibid. The principle of proportionality in the sense described here also appears in the jurisprudence of the ECtHR and is admittedly influenced by German constitutional law theory and practice: JA Frowein in idem and W Peukert (eds), *EMRK-Kommentar* (1996) 336 [17]. cf also R Kolb (2006) 39 RBDI 600–1.

[110] Talmon (n 10) 184. Also LB Sohn in Dupuy (n 61) 151. The ICJ's statement in *Expenses* (n 52) 168, quoted at n 107 above, can be seen as a confirmation of this. cf with respect to the EC Craig (n 97) 336–7. Erika de Wet expressly rejects the application of the principle with respect to Council measures at one point but then goes on to employ proportionality-based arguments: (n 87) 184–5, rejecting the application of a general principle of proportionality on Council action, but then conceding at 202–3 (and implicitly further at 218, 223–4) that 'some' notion of proportionality must be respected.

[111] Frowein and Krisch (n 6) 711. cf eidem in *Charter Commentary* (2002) 745–6. It is not unusual that the principle of proportionality should be considered positive law of a certain text, although the text itself never mentions the term. The 'desire' indicated by the Charter and noted by Frowein and Krisch is evident in the provisions of the relevant articles, in which it could be said that proportionality appears as 'latent' if not 'in thinly veiled form', to borrow phrases coined (although in another context) by M-A Eissen in RSJ Macdonald et al (eds), *The European System for the Protection of Human Rights* (1993) 125, 131.

[112] Talmon (n 10) 184 and fn 82; Frowein and Krisch (n 6) 711–12.

[113] See statements (n 101); Peru portrayed the STL as 'the only way' ultimately to promote peace and security in Lebanon (S/PV.5685 [2007] 6); cf Slovakia, US (ibid 7).

[114] Brownlie (n 70) 96–7; cf C Tomuschat (1994) 49 Europa Archiv 63; B Graefrath (1993) 47 NJ 434; F Berman in *Honour Bos* (1999) 175–6; see the discussion as to whether it is conducive, in order to restore international peace, to override democratic decision-making processes in F Mégret (2008) 21 LJIL 490–1 (commenting on the SC decision to establish the STL by means of a Chapter VII resolution in response to Lebanon's non-ratification of the Lebanon–UN STL Agreement within a set deadline).

proportionality, a further distinction must be made. Whereas it can be said that, given the wide margin of appreciation that the Council enjoys, the measures must be *manifestly out of all proportion* to the aims pursued in order for the Council to violate the principle as embodied in the Charter's positive law,[115] it is submitted that this proportionality test, while perhaps appropriate with respect to atypical or 'legislative' measures,[116] is not the one applicable to cases where the Council is imposing classical Article 41 measures, that is, sanctions against recalcitrant States. In those latter cases, a freestanding obligation under general international law—not superseded by the Charter for lack of any normative conflict between the two sources—dictates a stricter proportionality test.[117]

ii.　Concepts cognate to proportionality

Using language also highly reminiscent of the principle of proportionality, it has been suggested that the imposition of conditions on a MS which are not *necessary* or *appropriate* to achieve the object for which the power was granted (ie the maintenance of peace) may constitute *détournement de pouvoir* on the part of the Organization.[118] This is then juxtaposed to *ultra vires* action by stating that the latter constitutes action stretching the powers of the Organization beyond their proper limits, while *détournement de pouvoir* is action taken within those limits but for improper purpose.[119]

A similar distinction, transposed from domestic public law, is that between *excès de pouvoir*, as the public law variation of *abus de(s) droit(s)*,[120] and *usurpation de pouvoir*. The former refers to action within the 'proper domain' of the organ, that is, *intra vires*, but for an improper purpose in the special sub-species of *détournement*

---

[115]　Kirgis (n 60) 517; Frowein and Krisch (n 6) 712; Rosand (n 104) 557. cf ECJ cases (n 108). In C-84/95 *Bosphorus* [1996] ECR I-3953, the ECJ applied a test of proportionality with respect to the injury suffered by a foreign company because of the implementation in the EC of SC Art 41 measures, but found that the injury 'cannot be regarded as…disproportionate' [26 *in fine*].

[116]　cf Craig (n 97) 340. But see A Marschik in RSJ Macdonald and DM Johnston (eds), *Towards World Constitutionalism* (2005) 470, who considers that the establishment of ad hoc criminal tribunals 'was not the only means to achieve the goals' (presumably of maintenance of international peace), and points at the establishment of the SCSL and the ECCC as a suggestion of the 'unease among Council members as to the legality' of the establishment of ad hoc international tribunals.

[117]　See this chapter at Section II.3.ii.　　　[118]　JES Fawcett (1957) 33 BYIL 316.

[119]　Ibid 311. This definition brings *détournement de pouvoir* close to the doctrine of abuse of right (*abus de[s] droit[s]*), another concept cognate to proportionality: see P Guggenheim (1949) 74 RdC 252–3. cf, however, Pauwelyn (n 31) 288 who seems to consider that *ultra vires* action is action *within* the limited competence of the organization but not exercised in line with the conditions and restrictions 'that may have been imposed on this competence'.

[120]　According to N Politis (1925) 6 RdC 83, the theory of abuse of rights aims to delimit the exercise of subjective rights by individuals, while the theory of *excès de pouvoir* does the same with respect to the discretionary powers of public authorities. The PCIJ notably hinted to the theory of abuse of rights both in *Certain German Interests* [1926] PCIJ Ser A No 7 and in the *Free Zones* [1932] PCIJ Ser A/B No 46: cf CG Weeramantry (1997) 10 LJIL 324–5. It was Judge Álvarez who first spoke of a potential abuse of rights by the SC, specifically referring to the right of the veto, in *Competence of the GA* [1950] ICJ Rep 13 (diss op). In line with Politis' distinction above, in the first two instances before the PCIJ one would be dealing with a true case of abuse of rights, while in the last instance before the ICJ the case would be one of *excès de pouvoir*. cf finally Lauterpacht (n 90) 162–5.

de pouvoir, while the latter refers to action completely outside the scope of the powers granted to the organ.[121]

This distinction may be seen as tenuous, since the purpose for which a power has been granted arguably constitutes a limitation on the exercise of that power, especially when said purpose is explicitly stated in the provisions granting the power—that is, the Council has the power to take *any* non-forcible measures whatsoever under Article 41 (the enumeration of measures in the article is simply indicative)—but *only* with a view to maintaining international peace and security, in accordance with Article 39.[122]

Be that as it may, discretionary action taken by the Organization must be necessary and appropriate (ie proportional) to the objective pursued, and this can be based directly on the Charter provisions explicitly defining the purpose for which the discretionary power was granted; it is also supported by the alleged existence of a general principle of (international institutional) law that a discretionary power must be exercised for the purpose for which it was granted.[123]

3. Other obligations under the Charter

The SC is also under the obligation to respect the differentiation of its powers under Chapters VI and VII UNC when acting under Article 41.[124] With respect to pacific settlement of disputes, the Council only has the power to investigate,[125] and recommend appropriate procedures or methods of adjustment of any dispute,[126] or even terms of settlement,[127] but any settlement should be effected in accordance with international law,[128] by virtue of Article 24(2) read in conjunction with Article 1(1).[129] Furthermore, these recommendations do not have binding force, in accordance with Article 25, which refers solely to decisions.[130] This obligation is of particular importance, given the Council's tendency to make 'obscure transitions' from Chapter VI to Chapter VII.[131] Accordingly, recourse to measures under

---

[121] cf Politis (n 120) 83–4.

[122] cf cf Amerasinghe (1984) 44 ZaöRV 440, where it is stressed that this doctrine/general principle of law applies also to cases where the law *does not explicitly prohibit* irregular motives or purposes. cf also E Schmidt-Aßmann and C Möllers in Craig and Tomkins (n 97) 286, who consider the issue of *détournement* within the context of the principle of proportionality (with respect to German law).

[123] Fawcett (n 118) 311. cf Sarooshi (n 36) 16, 108. The establishment of a STL under Chapter VII has come under fire for being 'inappropriate' to deal with the threat (South Africa, China [n 102]); for constituting a misuse of Chapter VII powers (Indonesia [n 92]); or for promoting a specific view of Lebanese history and thereby constituting *détournement de pouvoir* (cf B Elberling [2008] 21 LJIL 529–38).

[124] cf *Repertory*, vol II (1955) 23.   [125] Art 34 UNC.   [126] Art 36 UNC.

[127] Art 37(2) UNC.   [128] Frowein and Krisch (n 6) 712.

[129] cf R Higgins (1970) 64 AJIL 8.

[130] Text at nn 39–44. Also R Higgins (1972) 21 ICLQ 281–2. A contrary view was expressed by counsel for the UK during oral pleadings in *Corfu Channel* (n 16) 54–5, who was, however, rather guarded, saying that he 'might be wrong' on this six times within a page and a half of verbatim record. Indeed, a number of judges disagreed: [1948] ICJ Rep 32 (sep op Basdevant et al). The UK sharply changed its position later, in the context of the *Namibia* case before the Council, contending that only Chapter VII decisions are binding.

[131] cf B Graefrath (1993) 4 EJIL 192.

Chapter VII in order to enforce a settlement recommended under Chapter VI may constitute a breach of the obligation of the Council to respect the differentiation of its powers under Chapters VI and VII.[132]

Somewhat related is the issue whether the Council can impinge on the authority of another principal organ of the UN under the Charter through a provision in a resolution under Chapter VII. An eloquent example, which has given rise to serious questions about the lawfulness of relevant SCRs,[133] is the Council's attempt to pre-empt the incurrence of costs by the Organization by reason of the Council's deferral of the situation in Darfur to the ICC. In SCR 1593 (2005) at [7], the Council '[recognized] that none of the expenses incurred . . . shall be borne by the United Nations . . .'. Notwithstanding the problems that such a clause may be creating with respect to Article 115 of the Rome Statute,[134] of which the UN is in any case not a party, the clause effectively negates the GA's competence over UN budgetary matters, which is exclusive in accordance with Article 17 UNC.[135] As a matter of Charter law, the Organization is bound to respect the division of powers among its organs.[136] A binding Chapter VII resolution that purports to re-write the Charter cannot but constitute a breach of the Organization's international obligations.

The Council is finally under an obligation to comply with a number of procedural rules under the Charter, particularly those referring to the right of veto, requisite majorities, and the like.[137] One would think that, given the latitude of interpretation of the substantive rules regulating the exercise of Council powers under Article 41, the importance of procedural limitations on Council action would be all the more crucial.[138] However, in view of the general presumption of legality of the decisions of UN organs and of the extremely deferential control of the ICJ,[139] procedural irregularities are not accorded any substantial influence with respect to the legality of the relevant decision, and are thus of limited practical significance.[140] More importantly, certain practice, if 'uniformly and consistently interpreted' by members of the Council 'as not constituting a bar to the adoption of resolutions', and if subsequently generally accepted by the Organization's membership, thus constituting general practice, has the effect of 'covering' procedural irregularities.[141] Still, certain significant procedural irregularities, such as the improper constitution of an organ, may taint the decisions promulgated by that organ, rendering them illegal.[142]

---

[132] Arangio-Ruiz (n 98) 47–8. cf B Martenczuk (1999) 10 EJIL 542; AL Paulus (2006) 10 ASIL Insights (3 November).

[133] R Cryer (2006) 19 LJIL 206–8.   [134] See ibid 206 for the relevant discussion.

[135] cf W Koschorreck in *Charter Commentary* (2002) 341, especially [43].

[136] cf *Expenses* (n 52) 230 (diss op Winiarski); D Ciobanu *Preliminary Objections* (1975) 47.

[137] *Namibia* (n 28) 22 [20]. cf Franck (n 92) 85.   [138] Bothe (n 91) 79.

[139] *Expenses* (n 52) 188; *Namibia* (n 28) 22 [20]; Gaja (n 65) 315.

[140] cf Pellet (n 35) 234.

[141] *Namibia* (n 28) 22 [22]; cf CA Stavropoulos (1967) 61 AJIL 737.

[142] In *Constitution of the Maritime Safety Committee* [1960] ICJ Rep 150, the Court found that the Committee of the (then) IMCO was 'not constituted in accordance with the Convention for the Establishment of the Organization' (171) but did not elaborate on the legal effects of this finding. In *Namibia* (n 28) 22 [20], the Court held that

Finally, the Council is under no legal obligation to comply with its previous resolutions, since no principle of *res judicata* applies. In case of a normative conflict, the maxim *lex posterior derogat legi priori* operates.

II. General International Law: The *Lex Generalis*

There is an apparent problem with respect to the overall relationship between UN law and general customary international law, including *jus cogens*, particularly in view of the augmenting claims of the Charter being a constitution of the international community.[143] First of all, there is a part of theory that considers the Council as limited by no obligations other than those imposed by the Charter itself,[144] informed at best in a general manner by the Purposes and Principles of the UN.[145] The problem, however, is more clearly exemplified by the attempt of another part of theory to present a significant number of general international legal norms as Charter law through a rather tentative notion of 'transcription' based on the Charter's Purposes and Principles. Many argue that the Council, when acting under Chapter VII, is under an obligation, by virtue of Article 24(2), to respect the Purposes and Principles of the UN, among which Article 1 lists conformity with international law and respect for human rights.[146] It is thus argued that the Council is bound by customary international law in general,[147] by IHL,[148] by the ICCPR and the ICESCR,[149] and so forth. In fact, at San Francisco the Great Powers successfully resisted certain proposals to amend Chapter VII, submitted with a view to making sure that Council decisions would not be arbitrary in nature, by stressing that the Council should not be expected to act arbitrarily, since under the terms of Article 24(2) it was required to act 'in accordance with the Purposes and Principles of the UN'.[150]

However, whereas Article 24(2) does stipulate that the Council shall act in accordance with the Purposes and Principles, and whereas Article 1(1) mentions

A resolution of a *properly constituted organ* of the United Nations which is passed in accordance with that organ's rules of procedure ... must be presumed to have been validly adopted. [emphasis added]

For a detailed discussion see further Chapter 7.II.2.ii, especially nn 127–35 and accompanying text.

[143] P-M Dupuy (1997) 1 MPUNYB 5. See generally B Fassbender, *The UNC as the Constitution of the International Community* (2009).

[144] Kelsen (n 29) 294–5; Talmon (n 10) 184.

[145] Frowein and Krisch (n 6) 712. cf Alvarez (n 41) 125.

[146] *Lockerbie* (n 85) 61 (diss op Weeramantry); *Bosnia Genocide* [1993] ICJ Rep 440 [101] (sep op Lauterpacht); N Elaraby in *Festschrift Eitel* (2003) 56, 62–3; A Reinisch (2001) 7 Global Governance 136; ME O'Connell (2002) 13 EJIL 70; E de Wet (2001) 14 LJIL 279; H-P Gasser (1996) 56 ZaöRV 880–1. Critically Koskenniemi (n 14) 327. This is ostensibly the approach the CFI took in T-315/01 *Kadi* [2005] ECR II-3649 [228]–[229]; T-306/01 *Yusuf* [2005] ECR II-3533. See also T-253/02 *Ayadi* [2006] ECR II-2139; T-49/04 *Hassan* [2006] ECR II-52.

[147] Reinisch (n 146) 136.   [148] Gasser (n 146) 880–1.

[149] I Cameron (2003) 72 NJIL 167.

[150] Goodrich et al (n 40) 292. This restriction is to be interpreted narrowly as referring only to Arts 1 and 2: Degni-Segui (n 68) 466–7.

among these 'conformity with . . . international law', the latter postulate refers only to the Organization's purpose to bring about settlement of disputes or adjustment of situations, not to enforcement action.[151] A proposal to add a proviso requiring conformity with international law specifically when the Council is discharging its primary responsibility was defeated at San Francisco,[152] since the US and the UK felt that the Council should not be constrained by international law in that case.[153]

Accordingly, it may be contended that general international law is irrelevant when the Council is acting under Article 41. However, one can retort that, even without Article 1(1), the SC is still bound by general international law, as discrete from Charter law, because it is a creation of that former law, and its subject.[154] It is also noted in this respect that customary rules, even if embodied in the Charter in any way, retain their separate identity.[155] A more detailed examination into possible obligations for the Organization by virtue of general international law is thus required.

1. *Jus cogens*

According to Verdross, *jus cogens* norms (or peremptory norms of general international law) do not exist to satisfy the needs of the individual States, but the higher interest of the whole international community, and are hence absolute.[156] Under Article 53 VCLT, 'a treaty is void if, at the time of its conclusion, it conflicts with a peremptory norm of general international law', which is defined as 'a norm accepted and recognized by the international community of States as a whole as a norm from which no derogation is permitted'; Article 64 VCLT provides that 'if a new peremptory norm of international law emerges, any existing treaty which is in conflict with that norm becomes void and terminates'. Whereas thus States may freely elect to contract out of the *jus dispositivum*, they cannot escape the operation of *jus cogens*. In order for the Charter to remain in harmony with both the peremptory norms that existed at the time of its entry into force, and the peremptory norms that emerged subsequently, it must be interpreted as not being in conflict with them; otherwise one would be forced to consider it void. In the absence of conflict between a *lex specialis* and a *lex generalis*, the latter continues to apply independently of the former. There are accordingly obligations under peremptory norms that are incumbent upon the UN and the Council acting under Chapter VII, which are independent from the obligations stemming

---

[151] Text at n 11; Kelsen (n 29) 729–30; R Wolfrum in *Charter Commentary* (2002) 43. Also the Court of Appeal in *Al Jedda* [2006] EWCA Civ 327 [71 *in fine*]. But see S/PV.4761 (2003) 11–12 (Pakistan).
[152] UNCIO VI 34, 318, 453, 702. Also Wolfrum (n 151) 43 and fns 28–9.
[153] UNCIO VI 29 (US), 25 (UK); Akande (n 9) 319–20.
[154] Among others K Skubiszewski in *Honour Jennings* (1996) 627; cf Pauwelyn (n 31) 324–5. The issue had already been raised no less than 20 years before Skubiszewski by F Morgenstern (1976–7) 48 BYIL 253.
[155] cf *North Sea* [1969] ICJ Rep 39 [63]; *Nicaragua* [1986] ICJ Rep 95 [177]; Dupuy (n 143) 15.
[156] A Verdross (1966) 60 AJIL 58.

from the Charter. These former obligations also operate with respect to decisions under Chapter VII, which constitute secondary law promulgated on the basis of the Charter.[157]

Jus cogens is then binding upon the Organization and the Council.[158] This is also confirmed by the operation of the maxim *nemo plus juris transferre potest quam ipse habet*: if States cannot escape the operation of *jus cogens*, they certainly cannot create an IO which is unbound by it.[159] There are two issues that need further clarification with respect to this point: first of all, it is contended that States could have delegated powers to an organization which they themselves do not possess, because the powers exercised by the collective totality is greater than the sum of the individual powers of States.[160] However, a permission to act contrary to a *jus cogens* norm cannot be presumed, and if a treaty explicitly authorizes a breach of *jus cogens*, for example if Article 103 is interpreted as giving resolutions that are binding under Article 25 the power to derogate from *jus cogens*, then it is void in accordance with Articles 53 and 64 VCLT.[161] This is reiterated by the ILC, according to which no IO may derogate from *jus cogens*: '[n]othing...precludes the wrongfulness of any act of an international organization which is not in conformity with an obligation arising under a peremptory norm of general international law'.[162] It could also be maintained that MS may acquiesce to violations of *jus cogens* by the Council.[163] Article 26 ARSIWA and Article 25 DARIO provide, however, that consent (be it specific or implied), and thus—*a majore ad minus*—also acquiescence, cannot preclude the wrongfulness of the breach of a peremptory norm by the relevant actor,[164] a view which is shared by a number of authors.[165] This is so because peremptory norms are not dependent on the will of any (aggrieved) State, but rather are a result of the common values of the international community as a whole.[166]

The maxim has been reiterated by the CFI, which found that the MS of the EC could not, by concluding a treaty, transfer to the Community more powers than they possessed, namely the power not to be bound by SCRs which are binding (Article 25 UNC) and which supersede all other international agreements, prior or subsequent (Article 103 UNC).[167] In the same case, the Court found that it was

empowered to check indirectly the lawfulness of the resolutions of the Security Council...with regard to *jus cogens* [which is] binding on all subjects of international

---

[157] *Bosnia Genocide* (n 146) 440 [100] (sep op Lauterpacht).

[158] cf Akande (n 9) 322; Orakhelashvili (n 30) 61; Doehring (n 7) 98–9; Pellet (n 35) 236–7.

[159] Arts 40–1 DARIO and Commentary, in particular to Art 41: UN Doc A/62/10 (2007) 218–20 [2]–[7] (provisionally adopted in that Report as Arts 44–5).

[160] cf Sarooshi, *Development* (n 56) 29–30; Crawford (n 10) 15.

[161] cf A Orakhelashvili, *Peremptory Norms in International Law* (2006) 431; also Lord Bingham obiter in *Al-Jedda* [2008] UKHL 58 [35]. Of course the VCLT does not per se apply to the UNC. For the customary status of Arts 53 and 64 see respectively E Suy and A Lagerwall in *Vienne Commentaire* (2006) 1908 [4]–[5] and 2304–14 [7]–[19].

[162] Art 25 DARIO.

[163] cf E Lauterpacht in *Honour McNair* (1965) 117–18.

[164] n 162; Art 26 ARSIWA and Commentary 122 [4] (specifically linking acquiescence to consent for the purposes of justifying a breach of *jus cogens*).

[165] Orakhelashvili (n 161) 402–4 and notes.

[166] Ibid 401. ARSIWA Commentary 122 [4].   [167] *Kadi* (n 146) [192]–[195].

law, including the bodies of the United Nations, and from which no derogation is possible.[168]

The CFI was followed almost to the point, as far as this reasoning is concerned, by the Swiss Federal Tribunal.[169] Significantly, the CFI considered that fundamental human rights principles constitute peremptory norms of international law,[170] a point on which the Swiss Federal Tribunal was more reserved.[171] The ECJ subsequently overruled the CFI, relying, however, on a strict separation between the UN and EC legal orders.[172]

Some scholars,[173] as well as the ICTY,[174] the CFI,[175] and national courts,[176] stop at this: the Council is bound by obligations stemming from the Charter and from *jus cogens* norms, but these are the *only* limits to Council action under Article 41. Beyond that, the Council is the beneficiary of a power of appreciation which cannot be the object of any type of control.[177]

2. *Jus dispositivum*

Normally the rules of general international law have the character of *jus dispositivum*, meaning they are not imperative but of a yielding nature.[178] It can be thus maintained that the Security Council may derogate from norms of general international law having the character of *jus dispositivum*,[179] to the extent that the Charter evidences an intention to allow for derogation from such norms.[180] There is a need to locate the relevant evidence.

The fact that Article 1(1) makes principles of international law explicitly binding on the Council acting under Chapter VI[181] could be interpreted *a contrario* to mean that States have derogated from *jus dispositivum* with respect to Chapter VII, allowing the Council to disregard it.[182] This is corroborated to some extent by the *travaux*, since attempts explicitly to subject the Council to international law when acting under Chapter VII failed.[183] This constitutes evidence that the Council may derogate from dispositive rules of customary

---

[168] Ibid [226].

[169] *Nada g SECO, Staatssekretariat für Wirtschaft* (CH 2007) ILDC 461 [5]–[7.2]. cf also *A c Segreteria di Stato dell'economia* (22 April 2008) 1A.48/2007 before the Swiss Federal Tribunal, which was delivered five months after *Nada*, and is virtually identical.

[170] *Kadi* (n 146) [226]; see, however, the critique to this finding of the CFI in M Bulterman (2006) 19 LJIL 769–70.

[171] *Nada* (n 169) [7.3].

[172] C-402/05 P *Kadi* [2008] ECR I-6351 [278]–[308]. Thus the ECJ does not engage head-on with the CFI's argument, and as such does not overrule it.

[173] S Talmon (2009) 62 RHDI 68; A Orakhelashvili (2007) 11 MPUNYB 175–90, giving *jus cogens* an extremely broad scope; Pellet (n 35) 237.

[174] *Tadić* (Appeals Chamber Judgment) ICTY-94-1 (15 July 1999) [296].

[175] *Kadi* (n 146) [230]. cf A Ciampi (2006) 110 RGDIP 112.

[176] *Al Jedda* (n 151) [71]; *Nada* (n 169) [7].

[177] Pellet (n 35) 237.   [178] Verdross (n 156) 58.

[179] E Klein in *Festschrift Mosler* (1983) 481.

[180] cf Akande (n 9) 317, 320; Orakhelashvili (n 161) 413–14.   [181] Text at nn 11, 150–2.

[182] See R Hofmann (2007) 42 BDGVR 21.   [183] Text at nn 11, 150–2.

international law while exercising its primary responsibility for the maintenance of international peace and security. A further piece of evidence in this regard can be found in the assumption of a general obligation of the MS under Article 25 to accept and perform the decisions of the Council. This may signify the States' consent for the Council to derogate from general international law in the interest of peace and security.[184]

A piece of evidence to the contrary, however, is Article 2(7) UNC, which provides for an exception from the principle of non-intervention, a principle codifying customary international law, in case of Council action under Chapter VII. *A contrario* one concludes that other pertinent obligations under general international law remain applicable,[185] because there would be no need for a specific provision allowing for derogation from general international law if the Council was generally allowed to disregard it when acting under Chapter VII. Furthermore, the *travaux* cannot offer definitive guidance with respect to the intention of States to allow the Council to abrogate from *jus dispositivum*: not only did relevant amendments fail due to the extremely cumbersome process of amending the Dumbarton Oaks proposals,[186] but the Rapporteur also made a point of appeasing States' fears with regard to possible derogations from general international law by explaining that 'there was no intention... to let [the] notion of justice and international law lose any of its weight and strength as an *overruling arm* of the whole Charter'.[187] It seems thus that the Charter does not, in any clear or undisputable manner, allow for derogation from *jus dispositivum*, except in the specific case of Article 2(7).[188]

These arguments notwithstanding, it is contended that the willingness of States to abrogate (and thus to allow the Council to abrogate) from general international law may be presumed.[189] Indeed, it is tenable that in the absence of clear evidence indicating the willingness to abrogate from *jus dispositivum* or the unwillingness to do so, and given that States have the power to abrogate, they could have (implicitly) conferred this power on the Council in the case of Chapter VII action. If, *arguendo*, such an approach were to be accepted, one would have to look for evidence of the Council's intention to depart from general international law in its decisions under Chapter VII specifically rather than in the Charter in general.[190]

---

[184] Doehring (n 7) 104.   [185] cf Higgins (n 51) 87–90.

[186] UNCIO VI 23; cf Spiropoulos (n 15) 263.   [187] UNCIO VI 22 [emphasis added].

[188] cf the statement by the ILC Chairperson to the Sixth Committee: *Repertory*, supp 3 vol IV (1973) 214.

[189] Doehring (n 7) 104.

[190] H-P Gasser in HHG Post (ed), *International Economic Law and Armed Conflict* (1994) 175; Orakhelashvili (n 30) 80; Alvarez (n 41) 135. In drawing the 'impermissible' analogy to municipal law one could point out that English courts will typically presume unwillingness on Parliament's part to invade certain features of England's unwritten constitution in the absence of unmistakable clarity to such effect, despite the principle of parliamentary supremacy. See JE Pfander (2003) 35 GWILR 612 and n 10; cf *Garland v British Rail* [1983] 2 AC 751 at 771 (HL) (Lord Diplock) and its discussion in *Ex parte Brind* [1991] 1 AC 696 at 760 (HL) (Lord Ackner). The position is similar in US law with respect to its relationship to international law, the *locus classicus* being *Murray v The Charming Betsy* 6 US 64 at 118 (1804). This latter principle is followed in many other jurisdictions: see E Benvenisti (1999–2000) 98 MichLR 191 and fn 105. For a reason why such analogies may not be so 'impermissible' after all see Sarooshi (n 36) 14–17; idem (2008) 5 IOLR 237–9; J Crawford

This should be done by utilizing interpretive methods to establish clear evidence to that effect.[191]

The ICTY in *Tadić* confirms this approach when it states that

> it is open to the Security Council—subject to respect for peremptory norms of international law (*jus cogens*)—to adopt definitions of crimes in the Statute which deviate from customary international law. Nevertheless, as a general principle, provisions of the Statute defining the crimes within the jurisdiction of the Tribunal should always be interpreted as reflecting customary international law, unless an intention to depart from customary international law is expressed in the terms of the Statute, or from other authoritative sources.[192]

The ICTR took a similar approach in *Akayesu*.[193] It is significant in this respect that members of the Council, including permanent members, have gone on record to voice their concern with respect to provisions in Chapter VII resolutions which can be interpreted to impose an abrogation from general international law.[194] However, the English Court of Appeal did not consider that a reference in a Chapter VII resolution to an obligation to observe international law, which could presumably point toward the Council's intent in that case not to abrogate from *jus dispositivum*, can override the clear language of Article 103 UNC, in the event that an obligation in the Charter or in a SCR is clearly in conflict with, for example, an obligation in a human rights treaty.[195] One thus has to turn to the question of the operation of Article 103 with respect to *jus dispositivum*.

i. *Article 103 UNC and* jus dispositivum

It has been suggested that Article 103 is a general supremacy clause, which refers to all sources of international law, with the possible exception of *jus cogens*,[196] otherwise it would upset the equality among sources and create problems in the case of treaties codifying custom or of treaties which have generated custom.[197] Adopting a similar line of argumentation, the EC Council and Commission

---

(2006) 319 RdC 345. On the presumption against normative conflict in (international) law see n 32 above. In the final analysis, if one goes on to presume a power of the Council to abrogate general international law that is of a dispositive nature, then still one should not presume that the Council has in fact exercised that power unless this is made abundantly clear, whether explicitly or by necessary implication.

[191] Orakhelashvili (n 30) 80. The interpretive methods to be used with respect to SCRs have received little attention in scholarly writings but see Wood (n 51); E Papastavridis (2007) 56 ICLQ 83.

[192] *Tadić* (n 174) [296]. cf also *ELSI* [1989] ICJ Rep 42 [50].

[193] *Akayesu* (Appeals Chamber Judgment) ICTR-96-4 (1 June 2001) [465]–[466].

[194] eg S/PV.4803 (2003) 4 (Germany), 7 (France).

[195] *Al Jedda* (n 151) [84]. No claims under *jus cogens* were raised in this case.

[196] UN Doc A/CN.4/L.676 (2005) 22 [51]. The supremacy of peremptory norms over treaties expressed in the ILC Commentary on the Law of Treaties between States and IOs has been supported by the Sixth Committee: *Repertory*, supp 6 vol VI (1999) 157. See also Lord Bingham in *Al-Jedda* (n 161) [35].

[197] Pellet (n 35) 235; Alvarez (n 41) 132. With different justification R Bernhardt in *Charter Commentary* (2002) 1298–9.

contended before the CFI that Article 103 supersedes all obligations under international law, be these customary or contractual;[198] the Court did not pronounce on the issue.[199]

Article 103, however, does not *a priori* preclude the Council being bound from general international law, particularly since it refers to treaty law only and thus does not aspire to establishing hierarchy between norms of international law, but simply to resolving normative conflicts stemming from treaties.[200] The preparatory works seem to support this conclusion, given that a formulation which provided for supremacy over all commitments, including those under general international law, was not successful.[201] Finally, the Council's practice is to refer simply to obligations under any 'international agreement' (or other contracts, licences, and permits) when (implicitly) invoking Article 103; it surely does not proclaim its resolutions' priority over all international law.[202] Conversely, quite often it stresses the obligation to comply with international law in these same resolutions.[203]

In any event, Article 103 accords precedence to the obligations of States under the Charter, but says nothing about the Organization's, and thus the Council's, international obligations.[204] The only operation that Article 103 can have with respect to the Council is when the latter is interpreting or concretizing MS obligations under the Charter.[205]

Since it is imperative to locate clear and specific evidence of an intention for derogation from general international law in the Charter, or alternatively in the decisions of the Council, one is allowed to present an argument for the non-derogation from the principles of general international law in the case of imposition of Chapter VII sanctions by the Council, given the lack of evidence to the contrary. Sanctions in this case are not understood to encompass such recent atypical measures as the imposition of general obligations in Resolution 1373 (2001) or the establishment of ad hoc judicial fora,[206] but rather refer to action taken against States and other actors in the more classical sense of imposition of embargoes,

---

[198] See *Kadi* (n 146) [156 *in fine*]. The argumentation of the UK Government in *Al Jedda* before the Court of Appeal was along the same lines.

[199] Conversely, the ECJ in *Kadi* (n 172) [300]–[309] considered that Art 103 UNC is a rule of hierarchy of the *international* legal order and cannot operate to supersede primary EC law.

[200] See HF Köck in *Festschrift Zemanek* (1994) 70–1; Payandeh (n 10) 45; Bowett (n 42) 80; Pauwelyn (n 31) 340. Sceptical Simma (n 43) 261. A more detailed argument on Art 103 not being a hierarchy rule is provided in A Tzanakopoulos in E de Wet and J Vidmar (eds), *Norm Conflicts and Hierarchy in Public International Law* (forthcoming 2011) at Section IV.1.

[201] See Combacau (n 66) 282; Bernhardt (n 197) 1293; Dupuy (n 143) 13 and fn 36.

[202] See SCRs 670 (1990); 748 (1992); 1127 (1997); 1160 (1998); 1267 (1999); 1298 (2000). Also 1456 (2003) [6]:

> States must ensure that any measure taken to combat terrorism *comply with all their obligations under international law*, and should adopt such measures in accordance with international law, in particular international human rights, refugee, and humanitarian law. [emphasis added]

[203] See SCR 1718 (2006); cf *Al Jedda* (n 151) [82]; but see [84].

[204] R Cryer and ND White (2002) 8 YIPO 154; cf Jenks (n 31) 439.

[205] Bowett (n 42) 80. See further this chapter at Section II.2.ii.

[206] It has been contended that the Council is only bound by the Charter and *jus cogens* when promulgating 'legislative' resolutions under Chapter VII: Marschik (n 116) 485.

asset freezes, and flight and travel bans, such as those imposed against Libya, Iraq, North Korea, Iran, or Al-Qaeda.

ii. Functional analogy between countermeasures and sanctions

Drawing a functional analogy between countermeasures and sanctions allows for the application of general international law regulating countermeasures to sanctions imposed by the Council. If the Charter provides for no indication of an intention of MS to contract out of general international law with respect to imposing measures aimed at inducing certain conduct, and if general international law regulates the imposition of such measures, as it does, then the relevant customary obligations are incumbent upon the Organization and thus the Council.

According to the ILC, countermeasures aim at inducing the recalcitrant State to comply with its international obligations.[207] On the other hand, whereas it has been suggested that coercive economic sanctions may have a punitive aim towards the recalcitrant State,[208] they are mainly employed as a means of inducing compliance of States judged as violating international law.[209] Most definitions of the term 'sanctions' coincide in that inducing compliance is in fact the main objective of such measures.[210] Even more importantly, their 'effectiveness' primarily denotes the success of sanctions in making the sanctioned party comply with the decisions of the SC,[211] while both types of measures are liable to abuse. Countermeasures can be abused in view of the 'factual inequalities between States',[212] while sanctions can result in abuse because of their magnitude and potentially detrimental effects. Significantly, SC sanctions have also been termed as 'collective countermeasures',[213] while the ILC had considered the term 'sanction' when discussing State responsibility, but finally preferred the term 'countermeasure' in order to reserve the term 'sanction' for reactive measures applied by an IO.[214]

There is thus a functional analogy between countermeasures and sanctions. The main objection to this contention is that countermeasures may only constitute the

---

[207] Art 49 ARSIWA and Commentary 130–1.

[208] E Zoller, *Peacetime Unilateral Remedies* (1984) 106; UN Doc A/63/10 (2008) 258 [152]. The punitive character of countermeasures has also been suggested: O Schachter (1984) 37 JIA 233, but has been rebutted by the ILC, ARSIWA Commentary 130 [1]. See also S/PV.3519 (1995) 4 (Honduras), 6 (Nigeria), 12 (France) for a rebuttal.

[209] S/PV.5500 (2006) 3 (US); S/PV.5474 (2006) 12 (Slovakia), 22 (Tanzania), 32–3 (Austria), (Resumption 1) 15 (Iraq), 17 (Venezuela); S/PV.4394 (2001) 4 (Germany); S/PV.3864 (1998) 18 (Portugal), 29 (France); S/PV.3519 (1995) 2 (Italy). Also D Cortright and GA Lopez in Malone (n 37) 170, 172; A Reinisch (2001) 95 AJIL 851; UN Doc A/63/10 (2008) 258–9 [152].

[210] S/PV.5474 (2006) 18 (Greece), 24 (France), 28 (Congo); S/PV.3519 (1995) 2 (Italy), 4 (Honduras), 12 (France). Also J Combacau in *EPIL*, vol 4 (2000) 312; Lavalle (n 104) 412; CC Joyner (2003) 4 ChicJIL 331. Interestingly, F Swindells (1997) 20 FILJ 1894–5 uses the term 'sanctions' to describe both countermeasures and UN sanctions, while specifically stating that 'sanctions' aim at deterring and rectifying violations of international legal norms.

[211] Statements (nn 208–10); Oette (n 72) 101.   [212] ARSIWA Commentary 128 [2].

[213] L Boisson de Chazournes (1995) 89 ASILProc 337; eadem *Les contre-mesures dans les relations internationales économiques* (1992).

[214] Talmon (n 28) 163; W Fiedler (1998) 37 BDGVR 12–13. cf the discussions in (1979) I YILC 56–63 and see UN Doc A/63/10 (2008) 259 [153].

response to an internationally wrongful act,[215] whereas the Council, while usually stating the breach of an international obligation when resorting to sanctions,[216] has also acted in many cases without any precise determination of the existence of an internationally wrongful act.[217] Furthermore, the Council may act pre-emptively in order to prevent a threat to the peace, without the need to identify that a certain international obligation incumbent upon a State has been breached.[218] Indeed, whereas Kelsen qualified Article 41 enforcement measures as 'sanctions', he expressed strong reservations about the propriety of this qualification.[219] He argued that Article 39 does not stipulate that the measures are to be directed against a MS that has violated an obligation under the Charter, or even prescribe that the measures shall be directed only against a MS guilty of a threat to the peace.[220]

The very premise that SC sanctions, as opposed to unilateral countermeasures, are not meant to constitute a response to an international wrong can be questioned. The ILC has defined sanctions as

reactive measures applied by virtue of a decision taken by an international organization following a breach of international obligations having serious consequences for the international community as a whole, and in particular ... certain measures which the United Nations is empowered to adopt, under the system established by the Charter, with a view to the maintenance of international peace and security.[221]

Thus, Council sanctions largely constitute a centralized or collective reaction of the international community to an international wrong, just as countermeasures constitute a decentralized reaction.[222]

According to Kelsen, the normative content of a rule is based on the prohibition of conduct which is threatened by sanctions: certain behaviour is a delict (illegal

[215] Art 49(1) ARSIWA.

[216] V Gowlland-Debbas (1994) 43 ICLQ 63–8 with relevant examples. See also P-M Dupuy in *Festschrift Bernhardt* (1995) 51.

[217] Talmon (n 28) 156; M Craven (2002) 13 EJIL 52.

[218] Frowein and Krisch (n 6) 705.

[219] Kelsen (n 29) 724. However, in *Principles of International Law* (1952) 46, Kelsen specifically states that Art 41 measures 'have the technical character of reprisals', reprisals sharing the definition that describes what is today called countermeasures: idem *Reine Rechtslehre* (2nd edn, 1960) 321.

[220] Kelsen (n 29) 729, 732–3.

[221] (1979) II(2) YILC 121 [21]; see also France in *Repertoire*, supp 1959–63 (1965) 267. cf G Arangio-Ruiz (1991) II(1) YILC 10 [15]. R Ago (1971) II(1) YILC 210 [40] left open the possibility that an internationally wrongful act may create a new (secondary) relationship between the author and an organization of States, which would have the faculty or duty to 'react against the internationally wrongful conduct by applying sanctions collectively decided upon'. cf the UN Legal Counsel in [1972] UNJY 194–5.

[222] ND White and A Abass in MD Evans (ed), *International Law* (2nd edn, 2006) 526; WA Kewenig (1982) 22 BDGVR 26; V Gowlland-Debbas in Byers (n 51) 277 and *passim*; M Bennouna in *Honour Bedjaoui* (1999) 558. Generally L-A Sicilianos, *Les réactions décentralisées à l'illicite* (1990). cf V Gowlland-Debbas in eadem (ed), *UN Sanctions and International Law* (2001) 9, according to whom whereas Art 41 measures were not intended to be restricted to cases of non-compliance with international law, the practice of the Council has moved considerably towards dealing with responsibility of States for breaches of international law; also Combacau (n 210) 314, according to whom 'every time a UN organ has used [sanctions], it has taken the precaution of an *a priori* characterization of the act against which it was reacting as a violation of international law'; finally Zoller (n 208) 106–7; R Higgins in Fox (n 10) 50.

act, wrong) if it is made the condition of a sanction, while certain behaviour is the content of a legal obligation if the contrary behaviour is the condition of a sanction (and as such a delict).[223] This applies also to rules conferring powers, the violation of which is sanctioned by invalidity or non-operation of the violating act,[224] as well as to permissive rules, which aim at clarifying that the conduct provided for shall not be sanctioned.[225]

Since the condition for the imposition of Article 41 sanctions is the existence of a threat to the peace in accordance with Article 39, there must be a general obligation incumbent upon MS not to conduct themselves in a way which constitutes a threat to the peace.[226] This could be claimed to constitute an obligation incumbent upon non-MS as well, not by virtue of Article 2(6), but because the Charter has given rise to a (peremptory) norm of general international law.[227] This general obligation, this *Blankettverpflichtung*,[228] will then be elaborated ad hoc and given specific content by the Council in the exercise of its primary responsibility through relevant decisions.[229] It can thus be presumed that binding Chapter VII SCRs constitute an elaboration of the obligations imposed by the Charter and possibly by general international law.[230]

The imposition of sanctions will then virtually always be a response to illegality because it will be addressing the non-compliance of a State with a derivative (or concretized)[231] obligation, imposed by the Council through a binding decision.[232]

---

[223] Kelsen (n 29) 706. cf idem *Allgemeine Theorie der Normen* (1979) 115; *Reine Rechtslehre* (1934) 25–6.

[224] See FA Mann (1976–7) 48 BYIL 6; Lauterpacht (n 163) 113–14. cf also G Abi-Saab in *Honour Skubiszewski* (1996) 63–5. But see further Chapter 7.II.2.ii below.

[225] According to Kelsen, if every norm establishes an 'ought', then 'ought' encompasses commands, empowerments, permissions, and derogations. See *Allgemeine Theorie* (n 223) 2–3.

[226] cf Combacau (n 66) 12–17; Graefrath (n 84) 242; Schilling (n 88) 89; Kelsen *Principles* (n 219) 54. cf also P-M Dupuy (1993) 97 RGDIP 625, according to whom '[i]l faut de plus constater que les faits justifiant la prise des mesures de l'article 41 sont *par définition* eux-mêmes des faits illicites' [emphasis added]. cf finally H Kelsen (1946) 31 IowaLR 521–2.

[227] cf TM Franck in *Festschrift Eitel* (2003) 97. cf also E Klein (1992) 30 AVR 104; R Lapidoth (1992) 30 AVR 121.

[228] On 'Blankettverpflichtung' see HG Niemeyer, *Einstweilige Verfügungen des Weltgerichtshofs* (1932) 41 seq.

[229] cf Kelsen (n 226) 521–2 and idem (n 29) 736. Significantly, in the former, earlier work, Kelsen does not include the famous statement that '[b]y declaring the conduct of a State to be a threat to... the peace, the Security Council may create new law' (cf also [n 29] 295). He does, however, maintain that enforcement measures may amount to new law (cf [n 226] 526). Whether the elaboration of precise rules from a general prescription amounts to 'creation of new law', and in what sense, is beyond the scope of this discussion. Suffice it to mention, however, that courts regularly distil specific rules from general prescriptions, and so do executives. It was claimed above (text at nn 84–94) that the determination of a threat to the peace is a legal determination. The claim that the term 'threat to the peace' corresponds to a general obligation conforms to the former claim. According to O Schachter in *Honor Kelsen* (1964) 271, legal determinations reached by UN political organs 'specify obligations of members'. cf finally TM Franck in Al-Nauimi and Meese (n 8) 627; Johnstone (n 51) 452.

[230] See eg S/PV.3864 (1998) 18 (Portugal); L-A Sicilianos in idem and LP Forlati (eds), *Les sanctions économiques* (2004) 9. cf DW Bowett (1994) 5 EJIL 92–3. On the derivative nature of SCRs see G Lysen (2003) 72 NJIL 293.

[231] On the term (*Konkretisierung*) and its use with respect to Council action under Chapter VII see M Herdegen in *Festschrift Bernhardt* (1995) 103 seq.

[232] JE Alvarez (1996) 90 AJIL 20–1.

It should be noted, however, that whilst sanctions always respond to some illegality, illegality is not always sanctioned,[233] as the Council is under no obligation to make a finding of a threat to the peace in all cases of potential existence of such a threat. This is also what happens with respect to decentralized countermeasures: States are under no obligation to sanction each breach they suffer, but if they do take countermeasures, it must be in response to a breach. Thus, whilst certain conduct must be wrongful if it is sanctioned, it may sometimes not be sanctioned even if it is wrongful.

The decision imposing sanctions will state the conditions for the termination of sanctions, thus *uno actu* (and implicitly) determining the specific obligations (aspects of the general obligation) which have been breached and demanding compliance.[234] Although this approach may seem formalistic, it vindicates the coherence of the legal system, and it is in harmony with the stated objective of Council sanctions to induce compliance. Compliance in a legal context can only be understood as compliance with a legal obligation.

Given this analogy, there exists a strong indicator of non-derogation from the *jus dispositivum*. The ILC provisions on the permissible content of countermeasures, in particular Articles 50(1)(b) and 51 ARSIWA, could then be deemed to give rise to international obligations of the Organization when the Council imposes sanctions, to the extent that they codify general international law.

3. Obligations under general international law

i. Human rights obligations

One of the most central arguments to the proponents of legally unrestrained, or virtually unrestrained, action of the SC when fulfilling its mandate to maintain international peace and security is that potential legal constraints would place it at a disadvantage when confronted with actors disregarding all legal rules.[235] A similar line of argumentation contends that the policing function of the Council under Chapter VII of the Charter is qualitatively different from that of individual States asserting their own rights through countermeasures, and thus cannot be submitted to the same legal restraints, just as the police in municipal law is not as restrained as any individual citizen resorting to self-help.[236]

However, the international system is highly decentralized,[237] in sharp contradistinction to the heavily centralized municipal systems. Accordingly,

---

[233] It should be recalled, in this connection, that a sanction may properly be characterized as a 'legal faculty': see Ago (n 221) 209 [37]. See also L Gross in idem, *Essays on International Law* (1993) 171. cf finally Abi-Saab (n 224) 75.

[234] Dominicé (n 33) 203–4. cf Higgins (n 129) 6; Bennouna (n 222) 559. See by way of example SCR 1054 (1996) [2]. cf finally JM Farrall, *UN Sanctions and the Rule of Law* (2007) 133–4 (overview and critique of SC practice on the matter).

[235] E Davidsson (2003) 7 IJHR 2. cf Oosthuizen (n 4) 562–3.

[236] cf UN Doc A/63/10 (2008) 258–9 [152]. See with respect to the policing function of the Council Dupuy (n 226) 624.

[237] Kelsen (n 29) 707.

resort to self-help and countermeasures in the international system is much more closely connected to a policing function, undertaken by each actor of the system for the vindication of its own rights, than it is in municipal systems. In the international system self-help and countermeasures constitute the rule, whereas centralized responses only the exception.[238] There is thus—in practice rather than in theory—no overriding qualitative difference between centralized and decentralized responses to illegality, which would advocate for sharply different rules regulating them.

According to Article 50(1)(b) and (d) ARSIWA '[c]ountermeasures shall not affect...obligations for the protection of fundamental human rights [and] other obligations under peremptory norms of general international law.' Whereas this could be interpreted to mean that countermeasures, and thus also Article 41 sanctions, may not affect only those obligations for the protection of fundamental human rights which have come to be accepted as having the status of peremptory norms, it is submitted that such a provision would have been redundant if obligations for the protection of fundamental human rights had in fact been recognized by the international community of States as a whole as norms from which no derogation is permitted.[239]

The Commission's commentary supports this conclusion. It clearly states that the provision of Article 50(d) 'does not qualify the preceding subparagraphs, *some* of which also *encompass* norms of a peremptory character'.[240] The Council is thus bound by obligations to respect fundamental human rights under general international law,[241] whether these be considered to have attained the status of *jus cogens* or not.

In its discussion of the notion of 'fundamental human rights' the Commission may be seen to allude to the concession that only these human rights obligations that cannot be derogated from in time of war or other public emergency can positively be held to constitute prohibited content of countermeasures.[242] The question could be posed thus, whether the Council can act unrestrained from fundamental human rights obligations when acting under Chapter VII through the (implicit) invocation of a 'state of emergency'.[243]

However, whereas derogation from human rights obligations is permitted in cases of 'public emergency', it has been noted that the notion of a totally unsupervised power to derogate is not compatible with human rights obligations.[244] The acceptance of the notion of derogation in human rights instruments cited by the Commission is conditioned on substantive and

---

[238] TM Franck (1988) 82 AJIL 705. Also Schachter (n 208) 231.

[239] cf Art 53 VCLT.

[240] ARSIWA Commentary 132–3 [9]; 'analogies can be drawn from *other* elements of general international law': ibid 132 [7] [emphasis added].

[241] See with respect to fundamental human rights norms belonging to the corpus of general international law: O Schachter (1982) 178 RdC 333 seq; T Meron, *Human Rights and Humanitarian Norms as Customary Law* (1989).

[242] ARSIWA Commentary 132 [6 *in fine*]. cf D McGoldrick in M Fitzmaurice and D Sarooshi (eds), *Issues of State Responsibility* (2004) 197.

[243] cf *Kadi* (n 146) [216].   [244] Cameron (n 149) 181.

procedural limitations on the power to derogate, which do not exist in the case of the Council.[245] The application of the relevant rule of Article 50(1)(b) clarifies the substantive limitations of any derogation by the Council: the latter cannot derogate from fundamental human rights obligations. This also seems in line with the principle that all fundamental human rights have a hard core, and no derogation may affect this core.

It is perhaps of some significance that the Commission, in its commentary to Article 50(1)(b) specifically refers to sanctions by IOs, although at the same time recognizing that the topic falls outside the scope of the task at hand, and takes note of CESCR General Comment 8, which provides that 'sanctions should always take full account of the provisions of the [ICESCR]'.[246] The Committee, as well as the Commission, which cites the Committee's view approvingly,[247] sustain thus both the close functional relationship between sanctions and countermeasures, and the applicability of the relevant limitations with regard to content in the context of both reactions.

It is accordingly apparent that international obligations are directly incumbent upon the Council under general international law, without the need for attempting to channel these obligations through the Charter:[248] the obligations exist under general international law, limiting the content of measures short of armed force, which aim at inducing compliance of a recalcitrant entity. Since the Charter cannot be shown to permit divergence from these norms, they apply to SC action for the imposition of sanctions directly, and their violation engages the responsibility of the UN.

ii. The principle of proportionality under general international law

A second point that can be clarified by the analogous application of the law regulating the permissible content of countermeasures is the appropriate proportionality test. The notions of proportionality are different in the context of IHL,[249] the international law of human rights,[250] the law of individual or collective self-defence,[251] and the law of countermeasures. The application of IHL (including the relevant proportionality test) to SC sanctions has been supported by some,[252] but contested by others.[253] One of the points of controversy has been the notion of proportionality in IHL, which is admittedly much looser than other notions of proportionality in different contexts, and allows for weighing the importance of

---

[245] See the instruments cited in ARSIWA Commentary 132 [6] at fn 761: all have special mechanisms for monitoring their application.

[246] UN Doc E/C.12/1997/8 (1997) [1].   [247] ARSIWA Commentary 132 [7].

[248] This is especially pertinent since the English Court of Appeal found that 'the Charter does not create any immediately enforceable human rights obligations': *Al Jedda* (n 151) [77].

[249] eg JM Henckaerts in M Hector and M Jellema (eds), *Protecting Civilians* (2001) 11.

[250] J Delbrück in *EPIL*, vol 3 (1997) 1140, 1143. Also de Wet (n 146) 295.

[251] Delbrück (n 250) 1141.

[252] WM Reisman and DL Stevick (1998) 9 EJIL 95; JG Gardam (1993) 87 AJIL 398. Also de Wet (n 146) 294–6; eadem (n 87) 223–4.

[253] O'Connell (n 146) 74–5. Also Davidsson (n 235) 38–9.

the military target with the potential cost to civilians, as well as even escalating the amount of force if the objective cannot be obtained with less.[254] Such a broad proportionality test is hardly in harmony with the objective of sanctions. Economic sanctions have indisputably caused substantial hardship to civilian populations in the target States.[255] To allow for a lax test with respect to sanctions would amount to a legitimization, at least to some degree, of that hardship, and to an unwarranted reiteration of a punitive character of sanctions. The broad and deferential qualities of the proportionality test in IHL is confirmed by the fact that the test is expressed in negative terms. This is significant, as the evolution of the countermeasures proportionality test will readily show.

The application of countermeasures proportionality in the law of sanctions allows for the application of a stricter test than that of IHL. For the ILC, considerations of proportionality were deemed relevant in determining what countermeasures may be applied and their degree of intensity. Proportionality is a well-established requirement for taking countermeasures.[256] However, the relevant test has evolved significantly since its first application with respect to countermeasures in the context of *Naulilaa*. In that case, the Tribunal stated that one should certainly consider as excessive, and therefore unlawful, reprisals out of all proportion to the act motivating them.[257] Thus, according to this test, countermeasures would have to be 'out of all proportion to the act motivating them' to be deemed unlawful. This is a very lenient test, which results in the State being able to take countermeasures that are disproportionate to a significant degree to the internationally wrongful act which injured it, as long as they are not 'out of all proportion'. In *Air Services*, the arbitral tribunal held that 'the measures taken by the [US] do not appear to be clearly disproportionate when compared to those taken by France'.[258] The formulation of this particular proportionality test is again in the negative, in effect confirming the *Naulilaa* dictum. This led former SR on State responsibility Riphagen to propose a draft article which stipulated that countermeasures 'should not be manifestly disproportionate' with regard to the gravity of the internationally wrongful act.[259]

However, in *Gabčíkovo-Nagymaros* the ICJ held that 'an important consideration is that the effects of a countermeasure must be commensurate with the injury suffered, taking account of the rights in question'.[260] The ILC recognized the evolution in the application of the principle of proportionality in the context of countermeasures, and elected to phrase Article 51 in terms identical to the aforementioned pronouncement of the Court. It stated that

---

[254] O'Connell (n 146) 75.　　[255] Davidsson (n 235) 1.

[256] ARSIWA Commentary 134 [2]. Arguably, the obligation for State action to be in conformity with the principle of proportionality may be traced back to the general obligation of good faith: cf GS Goodwin-Gill in Fitzmaurice and Sarooshi (n 242) 98. This obligation is also incumbent upon IOs under general international law: cf Sarooshi (n 36) 14–17 (who argues in favour of public law analogies in the law of IOs) and Lowe (n 84) 218 (who characterizes proportionality as a 'public law standard'). On public law analogies see also Crawford (n 190) 345 and in the law of IOs specifically Sarooshi (n 190) 237–9.

[257] *Naulilaa* (1928) 2 RIAA 1028.　　[258] *Air Service Agreement* (1978) 18 RIAA 444 [83].

[259] (1985) II(1) YILC 11.　　[260] *Gabčíkovo-Nagymaros* [1997] ICJ Rep 56 [85].

A positive formulation of the proportionality requirement is adopted in article 51 [because a] negative formulation might allow too much latitude, in a context where there is concern as to the possible abuse of countermeasures.[261]

Countermeasures are susceptible to a more restrictive requirement because they are measures that would otherwise be unlawful. The same, however, holds true for the imposition of sanctions under Article 41: the Council can obligate States to take measures that would otherwise be unlawful as well.[262] The fact that sanctions serve broader and perhaps more important purposes than countermeasures[263] can be accommodated, as far as the proportionality test is concerned, within the notion of weighing the measures resorted to with the 'importance of the interest protected' and the seriousness of the breach to which they constitute the response.

Thus, the principle of proportionality as formulated in the context of countermeasures is directly applicable to the Council when the latter is imposing sanctions, by virtue of general international law.[264] There is no interpretation of the Charter allowing for divergence from this principle. Conversely, the Charter can be said to either support or even embody the principle of proportionality,[265] which would then lead to the conclusion that the Council may not elect to avail itself from the application of the principle by specific provision in a Chapter VII resolution. In the former case, the aforementioned proportionality test applies as incumbent upon the Council by virtue of general international law. In the latter case, the principle of proportionality embodied in the Charter is to be interpreted—as far as means-ends (*stricto sensu*) proportionality is concerned—to allow only sanctions commensurate with the injury suffered by the international community through the threat to the peace, and not to condone measures which are simply 'not out of all proportion' to the objective pursued, that is, the cessation of the threat to the peace through compliance.[266]

III. Interim Conclusion

Whereas the origin of international obligations should be of no consequence for the task of attributing responsibility to a subject of international law, the source of obligations incumbent upon the UN for Council Article 41 action is of paramount importance. The two main sources of obligations are the rules of the Organization and general international law. If the Council breaches an obligation under the former category, its act is *ultra vires*, but benefits from an important presumption of legality.[267] In the latter case the act is *intra vires* but still illegal. The significance

---

[261] ARSIWA Commentary 135 [5].   [262] Talmon (n 28) 155.
[263] White and Abass (n 222) 526.
[264] cf MJ Herdegen (1994) 27 VJTL 157, who argues that the principle of proportionality has emerged as a 'general principle of law'.
[265] Text at nn 109–15.   [266] See the proportionality test applied in *Bosphorus* (n 115) [26].
[267] Text at n 139. See further Chapter 7.II.2 below.

of this distinction is not limited to the operation of the presumption of legality, however. It also allows for a partial clarification of the Organization's relationship to non-MS. In Simma's words, Article 2(6) '*somehow* subjects third States to the activities of the organization'.[268] Third States are said to be bound by Chapter VII action,[269] but cannot hold the Organization responsible for its breach of an obligation stemming from its Charter, as the latter is *pacta tertiis* for them.[270] However, in case of a breach of an *erga omnes* obligation of the Organization, or of any other obligation under general international law which is owed to non-MS, the principle of privity does not apply, and the non-MS will be able to invoke the Organization's responsibility in accordance with the relevant norms.

---

[268] Simma (n 43) 257 [emphasis added].
[269] J Delbrück in *Charter Commentary* (2002) 460.
[270] cf Art 34 VCLT; I Seidl-Hohenveldern (1961) 11 ÖZöR 501–2.

PART II

THE DETERMINATION OF RESPONSIBILITY

The United Nations can become responsible under international law for conduct of—or imposed by—the Security Council under Article 41 of the UN Charter. Scholars can intelligibly argue that the responsibility of the UN has been engaged. However, this does not amount to authoritative determination of responsibility. The second part of this study examines to what extent such authoritative determination is possible at the present stage of development of international law. Chapter 4 surveys the possibility of judicial determination of UN responsibility, while Chapter 5 discusses decentralized determination on the part of States.

4

Judicial Determination

If the UN Security Council can take measures that are binding on States, whether these are specific or of a general character, it only makes sense that the subjects of the law of that international organization, the UN Member States, can appeal against these acts,[1] lest it be conceded that they have vested the Council with unlimited powers over them. And the first—almost instinctive—reaction of any lawyer, if not of any person in general, will naturally be that such an appeal aiming to review the legality of 'administrative' or 'legislative' action should be launched before a court of law.[2]

The issue can, of course, be recast in the more traditional vernacular of classical international law: the UN is under certain international obligations, the breach of which by the Council as a UN organ—or by MS acting as the UN's agents—engages the Organization's responsibility.[3] This then invites the question over the determination of the engagement of responsibility; again a court of law would be the organ instinctively resorted to in order to determine that engagement.

This chapter discusses the prospects of judicial determination of the engagement of UN responsibility for wrongful SC non-forcible measures under Chapter VII. In the first instance, issues of terminology are dealt with, primarily because they have an impact on further substantive considerations (Section I). Subsequently, the questions whether a court has the power judicially to determine UN responsibility for Council action (Section II) or whether it may judicially review Council action for compliance with the applicable legal framework (Section III) are successively discussed.

---

[1] cf A Gros (1950) 36 GST 30; idem in *Hommage Scelle* (1950) 267; J Klabbers, *An Introduction to International Institutional Law* (2nd edn, 2009) 213, and cf 221–4.

[2] cf A Aust in E de Wet and A Nollkaemper (eds), *Review of the SC by MS* (2003) 35; V Gowlland-Debbas (1994) 88 AJIL 663; WM Reisman (1993) 87 AJIL 92. Critically though admitting review is desirable J Klabbers in RSJ Macdonald and DM Johnston (eds), *Towards World Constitutionalism* (2005) 809 seq; cf generally idem (2007) 4 IOLR 293. See also A Reinisch (2007) 42 BDGVR 43–4, who reiterates the point and speaks of review of normative acts (*rechtliche Akten*) being in the foreground when discussing the control of legality of conduct of international organizations. cf generally A Tsoutsos (1963) 16 RHDI 273; idem (1954) 7 RHDI 35 seq.

[3] See Chapters 2 and 3 above.

I. The Question of Qualification of Judicial Involvement

A court of law should normally be involved in determining whether an entity has acted illegally, says common sense and instinct. What is this (as yet unidentified) court of law asked to do, precisely, in the case of the UN Security Council? The answer can be cast in two distinct ways, both of them having at least some impact on the subsequent substantive considerations.

Most of the literature on the legality of SC action under Chapter VII UNC has focused on the issue of 'judicial review' of Council action. Discussions began in earnest with *Namibia*,[4] whereas the more general question of judicial review of the actions of UN principal organs had already been raised in the context of *Expenses*.[5] Interest in the issue was re-kindled with the resurrection of the Council after the Cold War, especially during the *Lockerbie* debacle in the 1990s,[6] and, in a more limited manner, in the context of the *Bosnian Genocide* case.[7] The ICTY in *Tadić* kept the discussion going.[8] The apogee of course is the *Kadi* case before the EC Courts,[9] where the exercise of 'judicial review' over Council action was seen as being undertaken for the first time by a court outside the general structure of the UN system.

'Judicial review' as a term has little in the way of specific substantive content. More frustratingly, it is widely used without any serious attempt at defining what *precisely* the term is supposed to mean. Definitions of such generality as 'the reviewing of legality of decisions of political organs by an independent court of law' are often propounded,[10] on the happy occasion that they are offered at all; and they beg more questions than they answer: for example, the review should test the legality of the act on the basis of *which* rules? And does *any* independent court have the power to undertake such review? What are the *effects* of the review? How is it *organized*?

Even in such very general terms, 'judicial review' of Council action for compliance with the legal framework to which the SC is subject casts the issue in *domestic public law terms*. It seems to refer to review of compliance of administrative or legislative action with 'higher rules', and as such it evokes notions of a *vertical, hierarchical* relationship so banal in domestic legal systems but still so extravagant in international law.[11] This verticality does not solely or necessarily refer to the superiority of the controlling organ over the organ whose actions are being

---

[4] [1971] ICJ Rep 16.   [5] [1962] ICJ Rep 151.   [6] [1992] ICJ Rep 3, 114.
[7] [1993] ICJ Rep 3.   [8] (Appeal on Jurisdiction) IT-94-1-AR72 (2 October 1995).
[9] T-315/01 *Kadi* [2005] ECR II-3649 (*CFI Kadi*); T-306/01 *Yusuf* [2005] ECR II-3533 is in substance identical, but reference is always to *Kadi*; C-402/05P and C-415/05P *Kadi* [2008] ECR I-6351 (*ECJ Kadi*). cf also T-253/02 *Ayadi* [2006] ECR II-2139; T-49/04 *Hassan* [2006] ECR II-52, largely following *CFI Kadi* and *Yusuf*; T-318/01 *Othman* [2009] ECR II-1627 following *ECJ Kadi*.
[10] See E de Wet, *The Chapter VII Powers* (2004) 69. cf A Reinisch in idem (ed), *Challenging Acts of IOs before National Courts* (2010) 5–6 with further references.
[11] cf V Gowlland-Debbas in de Wet and Nollkaemper (n 2) 66, who understands the term as a 'constitutional' process with 'compulsory' effect; Klabbers in Macdonald and Johnston (n 2) 825–6.

controlled; or to the superiority of the normative act against which the impugned act is tested; rather more importantly it refers to the hierarchical relationship between those 'governing' and those 'governed'—those who are subject to an instance of exercise of power, seeking to challenge it. In any case it should be kept in mind that not all 'administrative' or 'legislative' actions are judicially reviewable, even in domestic legal systems.[12]

The term 'judicial review' employed thus constitutes, it is argued, a term of art peculiar to the highly centralized domestic legal system, where the administrative or legislative action is usually subjected—to varying extents—to systematized control by the domestic hierarchy of courts. For example, general reference works such as the *New Oxford Companion to Law* and the *Oxford Dictionary of Law* mention solely domestic judicial review under the relevant entry;[13] and only the latter adds a short note on judicial review of EC acts by the ECJ,[14] the single excursion into anything other than the domestic legal system, understood as it were as the legal system of a sovereign State.

In an international law context, however, 'judicial review'—generally defined as above—can also be taken to mean the review by a competent court of the compliance of a subject of international law with its international obligations. In other words, the issue at hand could be cast, simply, as the determination by a court of the responsibility of the UN for wrongful SC action: this would be nothing else but 'the review by an independent court of law of the legality of the decisions of a (political) organ' of the UN.[15] Cast thus, judicial involvement evokes notions of *horizontality*: there are two (in principle) equal sides to the dispute, which is resolved by a disinterested third party competent to decide the dispute in accordance with the law.

Which of the two frameworks one will adopt is of particular importance with respect to the content of the discussion if not with respect to its outcome.[16] It is, however, submitted that the adoption of a framework—whether that of analogy with domestic public law or that of classical international law; whether the vertical or the horizontal one—is not a decision to be made *a priori*. This should rather be broached on the basis of an analysis of the respective roles of judicial review of SC action and of judicial determination of UN responsibility for Council action.

---

[12] See Chapter 3 above at nn 7–10. The distinction between an administrative and a legislative act may be important (and relatively easy) in domestic legal systems, since some may allow for judicial review of administrative but not of legislative acts. Still, such precise qualification is difficult and perhaps counter-productive in the context of IOs, and in particular the SC. Measures adopted under Art 41 UNC could be qualified as both administrative and legislative, depending on their particular properties in each case: see generally Chapter 1.II.1 above; S Talmon (2005) 99 AJIL 175.

[13] M Sunkin in P Cane and J Conaghan (eds), *The New Oxford Companion to Law* (2008) 653–5; 'Judicial Review' in EA Martin and J Law (eds), *The Oxford Dictionary of Law* (6th edn, 2006). See also, among many others, 'Judicial Review' in LB Curzon and PH Richards, *The Longman Dictionary of Law* (7th edn, 2007).

[14] Martin and Law (n 13).   [15] cf the definition offered by de Wet (n 10) 69.

[16] The distinction is drawn implicitly in DW Bowett (1994) 5 EJIL 91.

II. Judicial Determination of Responsibility

The judicial determination of international responsibility should be the starting point of the enquiry, if not because it is easier to discuss, then at least because it would be a more familiar concept to the international lawyer. It is the process whereby a competent disinterested third party, usually called a court or tribunal for convenience, determines the existence of an internationally wrongful act, and the corollary engagement of international responsibility,[17] with binding force for the parties to a dispute.[18]

This can be seen, for example, in Articles 36(2)(c)–(d) and 59 of the ICJ Statute. Although the enumeration of specific subject-matters in Article 36(2) 'has never played any role in practice',[19] it serves to confirm that the ICJ has the power to determine the responsibility of States under international law with binding force. According to the provision, the Court can decide all disputes between States that concern

(c) the existence of any fact which, if established, would constitute a breach of an international obligation;

(d) the nature or extent of the reparation to be made for the breach of an international obligation.

These two elements underline the power of the Court to determine the engagement and content of State responsibility in a dispute before it.[20] The decision of the Court is binding between the parties.[21]

A 'judicial determination' (or: authoritative determination) of responsibility can be made by *any* disinterested third party so competent. This is to be inferred from the discussion in the ILC on dispute settlement proceedings as a bar to countermeasures.[22] Article 52(3) ARSIWA provides that

Countermeasures may not be taken, and if already taken must be suspended without undue delay if…the internationally wrongful act has ceased; and…the dispute is pending before a court or tribunal which has the authority to make decisions binding on the parties.

The power to take countermeasures is a primordial feature of a decentralized system necessarily reliant on self-help for enforcement. It is an aspect of implementation of responsibility which can only be set aside through recourse to binding third-party settlement of the dispute, and then again only temporarily, unless there exists also centralized enforcement. The Commission has stated that the reference to a 'court or tribunal' in the provision is to be understood as 'any third party dispute

---

[17] See Art 1 ARSIWA; cf Art 3(1) DARIO.
[18] See eg R Bernhardt (1987) 47 ZaöRV 17–18; CPR Romano in L Boisson de Chazournes et al (eds), *IOs and International Dispute Settlement* (2002) 5.
[19] C Tomuschat in A Zimmermann et al (eds), *ICJ Statute Commentary* (2006) 631 [74].
[20] ARSIWA Commentary 87 [2].   [21] Art 59 ICJ Statute.
[22] For the discussion prior to the first reading draft see succinctly M Bennouna (1994) 5 EJIL 61–4.

settlement procedure, whatever its designation', but it does not refer to political organs, such as the SC.[23]

A 'judicial determination' of the responsibility of the UN would thus require that a disinterested third party, a 'court or tribunal', be vested with the power to make a binding decision on the Organization with respect to the engagement and/or content of its responsibility under international law in a specific case.[24]

There is currently no permanent court or tribunal, whether international or domestic, whether of general or of circumscribed/special subject-matter jurisdiction, whether of global or of only regional reach, vested with the power to make such a binding decision on the UN with respect to SC action under Chapter VII UNC. No court whatsoever has jurisdiction over the UN or its SC;[25] and thus no court can authoritatively, judicially, determine UN responsibility over a Council measure under Article 41.

The ICJ, the principal judicial organ of the UN, which would be the most obvious first port of call, does not have the power to adjudicate contentious cases where any party is anything other than a State.[26] There have been various proposals for an amendment to the relevant Article 34(1) of the Court's Statute so as to allow *locus standi* for international organizations.[27] It would probably make good sense to allow IOs to appear before the Court in contentious cases. In the final analysis, if organizations have rights and duties under international law and can bring international claims or have claims brought against them,[28] then there is no obvious reason for restricting the *ratione personae* jurisdiction of the ICJ to States.[29]

These pertinent proposals notwithstanding, the fact remains that the UN cannot be party to a case before the ICJ in contentious proceedings. This means that the Court cannot determine the responsibility of the UN under international law with binding force for the Organization:[30] under Article 59 of the Court's

---

[23] ARSIWA Commentary 137 [8].

[24] cf for criteria on designating an institution as an 'international court or tribunal' C Tomuschat in *Judicial Settlement of International Disputes* (1974) 290–307.

[25] JA Frowein in *Festschrift Tomuschat* (2006) 794.

[26] Art 34(1) ICJ Statute, causing an 'extraordinary anomaly' in that IOs cannot participate in contentious proceedings, according to RY Jennings (1995) 89 AJIL 504–5. It has been called a 'relic from the past' by G Abi-Saab in Boisson de Chazournes (n 18) 242. Indeed, already in 1946 CW Jenks commented that the drafting of Art 34 conveys 'a certain twinge of conscience' on the part of the drafters, who—not daring to give IOs *locus standi*—contented themselves with elevating them to something analogous to *amici curiae* in contentious proceedings: (1946) 32 GST 2.

[27] eg Art 6 of IDI resolution in 45-II AIDI (1954) 296–8 at 298; Jenks (n 26) 24–37; idem *The Prospects of International Adjudication* (1964) 208–24; E Lauterpacht, *Aspects of the Administration of International Justice* (1991) 60–6; J Sztucki in AS Muller et al (eds), *The ICJ—Its Future Role after Fifty Years* (1997) 141; PC Szasz in ibid 169; I Seidl-Hohenveldern in ibid 189; A Watts in DW Bowett et al (eds), *The ICJ—Process, Practice and Procedure* (1997) 66–7 [80]–[83]; J Crawford in ibid 118–21; K Wellens, *Remedies Against IOs* (2002) 236 seq.

[28] See, with respect to the UN, *Reparation* [1949] ICJ Rep 174.

[29] As Sztucki (n 27) 144 notes, if the subjects of any legal system are 'not necessarily identical in their nature or the extent of their rights' (*Reparation* [n 28] 178), one might add that they have equal access to courts, such differences notwithstanding. But see also 144 seq.

[30] It should be noted here, as indeed it is by DW Bowett in *Honour Jennings* (1996) 189–90, that the question of giving *locus standi* to IOs for their international responsibility to be determined judicially is a question *separate* from '[w]hether the Court is to become an organ of judicial review'.

Statute, its decision is only binding between the parties and in respect of the particular case before the Court. The exercise of contentious jurisdiction, even if it incidentally touches upon the legality or effects of acts (whether normative or operational) of UN organs, will take place in the framework of contentious proceedings between States.[31] The outcome will only be binding upon these States, not the Organization or any other State.[32] Even if the Court were to find the relevant UN acts to be in breach of international obligations of the Organization, this would not in any case amount to a 'judicial determination' of UN responsibility.

Things are seemingly even more straightforward when the Court is in advisory mode: there the Court is not even resolving a dispute,[33] but it is merely offering legal advice for the benefit of the requesting UN organ. This may well represent the Court's 'participation in the activities of the Organization',[34] but it cannot be considered to constitute judicial determination of responsibility. It may provide a solid basis for a decentralized invocation of responsibility;[35] but an authoritative determination it is not. The advisory opinion of the Court does not have any binding force (notwithstanding its potentially great persuasive force) even for the requesting organ.[36] Even if advisory proceedings serve essentially 'to clarify the law',[37] or to 'state the law',[38] and even if they may be considered 'powerful *political* tools',[39] the fact remains that no possibility of judicial determination of international responsibility may arise in such an instance. An AO may even help 'prevent disputes from arising',[40] but still it cannot resolve such a dispute between MS and the Organization in a legally binding manner, by attributing international

---

[31] cf generally *Lockerbie* (n 6).

[32] See *Northern Cameroons* [1963] ICJ Rep 33:

> If the Court were to proceed and were to hold that the Applicant's contentions were all sound on the merits... [t]he decisions of the General Assembly would not be reversed by the judgment of the Court[;]... the judgment *would not be binding on Nigeria, or on any other State, or on any organ of the United Nations*. These *truths* are not controverted by the Applicant. [emphasis added]

[33] cf *Eastern Carelia* [1923] PCIJ Ser B No 5 at 27–9. Though neither the PCIJ nor the ICJ has ever since refused to give an AO on the basis of the *Eastern Carelia* principle, this is not because the principle is now bad law, but rather because it has limited scope. Nonetheless, it is valuable here in its limited, technical sense: the AO does not resolve disputes, it gives non-binding advice. If an AO can be given on legal questions actually pending between two or more States, this is because it is *only* advisory *in nature*: see *Interpretation of Peace Treaties* [1950] ICJ Rep 71. But this does not in any case relate to a dispute between a State and the UN or any other Organization of the UN family. cf Lauterpacht (n 27) 60–1.

[34] *Interpretation of Peace Treaties* (n 33) 71.

[35] cf GG Fitzmaurice (1952) 29 BYIL 55.

[36] This is evident from the fact that no provision in the Charter or the ICJ Statute vests AOs with any such force—in contrast to Art 59 of the Statute, which provides for the binding force of decisions in contentious cases and to Art 94(1) UNC, according to which the UN MS undertake 'to comply with the decision of the International Court of Justice in any case' to which they happen to be parties.

[37] F Morgenstern (1976–7) 48 BYIL 254.

[38] Among others CD Gray, *Judicial Remedies in International Law* (1990) 100; cf Fitzmaurice (n 35) 54–5.

[39] Romano (n 18) 18.   [40] L Boisson de Chazournes in eadem (n 18) 107.

responsibility to one or the other. In the end it is just that: an opinion (learned as it may be), not a judgment.[41]

There is, of course, an exceptional situation, whereby the ICJ is to render an AO on a *dispute*[42] between a State and an IO, the parties to the dispute accepting the Court's opinion as binding.[43] This 'roundabout' of 'binding' AOs to settle disputes has been adopted in some treaties[44] in order to address the lack of *locus standi* of international organizations under Article 34 ICJ Statute.[45] In such cases the Court can in fact judicially determine the existence of an internationally wrongful act on the part of the IO and thus the engagement of its international responsibility. However, the scope of this power is extremely limited, as it refers to nothing but a miniscule number of primary obligations.

Similar considerations apply *mutatis mutandis* to all other international courts and tribunals of any character, and of course *a fortiori* to all domestic courts, from whose jurisdiction the UN enjoys in any case very broad immunity, at least with respect to its 'official' acts.[46] These are the acts that are correspondingly called 'sovereign' in the case of States. There is no doubt that a normative act of the SC, that is, a decision under Chapter VII UNC, will qualify as such an 'official' act. Even in more general terms, it is fair to say that domestic courts, being tied to the municipal legal order, 'cannot make findings that decide legal issues in the international legal order',[47] and in particular the UN legal order. Any domestic court decision on the responsibility of the UN would have no binding effect upon the Organization,[48] and as such would not constitute a judicial determination of the UN's international responsibility in the sense envisaged here.

This is not necessarily a dualist argument whereby acts in one legal order cannot affect another—separate—legal order, as it has been contended.[49] Even within

---

[41] See Jenks (n 27) 219. Even Gray, who claims ([n 38] 100–1) that there is no difference in substance between an AO and a judgment, concedes later on (at 112) that it is not realistic to say that the AO is a 'remedy' for or against the organization.

[42] cf *Applicability of the Convention on UN Privileges and Immunities* [1989] ICJ Rep 189 [32]–[33]: The Court notes obiter that the object of Art VIII s30 of the Convention 'is to provide a *dispute settlement mechanism*', the IO being, in certain circumstances, 'one of the *parties* to the difference' [emphasis added].

[43] See generally R Ago (1991) 85 AJIL 439.

[44] eg Convention on the Privileges and Immunities of the UN, Art VIII Section 30; Convention on the Privileges and Immunities of the Specialized Agencies, Art XI Section 32; Vienna Convention on the Law of Treaties between States and IOs (not yet in force), Art 66(2)(b)–(e); UN Convention against Illicit Traffic in Narcotic Drugs and Psychotropic Substances, Art 32(3) referring to 'regional economic integration organizations' potentially becoming parties to the treaty and obviously meaning primarily the EC (which has in fact become a party). Some bilateral Headquarters agreements for UN Specialized Agencies include similar provisions. See for brief comment H Ruiz Fabri in *Vienne Commentaire* (2006) 2435–6 [8].

[45] See Sztucki (n 27) 148–9; cf Seidl-Hohenveldern (n 27) 190; Szasz (n 27) 187–8 for a discussion on extending such a procedure of resolving disputes between States and IOs.

[46] See generally E Gaillard and I Pingel-Lenuzza (2002) 51 ICLQ 1; cf the Legal Counsel's claims at n 43 in Chapter 6 below.

[47] A Nollkaemper (2007) 101 AJIL 772.   [48] cf ibid 773.   [49] Ibid 774.

a unitary[50] legal order it is understandable how domestic courts cannot make a binding determination of the engagement of UN responsibility: the rules which vest the domestic court with the power to make binding decisions have simply not given it the power to make binding findings with respect to other States or IOs. Conversely, specific rules preclude such findings: States and IOs enjoy sovereign and functional immunity respectively.[51]

It appears thus that there can be no binding determination of UN responsibility for Council action under Article 41 in any currently available judicial forum. But this is not a particularly surprising conclusion, even if it is somewhat peculiar to the decentralized system that is international law. For in international law it is quite common that no court will have jurisdiction over a given dispute: it is not necessary that the breach and subsequent engagement of responsibility will fall to be judicially determined.[52] In fact, usually it will not.

But this would be too easy and too unsatisfying a conclusion to the present enquiry. Perhaps there is some type of judicial control over SC binding non-forcible action, akin to that of State organs' action under domestic public law: perhaps there are courts that can engage in judicial review of the Council.

III. 'Judicial Review' of Council Action

The notion of 'judicial review' is rather more problematic, on account of the strong analogies with domestic public law that it necessarily invites. It would be superfluous to recount here the issues associated with easy transpositions of domestic law concepts in the field of international law.[53] Judicial review has—in all probability—not assumed the character of a general principle of (international) law in the sense of Article 38(1)(c) ICJ Statute.[54] The tentative nature of judicial review as a general principle is no less due to its conspicuous, though implicit, association with the 'common cultural heritage' and 'shared individual and societal

---

[50] In the sense, eg used by H Mosler (1980–1) 4 HICLR 448: international legal order and domestic jurisdiction of States constitute 'components of a general system of law'. See generally H Kelsen (1958) 19 ZaöRV 234: the 'unity' of the legal system does not prejudge whether it will be the international or the domestic legal order (or any other legal order for that matter) that will be superimposed.

[51] There is an argument to be made that a domestic court may deny immunity to the act of an IO if it considers it to be *ultra vires*: K Schmalenbach, 'IOs or Institutions, Legal Remedies against Acts of Organs' in *MPEPIL* [24]. For the legal qualification of such action see Chapters 5 and 7 below.

[52] D Akande (1997) 46 ICLQ 325; see further Chapter 5.I below.

[53] But see the eloquent summary by M Shahabuddeen in *Honour Jennings* (1996) 102: the danger of too easily either accepting or rejecting the analogy is equally great and equally fatal. One should here again recall AV Lowe: the development of the law is, in the final analysis, 'a never-ending battle for control of the analogy' (in M Koskenniemi [ed], *International Law Aspects of the EU* [1998] 166).

[54] See extensively de Wet (n 10) ch 3, in particular 116–29. Also HK Kaikobad, *The ICJ and Judicial Review* (2000) 27; cf L Caflisch in N Al-Nauimi and R Meese (eds), *International Legal Issues* (1995) 637. But see MSM Amr, *The Role of the ICJ* (2003) 323.

values' of Western societies,[55] which, however, are not necessarily shared by the rest of the world.[56]

It is understandable that the domestic law concept of 'judicial review' exercises such a strong pull as to its transposition in the law of international organizations.[57] IOs can be seen as oscillating between the two extremes of the unstructured international engagement, which is a purely normative concept, and the 'shared destiny' that gives birth to federalism.[58] They have not quite reached that latter extreme, however, or at least the UN has not.[59] As such one should be wary of easy transposition.[60]

Still, the main problem of 'judicial review' is not so much its transposition into international law at large, nor is it its standing as a general principle under Article 38(1)(c). Rather, it is the precise content and definition of the concept, which is widely divergent even within the various domestic legal systems.[61] This gives rise to particular difficulties; for a concept to be transposed it must first be at least by and large defined.[62] In this sense, 'judicial review' must be understood and treated as a term of art, as being a 'separate or special institution',[63] and thus as having a 'separate or special meaning', if it is to have any meaning at all.

Judicial review corresponds to the notion of internal institutional control of legality, in the sense of a judicial organ of a (corporate) entity reviewing the actions of other organs of the same entity for compliance with the entity's legal framework, namely with the 'higher' rules, which usually concern the delimitation of powers in general, or the division of powers between organs.[64] There are a number of basic elements inherent in this understanding of judicial review: that it is exercised 'internally', within the partial legal order establishing, for example, a State or an IO (Subsection 1); that it tests the conformity of acts of organs of that partial legal order with 'higher' rules, whether of the partial legal order itself, or

---

[55] See M Cappelletti (1980) 53 SoCalLR 412. cf E McWhinney in *Festschrift Bernhardt* (1995) 708, who connects the notion of constitutional review to 'leading Western and Western-influenced States'.

[56] Whether for 'good' or 'bad' reasons is another matter altogether; cf JE Alvarez (1996) 90 AJIL 36.

[57] Just as notions of public law generally do—cf H-J Schlochauer, *Der Rechtsschutz gegenüber der Tätigkeit internationaler und übernationaler Behörden* (1952) 23; S Kadelbach and T Kleinlein (2007) 50 GYIL 342.

[58] CM Chaumont in *Mélanges Rolin* (1964) 57; cf U Scheuner in *Festschrift Verdross* (1960) 231.

[59] cf L Gross (1967) 120 RdC 425, partly disclaiming a possibility of inspiration from the ECJ on the basis of a distinction between organizations of integration and organizations of coordination.

[60] cf Scheuner (n 58) 232.

[61] On the divergences between domestic forms of judicial review cf Kaikobad (n 54) 17–22 and de Wet (n 10) 123–6; even within the same jurisdiction: see JE Alvarez in de Wet and Nollkaemper (n 2) 138–9. Generally see AR Brewer-Carías, *Judicial Review in Comparative Law* (1989) 91–3 and Parts IV–VI *passim*.

[62] cf Kaikobad (n 54) 27.   [63] cf J Crawford in *Honour Jennings* (1996) 590.

[64] cf the definitions in Kaikobad (n 54) 11, 27; E Lauterpacht in L Boisson de Chazournes and P Sands (eds), *International Law, the ICJ and Nuclear Weapons* (1999) 92; Bowett (n 30) 181, 190–1; Amr (n 54) 290. In this respect, judicial review is closely associated with constitutionalism, at least within the framework of domestic law: Cappelletti (n 55) 430–1; WF Murphy (1980) 53 So CalLR 758.

possibly of a superimposed legal order (Subsection 2).[65] A third point, revolves around the question whether the power of judicial review inheres in the judicial nature of a court of law, in the absence of an explicit limitation, or whether it exists only to the extent that it is explicitly conferred upon the court (Subsection 3). It is further necessary to consider if a court proceeding that does not result in a binding decision with respect to the act being reviewed can properly be characterized 'judicial review' (Subsection 4). Finally, it has to be determined whether judicial review must be offered systematically rather than incidentally and haphazardly in order to be considered judicial review proper (Subsection 5).

1. Internal review

The *locus classicus* for judicial review of constitutionality of acts of the legislature in a domestic legal system is the decision of the US Supreme Court in *Marbury v Madison*.[66] This case clearly demonstrates the basic tenets of the notion, as it refers to the 'internal' review (by one organ over another within the same legal order) of compliance with 'higher' law (the said legal order's Constitution), an 'inherent' power of the Court.

The first point—that of the 'internal' nature of judicial review—is relatively unproblematic in a domestic setting, as the domestic court is necessarily an organ of the State. As such, when it reviews the conformity of acts of other organs of the State with the 'higher' rules of the Constitution for example, the 'internal' quality of review is apparent. In that very 'internal setting', judicial review can be further categorized into a 'horizontal' and a 'vertical' species. The latter refers to review of acts of *subordinate*, whether the former to review of acts of *coordinate* organs.[67]

Judicial review of SC action by the ICJ has been widely discussed in theory, and even dealt with by the Court itself.[68] It is noteworthy that no such issue ever arose with the PCIJ, a judicial institution—it may be stressed—that shared by and large the same constituent instrument as the ICJ. This is arguably because the PCIJ was not a judicial organ of the League of Nations, but was established separately from the League.[69] The ICJ, however, is the principal judicial organ of

---

[65] On this point specifically with regard to IOs see Reinisch (n 2) 43–4: review of *internal* (on the basis of the constitutive instrument) and *external* legality (on the basis of general international law).

[66] 5 US 137 (1803).

[67] See GA Bermann (2004) 36 GWILR 557; CM Vázquez (2004) 36 GWILR 595–6. Review of acts of subordinate organs is connected to 'federalism', whereas that of coordinate organs refers to 'constitutionalism': cf Cappelletti (n 55) 430. In this sense, the ICJ is an organ coordinate to the Council: see E McWhinney (1992) 30 CYIL 264–5 and cf *Hostages* [1980] ICJ Rep 21–2 [40]; *Nicaragua* [1984] ICJ Rep 435–6 [95]; Art 12 UNC.

[68] *Expenses* (n 5) 168; *Namibia* (n 4) 45 [89]. Numerous separate and dissenting opinions in *Expenses, Namibia, Lockerbie,* and *Bosnia Genocide* deal with the issue of judicial review of the GA and the SC by the Court.

[69] J Crawford (2004) 36 GWILR 510; cf TO Elias, *New Horizons in International Law* (2nd edn, 1992) 267–8. According to the latter, the reason why there had been no case of judicial review by the PCIJ of League organs' actions was the lack of any *organic* link between the League and the Court; this 'made it *unthinkable* that the latter should *deign* to review the structures and competence' of the Council and Assembly, even if relevant questions were referred to it [emphasis added]. But see KJ Keith, *The Extent of the Advisory Jurisdiction of the ICJ* (1971) 143–4.

the UN,[70] and as such belongs to the same institution and thus the same (partial) legal order as the SC. The latter can be said for all other courts existing within the UN system *lato sensu*.[71]

The requirement for judicial review to be 'internal' can be demonstrated in the case of the UN system of organizations. IOs, including the UN, cannot be parties to disputes before the Court. Further, only the UN and its Specialized Agencies and related organizations may request AOs if so authorized by the GA or the SC.[72] This facility has been used creatively by some UN organs and Specialized Agencies to create a binding system of judicial review (through so-called 'binding' AOs).[73] This system includes both review of decisions of other courts by the ICJ (what one might call 'appellate review'),[74] and review of acts of political organs of the relevant Organizations of the UN family.

As far as 'appellate review' is concerned, ILOAT judgments may be reviewed by the ICJ on very narrow grounds through a binding AO requested by the ILO Governing Body or the Administrative Board of the Pensions Fund.[75] UNAT judgments could be challenged on wider grounds, including for error on a question of law relating to provisions of the UNC, by MS, the S-G, and even the person in respect of whom the judgment was rendered, through a request to the Committee on Applications for Review, which would then request a binding AO of the ICJ.[76] However, this form of appellate review is no longer available under the UNAT Statute.[77]

---

[70] See Art 92 UNC. E Hambro (1962) 15 RHDI 1 remarked that this difference could lead some to think that the new Court would be called upon to play a greater role in the international community than the PCIJ, but history would prove them wrong.

[71] ie in the sense of Art 57 seq UNC; thus, the UN (partial) legal order can be seen as a 'framework' legal order or 'umbrella': Kadelbach and Kleinlein (n 57) 319–20.

[72] Art 96(b) UNC. cf the opinion of the Secretariat in [1992] UNJY 465–6.

[73] While in most cases treated together (eg Ago [n 43]; F Seyersted [1964] 24 ZaöRV 113–17), these 'binding' AOs are different from the ones discussed under Section II above. In the latter instance they are used to resolve disputes between States and IOs as to the interpretation and application of a freestanding treaty, while in the case here contemplated they are aimed at truly reviewing the acts of a political organ of an IO or the decision of a court for compliance with its own constitutive instrument. Hence the 'internality'.

[74] In discussing relevant proceedings, Seidl-Hohenveldern (n 27) 191 notes that they require the ICJ virtually to play the role of a Court of Cassation. cf also generally Lauterpacht (n 27) 99–112. According to the latter (at 104–5) there is some possibility for recourse against a decision of an international tribunal 'arising from an extraneous instrument', ie 'by reason of the existence of some separate source of jurisdiction'. But this is not review properly so-called, as Lauterpacht himself concedes, but rather the lodging of a 'new case', 'arising out of the alleged misconduct of the first tribunal'. Appellate review in the sense here employed at once integrates the notions of internality *as well as* superiority of the reviewing organ (verticality). This is evident when Lauterpacht argues (at 111–12) that otherwise 'appeal...is merely the substitution of one person's view of the situation for that of another'. cf also Kaikobad (n 54) 12, distinguishing 'appeal' from 'review'. However, the review of decisions of political organs need not be vertical: in that case the reviewing organ is different *in nature* from the organ which took the decision, and this is enough to justify review—it need not also be different *in status* (ie superior).

[75] Art XII of the Statute.

[76] See Lauterpacht (n 27) 106–7; Seidl-Hohenveldern (n 27) 190–1. For extensive discussion see Kaikobad (n 54) Part III.

[77] Arts 11–12 of the Statute.

With respect to judicial review of acts of political organs, decisions of the ICAO Council on the interpretation or application of the 1944 Chicago Convention upon submission of a dispute by States parties are subject to appeal before the ICJ (or an ad hoc arbitral tribunal).[78] The Havana Charter, the constituent instrument for an International Trade Organization that never came into force, also envisaged endowing the Court with judicial review powers.[79] Judicial review of acts of political organs can of course take place on an ad hoc basis through AOs, when the political organ so requests. For example, the IMO constituent instrument provides that any dispute on its interpretation or application shall be settled by reference to the ICJ for an AO.[80] The provision has been used to request judicial review of acts of the (then IMCO) Assembly.[81] Similarly, in *Expenses* France sought an amendment to the request for an AO by the GA, which would have put the question of conformity of GA resolutions with the Charter directly before the Court.[82] It should be noted, however, that such possibilities are open solely to organizations that have a constitutional link with the UN,[83] as is also evident from a reading of Article 96(b) UNC in conjunction with Article 65(1) of the Court's Statute.

The ICJ obviously fulfils the requirement of internality for engaging in judicial review of Council decisions.[84] And possibly so do some other courts which have been established within the broader framework of the UN family, such as the ICTY, for example. In the first instance one might question altogether the propriety of examining the possibilities of review of Council action by any court other than the ICJ. For some, the mere utterance of the phrase 'judicial review of Council action under Chapter VII' may amount to hubris, let alone the concession that this may be undertaken by a court other than the UN principal judicial organ. Such an issue is one of those 'of immense importance and sensitivity that, quite frankly, one cannot imagine any other tribunal dealing with'.[85] As such, only the ICJ, or at least a court belonging to the UN structure, could undertake judicial review of actions of the SC or of any other UN principal organ.

Still, one could retort that a requirement of 'internality' in the exercise of judicial review may be seen as overly restrictive and excessively formalistic in an era of

---

[78] Art 84 of the Convention on International Civil Aviation.

[79] Art 96(2) provided that

> Any decision of the [ITO] Conference under this Charter shall, at the instance of any Member whose interests are prejudiced by the decision, be subject to *review* by the [ICJ] by means of a request…for an advisory opinion pursuant to the Statute of the Court. [emphasis added]

That the AO would be considered as binding on the ITO is clearly stated in para 5 of the same Art: See *Havana Charter for an International Trade Organization* in Final Act and Related Documents of the UN Conference on Trade and Employment (1948) UN Doc E/CONF.2/78.

[80] Art 70 of the Convention on the IMO. cf also Art 69.

[81] See *Constitution of the Maritime Safety Committee* [1960] ICJ Rep 150.

[82] See *Expenses* (n 5) 156.

[83] See Jenks (n 27) 219–20. Seidl-Hohenveldern (n 27) 203, after calling this way of submitting a dispute to the ICJ 'subterfuge', criticizes the lack of access by IOs not belonging to the UN system, even in this 'roundabout' manner, as unfairly discriminatory.

[84] cf J Rideau, *Juridictions internationales et contrôle du respect des traités constitutifs* (1969) 67–8.

[85] R Higgins in MD Evans (ed), *Remedies in International Law* (1998) 7, referring to *Lockerbie*.

increased interdependence in international relations and interpenetration between courts belonging to 'different' legal orders. Why should other courts, whether international or even domestic, abstain from engaging in such judicial review, if only in an indirect manner?

2. Hierarchical review

The requirement of 'internality' of judicial review is intertwined with the requirement of judicial control reviewing the compliance of the acts under scrutiny with 'higher'—that is to say, hierarchically superior—rules. Judicial review of an act can only consider the compliance of that act with superior law.[86] Assuming a pyramidal scheme, where the highest law is at the apex, all other law and normative acts produced at lower levels must be in conformity with the law at the higher levels. This is how the norms gain their validity.[87] The first real issue is whether the court that finds, interprets, and applies the 'higher' law, partakes in this superior status. In other words, whether the reviewing court, becoming the final arbiter of legality,[88] assumes a position of superiority over all other organs, whose acts it tests against the prescriptions of the law.

Theoretically, the ICJ could review Council acts for conformity with 'higher' law, that is, Charter law and applicable general international law, as described in Chapter 3 above.[89] The problem that the Court is not explicitly so empowered could be overcome by arguments to the effect that courts will appropriate such power to themselves by asserting the 'constitutional hegemony' of the fundamental law on the basis of which they operate.[90] The objection to such a move would be that the Court and the Council are coordinate organs, that is, there is no hierarchy between them and each is supreme in its own sphere of competence.[91] Exercise of review by the ICJ would not, however, necessarily render it hierarchically superior to the

---

[86] See M Cappelletti, *The Judicial Process in Comparative Perspective* (1989) 117–32; Kaikobad (n 54) 13. The distinction between superior and inferior law is the 'main foundation' of the doctrine of judicial review: G Dietze (1956–7) 55 MichLR 553–4.

[87] See generally H Kelsen, *Reine Rechtslehre* (2nd edn, 1960) 196 seq ('Rechtsdynamik') and in particular 228 seq ('Der Stufenbau der Rechtsordnung'); also RL Bindschedler in *Festschrift Verdross* (1960) 67. cf within IOs the separate opinion of Judge Mosler in *Application for Review of Judgment No 273* [1982] ICJ Rep 388 [8]. Still, that norms gain their validity when they are in conformity with higher rules does not finally decide the issue of the legal effects of *ultra vires* acts: these depend on the authoritative determination of a competent body: see further Chapters 5 and 7.II.2 below.

[88] Or the 'ultimate guardian' in the carefully chosen words of TM Franck (1992) 86 AJIL 519–23; cf idem in Al-Nauimi and Meese (n 54) 625. Not simply the 'general' or 'principal' guardian of legality as in the words of Judge Lachs in *Lockerbie* (n 6) 26–7 (sep op).

[89] Superior law does not have to be a written, rigid constitution. For one, an ordinary law is superior to an administrative act, just as a constitutional norm is superior to an ordinary law. In the case at hand, we are concerned with acts of the Council under the Charter and under applicable general international law. These acts must conform to both: see also H Thierry (1980) 167 RdC 414–19. For another, even States with flexible, unwritten constitutions have systems of judicial review: see Brewer-Carías (n 61) 104–6. This allows, for the time being, an evasion of the question whether the UNC can be considered a 'constitution'.

[90] See Section III.3 below on the argument that judicial review 'inheres' in the judicial function.

[91] Akande (n 52) 312–13. cf GR Watson (1993) 34 HILJ 39–40, who argues that review with *erga omnes* effect establishes the Court as the supreme organ. See Section III.4 below.

other principal organs.[92] Review is undertaken to test an act's conformity with 'higher law' rather than against the subjective opinion of the organ undertaking the review.[93] As such, it is conceivable that the ICJ could undertake judicial review of Council acts, even if not explicitly so empowered, for conformity with hierarchically superior law.

If that is the case, then there is no reason why any other court could not sit in judgment of Council decisions and test their compliance to 'higher' law.[94] The problem with any court other than the ICJ or other tribunal within the UN system is where it would find that 'higher' law, that is, according to which hierarchy, which pyramid of validity-flow, it would determine certain rules to be superior to those made by the Council. It now becomes apparent that the requirement of internality elaborated above comes to bear: this is not only because of the black-letter prescriptions of Articles 34 ICJ Statute and 96 UNC, but because any court outside the UN system may profoundly misconstrue—from the perspective of international law—the hierarchy of norms.

Any judicial organ of a State or an IO other than the UN or the Specialized Agencies, as well as any organ monitoring the implementation of an international treaty (if otherwise qualified as a judicial, rather than a quasi-judicial or political organ) will not be part of the UN machinery. As such it will operate within the contours of a specific partial, potentially self-proclaimed 'separate' or 'autonomous' legal order, with its 'own' hierarchy of norms.[95] For example, a domestic court will operate within the domestic legal order, and be bound to the domestic hierarchy of norms; the EC Courts within the EC legal order, being

---

[92] Caflisch (n 54) 656 argues that it would, as does by implication Thierry (n 89) 396, who finds that the Court is not placed 'above' the other UN organs precisely because it has no power 'to *decide* on the validity of resolutions' [emphasis in original].

[93] For this argument see Dietze (n 86) 542: refusal to apply a norm for incompatibility with a superior norm does not establish the reviewing organ as superior to the promulgating organ but merely safeguards the superiority of the norm. But see further 555–7. cf finally Brewer-Carías (n 61) 99–100. It can be said that the will of the States as law-makers is above the will of their agent, the Council, when it makes law (even if it is 'for the specific case'). The Roman civil law doctrinal approach is evident in this instance, law being treated as having 'objective existence', independent of the will of judges: see Kadelbach and Kleinlein (n 57) 312. This 'existence' is nothing but the law's 'validity': H Kelsen in *Festschrift Verdross* (1960) 157–8. Still an argument could be made that the power of review renders the Court superior, since the Court also makes law for the specific case, potentially arbitrarily—if authoritatively!—selecting one of the possible interpretations of a rule as the only definitive interpretation (cf Kelsen [n 87] 242 seq on the 'constitutive character' of judicial decisions). However, the Council (and the membership of the Organization) are not relegated to inferior status: the Council could make a new decision challenging the Court's interpretation; and the membership of the Organization can reject the Court's interpretation (see text at nn 4–10 in Chapter 5 on this latter point).

[94] This is what the CFI did in *Kadi* (n 9) [231]: It appears to have assumed its competence to review Council act on the basis that *jus cogens* is absolutely binding on the Council, ie it is higher law. It was directly cited and followed by the Swiss Bundesgericht in *Nada g SECO, Staatssekretariat für Wirtschaft* (14 November 2007) ILDC 461 (CH 2007) [5.3]–[5.4]. See critically on the point R Kolb (2008) 18 RSDIE 404 at fn 8; U Haltern (2007) 62 JZ 540; N Lavranos in idem and D Obradovic (eds), *Interface between EU Law and National Law* (2007) 355 seq; and cf V Bore Eveno (2006) 110 RGDIP 837–8, 845–55.

[95] cf Brewer-Carías (n 61) 90 explaining briefly, Kelsen-style, the usual hierarchy within a domestic legal order. cf also Mosler (n 50) 457 seq.

bound by the EC hierarchy; the ECtHR within the partial legal order established by the ECHR,[96] applying the hierarchy of norms to be derived from that latter instrument, and so forth.

As a result, any of these courts, when engaged in judicial review of an act properly before it,[97] will test its conformity with the 'higher' rules as determined by the hierarchy of the partial legal order to which it belongs. Theoretically, any court could (indirectly) review Council action for its compliance with 'higher' rules as these are set by the international legal order only in the following two cases: (i) if it conceives itself as operating within a unitary legal order, that is, if it ascribes to rules of international law the position that international law itself ascribes to them; or (ii) if the partial legal order—exceptionally—puts international law in such a supreme position in the classic pyramidal scheme. The CFI in *Kadi* can be seen as having managed (to some extent) precisely that.[98] Similarly, Dutch courts, for example, may set aside a constitutional provision if it is incompatible with a rule of international law contained in a self-executing treaty provision or a decision of an IO.[99] By contrast, the Indian constitution merely exhorts the State (and by implication domestic courts, as its organs) to endeavour to 'foster respect for international law and treaty obligations in the dealings of organized peoples with one another'.[100]

Cases where courts will conceive the legal order as unitary are the rarest of exceptions: in the final analysis, the CFI and the Dutch courts can still be seen as applying the hierarchy of norms established by their own partial legal order—this hierarchy just happens to coincide, in part, with that established under international law.[101] Otherwise, and normally, it is expected that partial legal

---

[96] An international treaty establishes, for those subject to it, a partial legal order (*Teilordnung*): H Kelsen, *Allgemeine Staatslehre* (1925) 174. The European Commission of Human Rights stated obiter that States parties aimed to establish 'a common public order' through the ECHR: *Austria v Italy* (1961) 4 YECHR 138. cf also the arguments of the applicant in the pending *Al Jedda* case before the ECtHR (app no 27021/08).

[97] This will usually be an internal act implementing a Council decision. To the extent that the implementing act essentially transposes the Council act, review of the former will constitute indirect review of the latter. A Council act will not usually come directly and per se before a court other than the ICJ in advisory mode, for lack of jurisdiction *ratione personae*. See further A Tzanakopoulos in Reinisch (n 10) 56–8 and Chapter 5.II.3.ii below.

[98] See *CFI Kadi* (n 9) [226]–[231], though when discussing the substance, rather than the hierarchy of the rules, the CFI is to be found lacking. The ECJ on the other hand took a completely different stance on the issue in its own *Kadi* decision (n 9) [305]–[309], construing the hierarchy of norms differently. See generally K Ziegler (2009) 9 HRLR 288; T Tridimas and J A Gutierrez-Fons (2008–9) 32 FILJ 660; S Griller (2008) 4 EuConst 537–9.

[99] CM Zoethout in eadem et al (eds), *Control in Constitutional Law* (1993) 158; cf A Nollkaemper in D Sloss (ed), *The Role of Domestic Courts in Treaty Enforcement* (2009) 333–5.

[100] Art 51(c) of the Constitution of India, entitled 'Promotion of International Peace and Security' and positioned in Part IV 'Directive Principles of State Policy'. For a discussion, including of relevant case law, see VG Hegde (2010) 23 LJIL 57–62 and cf N Jayawickrama in Sloss (n 99) 245–7.

[101] cf V Gowlland-Debbas in eadem (ed), *National Implementation of UN Sanctions* (2004) 34. See for an example in the relationship between EC law and domestic law the BVerfG in *2 BvE 2/08* (30 June 2009): the Court states that the primacy of Community law is allowed in the German legal order by the German legal order itself, through the act approving the participation of Germany (at [339]). For the Court thus it is the German legal order that confers primacy on EC law.

orders and their organs will proclaim their 'constitutional hegemony',[102] as the BVerfG did in *Solange I*, and as the ECJ did in *Kadi*, overruling the CFI.

3. Inherent nature of judicial review

There is an argument that judicial review inheres in the judicial function unless specifically excluded, in accordance with the common law tradition.[103] This is supported by the fact that some constitutions will explicitly prohibit review of constitutionality of laws.[104] The theoretical foundation of inherence of judicial review in the judicial function can be found in the maxim *lex superior derogat legi inferiori*, thus being corollary of the requirement that review be for compliance with higher law. If the judge is to apply two norms that conflict with each other, she must give preference to higher law,[105] and as such review inheres in her function.

However, in some European legal systems, the presumption of validity generated by the doctrine of separation of powers overrides any form of judicial review of constitutionality (it is not rebuttable), unless the power of review has been explicitly conferred on the court.[106] Kaikobad notes that when reviewing an act of a constitutional organ for conformity with the constitution, the court may, if it finds it lacking, proceed to strike it down and nullify its effects, '*provided, of course, that the constitution . . . confer[s] powers of annulment in* [sic] *the court*'.[107] Skubiszewski claims that 'in analogy to municipal law, for [judicial review] powers to exist there must be an express norm authorizing judicial review. These powers *cannot be implied*.'[108]

What is, then, the position under international law? To which municipal law—if to municipal law at all—should one draw the analogy? Kaikobad states that the action or decision of an international institution which is found to be inconsistent with the law, whether customary/general or conventional, stands to be nullified by the reviewing court '*provided*, of course, that the international tribunal is empowered to annul the action or decision in question'.[109] But about 60 pages down the line he goes back on that statement claiming that the fact that the ICJ is not endowed with express powers of judicial review is not a major difficulty: what

---

[102] cf Tridimas and Gutierrez-Fons (n 98) 684; AL Paulus in Sloss (n 99) 232, 241–2. But see also A Tzanakopoulos in OK Fauchald and A Nollkaemper (eds), *Unity or Fragmentation* (forthcoming 2011) at Section VI.

[103] See eg Crawford (n 69) 508–9.

[104] The Netherlands is such an example: Zoethout (n 99) 157–8; Nollkaemper (n 99) 334.

[105] See Cappelletti (n 86) 135; Akande (n 52) 326. This is implicit in the CFI's reasoning in *Kadi* and in the Swiss Bundesgericht's *Nada*: see n 94 above.

[106] See Cappelletti (n 86) 137; cf Dietze (n 86) 554–5: while in the US judicial review is considered a corollary of the separation of powers, in Europe it was, particularly before the Second World War, considered to involve a *confusion* of powers. As such, France traditionally denied a power of review of constitutionality of the courts. Interestingly, the USSR rejected the concept of judicial review as an aspect of the 'bourgeois doctrine' of separation of powers: M Cappelletti, *Judicial Review in the Contemporary World* (1971) 7.

[107] (n 54) 13 [emphasis added].

[108] In *Honour Jennings* (1996) 623 [emphasis added]; an identical position is adopted by Caflisch (n 54) 655; also Watson (n 91) 6.

[109] (n 54) 27–8 [emphasis in original].

is more important is that 'there is no express prohibition *against* the exercise of such powers'.[110] In fact both positions have been argued forcefully in theory on the basis of such analogical reasoning.[111]

It makes sense, given the profoundly diverse content of the notion of judicial review, that the position in international law should be as confusing as it is in any comparative approach to judicial review in the various municipal systems.[112] This in and of itself militates against easy admission of any court exercising 'inherent' powers of judicial review over Council decisions. Assuming, for the moment, that what is not prohibited is allowed, one could accept that at least incidental judicial review inheres in the judicial function of any tribunal vested with the power to find and apply the law to resolve a dispute, including domestic courts.[113] But even this is not enough to establish a system of judicial review.

4. Binding force of judicial review

Judicial review by a court must yield a binding result. This is admittedly too general a statement to be meaningful. Still, Abi-Saab has put the underlying rationale for the binding force of judicial review in cogent and powerful terms. He maintains that there is a 'fundamental qualitative difference' between a decision that produces a *res judicata* effect and one that does not (ie that is not binding). This fact alone 'makes a world of difference': 'If you are not the one who has the final word, it makes you always look behind your back, which greatly undermines independence.'[114] Since judicial review can only be undertaken by a court that is independent even under the most generic of definitions,[115] and that independence must be both procedural *and* substantive, only a process that results in a binding decision can be considered 'judicial review'. This already disqualifies ICJ AOs, which produce no binding force for any States or any organs of the UN.[116]

---

[110] Ibid 89 [emphasis in original]; cf Akande (n 52) 326–7; E Cannizzaro (2006) 3 IOLR 195–6.

[111] Usefully summarized in Amr (n 54) 302, 304 respectively. In Alvarez's words (n 56) 15, '[t]he importance of the supposed lack of constitutional warrant for judicial review lies in the eyes of the beholder'.

[112] See further for arguments on an inherent power of WTO Panels and its AB to review binding interpretations of the WTO Agreement by the Ministerial Conference and the General Council (a power that is supposed to be 'exclusive': Art IX[2] WTO Agreement), as well as of NAFTA arbitral tribunals to review binding interpretations of NAFTA by the Free Trade Commission: Reinisch (n 2) 50–2.

[113] The argument is made by Cannizzaro (n 110) 205 seq.

[114] Abi-Saab (n 26) 246–7.

[115] See the definition by de Wet (n 10) 69 and cf N Lavranos (2007) 76 NJIL 7 who, in discussing the right to judicial review, speaks of a 'formal right to obtain review . . . by an *independent* (judicial) body' [emphasis added].

[116] See text at nn 33–41; Gray (n 38) 100 argues that since both AOs and judgments

> state the law, surely the fact that the latter are expressly said to be binding while the former are not is of little significance. The binding *quality* even of the latter *depends on the willingness* of the States concerned to comply with the judgment. [emphasis added]

But the willingness of States to comply does not affect the *binding quality* of the judgment; it may affect its effects *in practice*, but not *in law*. And in the context of judicial review, it is the effect in law that matters, at least as much as the effect in practice. Lauterpacht (n 27) 114 on the other hand makes the point that AOs require the consent and cooperation of the very organ the conduct of which is being questioned. '[A] true international tribunal', he continues, 'should be allowed to

Judicial review is quite obviously binding when it can result in the annulment or invalidation of the measure attacked with effect *erga omnes*. In general terms, judicial review systems allow for an act of public authority to be directly brought before a court with a view to determining whether it is lawful and produces full legal effects, whether it is invalid (or void) and thus produces no legal effect since its inception, whether it is unlawful and thus can be voided, producing no legal effect for the future, or whether it is marred by such a fundamental procedural irregularity so as to be inexistent. Accordingly, the outcome of the court proceeding will be either to declare the inexistence or invalidity of the act, confirming its lack of legal effect *ex tunc*, or to void the act, depriving it of legal effect *ex nunc*, or to confirm the lawfulness of the act and its production of legal effect. The decision of the court is binding not only on the public authority that issued the act, but also *erga omnes*. It is the legal order that vests the decision of the tribunal in this instance with legal consequences, with binding force, thereby differentiating it from the opinion of a jurist as to the legality or validity of the act.[117] Without such provision by the legal order, the tribunal's opinion as to the legality or validity of the act would simply remain an opinion.

When the term 'judicial review' is used with specific reference to review of SC action, it seems to be understood as a process, the outcome of which may be the Council decision being declared 'illegal' or 'void'.[118] For such an outcome to constitute judicial review, it must be binding on the UN and the Council.[119] In this sense, there can be no judicial review of Council action by the ICJ: as Gowlland-Debbas notes, if by the term is meant 'a constitutional process of judicial review, *with compulsory effect*, it is clear that no analogous procedure is to be found in the structure of the UN'.[120] Indeed even the Court has accepted as much, not only through its explicit statement in *Namibia*,[121] but also in *Northern Cameroons*,[122] thus covering both modes of jurisdiction, advisory and contentious. Neither can there be of course any type of judicial review by any other existing international,

exercise a review jurisdiction without the need for the consent of the institution concerned'. This in fact confirms the necessity of both a *binding* decision, and of *independence* of the tribunal, as argued above, and highlights AOs as unsuitable for the exercise of judicial review.

[117]   See H Kelsen (1952) 4 ÖZöR 266; idem (n 87) 242 seq.

[118]   cf eg Akande (n 52) 310–11, 314; Alvarez (n 56) 3–5; generally A Gros in *Honneur Scelle* (1950) 267–8.

[119]   See Watson Institute Targeted Sanctions Project, 'Strengthening Targeted Sanctions through Fair and Clear Procedures' in UN Doc A/60/887—S/2006/331 (2006) 50.

[120]   Gowlland-Debbas (n 11) 66. cf also Kaikobad (n 54) 44–5. With respect to the system of 'binding' AOs through which the ICJ exercises review in some instances (see text at nn 73–9), Kaikobad (n 54) 45 clarifies that any effect of annulment that the opinion of the Court has in such instances is '*extraneous to*, rather than an integral aspect of the Court's powers' [emphasis added].

[121]   (n 4) 45 [89]: '*Undoubtedly*, the Court *does not possess powers of judicial review* or appeal in respect of the decisions taken by the United Nations organs concerned', ie the Assembly and the Council [emphasis added].

[122]   (n 32) 33:

> The decisions of the General Assembly *would not be reversed by the judgment of the Court*.
> The Trusteeship Agreement would not be revived and given new life by the judgment.
> [emphasis added]

regional, or domestic court, for the simple reason that none of them can issue a decision binding on the UN and the Council.[123]

Still, an argument could be made that incidental review of the legality of an act of the Council by the ICJ—as well as the incidental review of an act of any public authority by a domestic court—can result in a binding decision. When the ICJ reviews incidentally a decision of the Council meant to produce legal effect affecting the rights or duties of the States parties to a dispute before it, then the outcome of this review is a binding decision with *res judicata* effect.[124] This effect of course is limited to the parties before the Court and does not extend to the UN.[125] However, the fact remains that in such an instance the normative act of the SC, if found to be unlawful, is 'disapplied', that is, it is set aside and it is not recognized as producing any legal effect so as to affect the parties' legal position (*Rechtsposition*).[126]

In many domestic legal orders the courts do not have the power to declare (all) acts of public authorities as without legal effect *erga omnes*, but they may review them incidentally and refuse to apply them in a specific circumstance.[127] This is sometimes called 'diffused' (or decentralized) judicial review.[128] It is no less judicial

---

[123] There is an argument to be made that an ICJ AO carries so much weight that the UN act found lacking is all but deprived of its validity *in fact* if not *in law* (Thierry [n 89] 405 among others). A similar case could be made for the ICJ, the ECJ, the ECtHR, or a supreme domestic court making a relevant incidental (and/or indirect) finding in a contentious proceeding. The important issue is that the effect of the decision is an effect *in fact*, not *in law*; and as such it does not constitute judicial review any more than it constitutes judicial determination of responsibility. What it does constitute is a *good argument* for decentralized reaction: see Chapter 5 below.

[124] In *Interpretation of Judgments Nos 7 and 8* [1927] PCIJ Ser A No 13 at 20, the PCIJ stated that the intention of the declaratory judgment given is

> to ensure recognition of a situation at law, *once and for all* and with binding force as between the parties; so that the legal position thus established *cannot again be called into question in so far as the legal effects ensuing therefrom are concerned.* [emphasis added]

This dictum, which can be *a fortiori* extrapolated to cover not simply all declaratory judgments, but all *judgments* of the Court, allows the argument that, should the Court refuse to apply a binding Council resolution in a dispute between States, then this decision is *incapable* of ever changing the legal position of these States.

[125] Art 59 ICJ Statute.

[126] cf *Northern Cameroons* (n 32) 34:

> The Court's judgment must have some practical consequences in the sense that it can affect existing legal rights or obligations of the parties, thus removing uncertainty from their legal relations.

And in this connection it is interesting to note that, the Court's decision being binding on the parties, any obligations found or imposed enjoy the supremacy of Art 103, the application of which is not reserved to the acts of any specific organ, but covers all obligations under the Charter, including the obligation under Art 94(1): see J-M Sorel (1998) 102 RGDIP 713.

[127] Examples include the review of constitutionality of laws in the Greek legal system, where any court may (in fact is obligated to) refuse to apply a law on grounds of unconstitutionality, but this has only effect *inter partes* in the specific dispute, and does not affect the validity of the law *erga omnes*. It is then up to the legislature to withdraw the law or amend it: see S Flogaïtis in Zoethout (n 99) 148–50. A similar procedure exists in Mexico: Kaikobad (n 54) 49; as well as in Switzerland, Denmark, Sweden, Norway: Cappelletti (n 86) 133–4. See generally idem (n 106) 69 seq.

[128] Brewer-Carías (n 61) 91, 125 seq; Cappelletti (n 86) 132 seq. In decentralized review systems there is no particular court with special review jurisdiction—all courts may review acts or laws for conformity with higher law. The corollary of such a setting is that there is no special court with the

review for that.[129] The ICJ can undertake a similar function in a contentious proceeding, as it was called to do in both *Lockerbie*[130] and the *Genocide* cases.[131] It has arguably left such a possibility open. Similarly, any other court, international or domestic, may incidentally review Council measures in the sense described above—the ICTY has done so in *Tadić*,[132] while one could see the ICC engaging in such a discussion in the future.[133] Importantly, the CFI in *Kadi* explicitly recognized that it was engaged in indirect review of SCRs,[134] while the ECJ may be seen to have done so in *Bosphorus* and in *Kadi*.[135] Relevant considerations could apply to any domestic court faced with a case where one of the parties challenges the legality of a Council resolution.

In the cases of all these courts—with the exception of the ICJ and potentially other UN system courts—this incidental (and diffused, as well as *in casu* indirect) judicial review cannot be considered judicial review proper not because it is not

---

power to invalidate or declare law to be void *ab initio* with effect *erga omnes*, but all courts may set aside unconstitutional law in a specific case with effect *inter partes*.

[129] Brewer-Carías (n 61) 92–3; cf Kaikobad (n 54) 11, who states in this sense that '*direct formal annulment* is not crucial to the notion of judicial review' [emphasis added]. Indeed, as he goes on to note (at 36), the whole point of a measure or decision being a nullity is that it cannot create or affect 'the legal rights and obligations of the relevant parties'. This can be either *erga omnes*, or only *inter partes*; but in either case, ie if a measure or decision is simply set aside in the specific case but not annulled or acknowledged as producing no legal effect, it is still incapable of affecting the parties' legal rights *in casu*: cf 46 and Amr (n 54) 291. The feature is not unknown in international law: see FA Mann (1976–7) 48 BYIL 7, referring (in another context) to 'relative nullity' (ie *inter partes*) as opposed to 'absolute nullity' (*erga omnes*).

[130] (n 6) 14 [36]–[37]; 125–6 [38]–[39]; cf [1998] ICJ Rep 25 [42]; 130 [41].

[131] (n 7) 6 [2(m)–(p)]; [1993] ICJ Rep 328 [2(m)–(p)]. But not in *Northern Cameroons*: see (n 32) 33, citing counsel for the Republic of Cameroon. Still, the latter case led to authors seriously considering the potential of incidental judicial review in contentious proceedings for the first time: see T Furukawa in *Mélanges Reuter* (1981) 298–9. cf finally Art 189 UNCLOS: according to Reinisch (n 2) 49, the provision excludes judicial review.

[132] (n 8) [14]–[22] establishing its 'incidental' jurisdiction; [28]–[40] reviewing the legality of the measure.

[133] See eg D Sarooshi (2001) 32 NYIL 43–8; Reinisch (n 2) 64; A Zimmermann in *Festschrift Eitel* (2003) 276–7. cf on the STL M Milanović (2007) 5 JICJ 1150–2.

[134] *Kadi CFI* (n 9) [226].

[135] In *Kadi* (n 9), the ECJ claims not to be reviewing the relevant SCRs, even indirectly ([286]–[287]). However, the Court is able to make this claim because it denies that the SCRs are of such a nature as to exercise effective normative control over the EC, ie it argues that the EC is to transpose the SCRs by making use of a margin of discretion (at [298]), which in fact the EC in the instance does not possess. This is a basic point, already discussed in Chapter 2.II.2.ii above: whether the EC is given 'a free choice among the various possible models for transposition' or not, it would still have to freeze Kadi's assets: his name is in the Sanctions Committee's list; were the EC not to blacklist Kadi, it would cause the MS to breach their obligations under Art 25 UNC. Had the ECJ accepted—as the CFI did in *Kadi* (at [231])—the fact that there was no discretion in the instance, it would have been unable to claim that it is not 'indirectly reviewing' the relevant SC measures. In fact, the ECJ *is* reviewing the SC decision by reviewing the internal EC measure transposing it, but it is able to deny that by obliterating the distinction drawn by the CFI between *Kadi CFI* (this note) and T-228/02 *OMPI* [2006] ECR II-4665 [100]–[102], ie between SCRs 1267 seq and 1373. Even long before *Kadi*, in C-84/95 *Bosphorus* [1996] ECR I-3953 [26], the ECJ can be seen as indirectly reviewing Council sanctions when it finds that the impounding of an aircraft in implementation of SC measures 'cannot be regarded as inappropriate or disproportionate'. cf on the ECJ's incorrect premise for claiming discretion as to the method of implementation of SCRs in *Kadi*, L van den Herik and N Schrijver (2008) 5 IOLR 335; further Tzanakopoulos (n 97) 58–60; idem (2010) 8 JICJ 257–60.

binding, which in the sense described above it is, since it sets aside the Council measure with binding force for the parties to the dispute. Rather, it will not constitute judicial review because it fails to satisfy either the requirement of 'internality' or both the latter requirement and that of 'review for compliance with higher rules'. In the case of the ICJ, however, it appears that one could qualify it judicial review proper: it is internal, hierarchical, and binding, at least for the specific case. But all that is still not enough.

5. Systematic nature of judicial review

The discussion in the previous section on the effects (ie the binding force) of judicial review is inextricably linked to the requirement that such review be systematic, in the sense of ensuring some regularity of control. As Franck notes, the whole point of judicial review, its basic function, is to serve as a 'weapon of deterrence', its effectiveness demonstrated by the absence of occasions for its use.[136] But for it to function as such a weapon, its *regular availability* must be guaranteed; if it is only fortuitously exercised, then it can have no deterring effect. Indeed, Franck himself seems to consider that a court engaging in judicial review will do so regularly and will thus allow for the evolution of presumptions, rules of evidence, principles of judicial restraint, and the like through its jurisprudence.[137]

In cases where a court has the power to declare an act of a public authority as void or to strip it of legal effect by invalidating it, then the requirement of regularity of control is more lax because once the question comes before the relevant court, a result *erga omnes* and for all future instances will be produced.[138] Where a court does not have such a power to annul or to declare an act as having no legal effect *erga omnes*, it could still be accepted that the court may incidentally review an act challenged in a proceeding—but it can only refuse to apply it in that specific proceeding. It is in such a situation that the requirement of regularity becomes even more exacerbated than in the former instance. There would be a need for constant and systematic disapplication (setting-aside) of the offensive (unlawful) act in order to ensure the effectiveness of review and to force the promulgating organ to rescind the act that the court cannot itself annul, or to allow it to fall into desuetude.

In either case, the need for regularity is connected with the requirement for compulsory jurisdiction, otherwise cast as the right of access to a court. Domestic courts will exercise judicial review in either of the two modes described above (direct—incidental) in various configurations. For example, all public acts may be directly attacked; or some acts (eg administrative acts) may be subject to direct review, while others (eg laws or legislative acts) may only be subject to incidental review; or all acts may only be incidentally reviewed, and so forth. This constitutes judicial review properly so called, precisely because it is premised on the compulsory

---

[136] In Al-Nauimi and Meese (n 88) 631.   [137] Ibid.

[138] This may be the outcome not of a formal power to invalidate, but of the doctrine of *stare decisis*. In either case the result is *erga omnes*, and there is no need for drawing a distinction. cf Cappelletti (n 86) 139–40.

jurisdiction of domestic courts: in one way or another, and even if only incidental control is allowed, the question will eventually end up before a court.[139]

But this is precisely the problem with the ICJ as an organ of judicial review. Even if one (or itself) were to accept that it can review Council acts incidentally, any such 'review' by the ICJ cannot be—at present at least—systematic.[140] Conversely, the 'sporadic and incidental nature' of judicial review within the UN system is 'endemic'.[141] The Court has not been vested with compulsory contentious jurisdiction, with the concomitant result that the relevant questions of lawfulness of SC decisions will incidentally come before it about as frequently as they have since SC reinvigoration at the beginning of the 1990s, that is, twice every 20 years, and without any answer no less.[142] If one were to refer to the ICJ's advisory jurisdiction, then one would already be stopped at an earlier point in the enquiry, namely that requiring judicial review to produce binding legal effects, at the very least for the case at hand. But even this point notwithstanding, judicial review of Council action through AOs could never be systematic;[143] in the history of the Court since 1945 there has been only one case where the SC requested an AO, while it has turned down numerous proposals to request further opinions.[144] The GA could request an opinion on the legality of Council action;[145] but to rely on majority requests by a political organ for 'systematic' judicial review would seem an untenable argument.[146]

There can be systematic control only in courts with compulsory jurisdiction, such as domestic courts. There, one can bring a claim, if not directly against the Council

---

[139] cf Akande (n 52) 334.

[140] See T Schilling (1995) 33 AVR 96; Cannizzaro (n 110) 196; and cf RY Jennings (1997) 68 BYIL 52 noting that any court is normally obliged to consider and decide on arguments put before it, and these may be arguments of unlawfulness of a decision of the UN SC—the fact that the court will 'pass in one way or another on matters of this kind' will not amount to 'a step towards the establishment of a "*system* of judicial review" in the sense in which that is understood in some domestic jurisdictions' [emphasis added]. The *travaux* also support that the framers of the Charter, by not providing for authoritative interpretation, 'did not wish the Charter to authorize judicial review "as an established procedure"': Watson (n 91) 12.

[141] ND White in MA Baderin and R McCorquodale (eds), *Economic, Social and Cultural Rights in Action* (2007) 104. See already with regard to the unsuitability of the Court's contentious jurisdiction in this respect Schlochauer (n 57) 22.

[142] cf JE Alvarez (1995) 89 ASILProc 86, who calls the two cases 'aberrational' and questions the prospects for future challenges; Gowlland-Debbas (n 2) 670, who speaks of a 'fortuitous' process; Bore Eveno (n 94) 851 calls the process 'aléatoire'; Cannizzaro (n 110) 196.

[143] In the words of Gros (1950) 36 GST 31

>   the proceedings involved in obtaining an advisory opinion are far too slow to allow the decisions of an international organization to be referred to the International Court of Justice *at all frequently, or with any regularity.* [emphasis added]

And for more reasons why the advisory jurisdiction of the Court will not be frequently resorted to see generally R Higgins in *Honour Jennings* (1996) 567 seq. See also the reservations by Lauterpacht (n 27) 114.

[144] For an overview see Jenks (n 27) 32–3. In 1946–7 the Council forewent the opportunity to request opinions on collective measures under Chapter VII (against Spain) and on its competence (to deal with the Indonesian Question).

[145] See Akande (n 52) 328.

[146] Succinctly Bowett (n 16) 97–8, who notes the unsuitability of the GA as a 'guardian of legality'. Also Cannizzaro (n 110) 196.

measure, then usually against the domestic implementing measure. Numerous examples can be recalled: a claim can be brought against an EC implementing act of an SC measure before the EC Courts; against a domestic implementing measure before domestic courts; and even against domestic implementing measures before the ECtHR.[147] These courts can then strike down the offending implementing acts (EC and domestic courts) or find a violation of a fundamental human right (ECtHR) and in this way offer redress to the applicant.[148] However, review of the Council measure in such cases is only indirect, as it is the domestic implementing measure that is directly attacked.[149] Given that the domestic court's judgment does not affect the Council measure, its binding force, or the obligations of the State to comply under Article 25 UNC,[150] it can hardly be said that the systematic review of domestic implementing acts by domestic courts amounts to systematic judicial review of Council action. The review is neither internal, nor hierarchical, nor *stricto sensu* review of the Council act. It is the review of another, albeit relevant, act by another authority, for compliance with the law binding on that authority. In the final analysis the court's decision has no effects in international law, but it forces the State to disapply the Council measure in breach of its international obligations under Article 25 UNC.[151]

Whether there is a scarcity of judicial avenues for implementing responsibility at the international level necessarily depends on the specific area of law, as the responsibility of States for breaches of the ECHR, for example, or for breaches of WTO Agreements, is determined relatively easily through centralized compulsory international dispute-settlement mechanisms. In general, however, one cannot but accede to the statement that there is such a scarcity at the international level, which progressively leads to the ever more active involvement of domestic courts in questions touching upon international responsibility.[152]

---

[147] See for a detailed analysis Tzanakopoulos (n 97) and idem (n 135) *passim*. See further Chapter 5.II.3 below.

[148] As noted, '[t]here will always be some courts that will *interpose* their fundamental rights norms between a purported international command and domestic execution': D Halberstam and E Stein (2009) 46 CMLRev 66 [emphasis added]. For a legal qualification of this 'interposition' see Chapters 5 and 7 below, and cf the works mentioned in n 147 above.

[149] See the *dispositif* in *Kadi ECJ* (n 9); *A, K, M, Q and G v HM Treasury* [2008] EWHC 869 (Admin) [49] (Collins J); and *Hay v HM Treasury* [2009] EWHC 1677 (Admin); (UK 2009) ILDC 1367 [47] (Owen J). The two latter decisions were in part upheld by the UK Supreme Court in a joint appeal in *HM Treasury v Mohammed Jabar Ahmed and Others (FC); HM Treasury v Mohammed al-Ghabra (FC); R (Hani El Sayed Sabaei Youssef) v HM Treasury* [2010] UKSC 2: see [83] (Lord Hope, with whom Lord Walker and Lady Hale agree); [156] (Lord Phillips); [188] (Lord Rodger).

[150] cf *Certain German Interests* [1926] PCIJ Ser A No 7 at 19:

from the standpoint of International Law ... municipal laws *are merely facts* ... which constitute the activities of States, *in the same manner as do legal decisions* or administrative measures. [emphasis added]

[151] See Cannizzaro (n 110) 205; as well as n 135 above and Chapters 5 and 7 below. In the same sense, national courts cannot undertake 'review' of decisions of international courts, but they can opt not to apply them, thereby potentially engaging the State's international responsibility: cf Mosler (n 50) 451.

[152] See Nollkaemper (n 47) 762.

It is clear on the basis of the definition of 'judicial review' given above, that domestic or regional international courts do not have a power of review of SC decisions under Chapter VII. This is in particular because they fail to satisfy some or most of the elements of judicial review proper. Still, authors do not refrain from referring to 'review' of these decisions—they simply add a proviso that the term 'review' should be understood in a 'wider sense'.[153]

Conversely it is argued here that the use of the term is unhelpful and misleading. It is conceded that, given the lack of any centralized and formal review procedure at UN level, any domestic (or regional international) organ called upon to apply or implement the Council decision must have a residual power to determine the legality of said decision,[154] lest it be forced blindly to defer to the promulgation of a political organ not subject to any control. But this is not judicial review. It is an exercise by the relevant actor (be it a State or an IO) of its power of auto-interpretation and auto-determination. It does not carry with it the finality of a judicial finding or have any binding force for any other subject of international law. It is a unilateral act within the decentralized system, and branding it (something like) 'judicial review' vests it with an authority of which it is actually devoid.[155]

IV. Interim Conclusion

It appears thus that there is no possibility for judicial determination of UN responsibility for Council action. There is also no possibility for 'judicial review' properly so called, in the sense of judicial review of Council action in both a binding and systematic manner.[156] The ICJ may incidentally, or in a non-binding mode, pass upon the legality of Council action. This will offer a very solid basis for States to determine the engagement and invoke the responsibility of the UN in a decentralized manner,[157] but it will not constitute either a judicial determination of the UN's responsibility or judicial review of Council action.[158] Still, even if there was a possibility for systematic and binding judicial involvement, other factors

---

[153] See eg E de Wet and A Nollkaemper (2002) 45 GYIL 184–5.

[154] cf CH Schreuer (1978) 27 ICLQ 9.

[155] See Cannizzaro (n 110) 207 and further Chapter 5 below.

[156] The words of Reinisch (n 2) 44 are to the point:

> Pointiert... könnte man sagen: Rechtmäßigkeitskontrolle funktioniert zwar *nirgendwo so wirklich, dafür aber fast überall.* [emphasis added]

[157] When Gowlland-Debbas (n 2) 673 argues that a finding by the Court of an SCR being 'illegal or invalid, though not binding, would *undermine the legitimacy* of the acts in question' [emphasis added]. It is possible to argue further that this will furnish States with a reason not to comply, though not necessarily on the basis of the non-existence of an obligation to comply. cf Akande (n 52) 335–6: the undermining of the Council's legitimacy is characterized here as 'the most important effect' of a relevant ICJ decision. This is dealt with in Chapter 7 below.

[158] See Skubiszewski (n 108) 628 [8]; Elias (n 69) 287, 290–1. It can be argued that the declaration of an act as not being in conformity with (higher) law, even if coupled with powerlessness to do anything more than this, can be qualified as 'judicial review': see eg the power of UK courts to declare incompatibility with the Human Rights Act 1998 and cf NW Barber [2008] Public Law 13–14; Klabbers in Macdonald and Johnston (n 2) 833. Still, within the international legal order and in

would weigh in as well: both IOs and States seem reluctant to have constitutional questions decided by international courts, since such 'constitutional review' could upset the 'institutional balance'—especially when such balance is extremely complex, as is the case with the UN SC.[159]

But all this is in fact secondary in an examination of the engagement of UN responsibility. Both the existence of legal constraints upon the actions of the SC and the engagement of UN responsibility for wrongful acts of the Council are *independent* of the question as to whether there is any third-party review of the Organization's (and thus also the Council's) activities.[160] They serve, however, no small purpose. It has been said that it matters little whether judicial scrutiny of Council action 'can be aptly characterized as an exercise of judicial review with the connotations that the latter expression encompasses in domestic legal orders'.[161] The argument that it cannot, when coupled with the lack of authoritative determination of responsibility, serves to confirm the 'rule' (in the sense of experience) that in international law, such questions are decided extra-judicially, in a decentralized manner. In the final analysis, are States not still the *final* arbiters? Do they not still retain the vital functions of world governance, determination and enforcement?[162] The next chapter will examine exactly how the determination of UN responsibility for Council action takes place. Courts—particularly domestic and (regional) international courts—do play an important role in this extra-judicial determination.

view of the lack of any tangible effect, this is better qualified as an argument for those contemplating decentralized reaction: see Chapters 5 and 7 below.

[159] cf P Couvreur in *Honour Bedjaoui* (1999) 320.

[160] See V Gowlland-Debbas in M Byers (ed), *The Role of Law in International Politics* (2000) 307 and cf Chapter 3 above at nn 7–10.

[161] A Bianchi (2008) 19 EJIL 499 (referring to CFI's *Kadi* in the instance). Later in the same text, the author lays the weight of importance on the 'diffused reaction by the societal body' to 'an unprecedented agglomeration of power at the international level' (ibid). It is this 'diffused reaction' that the rest of this text attempts to put in legal terms, despite Bianchi's theory of 'spontaneous checks' along the lines of Ago's spontaneous law (ibid at n 38).

[162] See VS Mani in Macdonald and Johnston (n 2) 247.

5

Determination by States

Whereas there is some possibility of (indirect) 'judicial review' of Security Council action, this can certainly not serve as an adequate control mechanism. Notwithstanding its very limited scope, potential judicial review by the ICJ seems exceptional, haphazard, and quite improbable.[1] As Nicolas Valticos has pertinently stated, though in a somewhat different context, one cannot usefully reason by employing an improbability as a starting point.[2] Furthermore, such review does not constitute an authoritative determination of the Organization's international responsibility. As such, one must enquire further into mechanisms for the determination of UN responsibility for Council action.[3] If there are no judicial organs vested with the power to make such a determination in a manner binding for the UN, then the question as to who may undertake the determination subsists.

There is no UN organ vested with the power *authoritatively* to interpret the UNC. It is understood that 'each organ will interpret such parts of the Charter as are applicable to its particular functions',[4] but even this partial power of interpretation does not carry authoritative weight.[5] This is not only in line with the Charter's drafting history,[6] and the jurisprudence of the ICJ,[7] but also with the established principle that 'the right of giving an authoritative interpretation of a legal rule belongs solely to the person or body who has the power to modify or suppress it'.[8] Indeed, if an interpretation by any organ is not 'generally acceptable' by the membership of the Organization, it will be without binding force.[9] This is

---

[1] See Chapter 4 above; cf P Malanczuk in WP Heere (ed), *International Law and The Hague's 750th Anniversary* (1999) 98.

[2] N Valticos (1996) 43 RYDI 418: 'on ne saurait utilement raisonner à partir de l'improbable'.

[3] The lack of a forum to determine UN responsibility has also elicited different responses by theory. One author, eg seeks to establish the responsibility of States participating in or implementing the impugned decision, rather than examine how the UN is to be held responsible: see T Schilling (2004) 64 ZaöRV 344.

[4] UNCIO XIII 709. This is 'inevitable' in the course of day-to-day operation, as well as 'inherent' in the functioning of any body operating under an instrument defining its functions and powers.

[5] See M Herdegen in *Festschrift Bernhardt* (1995) 111.

[6] UNCIO XIII 710.   [7] *Expenses* [1962] ICJ Rep 168.

[8] *Jaworzina* [1923] PCIJ Ser B No 8 at 37. Since the only ones who can modify or suppress the provisions of the Charter are the MS in accordance with Arts 108–9, they are the only ones who can provide such an authoritative interpretation.

[9] UNCIO XIII 710. In detail (specifically with respect to the Council): Herdegen (n 5) 112–13.

particularly the case with decisions of non-plenary organs—even more so when they are not unanimous.[10]

What follows with logical necessity from the above statements is that any State can at any point dispute the Organization's interpretation of its constitutive instrument, and the lawfulness of any decision based on that interpretation.[11] Mindful of this possibility, which did not take long to materialize in the actual practice of the UN, the ICJ has established a presumption of legality of acts of the Organization's organs, while admitting the lack of power of any organ to render an authoritative interpretation.[12] This, of course, does not at all imply that every determination or interpretation by the SC is to be accepted as legally correct;[13] much to the contrary, it concedes that States retain their powers of (independent) appreciation.

This chapter discusses the appropriateness for States to determine for themselves the responsibility of the UN (Section I). It then examines the methods and exercise of this power of auto-determination (Section II).

I. States as *Judices in Causae Suae*

The lack of a forum to determine international responsibility is nothing new in international law. The 'low incidence of modern judicial and arbitral settlement' has been duly noted.[14] Practically, international law is applied extra-judicially in the great majority of cases,[15] with the exception of 'special regimes' such as those established in such divergent fields as international trade (eg WTO) and human rights (eg ECHR), which have opted for quasi-compulsory judicial dispute resolution.[16] Legally, there is no obligation to settle disputes by recourse to adjudication—simply to settle them peacefully, if at all.[17]

---

[10] R Bernhardt in *Honour Skubiszewski* (1996) 600, 607.

[11] cf AJP Tammes (1958) 94 RdC 349.

[12] *Expenses* (n 7) 168. But see further Chapter 7.II.2 below.

[13] G Gaja (1993) 97 RGDIP 315. cf Bernhardt (n 10) 604.

[14] CD Gray, *Judicial Remedies in International Law* (1990) 1.

[15] See generally JG Collier and AV Lowe, *The Settlement of Disputes in International Law* (1999) 20 seq; D Anderson in MD Evans (ed), *Remedies in International Law* (1998) 112; cf RY Jennings (1987) 47 ZaöRV 3–4. Some cogent reasons for this are provided by idem in *Judicial Settlement of International Disputes* (1974) 35–6. Also M Akehurst (1976) 25 ICLQ 809, according to whom 'at present judicial settlement is optional and seldom used' and—echoing Akehurst 30 years later—S Oeter in *Festschrift Tomuschat* (2006) 584: 'international dispute settlement still is to a large extent a diplomatic exercise, deliberately avoiding the delegation of authority to judicial organs'. A Watts (1993) 36 BYIL 41 refers to recourse to judicial settlement as a 'somewhat extreme situation'. This is no different with respect to IOs: P Klein, *La responsabilité des organisations internationales* (1998) 543–4. cf the PCIJ and the ICJ, which have clearly stated respectively that 'judicial settlement... is simply an alternative to the direct and friendly settlement of [international] disputes between the Parties' (*Free Zones* [1929] PCIJ Ser A No 22 at 13) and that 'any negotiation between the Parties with a view to achieving [such] a settlement is [thus] to be welcomed' (*Passage through the Great Belt* [1991] ICJ Rep 20 [35]).

[16] Quasi-compulsory because it is still based on the consent of subjects which, however, is necessarily provided at the outset, as a condition for joining the regime. cf Jennings (1987) 47 ZaöRV 3.

[17] See Art 33(1) UNC. cf H Mosler in *Judicial Settlement* (1974) 4.

In examining the appropriateness for States to determine for themselves the legality of Council action, and the subsequent engagement of UN responsibility, it is necessary to discuss their power of auto-interpretation of international law, which is understood to go hand-in-hand with the powers of auto-determination (or auto-decision) and auto-enforcement,[18] both under general international law (Subsection 1) and in the UNC context (Subsection 2).

1. Auto-interpretation in general international law

In the decentralized international legal system, the prima facie arbiter of legality of its own and anyone else's action is the State itself. The principle has been recognized by arbitral tribunals,[19] having been characterized as 'one of the most general principles of international law'.[20] The ICJ has also recognized the power of auto-determination of States. In the *Hostages* case, the Court specifically stated with respect to US measures in response to the incidents in Iran, that 'they were measures taken in response *to what the United States believed to be* grave and manifest violations of international law by Iran'.[21] In other cases, the Court confirmed further instances of exercise of the power of auto-determination of States.[22]

In fact, even the UNC has preserved this power. If no organ of the Organization may authoritatively interpret it, then the power of auto-interpretation is not removed from States. This is so even with respect to the use of armed force in the exercise of individual or collective self-defence.[23] Any State is empowered to determine that it has sustained an armed attack and that it can thus use force in self-defence under Article 51. Even where the Charter intends to take away the power of auto-determination, this only has temporary effects. If the Council steps in and takes 'necessary' measures, the right of self-defence ceases, thus putting an end to unilateral determination.[24] Still, whether the measures taken by the

---

[18] See generally JL Kunz (1960) 54 AJIL 325.

[19] See *Air Services* (1978) 18 RIAA 443 [81]: 'each State establishes for itself its legal situation vis-à-vis other States'; *Lac Lanoux* (1957) 12 RIAA 310 [16]: 'il appartient à chaque État d'apprécier, raisonnablement et de bonne foi, les situations et les règles qui le mettent en cause'. See also H Kelsen, *Reine Rechtslehre* (2nd edn, 1960) 324.

[20] *Lac Lanoux* (n 19) 310 [16].   [21] [1980] ICJ Rep 28 [53] [emphasis added].

[22] See *Reservations* [1951] ICJ Rep 26, where the Court stated that 'each State...is entitled to appraise the validity of the reservation, and it exercises this right individually'. In *Nicaragua* [1986] ICJ Rep 134 [268], the Court noted that

> while the United States might *form its own appraisal* of the situation as to respect of human rights in Nicaragua, the use of force could not be the appropriate method to monitor or ensure such respect. [emphasis added]

The French version is more instructive as it indicates a proper *power* of appreciation: '*peuvent* certes porter leur propre appréciation sur la situation' [emphasis added].

[23] Self-defence being a reaction against an internationally wrongful act, the State invoking it necessarily makes a determination of wrongful conduct by another State. L-A Sicilianos, *Les réactions décentralisées* (1990) 12, speaks of a 'conceptual unity' between countermeasures and self-defence. cf also JA Frowein (1994) 248 RdC 368–9.

[24] Under Art 51, the inherent right of self-defence is not impaired '*until* the Security Council has taken measures *necessary* to maintain international peace and security' [emphasis added]. See also Frowein (n 23) 371.

Council are truly 'necessary'—and adequate—to restore international peace, so as to remove from the attacked State the right to use force, must in the instance be a decision which is to be left to that State.

The power of auto-determination thus subsists even in the setting of SC action. The Council does not have final authority to interpret the Charter with binding force.[25] Its interpretations and determinations remain susceptible of exceeding its powers. *A minore ad majus*, the Council does not have the power authoritatively to interpret general international law. Its interpretations and determinations remain susceptible of constituting a breach of the Organization's obligations under that law. Accordingly, the State remains free to make its own interpretations and determinations. Still, it must be conceded that these statements carry ominous overtones of anarchy.[26] As such, some qualification is in order.

The power of States to determine for themselves their legal situation is a necessary corollary of the lack of compulsory, centralized law-determination in the international legal system. It would constitute a *reductio ad absurdum* to contend that States would have to refrain from auto-determination (and consequently self-help) despite the lack of effective 'aid from the legal community'.[27] As such, this power can only be *completely* abolished through the introduction of some type of third party disinterested determination of merits.[28] The addressees of the legal rule are, in the final analysis, the States. They necessarily interpret these rules themselves

---

[25] See text at nn 4–10. In *Expenses* (n 7) 168, the Court clearly said that UN organs determine their own jurisdiction '*in the first place at least*' [emphasis added]. In this respect, it is clear that the Court does not accept any finality of the determination; this becomes ever more apparent when compared with the dissent of Judge Morelli (n 7) 224, who argues that 'each organ of the United Nations is the *judge of its own competence*' [emphasis added]. The general principle, of which the majority opinion in *Expenses* is a particular application, has been clearly enunciated obiter by the PCIJ in *Interpretation of the Greco-Turkish Agreement* [1928] PCIJ Ser B No 16 at 20:

> as a general rule, any body possessing jurisdictional powers has the right *in the first place* itself to determine the extent of its jurisdiction. [emphasis added]

[26] See among others C Leben (1982) 28 AFDI 24; L Gross in idem, *International Law and Organization* (1993) 183.

[27] cf H Kelsen, *The Legal Process and International Order* (1935) 21.

[28] cf H Lauterpacht, *The Development of International Law* (1958) 159; JL Brierly (1932) 17 GST 70–1. See also P Malanczuk (1985) 45 ZaöRV 296; Sicilianos (n 23) 31. As the WTO AB noted in *Canada—Continued Suspension* [2008] WT/DS321/AB/R [371], it is the obligatory dispute resolution system of the WTO which precludes a MS from 'unilaterally determin[ing] that a violation has occurred' [emphasis added]. This is also what the arbitral tribunal in *Air Services* (n 19) 443 [81] can be interpreted to mean when excepting from the principle of auto-determination 'mechanisms created within the framework of international organisations': see E Zoller (1987) 81 AJIL 621–2. This centralizing function of compulsory determination of merits by a third party (*Drittinstanz*) also introduces an element of verticality in the international legal order: cf Sicilianos (n 23) 4 seq; K Ostenck, *Die Umsetzung von UN-Wirtschaftssanktionen* (2004) 8. In the context of the law of treaties, it has been noted that the only alternative to an agreement of the parties (as to the existence of invalidity of a treaty or to the bringing about its termination or suspension) is the 'sentence d'un juge international': F Capotorti (1971) 134 RdC 564. Under the VCLT, the only way to establish the invalidity or bring about the termination or suspension of a treaty is by agreement of the parties, whether implicit or explicit, or by binding third party resolution of the dispute: A Tzanakopoulos, 'Article 67' in O Corten and P Klein (eds), *The Vienna Conventions on the Law of Treaties* (forthcoming 2011) [11]–[21], in particular [17] and [20].

in the first instance,[29] and without an authority empowered to challenge and overturn their interpretations and determinations, this first instance also becomes de facto the last. This is corroborated by the fact that the ARSIWA did not finally subject the right to resort to countermeasures to compulsory dispute settlement,[30] although the ILC did allow for particular regimes to institute such a mechanism of centralization through the general saving clause on *lex specialis*.[31] Even lacking machinery for dispute settlement, it is possible for the power to be *partially* abolished within the contours of a 'self-contained' regime, which, however, must provide 'entirely efficacious means' against abuse, as the ICJ found in *Hostages*.[32]

The power of auto-interpretation of States is thus well established, but it seems to allow States to be judges in their own disputes. This brings forth a situation where an established principle (auto-determination) is in direct contradiction with another established principle of international law (and all law in general): *nemo judex in causa sua*.[33] That 'no one can be judge in his own suit' is, according to the PCIJ, a 'well-known rule' that 'holds good'.[34] The contradiction, however, is only apparent, not real: there is a basic limitation to the power of a State to determine the legal situation for itself. The exercise of this power is undertaken by each State *at its own risk*.[35]

The interpretation or determination of an interested State is not, in any instance, binding on any other subject of international law.[36] Just as a State may not create law *by itself*,[37] and may not *unilaterally release itself* from assumed obligations,[38] it may

---

[29] cf G Abi-Saab in *Festschrift Bernhardt* (1995) 14–15; generally J Pauwelyn, *Conflict of Norms in Public International Law* (2003) 93: 'norms of international law are seldom "finished products", simply requiring implementation'. This, of course, applies to all law—there is no such thing as an *acte claire*. An interesting parallel can be drawn with the power of UN political organs to determine their jurisdiction and thus to interpret the UNC: in San Francisco this power was characterized as 'inevitable' and 'inherent', because these organs were the addressees of the Charter's rules on competence and thus had to interpret them in order to function; see UNCIO XIII 709. In *Expenses* (n 7) 168, the Court also said that this power of auto-interpretation and auto-determination is inevitable.

[30] See the contributions in (1994) 5 EJIL 20–115.

[31] See Art 55 ARSIWA.

[32] See (n 21) 38 [83], 40 [86]. These 'entirely efficacious means' could be seen to exist in the particular case of diplomatic law, since a State retains the power of auto-determination but is limited as to the measures it can employ for self-enforcement under the provisions of the 'self-contained' regime: the declaration of a protected person as *persona non grata*. But even so the qualification of diplomatic law as a 'self-contained regime' is open to question: see B Simma and CJ Tams in *Vienne Commentaire* (2006) 2163–4 [51].

[33] Or *nemo judex in re sua*, among other variations.

[34] *Interpretation of Article 3 para 2 of the Treaty of Lausanne* [1925] PCIJ Ser B No 12 at 32.

[35] cf J Crawford (1994) 5 EJIL 66; A Orakhelashvili, *Peremptory Norms* (2006) 471.

[36] See Abi-Saab (n 29) 12; Gross (n 26) 186–7.

[37] At the very least, the concurring will of another State is required for a bilateral obligation to be created. In this sense, the organ of the international community competent to create, determine, and apply law is a *composite* organ, made up—on occasion—of at least two States (or their competent representatives), but still a *unitary* organ: H Kelsen, *Allgemeine Staatslehre* (1925) 174–5; Gross (n 26) 181, 190; Abi-Saab (n 29) 12. This is in line with the 'established principle' enunciated by the PCIJ that a rule can only be authoritatively interpreted by the one who can amend or repeal it: see n 8. Of course States may create obligations binding on themselves through unilateral acts, but these obligations are only incumbent upon their creator.

[38] The VCLT eg clearly demands the act of a composite organ—made up of the parties to a treaty—or a dispute settlement body for the establishment of invalidity or the bringing about of termination or suspension of a treaty: see Tzanakopoulos (n 28) [14]–[17] and [20].

not *determine the law with binding force* either. As such, a State is never empowered *finally* to decide a dispute. The possibility of authoritative law-determination by a competent third party is always present, at least theoretically, and in such a case it may be found that the State erred in its interpretation or application of the law, and subsequently engaged its own international responsibility.[39] This is in fact what happened in *Nicaragua*, for example, where the US claimed to have been acting in collective self-defence.[40] The Court found that there was no such justification for the use of force.[41]

In this sense, States put forward suggestions as to the interpretation of a legal rule and its application in a specific case. The competent law-applying organ will then authentically interpret and apply the rule. This may be any organ empowered by law to that effect. In the decentralized system of general international law, it will be a composite organ, made up of—at least two—States.[42] Where partial centralization has occurred, it will not be a composite but a collective organ, such as a tribunal, created and vested with that power by States. In the law of the UN, this composite organ is the Organization's membership, which must 'generally accept' Charter interpretations for them to acquire binding force.[43]

2. Amelioration through presumption in the Charter framework

The power of auto-determination is well established in general international law, but one may wonder whether its exercise has been precluded within an international organization such as the UN and, if not generally, then at least with respect to certain aspects of its functions, such as enforcement action. In this, both the practice of States as well as doctrinal considerations carry weight.

History shows that in San Francisco States already understood their power of auto-interpretation of the Charter as not precluded by the action of Charter organs.[44] Indeed, practice confirms that States have themselves undertaken to interpret SC decisions under Article 41. This is evident, for example, when Sweden froze all the assets of Swedish nationals targeted by SCRs 1267 (1999) seq, but continued to make payments of welfare benefits to these individuals under national law,[45] presumably considering that these could not fall within the ambit of its

---

[39] The Tribunal in *Lac Lanoux* (n 19) 310 [16] stated the principle of action at own risk quite explicitly:

en exerçant sa compétence, [l'État] *prendre le risque* de voir sa responsabilité internationale mise en cause *si il est établi* qu'elle n'a pas agi dans la limite de ses droits. [emphasis added]

[40] (n 22) 70 [126], 72 [130].

[41] Ibid 146 [292] (2). For a similar claim that was held to be unfounded see *Wall* [2004] ICJ Rep 194 [138]–[139].

[42] See in detail nn 37–8.

[43] See nn 4–10 and accompanying text. This is, besides, the reason why AOs of the Court are not vested with binding force under Arts 94(1) UNC; 59 ICJ Statute.

[44] This is evident from the fact that they endowed no organ with powers of authoritative interpretation, and precluded the binding force of any interpretation not 'generally acceptable': UNCIO XIII 709–10.

[45] See P Cramér in E de Wet and A Nollkaemper (eds), *Review of the SC by MS* (2003) 91.

obligations under the relevant resolutions.[46] Similarly, Belgium interpreted the SC sanctions ordering the freezing of funds in the Libyan case as not including the freezing of payments necessary for the functioning of embassies.[47] Such actions were justified by States on the basis of acting in conformity with international law.[48] Further, a number of States have claimed that there is no need for them to enact specific legislation in order to implement SCR 1540 (2004), as the materials identified in the resolution are not present in their territories.[49] Similarly, some States have interpreted SCR 1373 (2001) as not requiring them to adopt any additional legislation in addition to the domestic anti-terror laws already in existence.[50]

From a doctrinal point of view it can be said that the decision of the SC under Chapter VII—much like any other rule of international law—is addressed to States, on which it relies for its implementation. In this sense it is subject to the interpretation, and potentially the determination, of these States as the 'agents of execution'.[51] Apart from those who see the right of auto-interpretation as subsisting within the framework of the UN,[52] even authors who warn against allowing States to 'judge for themselves' whether the Council is acting in conformity with the law, do accept that States can interpret SCRs, and in particular are within their rights in interpreting a decision as requiring compliance with relevant customary obligations unless the Council makes its intent to derogate explicit in its decision.[53] In this these authors must accept that a State may also reach an interpretation of a resolution as not allowing under any circumstances compliance with a rule of *jus cogens*, for example, and thus determine it to be illegal.

It is not significant, in this connection, which organ of the State undertakes to exercise the State's power of auto-interpretation. It suffices that it is an organ of the State, and thus its actions are attributable to the State.[54] As such, whereas the interpretation of the obligation to freeze funds under Council decisions was made by the Swedish and Belgian administrative authorities, there are also cases where

---

[46] The Council later adopted SCR 1457 (2002), which (at [1]) provided for granting humanitarian exceptions from the freezing of assets system under SCRs 1267 seq. However, the Resolution required at least the consent of the relevant Sanctions Committee for the granting of exceptions (at [3]).

[47] See N Angelet (1999) 32 RBDI 174–5.

[48] See V Gowlland-Debbas in eadem (ed), *National Implementation of UN Sanctions* (2004) 52.

[49] See UN Doc S/2006/257 (2006) 3. However, the 1540 Committee seems to consider this as non-compliance: see ibid.

[50] Gowlland-Debbas (n 48) 69.

[51] cf M Lachs in *Mélanges Rolin* (1964) 167.

[52] cf eg OJ Lissitzyn, *The ICJ* (1951) 96; Tammes (n 11) 338; D Ciobanu (1972) 55 RivistaDI 440–1.

[53] See J Alvarez in de Wet and Nollkaemper (n 45) 124 in contrast to 135. See also Chapter 3.II.2 above.

[54] Art 4 ARSIWA. The US Supreme Court put this very eloquently in *Banco Nacional de Cuba v Sabbatino* 376 US 398 (1964) at 423, where it stated that 'the public law of nations can hardly dictate to a country which is in theory wronged how to treat that wrong within its domestic borders'. cf also C Tomuschat (1973) 33 ZaöRV 189:

> Nicht das Völkerrecht, sondern allein das nationale Recht entscheidet darüber, welche Staatsorgane zur Anordnung von ... Repressalie zuständig sind.

national courts have undertaken interpretations of SCRs. In these cases, the auto-interpretation of a SCR by the Court may amount to auto-determination by the State if it is in conflict with the Council's own interpretation of its act.

The Constitutional Court of Bosnia and Herzegovina claimed the power to interpret the SC-authorized powers of the UN High Representative under SCR 1031 (1995),[55] despite the fact that it was very deferential in its approach.[56] The Irish High Court interpreted SCR 820 (1993) as not having intended to penalize, deter, or sanction those peoples or States not having contributed to the tragic events in the former Yugoslavia,[57] and dismissed a Sanctions Committee decision that found a certain aircraft to fall within the terms of the resolution.[58] Belgian courts have interpreted SCR 687 (1991) as not subjecting debts incurred prior to the first Gulf War to the UNCC.[59] The Canadian Federal Court did not consider that SCR 1822 (2008) prohibited Canada from facilitating the return home of a Canadian national who was subject to an asset freeze and travel ban, even through the provision of financial aid for the airfare.[60] In *Othman*, the English High Court 'read into' domestic and EC measures implementing SCR 1333 (2000) an exemption to the freezing of assets, if the latter would result in a situation where the targeted individual's life or health would be at risk.[61] In all these latter instances the domestic courts effectively 'read' exceptions into the relevant SCRs. The ECJ, on the other hand, refused to read an exception into an EC act implementing SCR 1390 (2002), partly relying on the fact that there was no such exception in the resolution itself.[62] However, the ECJ *did* effectively 'pass the buck' to the domestic (German) court (which had referred the case): the domestic court was told not to apply the provision if in the case before it this would amount to 'disproportionate infringement' of the right to property.[63] Finally, French courts have referred to SCR 687 directly in order to determine the immunity of Iraq from execution.[64] These cases are merely a short list of examples.

---

[55] *Case No U 9/00* (3 November 2000) [5]–[6]; cf SCR 1031 (1995) [26]–[31], but in particular [27].

[56] *Case No U 9/00* (n 55) [10] seq. See also J Marko in de Wet and Nollkaemper (n 45) 117.

[57] *Bosphorus Hava v Minister for Transport* [1994] 2 ILRM 551 at 558.

[58] Ibid 557. The decision was appealed and the rest of the *Bosphorus* case played out in the ECJ on request for a preliminary ruling under Art 234 TEC (C-84/95 [1996] ECR I-3953). Conversely, in *Dubsky v Government of Ireland* (IE 2005) ILDC 485 [91] Mr Justice Macken found it obiter 'neither permissible nor appropriate for this Court to seek to interpret a [SCR]', but without elaborating any further.

[59] *Irak v SA Dumez* (27 February 1995) [1995] Journal des tribunaux 565 (Brussels Court of First Instance); *Leica AG v Central Bank of Iraq and Republic of Iraq* (15 February 2000) [2001] Journal des tribunaux 6 (Court of Appeal). See P d'Argent (2003) 36 RBDI 604.

[60] *Abdelrazik v The Minister of Foreign Affairs and the Attorney General of Canada* (4 June 2009) 2009 FC 580 [122]–[128], [162]–[165]; cf [51]–[53]. See for comment A Tzanakopoulos (2010) 8 JICJ 249.

[61] *R (Othman) v Secretary of State for Work and Pensions* [2001] EWHC Admin 1022 [56]–[57], [60]–[61].

[62] C-117/06 *Möllendorf* [2007] ECR I-8361 [54]–[56], [64]–[66].   [63] Ibid [79].

[64] *Dumez GTM c Etat irakien et autres* (15 July 1999) in (2000) 127 JDI 45. The case is noteworthy in that the Cour de cassation refers *directly* to SCR 687 (1991) and not to domestic measures of implementation in order to determine the legal status of Iraq: see the note by M Cosnard ibid 52; for

Further, it has been suggested that a domestic court would have the power to interpret a SCR as not requiring a State to derogate from customary law.[65] The same applies to the power of auto-determination, as a State may determine for itself that a violation of international law has taken place, whether through political or judicial organs, and subject of course to its own constitutional framework. In the end, the interpretation and determination are acts attributable to the State.

The power of auto-interpretation and auto-determination subsists for as long as there is no binding third party dispute settlement process, or at least for as long as the relevant regime is not 'self-contained' in the sense of providing 'entirely efficacious means' against abuse.[66] Neither can be said to be the case with respect to 'abuse' by the Council of its powers under the Charter or with respect to Council acts in violation of international law. The principle thus provides that States can determine for themselves whether a SCR is *ultra vires*, or whether action attributable to the Council is in violation of international law.[67]

Although the principle subsists, there are two considerations that serve to ameliorate the impact of its operation. Both could be said to constitute considerations applicable to any international organization, but they are pertinently clear in the framework of the UN. The first refers to the existence of a presumption of legality, while the other is connected to the cumulative force of collective decisions.

The right of States to determine for themselves whether the UN has acted illegally and whether the Organization's international responsibility has been engaged is nothing but the flip side of the presumption of legality[68] accorded to the decisions of UN organs. It is a result of the lack of authoritative control of legality of acts in international law.[69] The presumption of legality of UN acts established by the jurisprudence of the ICJ basically contends that only flagrantly or obviously *ultra vires* acts of a UN organ have the capacity to be called into question by MS.[70]

It has been noted that the presumption of legality cannot really be rebutted, given the broad purposes of the UN, except in the most blatant of cases.[71] While the distinction between manifestly *ultra vires* and not-so-manifestly *ultra vires* acts

a critique of the 'confusing' interpretation by the Court see ibid 52 seq. See also the decision of the Cour de cassation in (FR 2006) ILDC 771 [5].

[65] See Alvarez (n 53) 136–7.

[66] See text at n 32. This is the sense in which one should read Art 51 DARIO:

An injured State or [IO] which is a member of a responsible [IO] may not take counter-measures against that organization . . . unless: (a) The countermeasures are *not inconsistent with the rules of the organization*; and (b) *No appropriate means* are available *for otherwise inducing compliance* [with secondary obligations]. [emphasis added]

[67] cf Frowein (n 23) 384.

[68] The presumption of *legality* of UN acts is different from the presumption of their *validity*: see Chapter 7.II.2.ii below.

[69] cf T Kalala (1999) 32 RBDI 568. See Chapter 7.II.2–3 below.

[70] Bernhardt (n 10) 604; Herdegen (n 5) 119. For a detailed discussion see Chapter 7.II.2.ii below.

[71] J Klabbers, *An Introduction to International Institutional Law* (2nd edn, 2009) 215. cf D Ciobanu, *Preliminary Objections* (1975) 33 seq; E de Wet, *The Chapter VII Powers* (2004) 73. Judge Winiarski stated the point eloquently in his dissent in *Expenses* (n 7) 230: 'The Charter has set forth the purposes of the United Nations in very wide, and for that reason too indefinite, terms.'

is admittedly somewhat tenuous,[72] it does serve a useful purpose. The purpose is none other than to ameliorate the impact of the power of auto-interpretation and auto-determination of States: through the establishment of a presumption of legality, and by allowing only manifestly *ultra vires* acts to be called into question, a semblance of limitation of the power of auto-determination of States is introduced.[73]

Further, the impact of the exercise of the power of auto-determination of the legality of acts of another subject is necessarily limited de facto, when that other subject is a collective of States. Because traditional international law is based on a bilateral performance structure,[74] the power of auto-interpretation (of the Charter and of general international law) and auto-determination (of the existence of a breach and the engagement of responsibility) of the State exemplifies itself much more forcefully in bilateral relations than in a multilateral or institutional setting.

The power of auto-interpretation and auto-determination in a bilateral setting simply posits the interpretations or determinations of one State against those of another, with necessarily equal claims to validity and correctness.[75] It is for this reason that the power of auto-determination has been called the Achilles' heel of every attempt to regulate decentralized enforcement.[76] The situation in a multilateral or institutional setting is much more complex however: in the latter case the interpretation and determination of one State may coincide with those of other States or of the institution, or be isolated, with necessary impact on its claim to validity and correctness.[77] For example, the GA condemned as a violation of

[72] Bernhardt (n 10) 604. Arguably, the BVerfG has attempted a relevant distinction in *Maastricht*, when it declares that EU normative acts that are based on an interpretation or development of the TEU that is not supported by the TEU itself, as it has been ratified by the Federal Republic, shall be denied binding force: BVerfGE 89, 155, 188. The decision is to be interpreted as referring to normative acts that are 'wholly outside the scope' of the programme of integration or the basic norms of the rule of law: M Bothe in *Festschrift Bernhardt* (1995) 769. cf the *Lissabon* judgment: *2 BvE 2/08* (30 June 2009) [208]–[240].

[73] cf M Herdegen in de Wet and Nollkaemper (n 45) 80.

[74] See K Zemanek (2000) 4 MPUNYB 8 with further references.

[75] *Lac Lanoux* (n 19) 310 [16]:

[l'appréciation d'un état] peut se trouver en contradiction avec celle d'un autre état; dans ce cas, apparaît un différend que les parties cherchent normalement à résoudre . . .

See J Basdevant (1936) 58 RdC 589; Abi-Saab (n 29) 16; cf H Kelsen, *Reine Rechtslehre* (1934) 131; idem (n 19) 324; idem (n 27) 15:

A State injured by another State is the one to decide whether a violation of international law has taken place, and if the other State denies the breach which is imputed to it, there is . . . no objective procedure by which the dispute can be determined.

Also text at nn 35–9.

[76] See L-A Sicilianos (2005) 38 RBDI 456.

[77] The words of Judge Álvarez in *Competence of the GA* [1950] ICJ Rep 15 (diss op) are pertinent in this respect, although they refer primarily to interpretations by UN organs:

Legal texts can be interpreted by anyone; but when such an interpretation is made by an authorized organ, such as the [GA] of the [UN] or the [ICJ], it presents a *great practical* value and creates precedents. [emphasis added]

This can be extended to refer to States as well, and does not solely corroborate the point made at n 42 on interpretation by 'authorized' organs, for which cf Abi-Saab (n 29) 12, but it also underlines the *practical force and value* of an interpretation made by a plurality of actors or by a collective as opposed

the UNC the UK's unilateral (and lone) interpretation that the SCR imposing sanctions on Southern Rhodesia had fulfilled its purpose and thus measures could be terminated unilaterally.[78] But this does not in principle deny the existence of a power of auto-determination.[79]

Two basic tenets can thus be distilled: (i) States retain the power of auto-interpretation/determination of legality of SCRs, a power that they may exercise through any of their organs and subject to domestic constitutional arrangements; (ii) the power of auto-interpretation/determination is much more forceful when the dispute is a bilateral State-to-State dispute than when it posits a State against an IO, particularly a universal one such as the UN. The latter is true both *formally*—UN acts enjoy a strong presumption of legality—and *practically*—effectively the State is faced with the entire membership of the Organization.

It is then justified to contend that a State wishing to turn against the Organization, arguing that the latter's acts are illegal, will have to be able to put forward a very strong case.[80] This has two immediate potential consequences: (i) the State will seek to gather support for its position, thus attempting to act through or within a collective, such as a regional IO for example;[81] and (ii) the State will be more comfortable in forwarding a determination that is based on full legal consideration of the merits of the case, thus preferring to act through judicial, rather than through political or administrative organs in certain cases. These two potential consequences have in fact started to materialize in (an interpretation of the) practice, and are not necessarily mutually exclusive, but rather complementary. They both aim at somewhat reducing the 'intuitive'[82] nature of auto-interpretation and auto-determination, and at lending them a more 'objective' air.

---

to one arrived at by a single State. In discussing the legality of Council actions, authors have noted the significance of a collective reaction as opposed to a solitary claim of illegality by the target State: see Malanczuk (n 1) 97. In general, the gathering of a number of States behind a certain interpretation has the power of reducing the size of the 'puzzle of allegations' of P Weil (1992) 237 RdC 222.

[78] GAR 34/192 (1979) [9]. See generally AJ Kreczko (1980) 21 VaJIL 97.

[79] In a discussion, Bowett pointed out with respect to protest against decisions of IOs that States 'are able to' physically protest a decision, and they frequently do so. However, there is the question whether by being 'able' one means that the majority of States will think this protest a justified action or that an international tribunal would necessarily support the protesting States. In such a case, continued Bowett, one may come to different conclusions: (1970) 64 ASILProc 58. Effectively, Bowett distinguished between the *legal capacity* of States to protest and the *effectiveness* of that protest.

[80] cf E de Wet in eadem and Nollkaemper (n 45) 27.

[81] cf ibid 28 (in the form of a proposal); eadem (n 70) 382; Orakhelashvili (n 35) 472. This is because of what Abi-Saab (n 29) 19 has eloquently called 'l'effet exponentiel de l'agrégation de prises de position' by other States. It is confirmed in a relevant though separate context (third-State countermeasures) by JA Frowein in *Festschrift Mosler* (1983) 259:

> Auch wird hier der kollektiven Entscheidung von Staatengemeinschaftsorganen oder Staatengruppen gegenüber isolierten Maßnahmen im Prinzip der Vorrang gebühren müssen.

cf finally C Tomuschat (2006) 43 CMLRev 538.

[82] cf Zemanek (n 74) 44–5.

II. The Exercise of the Power of Auto-Determination

The power of auto-determination, as a corollary of the power of auto-interpretation, is exercised primarily through political organs of States, either alone or
cooperating in (regional) IOs (Subsection 1). But interpretation is not limited to
political organs, and as such neither is determination: it can also be exercised by
domestic courts (Subsection 2). Finally, these two methods of determination inter-
act (Subsection 3).

1. Determination through political organs

Under domestic constitutional arrangements, as also reflected in the relevant rules
of international law,[83] it is invariably political organs of the State, in particular
organs of the executive power, which are charged with conducting its foreign
affairs. As such, it makes good sense to assume that the power of auto-determination of the lawfulness of another subject's conduct will be exercised primarily by
executive political organs. This is particularly so since it is these organs that will
subsequently invoke another subject's responsibility and will decide to resort to
countermeasures.

Further, as the primary addressees of SCRs, it will be the political, that
is executive, administrative, and legislative organs of a State that will be called
upon, in the first instance, to interpret them.[84] Interpretation of SCRs by States
is not significantly different from probing their legality, if reference for both is
made to the requirements of the UNC and/or general international law.[85] Thus,
the instances of 'harmonized' interpretation of SCRs, such as the one referred to
above by Swedish authorities with respect to blacklisted individuals, are a legality
probe on the resolution and also a unilateral determination that the resolution, so
interpreted, is in conformity with legal requirements and will be so implemented.
Interpretation is a form of determination of legality of SC action. As much as
Council decisions are open to interpretation, they are also open to doubt as to their
legality.[86]

Determination of legality may also take place in a more straightforward manner
than merely through interpretation. It has been argued that political organs 'retain
the powers . . . to deny implementation' of SCRs.[87] Indeed, under Article 9 of
the Dutch Sanctions Act 1977, the competent ministers may grant exemption or
dispensation from rules and regulations that implement SCRs.[88] Such a decision

---

[83] See eg Art 7(2) VCLT.
[84] cf E de Wet and A Nollkaemper (2002) 45 GYIL 192. See also generally the contributions in
Gowlland-Debbas (n 48).
[85] cf G Nolte in M Byers (ed), *The Role of Law in International Politics* (2000) 319.
[86] cf T Eitel (2000) 4 MPUNYB 53.　　　　[87] See eg de Wet and Nollkaemper (n 84) 192.
[88] Ibid; *Act of 15 February 1980 on the Imposition of Sanctions against Certain States or Territories*
('Sanctions Act 1977') (Stb 1980 No 3) in (1981) 12 NYIL 292–3. Art 9 has been interpreted by the
Dutch courts to require a specific statement of the special interests that have led the authorities to
deny dispensation, refusal by means of simple reference to the SCR not being sufficient: *PJF de Kerf v*

could only be logically preceded by (and at the same time signify) a determination that the application of Council measures in a particular case would be illegal.[89] A number of States have voiced concerns over the processes for blacklisting under SCRs 1267 (1999) seq.[90] These are more or less direct challenges to the legality of certain Council measures under Article 41.

In this connection it is important to note that many authors have signalled the danger of States ceasing to cooperate with the Council if the latter's decisions are 'perceived as illegitimate', thereby significantly impacting the Council's 'effectiveness'.[91] Cast in these terms, State reaction to Council action appears rather as a political stance than as a legal determination. In fact it is qualified as a political consideration by some,[92] ultimately serving as a reason for the Council to exercise self-restraint.

The qualification of the reaction would be quite different if it was considered under a strictly legal perspective. Certainly, no one wants to see the Council relegated to ineffectiveness for lack of cooperation, but that is hardly a legal consideration. And 'perceptions' of 'legitimacy' can only play a limited role, as it is quite impossible to determine what is 'legitimate' and what is not, if not for anything else, for lack of an objective criterion of 'legitimacy'. As such, one may feel safer discussing the reaction based on the legality of the Council's action, at least when discussing it from an international law perspective.

From such a perspective, the interpretation and implementation of Council decisions 'in harmony with' the provisions of the Charter and general international law may be seen by the Council itself as a breach of the obligations imposed by said decisions. It was mentioned earlier that the SC provided for exemptions to the 1267 regime similar to those already implemented by the Swedish authorities,[93] and 'read into' the regime by the English High Court in *Othman*.[94] But theoretically, since the possibility of exemptions was established only at the end of 2002, and then again only through a procedure that required the consent, if not outright approval, of the relevant Sanctions Committee,[95] the Council could claim that Sweden and the UK were in breach of Article 25 UNC. This serves to confirm that auto-determination has potential legal consequences, which must be considered.[96]

Minister of Finance (19 August 1999) in (2000) 31 NYIL 309 at 313 [5] (Trade and Industry Appeal Tribunal).

[89] See *de Kerf* (n 88) 312 [4], where the appellant seeks an exemption as necessary for reasons of fairness.

[90] See JA Frowein in *Festschrift Tomuschat* (2006) 785–6; cf for the reaction of domestic courts Tzanakopoulos (n 60) *passim* and in more detail idem in A Reinisch, *Challenging Acts of IOs before National Courts* (2010) 54; as well as Subsections 2 and 3 below.

[91] See among others LM Hinojosa Martínez (2008) 57 ICLQ 352.

[92] In ibid 350 seq this consideration is qualified as political by being included in a subsection dealing with 'political limits' to SC powers.

[93] See nn 45–6 and accompanying text.   [94] See n 61 and accompanying text.

[95] SCR 1457 (2002) [1], [3].

[96] For which see Chapter 7 below. In the opinion of the UN Legal Counsel, an interpretation by Switzerland of SCR 253 (1968), with which the latter had unilaterally undertaken to comply, and its practice based on that interpretation, was in manifest violation of the SCR: [1977] UNJY 194 [5]; cf [1973] UNJY 148–9.

Dispensing with the whole issue by qualifying it as 'political' and limiting its consequences to factual considerations of effectiveness is hardly satisfactory.

However, such factual considerations also merit attention. Since the Council and the Organization are reliant on MS compliance for the effective discharge of their functions, particularly with respect to non-forcible measures under Article 41, widespread non-compliance, even if partial and effected through 'harmonized' interpretation and implementation, will be detrimental. Legally, thus, any non-compliance should be considered as being in breach of Article 25: this is further explained in Chapter 7 below. In the factual arena, however, it must be admitted that there is hardly a danger of detriment in view of claims of illegality or 'harmonized' interpretation by a single or a handful of States.

In most cases where a State is targeted by sanctions, it will claim that these are illegal. It is understandable that such determinations of illegality of Council conduct are not only not binding (as no unilateral determination is), but also do not carry much weight, particularly since they are also usually not based on detailed legal argument. One would expect the targeted State to claim illegality of the measures against it for a multitude of (almost invariably non-legal) reasons. As such, a determination of illegality by the targeted State alone will signify a dispute between the Organization and that State, but will be of limited effect if not shared by other States.

Still, when the determination of illegality of Council conduct takes place in a State that is not the target of sanctions, or when no State is the direct target of sanctions, the weight of the decision to (partially) disregard or modify Council measures will have more significant repercussions. Even more so if the determination takes place within the framework of an IO, resulting in a collective decision. Collective decisions—partially centralizing the power of auto-determination—'contribute to the quest for a more objective answer' to the pertinent legal questions.[97]

While the ideal forum for such an exercise would be the UN itself, given its virtual universality, it is understandable that States may also act through regional organizations to which they belong. This is in particular because contesting the decision of a UN organ before the same or another UN organ cannot yield any significant results: as established, each UN organ determines, at least in the first instance, its own jurisdiction. It is to be expected that the organ which took the decision will not reconsider save in marginal cases, whereas another organ will have to defer to the deciding organ's power to determine its own jurisdiction. Further, such an 'internal recourse' does not amount to auto-determination in any case.[98]

In the most significant case to date of a decision to disregard SC sanctions that were auto-determined to be illegal, the political organs of the auto-determining States found it necessary to cooperate within the framework of a regional IO. The 53 MS of the (then) OAU clearly found SC sanctions against Libya imposed by Resolutions 748 (1992) and 883 (1993) to be in violation of a number of Charter

---

[97] E Klein (1992) 30 AVR 102.

[98] See Ciobanu (n 71) 163 seq, 173 seq, where he distinguishes between the 'political' determination, taking place *within* the UN organ and *by* the organ itself, and the auto-determinative 'right of last resort'. cf generally K Wellens, *Remedies Against IOs* (2002) 66 seq.

provisions and of general international law.[99] Consequently, they decided not to comply with them any longer.[100] Before they could make good on their threat, the Council backtracked, suspending the sanctions.[101]

The OAU threat to disobey the Council was certainly not the only case of collective auto-determination of illegality of Council action. The OIC, in successive resolutions of the Conference of Foreign Ministers, and in its Heads of State Declaration on Bosnia and Herzegovina between 1993 and 1995, determined that SCR 713 (1991) [6] imposing an arms embargo on the former Yugoslavia was illegal, to the extent that it impeded Bosnia's exercise of its inherent right of self-defence under Article 51 UNC.[102] Thereupon it reaffirmed that the OIC MS, more than 50, did not consider themselves '*de jure*' obligated to respect the illegal embargo,[103] and called upon all MS of the UN to help Bosnia, including through supply of arms.[104]

The auto-determination by political organs of States or regional IOs of the legality of SC decisions is a fact and cannot be denied. It may lead (and has led)[105] to States disregarding Council decisions. The question of how this 'disobedience' is to be legally qualified is discussed in Chapter 7 below.

2. Determination through judicial organs

Instances of threatened disobedience by States led to early calls for more attention to be paid to their role as the ultimate interpreters of SC action, acting either alone or through representative groups or regional IOs.[106] But, at the same time, it was acknowledged that challenges to SCRs may not come solely from political organs of the States.[107] While political organs are the first 'points of contact' with respect to the interpretation of a SCR, they are certainly not the only organs of the State that may be called upon to interpret them. The relevant question may well come before a domestic court.

Some domestic courts have traditionally avoided determining the existence of a breach of international law by another State, treating this as the prerogative of the executive. For instance, French courts have refused to take the initiative of not applying an international treaty in response to a breach or non-application by another State, reserving to the executive the power to determine the existence of a

---

[99] AHG/Dec.127 (XXXIV) (8–10 June 1998) [2]. Further S/PV.3684 (1998) 6–11; Chapter 7. II.3.ii.c below.

[100] AHG/Dec.127 (XXXIV) (n 99) [2].   [101] See SCR 1192 (1998) [8].

[102] Res No 6/22-P (10–12 December 1994) [7]; cf Res No 7/21-P (25–29 April 1993) 12th preamb; Res No 6/23-P (9–12 December 1995) [12]–[15]. See also OIC Heads of State and Government Declaration on Bosnia and Herzegovina at Seventh Islamic Summit Conference (13, 15 December 1994) [4].

[103] Res No 6/23-P (n 102) [14].

[104] Res No 7/21-P (n 102) [12]; 6/22-P (n 102) [5]–[6]; 6/23-P (n 102) [13]; Summit Declaration (n 102) [1].

[105] See eg LF Damrosch (1997) 269 RdC 125.   [106] See Nolte (n 85) 318.

[107] Ibid 320. See also JA Frowein in *Festschrift Eitel* (2003) 128 seq; A Pellet in *Colloque de Rennes* (1995) 227–8; Gowlland-Debbas (n 48) 34.

breach.[108] This, however, has more to do with internal constitutional arrangements than with a denial by courts of their capacity to exercise the State's power of auto-determination.[109] Much to the contrary, these decisions could be interpreted as meaning that, constitutional arrangements allowing, even a domestic court could determine—at least indirectly—the existence of an internationally wrongful act, and thus the engagement of responsibility.[110]

Indeed, US courts, including the Supreme Court, have explicitly accepted in *Sabbatino* that international law does not prohibit them from determining whether the act of another State is in violation of international law.[111] They abstain from such determinations on the basis of the 'act of State' doctrine, which, however, is not 'compelled' by international law,[112] but rather constitutes a 'self-imposed restraint', one with 'constitutional underpinnings' related to constitutional separation of powers.[113] Still, the US courts noted that other domestic courts will go on to determine the legality of acts of foreign States under international law.[114]

And, indeed, the English courts have accepted, though they normally apply the act of State doctrine, an exception in favour of English public policy, which is held to be wide enough to take account of clearly established breaches of international law.[115] The court's determination of an act as being a 'clearly established breach of international law', even if it refers to international authority, such as a SCR, does not cease to be an exercise in the power of auto-determination. And, in any case, it constitutes a finding that another subject of international law has breached its international obligations.

To invoke a further example, the Greek Council of State has found that it has the power to determine whether a specific provision in a treaty is reciprocally

---

[108] See Sicilianos (n 23) 21–2; see also *Rekhou (Req No 15.092)* in (1982) 109 JDI 439; (1982) 86 RGDIP 408 (Conseil d'État); *Kryla c dame Lisak* in (1984) 111 JDI 860; (1985) 89 RGDIP 540 (Cour de cassation).

[109] For instance, in both the cases cited above (n 108), the French courts denied they had the power *under the French Constitution* (Art 55) to determine the existence of a breach of the treaty in question, the relevant power ostensibly being allocated to the executive. For the different evasive tactics or 'avoidance techniques' employed by domestic courts to defer an international law question to the executive see E Benvenisti (1999–2000) 98 MichLR 188–9 and cf 193–4; cf with particular focus on challenges against acts of international organizations A Reinisch, *International Organizations before National Courts* (2000) *passim* and at 391 for a summary.

[110] In that sense there may be something to the statement that in recent cases, such as *R (Campaign for Nuclear Disarmament) v Prime Minister* [2002] EWHC 2777 (Admin) and *R (Abbasi and another) v Secretary of State for Foreign and Commonwealth Affairs* [2002] EWCA Civ 1598, English courts have allowed extensive international legal argument, when some years ago the objection of non-justiciability would have prevailed without much discussion: see D Williams (2004) 11 IJGLS 62.

[111] US District Court in 193 F Supp 375 (1961) at 380–2 (SDNY); Court of Appeal in 307 F 2d 845 (2d Cir 1962) at 855; Supreme Court (n 54) at 421–3.

[112] Supreme Court (n 54) 421.

[113] Ibid 423–4. cf the works by Benvenisti and Reinisch cited in n 109 above.

[114] District Court, *Sabbatino* (n 111) 380 and fn 6. Significantly, US courts admit exceptions to the act of State doctrine for 'unofficial acts', namely for grave human rights violations almost invariably under the ATCA: see A Bianchi in *Honour Caflisch* (2007) 142–4.

[115] See *Kuwait Airways Corp v Iraqi Airways Co (Nos 4 and 5)* [2002] UKHL 19; [2002] 2 AC 883 [323], [331]–[332], [376], [382], by and large confirming the analysis of Mance J in *Kuwait Airways Corp v Iraqi Airways Co and Another* [1999] CLC 31 (QB) at 59–60 (significantly citing *Sabbatino* [n 54]), 73–7.

implemented in law and in fact by another State party, and thus to decide not to apply the provision in a case before it for lack of the condition of reciprocity.[116] Similarly, Greek courts have determined that they cannot execute European Arrest Warrants issued by the German authorities after the BVerfG struck down the domestic implementing legislation of the relevant EU Council Framework Decision.[117] This was because Germany no longer provided for the transposition of the Framework Decision in its domestic law, and thus there was no reciprocity.[118]

It should be noted in this connection that reciprocity is a principle of international law intimately connected with the decentralized nature of the international legal order, the 'principal *leitmotif*' in a system of auto-determination and self-help.[119] According to the principle, 'a State basing a claim on a particular norm of international law must accept that rule also as binding upon itself'.[120] Thus in invoking the principle of reciprocity, domestic courts undertake to determine whether another State has in fact and in law applied the international legal norm. This is what the Greek courts did in the cases mentioned above, and it amounts to an (indirect) determination of another State's international responsibility. In the subsequent refusal to apply the rule invoked before it, the domestic court may even be seen as taking a reciprocal countermeasure.[121]

The UN Legal Counsel has accepted, in principle, that there is a possibility that a domestic court may determine the Organization's responsibility.[122] There are even cases where domestic courts could in fact be construed as having determined the existence of an internationally wrongful act *on the part of an IO*.[123] In *Ms Siedler v WEU*, the Brussels Labour Court of Appeal found that the internal procedure of the WEU did not offer guarantees of fair and equitable process as far as its internal procedure for the settlement of administrative disputes was concerned.[124] This was ostensibly in violation of the general principle that there should be no denial of

---

[116] See eg *Συμβούλιο της Επικρατείας 3562/2000* in [2002] Φορολογική Επιθεώρηση 549 (Council of State); *Διοικητικό Εφετείο Πειραιώς 908/1999* in [2000] Διοικητική Δίκη 955 (Administrative Court of Appeal of Piraeus). This jurisprudence is constant.

[117] *Council Framework Decision of 13 June 2002 on the European Arrest Warrant and the Surrender Procedures between Member States* (2002/584/JHA) [2002] OJ L 190/1. See BVerfGE 113, 273.

[118] *Συμβούλιο Εφετών Θεσσαλονίκης 1677/2005* in [2006] Αρμενόπουλος 450; [2006] Ποινικά Χρονικά 71 (*Thessaloniki Court of Appeal sitting in Council*). On the Spanish reaction to the BVerfG decision and relevant developments see E van Sliedregt (2007) 3 EuConst 245.

[119] B Simma in *EPIL*, vol 4 (2000) 30–1.   [120] Ibid 31.

[121] See further Chapter 7.III.3 below.

[122] See the response to a UNEP Deputy Director, where the UN Legal Counsel maintains that by filing a claim in domestic courts against private entities of MS for depletion of the ozone layer, the UN

> would no longer be immune from counterclaims…that the Organization shares the responsibility for depletion of the ozone layer inasmuch as it has failed to promulgate adequate international standards in this regard. ([1995] UNJY 412 [5])

[123] That national courts may be called upon to interpret the constituent instruments of IOs is nothing new: see cf Amerasinghe (1994) 65 BYIL 181. Neither is the discussion by national courts of an organization's immunity from domestic legal process: see extensively A Reinisch, *IOs before National Courts* (2000) 177 seq. What is important, however, is whether the national court's approach to the issues could amount to the determination of an internationally wrongful act.

[124] See (BE 2003) ILDC 53; [2004] Journal des tribunaux 617.

justice and of the right to a fair trial of every person consecrated in Article 6(1) ECHR and Article 14(1) ICCPR, and as such the WEU was made to submit to national jurisdiction.[125]

There are further examples of domestic courts having determined the legality of acts of the UN specifically. A prize court in the (then) United Arab Republic clearly—albeit incidentally—stated in 1960 that the GAR partitioning Palestine was outside the competence of the UN.[126] The defendant before the New South Wales Appeal Court in *Burns v The King* claimed that he was not guilty of sedition in publishing a series of articles on the Korean War: the decision of the SC was claimed to have been illegal due to the absence of the USSR when the decision was made.[127] The Court addressed a number of questions to the Australian Foreign Office, enquiring on the legal authority relied upon for participation in hostilities in Korea and on the States present 'as required by Article 27 when the resolution was carried that North Korea was the aggressor', and seems to have been satisfied on the legality of the hostilities and Australian participation in them, since it dismissed the defendant's appeal.[128] Had the court in this case found otherwise, it would have determined the responsibility of the UN for a violation of its Charter through the promulgation by the Council of an illegal Chapter VII resolution.

3. The interaction between judicial and political determination

Whereas there will necessarily be interaction between the judicial and political auto-determination of international responsibility of the UN for wrongful Council action under Article 41, it is useful to look first at the clearer (but most rare) case where the Council measure is directly attacked (i), before discussing the increasingly more frequent attack against the Council measure through an attack against the domestic implementing measure (ii).

i. The Security Council measure is directly attacked

On rare occasions, SC measures have been directly attacked before national courts. In 2001, Slobodan Milošević applied to the President of The Hague District Court, seeking an order that the Netherlands release him from custody.[129] He based his application on the illegality of the establishment of the ICTY.[130] The President of The Hague District Court relied on the fact that the ICTY had already confirmed the legality of its establishment under international law, and found finally that the court did not have jurisdiction to order the release.[131] A similar approach was taken by the US Court of Appeals for the Fifth Circuit in *Ntakirutimana v Reno*, where the argument that the SC was not empowered under the Charter to establish the

---

[125] See ibid [40]. The Court refers expressly to the two international instruments and to the general principle of law according to which denial of justice must be avoided.

[126] *Navire 'Inge Toft'* (10 September 1960) in (1960) 16 REDI 129; 31 ILR 517.

[127] (6 April 1951) 20 ILR 597.   [128] Ibid 597–8 (reporting of the case was limited).

[129] *Milošević v The Netherlands* (Interlocutory Injunction) KG 01/975 (2001) 48 NILR 357.

[130] Ibid 358–9 [2].   [131] Ibid 360–1 [3]–[4].

ICTR and thus the US should not surrender Ntakirutimana to the Tribunal was found to be outside the scope of judicial review.[132] The Croatian Constitutional Court has denied that it has competence to review acts of UN organs.[133]

It is, however, not beyond contemplation that a domestic court faced with a direct attack against a SC measure will disregard it, entertaining claims to its illegality, be it under international law or even under domestic law. If the domestic court finds the measure illegal because it is in violation of the UNC or general international law, it directly exercises the State's power of auto-determination: it has determined that another subject of international law has perpetrated an internationally wrongful act (which necessarily entails its international responsibility).

If, on the other hand, the finding is based on domestic law (including international obligations incumbent on the State and incorporated or reflected in its domestic law), then the issue is more complicated. Effectively one is faced with a situation similar to the one created by the *Solange I* decision of the BVerfG,[134] where, from the perspective of international law and the pyramidal flow of validity, 'lower' (domestic) law has been relied upon to overcome 'higher' (international, or, in the *Solange I* case, partial international [Community]) law. The court has not determined that the UN has breached international law, and as such has not exercised the power of auto-determination. The State's executive organs must now come into play.

In any of the two cases, the executive organs of the State will be bound to disregard the Council measure and comply with the court's decision (after having exhausted all possibilities of appeal).[135] The State cannot plead that under its domestic law it is bound by its own court's decision, as this cannot release it from its international obligations,[136] and in particular the obligation to comply with binding SCRs under Article 25 UNC. As such, the State will be forced to forward a claim, through its political (executive) organs, that the Council measure was in breach of international law and was therefore not complied with.[137]

In the case where the court's decision relies on international law arguments to find the Council measure illegal and as such inapplicable, the political organs may accede to the reasoning of the court in their international claim. In the case where the court's decision is founded solely on considerations of domestic law, the political organs—not being able to plead domestic law internationally—will be forced to translate the argument in international legal terms. In either case, however, the court's decision will have forced the State's political organs to exercise the power of

---

[132]   184 F 3d 419 (5th Cir 1999) at 430.

[133]   Though in particular with respect to their compliance with domestic law, especially on human rights: *Bobetko Report* (HR 2002) ILDC 383 [3].

[134]   BVerfGE 37, 271. cf *Lissabon* (n 72).

[135]   cf the UN Legal Counsel in [1991] UNJY 320 [5]. In *Tachiona v US* 386 F 3d 205 at 212 (2d Cir 2004), the US Court of Appeal accepted that the US Government had the requisite legal interest to appeal a decision from a lower court which effectively put the US in breach of its international obligations.

[136]   cf Arts 3 ARSIWA; 27 VCLT.

[137]   For the justification of non-compliance under international law see Chapter 7 below.

auto-determination of UN responsibility, lest the State appear wantonly to violate international law.

A similar approach can be taken, it is submitted, even when the Council measure is indirectly attacked through an attack against the domestic implementing measures. However, as the indirect nature of the attack perplexes matters to a certain extent, it is advisable to examine the matter more closely.

ii. The Security Council measure is attacked through the implementing measure

Security Council measures are not self-executing in the municipal legal orders of MS;[138] as such, States are under an international obligation to take all requisite domestic measures to ensure the implementation of SCRs. Where States have transferred the relevant powers, particularly with respect to the implementation of economic measures, to a (regional) IO, such as the EC/EU, it will be that organization which will adopt the implementing measures. The latter can be treated for present purposes as tantamount to domestic measures.

Such domestic implementing measures are susceptible of being attacked in domestic courts,[139] including in the particular instance EC Courts and the ECtHR. When so attacked, the domestic court may be called upon not only to decide on the legality or the interpretation of the domestic measure, but also indirectly on the legality or the interpretation of the Council measure being implemented. This will be the case, in particular, where the implementing measure will effectively be a 'transposition' of the Council measure, the implementing authority not having availed itself of any margin of discretion, whether such margin is allowed under the Council decision or not.[140]

The possibilities in this respect are many. The domestic court may simply interpret the domestic implementing measure, and with it the Council measure. Such interpretation may be wholly uncontroversial. Dutch courts found for example that the 1267 sanctions regime did not impose the dissolution of a listed legal entity and the release of its accounts to the State, contrary to what the Dutch Prosecution

---

[138] Gowlland-Debbas (n 48) 33–4 and 37 seq. cf the English Court of Appeal in *A, K, M, Q and G v HM Treasury* [2008] EWCA Civ 1187 [109]–[110]; and the Irish High Court in *Bosphorus* (n 57) 557.

[139] See generally on challenges against the 1267 regime the reports of the Analytical Support and Sanctions Monitoring Team to the 1267 Committee in UN Docs S/2009/502 (2009) 16–17 [36]–[38] and 32–4 (Annex I); S/2009/245 (2009) 37–9 (Annex I); S/2008/324 (2008) 36–7 (Annex I); S/2007/677 (2007) 40–2 (Annex I); S/2007/132 (2007) 14 [35]–[36] and 38–40 (Annex I); S/2006/750 (2006) 47–50 (Annex III); S/2006/154 (2006) 45–7 (Annex); S/2005/572 (2005) 48–51 (Annex II); S/2005/83 (2005) 16–17 [50]–[52]. See finally Frowein (n 107) 132; Tzanakopoulos (n 90) 56–8.

[140] Even the domestic court's finding that a margin of discretion is allowed under the decision may be seen by the Council as resulting in a violation of its decision, as it may consider that the latter was not supposed to be interpreted as allowing any discretion to MS. See in detail Tzanakopoulos (n 90) 58–60.

Service contended.[141] Similarly the Lahore High Court did not accept that preventive detention was an obligation imposed under the 1267 regime.[142] The ECJ engaged in interpretation in *Bosphorus*.[143] In finding the implementing measure and thus also the Council measure as imposing a limitation on the right to property that was proportional in the circumstances,[144] the Court effectively confirmed the legality of both measures. Had the Court found otherwise, that is, that the limitation was disproportionate, it would have effectively disregarded the Council measure in the case: the domestic court would be obligated to follow the ECJ's interpretation, and thus to (partially) disregard the Council measure. In the eyes of the Council, this could amount—if not accepted as a sound interpretation—to the violation of the relevant State's obligation under the resolution and Article 25.

There is, however, a possibility that courts will endeavour to 'harmonize' the interpretation, that is, interpret the implementing measure in a way that is—in their view—in harmony with international or domestic law, thereby potentially modifying (in the eyes of the Council) and thus (partially) violating the Council measure.[145] To paraphrase Lauterpacht, 'the difference between disregarding a rule...in deference to [another rule] and interpreting it (possibly out of existence) in the light of [that other rule]' may be but a play on words.[146] An example is provided by *R (M) (FC) v HM Treasury and two other actions*,[147] where a committee of the House of Lords, while advising the House to refer to the ECJ for a preliminary ruling,[148] went on to interpret Regulation (EC) 881/2002 implementing SCR 1390 (2002), and in particular its paragraph 2(2), finding that the Treasury's construction of the provision 'is not required to give effect to the purpose of the [SCR]',[149] and 'produces a disproportionate and oppressive result'.[150] In the instance, the House of Lords' interpretation was confirmed by the ECJ.[151] Again this would force the State to comply with the Court and risk being found in breach of its obligations under the relevant SCR and the UNC.

---

[141] *Stichting Al-Haramain Humanitarian Aid* case, reported in UN Docs S/2006/154 (2006) 46 [8]–[9]; and S/2006/750 (2006) 48 [5].

[142] *Hafiz Muhammad Saeed and Others v Government of the Punjab, Home Department and Others* (2 June 2009) Writ Petition No 6208/2009 [20], [21 *in fine*], [23].

[143] (n 58) [6], [13] seq.

[144] Ibid [26]. cf, however, *Möllendorf* (n 62) [79], where the ECJ leaves the issue of proportionality to be determined by the domestic court.

[145] This is what the Irish High Court did in *Bosphorus* (n 57), which resulted in proceedings before the ECJ. See text at nn 57–8. cf I Canor (1998) 35 CMLRev 155–6, who argues that 'every [domestic] legal system should...apply its own constitutional and administrative principles' to interpret SCRs, though accepting that this may lead to 'different legal results' in different cases. It is submitted that if these 'results' are irreconcilable with the SCR, then there is a breach.

[146] (n 28) 166.   [147] [2008] UKHL 26.

[148] Ibid [2].   [149] Ibid [12].

[150] Ibid [15]. Similarly, in *A, K, M, Q and G v HM Treasury* [2008] EWHC 869 (Admin) [39]–[40], Mr Justice Collins undertakes direct interpretation of SCR 1373 (2001) [1(c)] to find that the Terrorism (United Nations Measures) Order 2006/2657 does not constitute a necessary means to apply the resolution and must be quashed (ibid [49]), though the decision does not actually quash the order, as it merely disposes of preliminary questions. The order is in fact partially quashed on appeal in *HM Treasury v Mohammed Jabar Ahmed and Others (FC); HM Treasury v Mohammed al-Ghabra (FC); R (Hani El Sayed Sabaei Youssef) v HM Treasury* [2010] UKSC 2.

[151] C-340/08 [2010] ECR I-0000; [2010] OJ C 191/6–7.

In *Othman*, the English High Court 'read into' domestic and EC measures implementing SCR 1333 (2000) an exemption to the freezing of assets if the latter would result in a situation where the individual's life or health would be at risk.[152] Of course no such exemption was provided for under the 1267 regime at the time, and Mr Justice Collins had to resort to the 'law of humanity' and to the absurdity of a need to ask the Sanctions Committee for such an exemption, which could also not be granted particularly speedily.[153] The interpretation by the judge, reasonable as it may seem, was at the time technically incorrect. This is confirmed by the fact that the SC passed a resolution allowing for exemptions to the asset freeze as regards basic expenses only on 20 December 2002,[154] and then again requiring at least consent, if not outright approval, by the Sanctions Committee.[155] The High Court's decision was delivered in November 2001, more than a year before SCR 1452 (2002).

It could be argued that the SC retrospectively confirmed, in part, the correctness of the High Court's interpretation (as well as that of the Swedish authorities mentioned above).[156] But it is clear that for a critical period of more than one year the SC would not have accepted the power of a State independently to grant exemptions from the asset freeze. Otherwise it would have felt no need to pass a resolution explicitly allowing such action—with the added requirement that the Sanctions Committee also consent to the exemption.

In *Abdelrazik*, Canada defended its denial of allowing or assisting one of its nationals to return to the country by relying on the fact that the person was listed by the 1267 Sanctions Committee and thus was subject to a travel ban and an asset freeze.[157] Mr Justice Zinn, however, interpreted the measures under the relevant SCR 1822 (2008) not to be an obstacle to Abdelrazik's return to Canada, at government expense if required.[158] He further ordered that the person attend a hearing before the court, for the latter to satisfy itself that Abdelrazik had in fact returned to Canada.[159] The interpretation of the resolution by the Canadian court is of course not determinative of the position under international law. However, the court forced Canada to act in accordance with that interpretation. The SC may well find such interpretation to be incorrect, and thus determine that Canada has acted in breach of the resolution and the UN Charter in complying with the court decision.[160]

A further possibility is that the court may outright find the implementing measure to be in violation of international or domestic law. The EC implementing measures were attacked in *Kadi* on the basis of the violation of the applicant's fundamental rights.[161] If the CFI had accepted the relevant arguments, even within the very limited scope of review it allowed itself, that is, if it had found that the implementing measures and thus also the Council decisions were in breach

---

[152] *Othman* (n 61) [57].   [153] Ibid [56], [60]–[61].   [154] SCR 1452 (2002) [1].
[155] Ibid [3].   [156] See text at nn 45–6 and 93–5 above.
[157] (n 60) [3] and [120]–[121]; cf [162].
[158] Ibid [123]–[129], in particular [127]; and [163]–[165].   [159] Ibid [167].
[160] See for further comment Tzanakopoulos (n 60) 249 seq.
[161] T-315/01 [2005] ECR II-3649 [59], [138]–[152].

of obligations under peremptory norms of international law,[162] and had struck down the implementing measures, effectively it would have forced all EC MS not to comply with their obligations under the relevant SCRs and the UNC, at least until such time as new implementing measures were adopted (which of course does not preclude that they would be attacked again).

The situation is no different when the decision to strike down the implementing measures is based solely on considerations under EC law. This is what the ECJ did on appeal in *Kadi*,[163] following—in effect—the Advocate-General,[164] with the CFI following it in *Othman*.[165] The same applies also when the decision to strike down the implementing measures is made under domestic law in the case of a domestic court:[166] again the State(s) would be forced not to comply with their international obligations under the resolution and the Charter.[167] The only thing

---

[162] cf ibid [209]–[232]. On the standard of review see Tzanakopoulos (n 90) 61–3.

[163] C-402/05 P *Kadi* [2008] ECR I-6351 [281]–[326].

[164] See *Kadi* (n 163) (Opinion of A-G Poiares Maduro) [41]–[55]. Admittedly, the Court does not wholly accede to the reasoning of the A-G, but it does reach the same result of annulling the relevant implementing acts on the basis of EC law considerations.

[165] T-318/01 [2009] ECR II-1627 [94], where the CFI put the MS immediately in breach of the SCR and the UNC by annulling the implementing measure without providing (at [95]–[99]) for the *Kadi* (n 163) [373]–[376] suspension.

[166] In *Ntakirutimana* (n 132) 424–7, the US executive's power to surrender Ntakirutimana to the ICTR on the basis of a domestic statute rather than an international treaty was challenged as unconstitutional, but the Fifth Circuit Court of Appeals did not accede to the claim. If it had accepted the argument, the US would have been forced to deny surrendering Ntakirutimana to the ICTR in violation of the relevant SCR 955 (1994), although this consideration does not figure in the Court's judgment. But see the dissent of Judge DeMoss (ibid 431 at 434–8). Similar considerations apply in *Croatia v N-T* (HR 1999) ILDC 384, where a Croatian indicted by the ICTY sought to avoid being surrendered to the Tribunal. The Croatian Supreme Court found that it was bound by the 'coercive measure' under Art 41 UNC (ibid [17]); a contrary decision would have put Croatia in breach of SCR 827 (1994). In *Rukundo v Federal Office of Justice* (CH 2001) ILDC 348 the Swiss Federal Tribunal upheld Rukundo's transfer to the ICTR (at [3]) but rejected the transfer of some of the documents seized, which it held had no evidentiary value for the ICTR (at [4]). This independent determination of the evidentiary value of material seized and to be transferred to the ICTR by the Swiss court could be seen as a breach of Swiss obligations under the relevant SCRs. See generally on challenges to international criminal tribunals before domestic courts J d'Aspremont and C Brölmann in Reinisch (n 90) 111 seq, especially 116–17 on the 'absolute' obligation to cooperate with the ICTY and ICTR under Art 28 of their respective Statutes.

In a case brought before the Turkish courts by Al-Qadi (our well-known Mr Kadi), the 10th Division of the Council of State, sitting as a court of first instance, annulled the domestic implementing measures taken pursuant to SCRs 1267 (1999) and 1333 (2000) against the applicant, on the basis that under Turkish law, the freezing of assets can only be initiated by a court decision, and not an administrative one: see UN Doc S/2007/132 (2007) 39 [8]. This would have put Turkey in breach of the relevant Council decisions. Still, the Council of State sitting as a court of appeal reversed the decision annulling the administrative act in Decision No 115/2007 (22 February 2007) [in Turkish]; (TK 2007) ILDC 311, finding that blacklisting by the SC allows for measures to be taken without judicial proceedings. The High Court for the southern province of Sindh in Pakistan found in favour of the Al Rashid Trust, which is subject to the 1267 sanctions regime, on a domestic law technicality, finding the freezing order against it unlawful for lack of the requisite notification (see UN Doc S/2006/750 [2007] 48 [6]). This would have forced Pakistan into non-compliance with the Council's Chapter VII decisions under the 1267 regime, but the judgment was appealed and the case is still pending before the Supreme Court (see UN Doc S/2009/502 [2009] 33 [9]).

[167] This is exactly what happened in *Bradley v Commonwealth of Australia and Another* (10 September 1973) (1973) 1 ALR 241. The Postmaster-General of Australia adopted measures against a South African employed by the Rhodesian Department of Information and operating the

that would be different in such a case is that the State political organs would have to translate the reasoning into international legal argument.[168] This may be easier than it first sounds: there is an argument that the EC/domestic law relied upon in the instances above—referring, as it does, to a hard core of fundamental human rights—has a certain universal 'radiance', due to the status of these rights as positive general international law.[169]

Up until recently there had been few decisions openly disregarding Council sanctions.[170] At the end of the first decade of the twenty-first century, the ECJ finally dared to strike down domestic measures of implementation,[171] followed by the CFI,[172] the English High Court,[173] and the UK Supreme Court.[174] The Irish High Court as well as the Turkish Council of State have also come rather close.[175] Additionally, the Canadian Federal Court has 'interpreted away' the international obligations of Canada under SCR 1822 (2008) so as partially to circumvent the asset freeze and travel ban,[176] while The Hague District Court has reviewed domestic implementing measures, which it then found not to have been strictly imposed by SCR 1737 (2006).[177] There is reason to believe that further developments are *ante portas*. The Swiss Bundesgericht has sent ominous signals to that effect. Though acceding by and large to the CFI reasoning in *Kadi*,[178] it has conceded in *Nada* that there is no means of redress for listed individuals, while the UN de-listing procedures are not in compliance with Swiss constitutional law,

'Rhodesia Information Center' in Sydney, pursuant to SCR 277 (1970) [11]. The High Court of Australia found that since the SCR had not been transposed into Australian law, the Postmaster had acted illegally, irrespective of the fact that Australia was internationally bound to implement SCR 277 under Art 25 UNC: ibid 259–60. It thus ordered the Postmaster-General to withdraw the measures: ibid 268. This clearly compelled the Australian executive to 'act contrary to [Australia's] international obligations' and exposed Australia to international responsibility: CH Schreuer (1978) 27 ICLQ 12. See also Maduro (n 164) [30]. cf V Gowlland-Debbas in de Wet and Nollkaemper (n 45) 68; Cramér (n 45) 96; RA Wessel (2008) 5 IOLR 326–7. cf also *Tachiona* (n 135) 212.

[168] cf Maduro (n 164) [39]:

> To the extent that [a ruling annulling the Community implementation measures] would prevent the Community and its [MS] from implementing [SCRs], the legal consequences within the international legal order remain to be determined by the rules of public international law.

Thus,

> it is true that the restrictions which the general principles of Community law impose on the actions of the institutions may inconvenience the Community and its [MS] *in their dealings on the international stage.* [emphasis added]

[169] See A Tzanakopoulos in OK Fauchald and A Nollkaemper (eds), *Unity or Fragmentation* (forthcoming 2011) at section VI; idem (n 60) 261–4; idem (n 90) 73–4; cf R Kolb (2008) 18 RSDIE 407–8; T Rensmann in *Festschrift Tomuschat* (2006) 261 (arguing on *Solange*).

[170] *Bradley v Commonwealth* (n 167). One must also not forget *Diggs v Shultz* 470 F 2d 461 (DC Cir 1972), where the Court of Appeals gave precedence to the domestic Byrd Amendment over SC sanctions against Southern Rhodesia, admitting the corresponding necessary violation of the UNC (at 466).

[171] *Kadi* (n 163) [372].   [172] *Othman* (n 165) [94].

[173] *Hay v HM Treasury* [2009] EWHC 1677 (Admin).

[174] *HM Treasury v Mohammed Jabar Ahmed and Others* (n 150).

[175] See *Bosphorus* (n 57) and text at n 58; Decision No 115/2007 (n 166) and text at same note.

[176] *Abdelrazik* (n 60).   [177] *A and Others* (NL 2010) ILDC 1463 [4.6].

[178] *Nada* (CH 2007) ILDC 461 [5.4].

the ECHR, and the ICCPR.[179] A relevant application has been brought before the ECtHR by Nada.[180] Similarly, UK courts have noted that the de-listing procedure 'does not begin to achieve fairness' for the person listed,[181] before finally striking down domestic implementing measures.[182] The Canadian judge in *Abdelrazik* likened the situation of a person subject to the 1267 sanctions regime to that of Josef K in Franz Kafka's *The Trial*.[183] The ECJ also strongly criticized the de-listing procedure before annulling the EC implementing acts in *Kadi*,[184] thereby confirming expectations that it will be much less deferential in the future, compared to earlier cases such as *Bosphorus*.[185] Up until recently, courts seemed not to want to put the exercise of auto-determination in full motion with respect to SC Chapter VII measures; but they have already changed their mind.[186]

III. Interim Conclusion

Recent developments that have seen an increasing number of cases in effect challenging the legality of SCRs being brought before domestic and regional courts, are said to 'reflect a general desire of UN [MS] to curb the Council's assertiveness or at least to add commensurate guarantees...to its constantly extending powers'.[187] It is submitted that this is in fact the case, which is also in line with the general trend of municipal courts asserting a more robust role in the enforcement of international norms, particularly in the field of human rights.[188] States may wish to exercise their powers of auto-determination by relying on the full examination of the merits of a test case by a court of law, rather than simply by mounting a challenge that would be—for lack of authoritative determination—seen against a

---

[179] Ibid [8.3].

[180] See UN Doc A/62/881—S/2008/428 (2008) 4.

[181] See *A, K, M, Q and G* (n 150) [18]; Mr Justice Collins regrets that '[m]uch as [he] would like to, [he does] not think [he] can go as far as the Advocate-General in *Kadi*': ibid [36]. However, he goes on to state that 'there should be a power in the court to decide whether the basis for listing existed, *which would then bind the Government to support de-listing*' [emphasis added].

[182] And indeed, in following up Mr Justice Collins's comments (immediately above), the UK Supreme Court issued a damning indictment of the 1267 de-listing procedure, even after this had been 'upgraded' through the introduction of an Office of the Ombudsperson in SCR 1904 (2009): *HM Treasury v Mohammed Jabar Ahmed and Others* (n 150) [78] (Lord Hope, with whom Lord Walker and Lady Hale agree); [181] (Lord Rodger); [239] (Lord Mance).

[183] *Abdelrazik* (n 60) [51]–[53].   [184] (n 163) [321] seq, in particular [324]–[325].

[185] cf PJG Kapteyn in de Wet and Nollkaemper (n 45) 61.

[186] It is instructive that in its assessment of legal challenges to the 1267 sanctions regime in May 2009 the 1267 Monitoring Team considered that future challenges are 'less likely and less likely to be successful': UN Doc S/2009/245 (2009) 12 [25]. Less than five months later, in October 2009, the 1267 Monitoring Team commented that the appeal brought by Kadi against the (fresh) EC Regulation subjecting him to an asset freeze and travel ban in accordance with SCR obligations, as well as the CFI's decision in *Othman* (n 165), and the decisions in *Hay* (n 173) and *A, K, M, Q and G* (n 150) (HC) and (n 138) (CA) 'may alter the terms of the wider discussion of the fairness of the regime and the need for reform' (UN Doc S/2009/502 [2009] 16 [36]) and will put 'additional pressure on the regime' (ibid 16–17 [37]–[38]). That, by any standard, is quite a volte-face.

[187] G Thallinger (2007) 67 ZaöRV 1034–5. cf generally H Keller and A Fischer (2009) 9 HRLR 257.

[188] cf Bianchi (n 114) 149.

political rather than a legal backdrop. Or, alternatively, domestic courts are taking it upon themselves to force their States into reacting against Council measures that can be seen as violating fundamental human rights (that are also part of general international law).[189]

Much like the behaviour of a State, the behaviour of an IO is also

not easily challenged on grounds of 'policy'; it is clearly preferable, *if one wishes to gain the support of those not directly involved*, to show it as a departure from legal obligations.[190]

In that, the determination of UN responsibility for Council action through a domestic or regional international court serves a double function: it does not solely posit the challenge on legal grounds,[191] but also attempts to rally support for the advocated legal arguments.

In effect, the challenge of legality of Council measures, whether through political or judicial organs, whether directly or indirectly, amounts to the exercise of the power of auto-determination of States that a violation of international law has occurred. The necessary corollary of an internationally wrongful act in the form of an illegal Council decision is the engagement of international responsibility of the UN. What remains to be examined is what consequences this auto-determined international responsibility of the UN for wrongful Council measures under Article 41 entails.

---

[189] See n 169 above.   [190] R Higgins (1970) 64 AJIL 17 [emphasis added].

[191] In the sense that it 'allows for the dismissal of unilateral and subjective evaluations in favour of a legal evaluation undertaken by a third party exercising a judicial function': see L Boisson de Chazournes in *Festschrift Tomuschat* (2006) 281. Although Boisson de Chazournes is referring to the ICJ in the exercise of its advisory jurisdiction, the statement is equally applicable to domestic or other courts, notwithstanding the fact that it does not amount to authoritative determination of responsibility, as explained in Chapter 4.II above. This is because even a domestic court is a 'third party' (to the extent that it is a third party when deciding disputes between individuals and the State of which it forms part, for example), and it most certainly exercises a 'judicial function'. cf the definition of international judicial role by Y Shany, *National Courts as International Actors: Jurisdictional Implications* (2008–9) 13.

PART III

THE CONSEQUENCES OF RESPONSIBILITY

The last part examines the 'consequences' for the United Nations of the emergence of the secondary regime of international responsibility. Chapter 6 discusses the content of UN responsibility, that is, the secondary obligations incumbent upon the Organization. The final chapter, Chapter 7, puts forward an argument as to the implementation of UN responsibility in a decentralized manner, predominantly by its own Member States.

6

The Content of International Responsibility

With the commission of an internationally wrongful act on the part of the UN through non-forcible Chapter VII Security Council action a new legal relationship emerges. The UN is no longer solely under the obligation to conform to the primary rule breached, but is also under secondary obligations to cease the wrongful conduct and to offer reparation.[1] These secondary obligations correspond to secondary rights of the (directly or 'indirectly') injured State(s) and/or IO(s). The content of the Organization's responsibility must be discussed before examining the avenues for the implementation of that responsibility. This chapter thus focuses on the secondary obligations to cease the internationally wrongful act if it is continuing (Section I) and to offer reparation (Section II).

I. Cessation: Between Performance and Restitution

The obligation to cease a continuing internationally wrongful act is particularly important in the context of Council action under Chapter VII. If the internationally wrongful act is a normative ('juridical') act of the Council, such as the promulgation of a resolution in violation of the Charter or of applicable rules of general international law, then the internationally wrongful act is continuing for as long as the resolution is in force and produces legal effect.[2] If, on the other hand, the wrongful act is an implementing act by States, which, however, is necessitated by a resolution and which results in a breach of the Charter or of general international law,[3] then the wrongful act will be continuing for as long as the States continue to implement that resolution. The States and/or IOs to which the breached obligation is owed will then have the (secondary) right to demand the cessation of the wrongful act, irrespective of whether they can be considered 'directly' or 'specifically' injured by the breach.[4]

---

[1] Arts 30–1 ARSIWA; 29–30 DARIO. See also ARSIWA Commentary 87 [2], referring to the 'core legal consequences' of an internationally wrongful act.

[2] cf ARSIWA Commentary 60 [3]: the maintenance in effect of a normative act producing legal effects incompatible with the international obligations of the enacting subject of international law constitutes a continuing wrongful act.

[3] In such instances of *normative* control, the impugned conduct, even though taken by State organs, should be considered as being attributable to the Council: see Chapter 2.II.2.ii above.

[4] See Arts 48 ARSIWA; 48 DARIO.

If, however, the UN—like any other State or IO—is under a continued duty of performance of its 'primary' international obligations even in the event that it has in fact breached them,[5] then one cannot help but wonder whether the 'secondary' obligation of cessation of continuing wrongful conduct[6] has any real substance—is it not in fact part of the same primary obligation, the performance of which the UN is anyway under a duty to continue?[7] Indeed, the ILC, in its Commentary to DARIO, treats cessation not as a true secondary obligation, but merely as a corollary of the continued duty of performance.[8] In the Commentary to ARSIWA, on the other hand, the ILC seems to have treated cessation as a true secondary obligation.[9]

Presumably the distinction is the following: the 'continued duty of performance' aims to underline the fact that a breach of a primary obligation does not per se terminate the primary obligation.[10] As such, it refers to all conduct of the responsible international legal entity prescribed, prohibited, or authorized by the primary obligation, and not to any specific conduct. The secondary obligation of cessation, on the other hand, targets specific wrongful conduct and arises only on the occasion and as a consequence of such wrongful conduct[11]—but its underlying legal basis is the continued duty of performance.[12]

The distinction may seem of limited importance and the discussion largely academic. It is true that by demanding cessation of the wrongful act one is demanding no more than the resumption of compliance with the primary obligation.[13] It is equally true, however, that by demanding cessation of the wrongful act one is already seeking a (limited) remedy, for example (potentially partial) restitution, from which cessation may in practice be indistinguishable, in particular with respect to a primary obligation which continues to be in force.[14] One could argue that cessation is *in and of itself* a limited form of remedy.[15] Both

---

[5] See Arts 29 ARSIWA; 28 DARIO.   [6] See Arts 30 ARSIWA; 29 DARIO.

[7] cf C Deman (1990) 23 RBDI 477.

[8] Cessation is 'not a new obligation arising as a consequence of the wrongful act': UN Doc A/62/10 (2007) 202 [2].

[9] ARSIWA Commentary 89 [6].   [10] Ibid 88 [2]–[3].

[11] Ibid 89 [6]. cf the distinction in *Wall* [2004] ICJ Rep 197: at [149] the Court underlines the continued duty of Israel to perform its international obligations with respect to self-determination, IHL, and international human rights law. At [150] on the other hand, it stresses the obligation of cessation, which at 197–8 [151] it finds to encompass, inter alia, an obligation to cease the construction works.

[12] *Avena* [2004] ICJ Rep 127 [79] (sep op Sepúlveda); cf P d'Argent in *Festschrift Tomuschat* (2006) 466 who comments in this respect that 'obeying existing rules is not a specific legal consequence' of the wrongful act.

[13] UN Doc A/62/10 (2007) 202 [2]; cf ARSIWA Commentary 88 [1]: 'Cessation is … the negative aspect of future performance'.

[14] ARSIWA Commentary 89 [7] and text at n 21 below. cf *Wall* (n 11) 197–8.

[15] eg B Graefrath (1984) 185 RdC 73 treats cessation as part of the claim to reparation. So does the ECtHR in *Assanidze* (GC) App No 71503/01 (2004) [202]:

> As regards the measures which the Georgian State must take … in order to *put an end to the violation* that has been found, [the very nature of the latter] does not leave any real choice as to the measures required to *remedy* it. [emphasis added]

cf *Ilaşcu* (GC) App No 48787/99 (2004) [490]. cf finally *Hostages* [1980] ICJ Rep 44 [95(3)] where the Court qualifies cessation as 'redress'; and the UN Legal Counsel in [1987] UNJY 209.

the ARSIWA and the DARIO Commentaries admit and underline that in the case of a continuing internationally wrongful act, cessation of the wrongful conduct will often be 'the main object pursued' by the (directly or 'indirectly') injured State(s) or IO(s).[16]

In the context of SC wrongful conduct under Chapter VII, cessation will involve the 'overturning' of an unlawful normative act—unlawful either because it was promulgated in violation of applicable international law, or because it necessitates implementing acts in violation of that law. Indeed, it is obvious that in most cases this will be the 'main object pursued' by the reacting States or IOs: they will seek to ensure that the offending resolution will either be retracted by the Council or will cease to be implemented.[17] This brings up the related question whether cessation can be distinguished from reparation in cases where the wrongful conduct is the promulgation of a normative act. In particular, reparation in such cases will primarily take the form of 'juridical' restitution, which will be virtually indistinguishable from cessation.

The problem does not arise in every case, of course; cessation and restitution can be clearly distinguished in the following sense: the secondary obligation of cessation arises only for continuing wrongful acts, while the secondary obligation to offer restitution exists in principle for all wrongful acts, whether continuing or completed.[18] Further, the obligation to cease a wrongful act is absolute and unconditional;[19] but restitution, as all forms of reparation, is subject to a number of constraints.[20] In view of that latter consideration, it is crucial whether the secondary obligation of withdrawing an offending normative act is qualified as 'cessation' or 'restitution'.[21] An internationally responsible actor will be able to argue that restitution is overly cumbersome; or it may 'induce' the beneficiary of the obligation to opt for another form of reparation; that is, in either case it will potentially be able to 'buy its way out'.

In the particular case of normative acts, cessation and restitution will always coincide,[22] at least in part. If the keeping in force of a normative act constitutes

[16] UN Doc A/62/10 (2007) 202 [2]; cf ARSIWA Commentary 89 [4]: 'Cessation is often the *main focus* of the controversy produced by conduct in breach of an international obligation' [emphasis added].

[17] eg Libya asked for the sanctions against it to be 'rescinded', while in the same breath it also asked for suspension of their implementation in S/PV.3684 (1998) 11. Similarly, the OAU asked repeatedly for the Libyan sanctions to be lifted: eg AHG/Dec.127 (XXXIV) (1998) [2]; as did the OIC regarding the arms embargo on the former Yugoslavia, with respect to the territory of Bosnia: eg Res No 7/21-P (1993) [11].

[18] See nn 27–8 below. cf *Avena* (n 12) 68 [148] where the wrongful conduct was found not to be of a continuing character, and thus the Court found no secondary obligation of cessation, though it determined the existence of certain secondary obligations of 'juridical' restitution, discussed in this chapter at Section III below. cf further *Armed Activities (DRC v Uganda)* [2005] ICJ Rep 254–5 [254].

[19] cf G Arangio Ruiz (1988) II(1) YILC 20 [57].

[20] See nn 29–30 below.　　[21] ARSIWA Commentary 89 [7].

[22] See the admission by the ILC that, in practice, in many instances it will be very difficult if at all possible to distinguish the cessation of the wrongful conduct from restitution: ARSIWA Commentary 98 [6]; and cf the Libyan statement in the SC (n 17): it can be argued that the suspension of sanctions that Libya requests is a request for 'cessation', while its call to the Council to rescind

wrongful conduct, then there is no other way to cease the wrongful conduct than to repeal or rescind the normative act.[23] This is evident when the ICJ holds that Israeli legislative acts regarding the construction of the Wall in the occupied Palestinian territories and the establishment of its associated regime must 'be repealed or rendered ineffective' as part of Israel's secondary obligation to cease its wrongful conduct.[24] In *Avena*, on the other hand, the wrongful conduct is not the criminal convictions of certain Mexican nationals per se, but the fact that the convictions were arrived at in violation of the VCCR. As such, the Court does not require their annulment or repeal, but merely the establishment of a judicial process to offer review and reconsideration, in order to re-establish the situation that would have existed had the VCCR not been violated.[25]

While repealing the offending normative act will be necessary in order to comply with the secondary obligation of cessation, it will at the same time amount to full or partial reparation through 'juridical' restitution.[26] The issue of reparation, and of 'juridical' restitution in particular, is discussed in the following section, but with an important disclaimer: to the extent that cessation and restitution coincide, the limitations on restitution do not apply.

II. Reparation

Restitution is traditionally regarded as the principal form of reparation, following the celebrated PCIJ dictum in *Chorzów Factory*,[27] aiming most directly at 'wiping

the sanctions is a claim for 'juridical restitution'. The OIC can be seen as seeking at once cessation and juridical restitution in Res No 7/21-P (1993) [11], where it requests the Council 'to exempt, without any further delay, the Republic of Bosnia and Herzegovina from the arms embargo as imposed on the former Yugoslavia under [SCR] 713 (1991)'. And domestic courts can be interpreted as requesting cessation and partial juridical restitution when they determine the 1267 sanctions regime as not offering adequate judicial guarantees and they implicitly call for its reform: see nn 178–86 and accompanying text in Chapter 5 above and cf n 41 below.

[23] Even if one accepts the formal distinction sometimes made, that cessation refers to conduct *ex nunc*, ie for the future, while restitution refers to effects *ex tunc* (see eg W Riphagen [1985] II[1] YILC 9 [6]–[8]; Deman [n 7] 487–8), in the case of a normative act cessation *ex nunc* is impossible without repeal, which in effect re-establishes the *status quo ante* (at least to an extent).

[24] *Wall* (n 11) 197–8 [151]. When discussing reparation, the Court only refers to restitution through the return of land taken and compensation for damage caused by the construction of the Wall (198 [153]). This is arguably because 'juridical' restitution will already have been effected, to the extent possible, through Israel's cessation of the wrongful conduct, as this secondary obligation was determined by the Court to include the repeal of legislative and regulatory acts related to the construction.

[25] (n 12) 60 [121]. This, in the context of *Avena* where the violation is continuing, can be qualified as cessation; in the context of *LaGrand* [2001] ICJ Rep 514 [215], however, where the violation could not be meaningfully understood as continuing with respect to Germany, the same obligation can be qualified as an obligation to offer assurances and guarantees of non-repetition: cf CJ Tams (2002) 27 YJIL 441–4; idem (2002) 13 EJIL 1257–9; this serves to confirm the interpenetration or (con)fusion of different secondary obligations (read: 'remedies' *lato sensu*).

[26] cf W Riphagen (1981) II(1) YILC 86 [57] who notes that the secondary obligation to cease may include conduct characterized by some as *restitutio in integrum*; and Graefrath (n 15) 85 who comments that 'quite often cessation of the violation *can already be regarded as part of* the restitution' [emphasis added].

[27] [1928] PCIJ Ser A No 13 at 47.

out' the consequences of the wrongful act and the re-establishment of the *status quo ante*.[28] The two other forms of reparation, namely compensation and satisfaction, are to be considered only when restitution is not adequate in order to achieve 'full' reparation,[29] when it is impossible or overly burdensome,[30] or when it is not actually claimed by the injured State(s) and/or IO(s).[31] Despite, however, being first in line, and despite being most often claimed by States in practice,[32] restitution is hardly ever implemented as a form of reparation.[33] In particular with respect to IOs, where practice is scarce to say the least, it is instructive that the ILC does not even comment on the article concerning restitution. Rather, it goes on immediately to consider compensation as 'the form of reparation most frequently made by international organizations'.[34]

In the context of SC action, however, it appears that compensation is the form of reparation with the least relevance or, pragmatically, with the slimmest prospects of being claimed—let alone offered. Since the internationally wrongful act is a normative act, the injured States will be primarily concerned, as already mentioned, with the cessation of the breach, that is, with stripping the normative act of its legal effects. This is, in effect, tantamount to 'juridical' restitution (Subsection 1).[35] Further, the role of satisfaction in safeguarding the rights of States should not be underestimated (Subsection 2). The fact that, following such eventualities, States may pursue 'full' reparation by claiming compensation for quantifiable damage sustained by the adoption or implementation of the wrongful measure is beyond the scope of this study. It would require lengthy analysis as to issues of causal link, remoteness, quantum, and the like, thereby detracting from the immediate objective, namely to determine the forms of reparation that States may realistically want to achieve through decentralized reactions against the Security Council.

1. 'Juridical' restitution

An aspect of restitution can be the material restoration or return of territory, persons, or property.[36] Such instances are not inconceivable if a Council measure under Chapter VII is found to amount to an internationally wrongful act. For example when the UN is administering a territory under a Council decision pursuant to Chapter VII, restitution could potentially require the restoration of the relevant territory to the State that has the right to exercise sovereignty over it (if there is one). Humanitarian goods (such as foodstuffs or medicine)

---

[28] cf ARSIWA Commentary 96–7 [1]–[3].
[29] In many instances full reparation can only be achieved by employing a combination of some or all the possible forms of reparation: ibid 95 [2].
[30] cf ibid 96 [5]; 97 [4].   [31] cf ibid 96 [4].   [32] Ibid 97 [3].
[33] See CD Gray (1999) 10 EJIL 416 and fns 8–9, 418.
[34] UN Doc A/62/10 (2007) 209. cf ARSIWA Commentary 99 [2], according to which compensation 'is perhaps the most commonly sought [form of reparation]' in international practice'.
[35] See text at n 22 seq.
[36] See for the phraseology ARSIWA Commentary 97 [5]. cf *Temple of Preah Vihear* [1962] ICJ Rep 36–7. The Council has itself demanded such forms of reparation: SCR 686 (1991) [2(c)–(d)].

seized in implementation of a comprehensive embargo (eg providing for no humanitarian exceptions) could be considered as items that need to be 'restored' to the intended recipient State, while similar considerations could apply to payments withheld from blacklisted individuals if these are needed for basic sustenance.[37] When a person indicted by an ad hoc international criminal court (unlawfully) established by the Council is being held awaiting trial, the Council would be required, in order to effect restitution, to return the person in custody to their home State.

In most of these examples, however, it is the MS that seized the goods or the monies or that holds the indicted individual that must take action to effect restitution on the part of the Council. Still, that MS cannot so act lest it be found in violation of the relevant SCR(s) and Article 25 UNC.[38] As such, some action is required on the part of the Council: since it cannot effect restitution itself (as it does not hold the goods, or the monies, or the person), it must somehow 'liberate' the MS that is acting pursuant to Council orders from the obligation to comply with those orders.

Restitution can in fact be effected, in such instances, by employing another modality; namely by effecting 'juridical' restitution. This 'juridical' restitution can be defined as restitution through the 'reversal of some juridical act', or even more specifically as

the revocation, annulment or amendment of a . . . provision enacted in violation of a rule of international law [or] the rescinding or reconsideration of an administrative . . . measure unlawfully adopted . . . [39]

The 'reversal' could consist thus, in the cases described above, in the adoption of a new binding decision, countermanding the problematic obligation in the first decision (eg through amending it). This would allow and obligate the MS to cease its offending conduct (which is in fact attributable to the Council, as it is effectively

---

[37] The Council has, of course, addressed such grossly problematic measures by employing humanitarian exceptions. However, in the case of the 1267 sanctions regime eg this was only after MS, whether through their executives or through their courts, had reacted against the Council measures by granting themselves (and unilaterally) dispensation for basic expenses: see text at nn 45–6; nn 93–5; and n 156 in Chapter 5 above on the Swedish authorities and the English court reaction in *Othman*. The Council's granting of exemptions from the sanctions regime can even be seen as redress in response to State reaction. Still the exceptions may, eg not go far enough and thus render the measure disproportionate and, consequently, unlawful.

[38] cf the President of The Hague District Court in *Milošević v The Netherlands* (Interlocutory Injunction) KG 01/975 (2001) 48 NILR 361 [3.5]–[3.6]: that a potential order for the release of Milošević from the custody of the ICTY would violate the UNC is implicit in the Court's finding that it lacks jurisdiction. cf also the opinion of the UN Legal Counsel that States using frozen Iraqi funds held by them to finance the sale or supply of medicine to Iraq directly (as opposed to through a transfer to a sub-account of the escrow account established by SCR 712 [1991]) would be in violation of SCR 778 (1992) [11]: [1993] UNJY 446–7.

[39] cf ARSIWA Commentary 97 [5]; FV García Amador (1961) II YILC 17–18 [68]–[69].

normatively controlled by it),[40] and would amount to the Council effecting partial restitution.[41]

In the event that the internationally wrongful act of the Council is not the result of the implementation of its Chapter VII resolution, but rather the passing of the resolution itself, there is no other modality to effect restitution than the 'reversal' of the offending juridical act. In the instance the Council would be under a secondary obligation to offer juridical restitution by withdrawing or revoking the offending resolution through a new decision.[42] The UN itself has presented States on numerous occasions with claims for 'juridical' and material restitution on the basis of violations of their international obligations towards the Organization, usually with respect to its privileges and immunities.[43] There is no reason why this should not work the other way around.

---

[40] See Chapter 2.II.2.ii above. The MS would not just be *allowed* to cease, it would be *obligated* to do so: non-forcible measures under Art 41 will usually constitute breaches of international law if undertaken by a State unilaterally (unless they can be qualified as countermeasures or retorsion). Their legal basis is the binding decision of the Council; once deprived of this legal basis, the measures would constitute a breach of international obligations of the State taking them, engaging its own responsibility. As such, the MS will be 'normatively' forced to stop them or face the consequences of the engagement of responsibility.

[41] It is true that, in the event eg that a State has sought illegally to annex territory through the use of force, it must, in order to effect restitution by returning the territory seized, rescind all relevant domestic legal acts purportedly annexing the territory. This will remove the (domestic) legal foundation and allow actual restitution. In this sense, juridical restitution is always required ahead of restitution of property or territory: see SCR 686 (1991) [2(a)]. cf García Amador (n 39). Unlike the case of a State, in the case of the SC, the actor effecting juridical restitution will be different from the actor actually returning territory or property (the UN and MS respectively).

An example of the Council having attempted to make partial juridical restitution can be seen in SCR 1904 (2009). After '[t]*aking note* of challenges, both legal and otherwise, to the measures implemented by [MS] under the [1267 sanctions regime]' (at ninth preamble), the Council established an 'Office of the Ombudsperson' to receive de-listing requests and report to the Sanctions Committee which has final decision on the requests 'in an independent and impartial manner' (at [20] and Annex II). This was explicitly in response to challenges by MS (including through their courts) that the 1267 regime did not provide for adequate safeguards while imposing severe restrictions on individuals: cf nn 170–86 and accompanying text in Chapter 5 above and in detail A Tzanakopoulos (2010) 8 JICJ 249 and idem in A Reinisch (ed), *Challenging Acts of IOs before National Courts* (2010) 54. The Council sought, by amending the offending normative acts, to address the problem, thereby offering partial restitution. It did not succeed in doing so, as is evident from the UK Supreme Court reaction to even the amended 1267 regime in *HM Treasury v Mohammed Jabar Ahmed and Others (FC); HM Treasury v Mohammed al-Ghabra (FC); R (Hani El Sayed Sabaei Youssef) v HM Treasury* [2010] UKSC 2, in particular [78] (Lord Hope, with whom Lord Walker and Lady Hale agree); [181] (Lord Rodger); [239] (Lord Mance).

[42] Note the primacy of juridical restitution in WTO law. Lacking a solution 'mutually acceptable to the parties' (in which case there would exist no dispute), the 'withdrawal of the measures concerned' is determined as 'the *first* objective of the dispute settlement mechanism': DSU Art 3(7) [emphasis added]; cf Art 22(1):

> neither compensation nor the suspension of concessions or other obligations is preferred to full implementation of a recommendation *to bring a measure into conformity* with the covered agreements. [emphasis added]

Withdrawal and bringing a measure into conformity with the international obligations amount to juridical restitution.

[43] See eg the Note verbale of the Legal Counsel requesting that a State take steps to respect the Organization's and FAO's immunity from jurisdiction, dismiss a pending case, and withdraw an

Theoretically, a tribunal could effect what amounts to juridical restitution 'by determining the legal position *with binding force* for the parties'.[44] The PCIJ could be seen as having done that in *Eastern Greenland*.[45] But this was only possible because in the instance the domestic legal act purported to produce *international legal effects*. The Norwegian declaration of occupation was held to be 'invalid',[46] but the Court's decision did not really invalidate the Norwegian declaration within the Norwegian legal order; it merely found that it produced no legal effects on the international plane, that is, it made it impossible for Norway to rely on it against Denmark.[47] This finding was binding on the parties. At the same time, the Court can be seen as implicitly imposing an obligation on Norway to withdraw the act.[48]

In general, an international court's decision cannot 'pierce through' a municipal legal order, denying legal effects to acts within that order.[49] As such, when juridical restitution is sought with respect to a domestic legal act meant to produce effects within the municipal legal order, different considerations apply. The Court cannot effect such juridical restitution itself, but can define (and prescribe) how this restitution is to be effected.

In *LaGrand*, the ICJ discussed the juridical restitution that the US would have to offer in case of future violations of the VCCR and found that

> it would be incumbent upon the [US] *to allow the review and reconsideration of the conviction and sentence*, . . . [an obligation that] can be carried out in various ways. The choice of means must be left to the [US].[50]

When Mexico, clearly seeking juridical restitution in *Avena*, asked the Court to adjudge and declare that 'this restitution consists of the obligation to restore the *status quo ante* by *annulling or otherwise depriving of full force or effect* the conviction

---

execution order which embargoed funds of the WFP, thereby returning the funds: [2004] UNJY 328. cf ibid 336–9, where the Legal Counsel asks for the exemption of MONUC personnel from fees in accordance with obligations under the Convention on Privileges and Immunities, arguably thus demanding only cessation of the illegal practice of imposing the fees but no restitution, whether juridical or material; cf in UNJY: [1988] 305, 308 [12]; [1977] 239; [1964] 265 [5]. Juridical restitution may, however, be implied in the claim. See further on restitution claims in UNJY: [1998] 480–1; [1995] 403–4; [1993] 362 [6]; [1992] 474; [1990] 289 [5]; [1989] 361; [1987] 210; [1982] 210; [1978] 187; [1974] 146; [1973] 136 [24]; [1966] 224.

[44] ARSIWA Commentary 97 [5].
[45] [1933] PCIJ Ser A/B No 53 at 22.   [46] Ibid 75; cf 64.
[47] It is also of some importance that the Court was considering the relative strength of claims over territory, cf ibid 46.
[48] cf *Free Zones* [1932] PCIJ Ser A/B No 46 at 172, where the Court imposed an obligation on France to establish and maintain a specific legal regime.
[49] Or imposing a directly enforceable obligation within that order. Such a direct effect within the domestic legal order is provided or not provided for *by the relevant domestic legal order itself*: cf *Interpretation of* Avena [2009] ICJ Rep [44]. cf also *Papamichalopoulos* (ECtHR [Just Satisfaction]) App No 14556/89 [34]:

> If the nature of the breach allows for *restitutio in integrum*, it is for the respondent State to effect it, *the Court having neither the power nor the practical possibility of doing so itself.* [emphasis added]

cf generally H Urbanek (1961) 11 ÖZöR 72 seq.
[50] (n 25) 514 [125] [emphasis added]. This is confirmed in *Avena* (n 12) 60 [121]. See also n 25.

and sentences of [Mexican nationals]' made in violation of the VCCR,[51] it was not claiming that the Court had the power to annul the US convictions—it was merely asking the Court to find that the US was under an obligation to effect juridical restitution along those lines. And indeed the Court confirmed that juridical restitution was due, though not along the lines of annulment claimed by Mexico: it found that juridical restitution was to be effected, much like in *LaGrand*, through the implementation of a system of effective judicial review and reconsideration.[52] This merely meant that restitution *in casu* did not extend to annulment, but to the implementation of review measures on the part of the US.[53] In *Arrest Warrant* the Court ordered Belgium to cancel the warrant issued by its judicial authorities in violation of international law (but could not annul the warrant itself);[54] that is, it defined the manner in which Belgium was to effect (juridical) restitution.

The UN cannot be a party before the Court, and as such it will be able to rely on a SCR as against all MS, irrespective of the Court setting aside the same SCR in a case between States parties to a dispute before it. Further, the Council cannot be obligated by the Court to amend, withdraw, or rescind, or even reconsider a SCR. Nor can it be obligated, for example, to adopt a system of judicial review of targeted sanctions imposed against individuals. This is because the Court lacks the power to determine with binding force the secondary obligations incumbent upon the UN as a result of violations of international law on its part.[55] However, this does not mean that the UN is under no secondary international obligations to effect juridical restitution. This can be seen in the example of the (then) IMCO: when the ICJ found that an act of the Organization was in violation of its constitutive instrument, it did not elaborate on the legal consequences.[56] However, the Organization remedied the deficiency by adopting a new act, overturning the unlawful one, and following the Court's interpretation of the relevant provisions. In effect the Organization complied with its secondary obligation of offering 'juridical' restitution, even though the Court did not pronounce on the issue.

It has been argued that domestic courts may effect juridical restitution by, for example, suppressing incriminating evidence in the case of a violation of an alien's rights under the VCCR,[57] or annulling an internationally wrongful domestic normative act. While it may be true that the act of a domestic court, being attributable to the State, may in fact amount to juridical restitution, given in particular that it is binding on the State, no municipal court could ever effect

---

[51] (n 12) 58 [116]–[117] [emphasis added]. cf claims by Paraguay in *Breard* [1998] ICJ Rep 250–1 [5]; Germany in *LaGrand* [1999] ICJ Rep 11 [5].

[52] (n 12) 60 [123].

[53] Which the Court defined as having to be 'judicial' as opposed to 'executive' in nature: ibid 65–6 [138]–[143]. See further n 18 and text at n 25.

[54] [2002] ICJ Rep 32 [76]; cf 33 [78(3)]. However, the problem in this case revolves around whether the violation is of a continuing character. If it is, as the Court implies, then the obligation to cancel the arrest warrant would more appropriately come under the secondary obligation of cessation; cf the joint separate opinion of Higgins, Kooijmans, and Buergenthal (ibid 89 [89]), who find that there is no continuing violation since Yerodia was no longer covered by immunity at the time.

[55] See Chapter 4.I above.   [56] [1960] ICJ Rep 150.

[57] See FL Kirgis (2001) 95 AJIL 342; cf 345–6.

juridical restitution on the part of the Council or impose an obligation upon it to that end.[58]

This distinction can be clearly drawn in the cases relating to sanctions implementation within the legal order of the EC. The CFI, in annulling in part the EC Regulation with respect to the OMPI,[59] could be interpreted as having effected juridical restitution on the part of the EC for a violation of international law (right to effective judicial protection). This is because the relevant SCRs imposed an obligation on the EC to blacklist individuals, but *not any specific individuals*. The EC decision to blacklist the OMPI, without being strictly bound to do so by the SC,[60] and without allowing for due process, arguably constitutes not only a violation of EC law, but also a violation of the ECHR and possibly the ICCPR and general international law.[61] The CFI's annulment of the offending part of the Regulation amounts to juridical restitution for such a breach of international law.

On the other hand, the ECJ's annulment of the EC Regulation with respect to Kadi and Al Barakaat does not constitute juridical restitution:[62] the conduct which is in breach of international law in this case (the blacklisting of Kadi and the Foundation) is attributable to the SC, which has imposed a strict obligation on the EC.[63] By annulling in part the implementing measure, the ECJ—by its own admission—does not affect the relevant SCRs,[64] which continue to produce legal effects. It merely puts the EC and its MS in breach of their obligations under the SCRs and Article 25 UNC.[65]

As such, the only body which can effect juridical restitution for wrongful Council non-forcible action under Chapter VII is the Council itself. Neither the ICJ nor any other court can have a binding impact on the legal effects of Council decisions, nor can they impose obligations on the Council to withdraw, rescind, reconsider, or otherwise adopt measures to address the international legal shortcomings of its decisions. But it cannot be stressed enough that relevant

---

[58] But it could formulate a relevant claim: see n 22 and n 41 above and Chapter 7.III.3 below. In any event, as noted already by the PCIJ and in Chapter 4.III above,

> from the standpoint of International Law…municipal laws *are merely facts*…which constitute the activities of States, *in the same manner as do legal decisions* or administrative measures: *Certain German Interests* [1926] Ser A No 7 at 19 [emphasis added].

[59] T-228/02 *OMPI* [2006] ECR II-4665 [173]–[174].   [60] cf ibid [100]–[102].

[61] cf the argument made at n 169 and accompanying text in Chapter 5.II.3.ii above.

[62] C-402/05 *Kadi* [2008] ECR I-6351 [369]–[372]. The same considerations apply to the UK Supreme Court's partial annulment of the domestic Order in Council implementing the 1267 sanctions regime in *HM Treasury v Mohammed Jabar Ahmed and Others* (n 41).

[63] See Chapter 2.II.2.ii above on the concept of effective *normative* control. The ECJ admittedly does not fully appreciate the distinction drawn by the CFI in *OMPI* (n 59) [100]–[102]: it says that it is open to the Community to comply with the SCRs without violating the right of effective judicial protection ([n 62] [298] seq); assume, however, that the EC provided for a review procedure, and Kadi eg was able to show that there was no reason for him to be blacklisted; what would the EC do? Not include him in the blacklist? If it did so, it would cause 27 MS (and itself) to be in breach of the SCR and Art 25 UNC. cf the A-G in *Kadi* (n 62) [30]. The distinction is clearly drawn by the UK Supreme Court in *HM Treasury v Mohammed Jabar Ahmed and Others* (n 41) [148] (Lord Phillips); [168] (Lord Rodger); [196] seq (Lord Brown).

[64] cf *Kadi* (n 62) [286]–[287].

[65] See Chapter 7.III.3 below; this is, eg what the CFI does in T-318/01 *Othman* [2009] ECR II-1627.

secondary obligations along these lines *do* exist and are binding upon the Council by *automatic* operation of international law.[66] The lack of a judicial instance merely makes the determination of their emergence and of their precise content more difficult.

2. Satisfaction

Satisfaction is sometimes regarded as an unimportant and somewhat obscure form of reparation.[67] It is, however, commonly resorted to—as evidenced by the practice of requesting and obtaining declaratory judgments from international tribunals. It is also anything but exceptional in the context of international organizations: in fact, the DARIO Commentary on the forms of reparation cites the most instances of practice with respect to satisfaction offered by IOs—as opposed to not commenting at all on restitution and mentioning the Congo example with respect to compensation.[68]

As Gray notes, declaratory judgments have taken on a new importance in the practice of the ICJ, as opposed to that of the PCIJ: they have been granted as satisfaction, in implementation of the responsibility of the State found to have violated international law.[69] The importance of satisfaction as a form of reparation is highlighted by the fact that in a number of cases where States could have claimed pecuniary compensation on behalf of nationals, they did not do so but 'felt it more appropriate' to seek only a declaratory judgment; this was because 'what was important to them was a declaration of their legal rights'.[70] According to Brownlie, and this is the crucial part, *all* judgments 'are declaratory of the existence of international obligations...or of the absence of legal justification (State responsibility)'.[71] This can be taken to mean that whereas all judgments will include a declaration as to the legal position of the parties and thus will determine their potential international responsibility, sometimes they will not go further: the declaration will at once also be the remedy.[72]

While this discussion refers to *judicial* remedies, it highlights the importance of satisfaction as a form or reparation even in the decentralized implementation of responsibility. An acknowledgement of the internationally wrongful act and

---

[66] Arts 1 ARSIWA; 3 DARIO; cf ARSIWA Commentary 119 [2], 116.

[67] The ILC calls it 'not a standard form of reparation' having a 'rather exceptional character': ARSIWA Commentary 105 [1]. cf C Dominicé in *Mélanges Perrin* (1984) 91–2.

[68] UN Doc A/62/10 (2007) 209–12.

[69] CD Gray, *Judicial Remedies in International Law* (1990) 98. See eg *Mutual Assistance* [2008] ICJ Rep 245 [204].

[70] Gray (n 69) 100. cf ARSIWA Commentary 106–7 [6].

[71] I Brownlie in *Honour Jennings* (1996) 560. He therefore denies the existence of a separate category of 'declaratory judgments'.

[72] eg in *Modinos* (Judgment) App No 15070/89, the ECtHR found a Cypriot law to constitute a breach of Cypriot obligations under the ECHR ([23]–[26]), but considered that the finding of breach constituted 'sufficient just satisfaction' for the claimant ([30]). At the same time, however, Cyprus was clearly under an obligation to cease the breach and offer juridical restitution by rescinding the offending piece of legislation. This serves not only to highlight the potential for further claims against Cyprus, but also to underline the close connection between cessation and juridical restitution already noted (text at n 22 seq). See also E Fasoli (2008) 7 LPICT 192.

an apology on the part of the responsible subject are constitutive elements of satisfaction in the extra-judicial context.[73] This admission and apology not only serve as a sort of reparation for moral harm of the injured State, they also serve as a method of precluding the establishment of precedent, and this can be all the more important within the setting of an IO. If the UN admits that a Council measure (even if now elapsed) was in breach of UN obligations under international law, the admission effectively estops the Council from adopting a similar measure in the future. Or, in any event, it furnishes States with a potent argument against the legality of a similar measure being adopted. Thus, the value of the admission and apology can hardly be overemphasized.[74]

III. Interim Conclusion

International responsibility is engaged *automatically* on the perpetration of an international wrong. It arises 'by operation of law on the commission of an internationally wrongful act'. Therefore, the content of international responsibility of the UN for wrongful acts of the SC can intelligibly be cast in terms of secondary obligations of the UN to cease the wrongful act and, what *in casu* will amount much to the same, offer reparation in terms mainly of 'juridical' restitution and perhaps satisfaction. However, this says little about who and in what way can claim these remedies from the UN. Invocation of the international responsibility of a subject is necessary, since it determines which other subjects are entitled to take action with respect to the violation, in order to secure the performance of the secondary obligations of cessation and reparation.[75]

Invocation is, according to the ILC, and for the purposes of ARSIWA, the taking of measures of a 'relatively formal character', such as presenting a claim against another State or commencing proceedings before an international jurisdiction, but cannot be mere criticism or simple calls for the observance of an obligation, or even protest in some circumstances.[76] This makes sense, as invocation is grounded on a specific entitlement, a right, which is generally reserved to the subject injured by the internationally wrongful act.[77] Further, it connotes that the subject invoking the responsibility of another subject wishes to avail itself of the secondary rights of cessation and reparation.

Invocation, thus, as a 'relatively formal' process, will necessarily presuppose and imply—if it does not explicitly state—the (auto-)determination by the acting subject that the intended target has perpetrated an internationally wrongful act, which engages its responsibility. This becomes particularly problematic in respect of invocation of responsibility for breaches of obligations *erga omnes*: the concept of such obligations has emerged with no support from, or serious attempts at,

---

[73] cf Dominicé (n 67) 114–15.
[74] cf also UN Doc A/62/10 (2007) 212 [2]–[3] referring to UN practice.
[75] ARSIWA Commentary 116.   [76] See ibid 117 [2].
[77] Ibid; but see CJ Tams, *Enforcing Obligations* Erga Omnes (2005) 38–9.

adequate institution-building.[78] As such, it too is subject to the power of auto-determination and (presumably) self-enforcement of States.[79] The SC could be approached as a mechanism for collective law-enforcement.[80] But such a view of the Council's function is far from generally accepted.[81] And, in any event, in the instance under scrutiny here, the question of who enforces 'community norms' against the principal 'enforcer' is posed with some force.

Thus, in a rather ironic re-adjustment of traditional approaches, the role of enforcing community norms against the Security Council is still left to the individual auto-determination of duties and self-enforcement of rights by States themselves. It is to such decentralized implementation of the international responsibility of the UN for non-forcible measures under Article 41 UNC that the final chapter now turns.

---

[78] B Simma (1994) 250 RdC 249; also K Zemanek (2000) 4 MPUNYB 12–17.

[79] As is well known, the ILC avoided, in adopting Art 54 ARSIWA, to take a position on whether 'third'/'indirectly injured'/'States other than the injured State' may resort to countermeasures. See further Chapter 7.IV below.

[80] cf V Gowlland-Debbas in M Byers (ed), *The Role of Law in International Politics* (2000) 285–6.

[81] cf Zemanek (n 78) 45–7.

7

Implementation through Self-Enforcement

The implementation of international responsibility is nothing but the effectuation of the secondary obligations of cessation and reparation.[1] And it is precisely for this purpose that decentralized countermeasures are accepted in international law.[2] This chapter discusses whether States, be it members or non-members of the UN, can resort to countermeasures against the Organization in response to a wrongful act perpetrated by its Security Council acting under Article 41 of the UN Charter.

Countermeasures are breaches of international obligations on the part of a subject of international law, which are taken in response to a previous internationally wrongful act by another subject, in order to induce the recalcitrant subject to comply with its international obligations.[3] In that, they are a mechanism for the ('private' or decentralized) enforcement of international law. At the same time, they are a reaction,[4] a 'response' to the violation of international law by way of a further breach, the wrongfulness of which is precluded.[5] They are thus also an excuse for non-compliance with an international obligation of the reacting subject.

Countermeasures are available for the enforcement of international obligations, even when there exists binding third-party determination of the engagement of international responsibility,[6] except where they have been subjected to specific limitations.[7] This chapter will first enquire whether countermeasures by States against an IO are theoretically conceivable (Section I). It will then go on to examine

---

[1] ARSIWA Commentary 116.

[2] See *Gabčíkovo-Nagymaros* [1997] ICJ Rep 56–7 [87]; Art 49(1) ARSIWA and Commentary 130 [1].

[3] cf the definitions of countermeasures and reprisals in ARSIWA Commentary 128 [1]; R Ago (1979) II(1) YILC 39 [78]; the opinions of members of the ILC in (1979) I YILC 56–63; its Report in (1979) II(2) YILC 115 [1]; Art 1 of the IDI Resolution on 'Régime des représailles en temps de paix' in (1934) 38 AIDI 708; N Politis in ibid 7–8 [10]; H Kelsen, *Reine Rechtslehre* (2nd edn, 1960) 321. cf also C Leben (1982) 28 AFDI 14 [7].

[4] L-A Sicilianos, *Les réactions décentralisées* (1990) 247 seq. On the meaning of the term 'enforcement' see CJ Tams in G Ulfstein (ed), *Making Treaties Work* (2007) 391–6, 407.

[5] A Bleckmann in *Festschrift Schlochauer* (1981) 193.

[6] They are also available, eg within the context of the ECHR in case of non-compliance with a ECtHR decision. See T Stein (1987) 47 ZaöRV 106–7. cf K Zemanek (1987) 47 ZaöRV 41.

[7] As is the case, eg within the framework of the WTO, where resort to unilateral countermeasures in view of non-compliance with the decision of the DSB is multilaterally approved and monitored. See generally J Pauwelyn (2000) 94 AJIL 335 seq, 339.

whether the widely proposed 'last resort' of disobedience can be legally qualified as a countermeasure (Section II), before finally discussing the potential availability of other countermeasures (Section III), as well as 'lawful' measures that can be taken by States 'other than the injured State' (Section IV).

I. Availability of Countermeasures

Countermeasures evolved in a bilateral framework, and bilateralism is thus inherent in their nature and application:[8] one subject takes measures against another subject, because the latter violated some subjective right of the former. There is no theoretical problem in contemplating countermeasures being taken in the relations between an IO and non-MS (third States). In fact, such a possibility had been accepted quite early on, as intimately connected with the quality of an organization as a subject of international law.[9]

However, it is natural to question whether such a 'traditional' instrumentality of international law can be said to apply in the relationship between an international organization and its MS. Whereas all the MS retain their international legal personality, and whereas the international organization has a separate international legal personality, it is still somewhat counterintuitive to imagine the States that have created the IO taking measures against it. The verticality of the relationship, when the organization has the power to take binding measures (as is the case with the UN when the SC acts under Chapter VII) creates a situation where MS are subject to the organization. In traditional State-to-State relations the subjects are on the same level, being sovereign and equal. This consideration does not deny, in principle, the availability of countermeasures in the organization–MS relationship, as will be shown immediately. But it does inform the particular 'form' of countermeasure available in the instance.

The capacity of resorting to countermeasures is inherent in the international legal personality enjoyed by IOs,[10] and thus also by the UN. In fact this is true for all mechanisms of invocation and implementation of international responsibility, such as protest or the presentation of an international claim, whether directed against a MS, a third State, or any other subject of international law.[11] Accordingly, the UN must have the capacity not only to take countermeasures against a State

---

[8] See K Sachariew (1988) 35 NILR 286; JA Frowein (1994) 248 RdC 353.

[9] In fact W Wengler (1951–3) 51 Friedens-Warte 142, considers that IOs are subjects of international law to the extent that they can be made the targets of sanctions under international law alongside States. And if the UN can invoke the responsibility of Israel and claim reparation for injury (*Reparation* [1949] ICJ Rep 179–85), this means that the UN can back this with countermeasures. But the opposite must also be true. cf W Meng (1985) 45 ZaöRV 328. See also the comments by UNESCO and WHO in UN Doc A/CN.4/609 (2009) 10–11, supporting in principle the availability of countermeasures against IOs.

[10] C Dominicé in *Honour Skubiszewski* (1996) 163.

[11] In answering the question whether the UN could bring an international claim against a State, the ICJ first sought to establish whether the Organization enjoyed international legal personality: *Reparation* (n 9) 177–9. Further, the Court did not provide a different answer based on whether the claim was to be directed against a MS or a third State: ibid 184–5.

or another IO,[12] but also to sustain such countermeasures, to be their object or recipient.[13] This is evident from the fact that the UN has been in practice the target of both protests and international claims. The Organization has thus the capacity to be targeted by countermeasures.[14]

Countermeasures can be taken by States against the Organization by logical necessity. As it has been established thus far, there is no possibility for an objective determination of whether the Organization has perpetrated an international wrong, save in the most exceptional circumstances. In any case, there is no central, compulsory, third-party determination of engagement of responsibility.[15] As such, the issue necessarily rests with the power of auto-interpretation of (Member) States, which is understood to include the power of auto-enforcement.[16] It can only follow that the States (both members and non-members) also retain their power to resort to countermeasures against the Organization in the event of a breach. According to Kelsen, '[s]elf-help cannot be eliminated, nor can it be curtailed until the...question of auto-decision [as to] right or wrong has been disposed of'.[17] Indeed, the centralization of the determination of the existence of a breach and its legal consequences is necessarily prior to the centralization of the application of sanction—whereas there can be centralization of the former without centralization of the latter,[18] the opposite is not true.[19]

Further, there is nothing in the Charter to exclude the possibility of MS taking countermeasures against the Organization. It can, of course, be claimed that the constituent instrument creates a 'self-contained regime', and as such supersedes the general rules on countermeasures as *lex specialis*,[20] at least with respect to MS.[21] However, the general rules of countermeasures provide for an enforcement mechanism that special systems may lack, even if they provide for special secondary rules to complement primary obligations.[22] In such cases, 'fallback' on

---

[12] Ago (n 3) 44 [94] states, in introducing (then) Art 30 (dealing with countermeasures as a circumstance precluding wrongfulness), that IOs can take countermeasures in their own name against a State that has breached an obligation owed to them. See also Meng (n 9) 349–50.

[13] See H Kelsen, *Principles of International Law* (1952) 174. Similarly Wengler (n 9) 142. According to Meng (n 9) 328, the capacity to commit an internationally wrongful act (*Deliktsfähigkeit*), inherent in subjecthood, is meaningless if there are no consequences. cf Art 50(1) DARIO; proposed Art 52(1) DARIO in G Gaja (2008) UN Doc A/CN.4/597 at 17–18 [48]; DC-adopted Art 54(1) in UN Doc A/CN.4/L.725/Add.1 (2008).

[14] ie it has the *Passivlegitimation* or *légitimation passive*. See Gaja (n 13) 15 [41].

[15] See Chapter 4 above.   [16] See Chapter 5.I above.

[17] H Kelsen, *The Legal Process and International Order* (1935) 23. cf H Mosler (1981) 4 HICLR 425, according to whom it is uniform law and its application by the judiciary 'whose highest court in the hierarchy guarantees...enforcement' that primarily converts a 'society' into a 'legal community'.

[18] Witness the system of trade sanctions in the framework of the WTO and its DSU (Art 22) and cf nn 6–7 above. cf also Kelsen (n 17) 20, who points out that it has historically been so.

[19] Witness the incomplete centralization of the use of non-forcible measures under the UNC: whereas States are prohibited from using force except in self-defence under Art 51, they may still resort to countermeasures in parallel to measures taken by the Organization under Art 41. cf Art 49 ARSIWA; Chapter 3 above at nn 45–7.

[20] See Art 55 ARSIWA. cf Gaja (n 13) 15–16 [43]; Meng (n 9) 326.

[21] cf Art 51 DARIO; proposed Art 52(4) DARIO (n 13) 18 [48]; DC-adopted Art 55 in UN Doc A/CN.4/L.743 (2009); UN Doc A/63/10 (2008) 250–1 [130].

[22] B Simma and D Pulkowski (2006) 17 EJIL 507–9.

the general international law of countermeasures is admissible.[23] Since the 'rules of the organization', that is, the UNC, do not explicitly prohibit countermeasures, and since they provide no appropriate means for otherwise inducing compliance of the UN with its obligation of cessation and reparation,[24] the availability of countermeasures by MS against the UN must be affirmed.[25]

II. Disobedience

The survey has so far revealed that the avenues for obtaining an authoritative determination of illegality of SC action are limited at best, and for the time being rather hypothetical. The extra-judicial determination on the part of States is the only avenue that remains, and this has led many to argue that the last resort, the *ultimum refugium* of States is non-compliance with Council decisions that are illegal.[26] In fact this has been argued with reference to illegal acts of other UN organs and of other IOs as well.[27] States and their national administrations are every IO's 'life-supporting system',[28] and it is particularly the SC that relies on MS obedience for the implementation of its normative acts.

The crucial question is how this *ultima ratio* of non-compliance is to be legally qualified. Some have termed it civil disobedience,[29] which probably does not amount to a legal qualification. Others, admittedly more numerous, rely on the construction that an *ultra vires* Council resolution does not command any duty of compliance under Article 25 UNC and can thus be treated as a nullity (as being

---

[23] Ibid 509. cf also Zemanek (n 6) 40–1, who implicitly denies—while discussing the distinction between 'self-contained regimes' and open sub-systems—that the Charter forms such a regime and thus precludes countermeasures; as well as K Doehring (1987) 47 ZaöRV 47.

[24] cf Art 51 DARIO.

[25] cf text at nn 66–7 in Chapter 5.I.2 above.

[26] See eg C Dominicé (1996) 43 RYDI 210; H-P Gasser (1996) 56 ZaöRV 883; E de Wet in eadem and A Nollkaemper (eds), *Review of the SC by MS* (2003) 24 seq; PJG Kapteyn in ibid 62; J Alvarez in ibid 141, according to whom this 'political check' is the 'only real remedy'; A Orakhelashvili (2007) 11 MPUNYB 191–5. See finally Art 51 DARIO; and comments by UNESCO (n 9) 10.

[27] The 'right of last resort' of disobedience has been maintained to exist with respect to all decisions of political organs of the UN: D Ciobanu, *Preliminary Objections* (1975) 173–5; cf *Expenses* [1962] ICJ Rep 232 (diss op Winiarski), who finds that this resort is 'exceptional' but nonetheless 'inevitable' for lack of third-party determination, and 'recognized as such by general international law'; and 304 (diss op Bustamante), according to whom

> the conditional link between the duty to accept institutional decisions and the conformity of those decisions with the Charter...lays down a fundamental basic rule which is generally applicable to the whole system of the Charter.

The last resort of disobedience has also been considered (but then rejected) as a general right of States participating in IOs by E Osieke (1979) 28 ICLQ 25. But see *Interpretation of Agreement* [1980] ICJ Rep 104 (sep op Gros), who finds that 'the practice of international organizations has shown that recourse is had in such circumstances [of an unlawful act of an IO] to a refusal to carry out such act'. See also LM Hinojosa Martínez (2008) 57 ICLQ 355.

[28] For the expression see R Sadurska and CM Chinkin (1990) 30 VaJIL 888.

[29] See T Kalala (1999) 32 RBDI 545, who admittedly uses the term only in the title and then proceeds for the most part to examine traditional legal justifications of disobedience; and cf ND White (2004) 75 BYIL 382.

invalid) by States.[30] It is the purpose of this section to determine whether this disobedience rather constitutes a countermeasure against the IO.

1. Disobedience as civil disobedience

Even before attempting to define the term 'civil disobedience' in order to examine whether non-compliance with Council measures can be properly qualified as such, one must face the rather more pressing objection that civil disobedience is a concept that emerges with respect to actions of citizens within a State, and constitutes a form of protest against the exercise of State power.[31] Already at this stage the parallels with State disobedience of Council measures seem to break down. The UN is not a State, let alone a super-State,[32] and States themselves are sovereign, not subject to any other sovereign. This is at least what the traditional doctrine of international law teaches.

Still, pragmatically, the SC wields enormous, vaguely limited, and ill-controlled power under Chapter VII.[33] It has been likened to the Leviathan in this respect.[34] The Council addresses its orders to States, whether to implement or to endure, in a similar way as the State addresses its orders to those under its jurisdiction. And it has been noted that 'in times of danger—or of terror—public powers insist on unconditional obedience'.[35] There can be little doubt that (many think) we live in such times. At least schematically, there is enough to call for a more thorough examination of whether this concept of 'civil disobedience', originally developed within the State, may find any useful application in the relationship between the UN and its MS.

i. The term 'civil disobedience'

Civil disobedience is not a *terminus technicus*, in any event not in international law. It is rather a political term, and a controversial one at that, which resists easy classification and definition.[36] It has been employed mainly in, or rather *around*, domestic law, in order to signify a deliberate, open (public), violation of any law that protects or allows injustice.[37] In this sense, it constitutes a particular form of

---

[30] See Section II.2 below.

[31] See J Rawls, *A Theory of Justice* (1991) 319. According to another definition, civil disobedience is the last resort of 'society' against the 'State': cf MJ Falcón y Tella *Civil Disobedience* (2004) xxvii.

[32] *Reparation* (n 9) 179. But see I Brownlie in *Honour McMahon* (1974) 26.

[33] See Chapters 1, 3, and 4 above, respectively.

[34] M Koskenniemi (1995) 6 EJIL 326. But see B Fassbender (2000) 11 EJIL 220.

[35] M Koskenniemi in Falcón y Tella (n 31) xv.

[36] K Johnson (1979) 12 ARSP-Beiheft 33.

[37] See eg NW Puner (1968) 43 NYULR 651–2. cf the definition by Rawls (n 31) 320: 'a public, nonviolent, conscientious yet political act contrary to law usually done with the aim of bringing about a change in the law or policies of the government', closely following HA Bedau (1961) 58 Journal of Philosophy 661. The approach of Lord Hoffmann in *R v Jones* [2006] UKHL 16 at [89] affirms the most important elements of this definition.

protest by individuals against the conduct of the State.[38] In attempting to establish the general scope of the notion of 'civil disobedience', it is useful to limit the discussion to the 'lowest common denominator' of all the relevant properties of the term identified by the literature, before applying it to reactions against SC decisions.

Disobedience is located within a spectrum of (politically motivated) resistance,[39] as a reaction against illegitimate concentration of power and/or against arbitrariness, which ranges from simple protest to disobedience to revolution to terrorism.[40] Its first important trait is that it presupposes some form of constitutional order or framework, in which to take place.[41] This is implied in the fact that civil disobedience has not been discussed *in abstracto*, but as a reaction to the exercise of State power, and within a particular State at that. The existence of a constitutional order *lato sensu*, in the sense of an order allocating powers to particular organs and commanding obedience to (or compliance with) their decisions is thus the first, presupposed, requirement for qualifying non-compliance with a legal obligation as civil disobedience.

Protest, located at one extreme of the 'dissenter's spectrum', is not in itself unlawful, if it is followed by obedience.[42] Another important property of civil disobedience then is that it must be unlawful; it must amount to the breach of a legal obligation.[43] This is evident, because valid law necessarily commands obedience: a norm *ought* to be observed, and when not observed it *ought* to be applied.[44] However, it is not required that the civilly disobedient breach the same law that is being protested.[45] In any case, what is important is that civil disobedience is unlawful because there is no legal rule that allows for—or justifies—the violation of the rule disobeyed by the civilly disobedient.[46] In fact, this is the most important property of the notion, the qualitative difference that sets apart civil disobedience from other, milder forms of protest.

Whereas the property of civil disobedience as action in violation of the law is not in dispute, it is closely connected with other relevant considerations, such as whether the illegality need be only prima facie illegality, or whether the act must be *finally* illegal.[47] This distinction is important: some actions of disobedience aim

---

[38] See T Laker, *Ziviler Ungehorsam* (1986) 161.

[39] The words 'political motivation' are in parentheses because any conscious reaction or act of resistance to authority is ostensibly *lato sensu* politically motivated.

[40] K Roth in idem and B Ladwig, *Recht auf Widerstand?* (2006) 8–9.

[41] cf Rawls (n 31) 319; MJ Falcón y Tella (2002) 13 FYIL 25; J Raz, *The Authority of Law* (1979) 263.

[42] HA Bedau in idem (ed), *Civil Disobedience in Focus* (1991) 5.

[43] See Bedau (n 37) 653–4; Puner (n 37) 651–2; Rawls (n 31) 336; Laker (n 38) 162; Falcón y Tella (n 41) 22; B Ladwig in Roth and Ladwig (n 40) 60–1.

[44] H Kelsen, *Allgemeine Theorie der Normen* (1979) 3.

[45] Bedau (n 37) 657; Puner (n 37) 653–5; Rawls (n 31) 320; Laker (n 38) 164–5. This is because the protested law or act of government cannot be disobeyed, if it is not addressed to the disobedient—see eg *R v Jones* (n 37).

[46] Falcón y Tella (n 41) 21.

[47] See Laker (n 38) 163 seq. This is particularly so in civil law systems, which distinguish between the *Tatbestandserfüllung* and *Rechtswidrigkeit*, but is also not unknown in international law, where an act is prima facie internationally wrongful where conduct attributable to a subject constitutes

at having the protested law or act reviewed in court.[48] If the court finds the law unconstitutional or invalid, or the act illegal, then no real disobedience has taken place;[49] or a circumstance precluding wrongfulness of disobedience may apply.[50] Many authors consider these to be acts of civil disobedience nonetheless.[51] Further, if civil disobedience is necessarily unlawful, the issue of its justification belongs to the realm of the extra-legal (or *para*-legal according to some).[52] Only moral justifications are available for civil disobedience,[53] with the subjectivity that such an enquiry necessarily brings.[54]

Whereas all other properties of the term are generally accepted, as is apparent from the definition, their precise scope is to some extent disputed. Disobedience needs to be open and public, as this highlights its communicative character as a form of protest and appeal to the authorities; but it may also take place in hiding under certain circumstances.[55] The public character of the act of disobedience is usually accompanied by voluntary submission to sanction in the sense that the authorities can react to the reaction; but this need not always be the case.[56] Disobedience is generally non-violent or peaceful, but some consider it may even evolve to a full-scale rebellion.[57] As it is not the object of this work to define the exact contours of the scope of civil disobedience, but rather to use it as an explicative tool of State reactions to SC measures, these properties should be treated as established and discussed only in view of examples.

Finally, civil disobedience is always portrayed as a last resort—no other means of redress must exist, or if it does, it must have proved of no avail.[58] This serves as the connecting point with the application of the notion in the context of SC action. The last resort of States against binding measures of the Council is, as is widely held,[59] non-compliance. Could this be qualified as 'civil disobedience'?

---

a breach of its international obligations, but the wrongfulness of the act is *precluded* in specific circumstances.

[48] *R v Jones* (n 37) serves again as a pertinent example. See particularly the comments by Lord Hoffmann at [90] seq.

[49] See eg *Wright v Georgia* 373 US 284 (1963) and its discussion in Puner (n 37) 674–6.

[50] This was the claim in *R v Jones* (n 37) [2] (Lord Bingham).

[51] Laker (n 38) 164; Puner (n 37) 663 seq.   [52] See Falcón y Tella (n 41) 30.

[53] eg Rawls (n 31) 337 seq; R Dworkin, *Taking Rights Seriously* (1978) 217–19. Lord Hoffmann stated in *R v Jones* (n 37) [89] that those who practice civil disobedience do it to 'affirm their *belief in the injustice* of a law or government action' [emphasis added].

[54] However, it is important to note that sometimes acts of civil disobedience are justified not on the basis of the 'unjust', but rather the *illegal* character of the law or act protested. They are, however, cast into the realm of the extra-legal, because their legal justification refers not to domestic, but rather to international, law. See generally *R v Jones* (n 37) [10], where the appellants sought to justify their actions on the basis of 'reasonable force to prevent the commission of a crime', the crime being the crime of aggression under international law. cf also N Chomsky in idem, *For Reasons of State* (1973) 75–6, on civil disobedience 'against the waging of an illegal war' (in Indochina).

[55] See eg K Greenawalt, *Conflicts of Law and Morality* (1989) 239.

[56] See eg Raz (n 41) 265.   [57] See generally Laker (n 38) 173 seq.

[58] See Falcón y Tella (n 31) 7; Greenawalt (n 55) 229; Rawls (n 31) 327; WS Coffin and MI Leibman *Civil Disobedience* (1972) 45.

[59] See n 26 above and accompanying text.

ii. Application in the context of Security Council binding action

In international law, the term 'civil disobedience' has been used to describe refusal to comply with binding SC decisions on at least one occasion.[60] But the question is why spend time considering this qualification—after all, it may only have been a figure of speech, a literary *modicum* to draw attention to the relevant discussion. It is not, however. Civil disobedience comes into play, because Council action is not simply conduct that is susceptible of being in violation of the law. It is also *normative* conduct that establishes obligations for States under Article 25 UNC. In one way or another, it makes law binding on them.[61] And where law is made, the question of disobedience of that law is bound to arise. One could argue that the concept is congruent with the nature of the relations of MS toward the Organization. This relationship is more akin to the one between the citizen and the State,[62] than between two subjects of international law on the same level, precisely because of the normative power exercised by the Council upon MS.[63]

The first step for the application of the notion is to establish the existence of a constitutional framework. Many a time the UNC has been likened to a domestic constitution, or at least has been considered as setting up a constitutional framework for the UN membership, if not for the international community, ill-defined as it is.[64] The discussion on the control of constitutionality of SCRs can be seen as a consequence of this parallelism.[65] The characterization of non-compliance with SCRs as 'civil disobedience' is another such offshoot of a constitutional approach. For present purposes, it need only be accepted that the Charter sets up

[60] See Kalala (n 29) 545, as well as text in the same note. At the same time, the press reported diplomats in the UN describing the 1998 OAU action as an 'enormous act of civil disobedience': C Turner, 'Security Council Frustrated, Divided', *Seattle Times*, 26 November 1998. Alvarez (n 26) 141 uses the term 'political act of defiance', which at least comes close to what is generally understood under 'civil disobedience'. cf finally J Crawford (2006) 319 RdC 383 who writes that rights conferred upon MS by the Charter cannot be vindicated against the SC or the GA 'by means other than persuasion or by *civil, or uncivil, disobedience*' [emphasis added].

[61] 'Law' being understood in the present instance as a norm that commands obedience, whether it refers to a specific case or to an unlimited number of cases, whether it is limited in time and/or space or not, and whether it is addressed to a specific subject or an unlimited number of subjects. See, with respect to whether a binding SCR creates 'law' or merely international obligations R Higgins (1970) 64 ASILProc 43–4, 45.

[62] See E Zoller (1987) 81 AJIL 625; E de Wet, *The Chapter VII Powers* (2004) 91. In this one could refer to the distinction between civil law and public law, the former being (decreasingly, but still in principle) law between equals, the latter law between unequals: see G Morange in *Honneur Scelle*, vol 2 (1950) 900.

[63] As H Kelsen, *Law of the UN* (1950) 280 pertinently stated '[MS] are *subordinated* to the [SC]' [emphasis added]. cf Dominicé (n 26) 198, who notes the 'vertical' relationship of authority and subordination between MS and the Organization.

[64] See generally J Crawford in H Fox (ed), *The Changing Constitution of the UN* (1997) 3; P-M Dupuy (1997) 1 MPUNYB 1; B Fassbender (1998) 36 CJTL 529; idem, *The UNC as the Constitution of the International Community* (2009); TM Franck in *Festschrift Eitel* (2003) 95; S Szurek in *Charte Commentaire* (2005) 29; RSJ Macdonald in idem and Johnston (eds), *Towards World Constitutionalism* (2005) 853; E de Wet (2006) 55 ICLQ 51. There are even claims that the 'constitution' is not simply the Charter, but it includes also the constitutive instruments of other Specialized Agencies in the UN system: ND White in NM Blokker and HG Schermers (eds), *Proliferation of IOs* (2001) 96–100.

[65] See Chapter 4.III above.

a constitutional framework for the Organization and its membership,[66] at least *lato sensu*,[67] in that it confers certain powers on the Organization, allocates them to its organs, and obliges the members to comply with specific decisions by these organs.[68]

The main properties of civil disobedience should then be tested against examples of open and principled disobedience of Council sanctions by States. Faced with the obligation to impose and maintain sanctions on Libya, the 53 MS of the (then) OAU condemned, through the Organization, the 'unjust' sanctions and repeatedly pleaded for their reconsideration,[69] before eventually deciding to disobey them.[70] In acting thus they publicly proclaimed their decision to disobey, and they could also be presumed as having voluntarily accepted the potential sanctions for such conduct, as nothing could stop the Council from reacting to their disobedience.[71] Further, they did not employ any forcible means, and in that their disobedience was peaceful.

Similarly, the OIC MS proclaimed, through the Organization, that the arms embargo on the former Yugoslavia imposed by the SC was illegal as far as it impeded Bosnia and Herzegovina's right of self-defence:[72] they thus called upon all UN MS to disobey the embargo as regards Bosnia.[73]

There is an argument to be made that civil disobedience (and other forms of resistance) is a way for the right-holders to remind the political units to which they are subject of their rights.[74] If this is so, the terms are broad enough to accommodate as right-holders both States *and* citizens, and as superimposed political units both IOs *and* States.[75] The concept so far seems not only applicable, but very inviting indeed—there is an element of attraction in characterizing MS disobedience of

---

[66] cf *Milutinović et al* (Motion Challenging Jurisdiction) IT-99-37-PT (6 May 2003) [62].

[67] Or in the 'weak' sense: see Crawford (n 64) 8; idem (n 60) 372.

[68] cf M Happold (2003) 16 LJIL 595; J Rideau, *Juridictions internationales et contrôle du respect des traités constitutifs* (1969) 4–11, 21–33.

[69] See CM/Res.1566 (LXI) (23–27 January 1995). The Council of Ministers expresses, in the 8th preamb, its great concern 'about the human and material damage [the Libyan people] ... are suffering as a result of the *unjust* sanctions imposed on Libya pursuant to [SCRs] 748 (1992) and 883 (1993)' [emphasis added]. In its 6th operative clause the resolution reiterates an appeal to the Council to reconsider the relevant resolutions imposing sanctions, after having considered, in the 2nd operative clause, the threat to impose further sanctions as 'a method in dealing with other States in violation of the Charters of the OAU and the UN, as well as international laws and standards'. On civil disobedience as an appeal or a plea for reconsideration see: Bedau (n 42) 6–7; Rawls (n 31) 339; and generally P Singer in Bedau (n 42) 122.

[70] AHG/Dec.127 (XXXIV) (8–10 June 1998) [2].

[71] See Kalala (n 29) 572–4. Significantly, in the preamble to SCR 269 (1969) the Council clearly stated that it is '[m]indful of its responsibility *to take necessary action to secure strict compliance* with the obligations entered into by [MS] ... under ... Article 25 [UNC]', ie the obligation to 'accept and carry out' Council decisions [emphasis added].

[72] Res No 6/22-P (10–12 December 1994) [7]; cf Res No 7/21-P (25–29 April 1993) 12th preamb; Res No 6/23-P (9–12 December 1995) [12]–[15]. See also OIC Heads of State and Government Declaration on Bosnia and Herzegovina at Seventh Islamic Summit Conference (13, 15 December 1994) [4].

[73] Res Nos 7/21-P (n 72) [12]; 6/22-P (n 72) [5]–[6]; 6/23-P (n 72) [13]; Summit Declaration (n 72) [1].

[74] cf T Honoré (1988) 8 OJLS 39.   [75] Ibid 36 at fn 7.

SCRs as civil disobedience. Inviting as it may be, however, the application of the concept calls for the consideration of its most central property: that of illegality of the act of disobedience.

There is no doubt that, under Article 25 UNC, States have agreed to 'accept and carry out the decisions of the [SC]'. As such they are under an obligation, at least prima facie, to comply with SCRs under Article 41. The crucial question, however, is whether States can disobey such a decision and rely on some legal justification for their conduct. If this is possible, then there is no illegal conduct on their part. As such, no issue of civil disobedience, justifiable on purely extra-legal, moral grounds, can arise. Acts of civil disobedience must be necessarily illegal; otherwise one is faced with the oxymoron of a 'legal illegality'.[76]

In a highly centralized, domestic legal order, acts of disobedience that are prima facie illegal will find their way to court, which will decide whether the protested law or act is unlawful, and thus there was no disobedience (for one cannot disobey an unlawful act, which is either invalid or at least non-applicable in the circumstances); or they will determine whether the wrongfulness of the act of the disobedient is precluded on some legal grounds.[77] In that, domestic courts will decide on the limits of self-help.[78]

Before finally determining whether non-compliance with binding SCRs constitutes 'civil disobedience' on the part of States towards the Organization, it must be examined whether Article 25 allows for non-compliance with decisions in certain cases (Subsection 2); or alternatively whether the wrongfulness of non-compliance is legally precluded—that is, the question of the availability and limits of self-help must be broached (Subsection 3). Only if these questions are answered in the negative is a discussion of the possibility of civil disobedience to resume—but in a philosophical or political, rather than a legal context. This is because civil disobedience is a breach of law, but a *morally justifiable* breach, perhaps; it is not a reaction within the legal framework. But first, the potential legal justifications for disobedience must be dispensed with.

---

[76] cf Laker (n 38) 163.

[77] See text at n 47 above. Significantly, in some domestic legal orders, there exists a normatively consecrated 'right of resistance'. Art 20(4) of the German Constitution provides for such a right of last resort against anyone 'seeking to abolish [the] constitutional order'. This is a supra-positive right, which has been codified in positive law: among others F Klein in B Schmidt-Bleibtreu and F Klein, *Kommentar zum Grundgesetz* (1980) 404 [21]. It is an exceptional right, to be exercised in anomalous circumstances: R Herzog in T Maunz and G Dürig (eds), *Grundgesetz Kommentar*, vol 3 (2007) 20–328 [5]. Because of its exceptional character it will normally not cover acts of civil disobedience, except perhaps in extreme cases: cf R Gröschner in H Dreier (ed), *Grundgesetz—Kommentar*, vol 2 (1998) 218 [17]; M Sachs in idem (ed), *Grundgesetz Kommentar* (1999) 798 [169] with references to case law of the BVerfG. Art 120(4), the very final clause of the Greek Constitution, provides that the

> Observance of the Constitution is entrusted to the patriotism of the Greeks who shall have the right *and the duty* to resist *by all possible means* against anyone who attempts the violent abolition of the Constitution. [emphasis added]

See also Portuguese Constitution Art 21; Lithuanian Constitution Art 3; Slovakian Constitution Art 32. On the relevant constitutional provisions in African States see DA Mindaoudou (1995) 7 RADIC 417.

[78] See *R v Jones* (n 37) [70] seq (Lord Hoffmann).

2. Disobedience as allowed under Article 25 UNC

Non-compliance with (or disobedience to) SC binding non-forcible measures has been legally justified as flowing from the fact that a resolution that is *ultra vires* does not command a duty of compliance under Article 25 UNC.[79] This is what Judge Bustamante called, in his dissent in *Expenses*, the 'conditional link' between obedience of States to institutional decisions and the compliance of those decisions with the terms of the Charter.[80] This conditional link is 'enshrined' in Article 25.[81] As such, States are under no obligation to comply with, which is to say that they are free to disobey, a decision that is not in conformity with the Charter. Non-compliance in such a case is alleged not to constitute a breach of obligation—it is non-compliance *allowed* by the Charter; thus *allowed* by international law. Even more so, non-compliance can be seen as *imposed* by international law, if compliance with the decision would lead to the violation of rights of another MS under international law.[82]

i. Article 25 as an 'open licence' for disobedience

There are numerous problems with asserting that UN MS are under no obligation to comply with SCRs that are not in conformity with the Charter. The basic argument is found in the provision of Article 25, and this is where the problems start. For one, not everyone agrees that Article 25 UNC is 'an open licence for [MS] to judge for themselves' whether SCRs are in conformity with the Charter.[83] In fact, it is precisely whether the phrase 'in accordance with the present Charter' grants such an open licence that constitutes the 'essential problem' in the interpretation of Article 25.[84]

Article 25 provides that UN MS 'agree to accept and carry out the decisions of the Security Council *in accordance with the…Charter*'.[85] The exact scope of this obligation to accept and carry out Council decisions is the matter of controversy, in view of the qualification posited by the closing phrase of the provision. Some consider that the qualification refers to the *way* in which States are to accept and carry out the Council's decisions, while others see it as qualifying the *decisions* of the Council, which States agree to 'accept and carry out'.

With regard to the first reading of the provision, it is not quite clear how it makes for a meaningful construction of Article 25. Arguably, the qualification of the last phrase of the provision is to define the *manner* in which States must

---

[79] Text at nn 39–44 in Chapter 3 above. Also T Schilling (1995) 33 AVR 96; D Akande (1997) 46 ICLQ 333–5; de Wet (n 26) 25–7; eadem (n 62) 375 seq; M Herdegen in de Wet and Nollkaemper (n 26) 80; DH Joyner (2007) 20 LJIL 512–15; K Parameswaran (2008) 46 AVR 187–9; cf UN Doc A/CN.4/L.682 (2006) 169 [331].

[80] (n 27) 304.   [81] Ibid.

[82] See W Wengler (1957) 47-I AIDI 22–3.

[83] See Alvarez (n 26) 125. Even proponents of the interpretation of Art 25 as allowing non-compliance with the *ultra vires* decisions reserve the point of auto-determination: Akande (n 79) 335–6.

[84] J Delbrück in *Charter Commentary* (2002) 459 [17].

[85] Emphasis added.

implement their obligation to accept and carry out the decisions of the Council.[86] But in *which manner* could States possibly carry out these decisions *other than* in accordance with the Charter? If the final phrase of the provision is to be understood as imposing an effective limitation on the margin of discretion of States, one would have to assume that a State could theoretically be allowed under Article 25 to carry out a decision of the Council through means or in a way that otherwise violates the Charter. This leads to an *absurdum*. A State could not be allowed to comply with a decision of the Organization while at the same time violating other assumed obligations under the same Organization's Charter. One is thus forced to accept that, under this construction, the qualification in Article 25 is to be reduced to redundancy.[87] It merely states the self-evident: States, in complying with Council decisions, must also respect and apply the other provisions of the Charter. This cannot be accepted if another reading of the provision would vest it with an *effet utile*.

The other possible construction of Article 25 is that the last phrase qualifies the decisions of the Council that are to be complied with. Because of the double meaning of the word 'decision' in the Charter, which may refer to either a resolution of the Council in general, including a resolution in the nature of a recommendation, or a decision properly so called, the final phrase in Article 25 can be read as meaning that only those decisions of the Council which are vested with binding force under other provisions of the Charter are to be accepted and carried out by MS.[88] In fact, the relevant provision was redrafted in San Francisco precisely to clarify this point,[89] while *Namibia* also lends support to this interpretation.[90]

This reading of Article 25 is extended by some to the effect of delimiting the scope of the obligation under Article 25: only those decisions taken in accordance with the Charter, namely *intra vires* decisions, are to be accepted and carried out.[91] *Ultra vires* decisions, conversely, can lay no claim to binding force. States have specifically agreed to carry out only those decisions that are in accordance with the Charter. This may seem trite; it would make little sense if States agreed to be bound by decisions that are *not* in accordance with the Charter.

---

[86] E Suy and N Angelet in *Charte Commentaire* (2005) 917. In that, the last phrase refers to the 'modalities of execution'.

[87] According to ibid, the *effet utile* of such a construction is the implicit *renvoi* to Arts 48–9 and 103. This *renvoi*, however, is redundant, as these provisions would apply in any case when the conditions for their application are met. Further, it is also possibly erroneous, given that Arts 48–9 constitute a 'specification' of the obligation under Art 25 with respect to decisions taken under Arts 41–2 *only*. But Art 25 has been accepted to apply to decisions taken outside Chapter VII, even if in exceptional circumstances. See Kelsen (n 63) 97–8.

[88] See M Krökel, *Die Bindungswirkung von Resolutionen des Sicherheitsrates* (1977) 163; Delbrück (n 84) 458 [14]; D Schweigman, *The Authority of the SC* (2001) 33. cf Kelsen (n 63) 95–6, 293.

[89] See LM Goodrich et al, *UNC* (1969) 208; R Higgins (1972) 21 ICLQ 278.

[90] [1971] ICJ Rep 53 [114]:

the question whether [Art 25 powers] have in fact been exercised is to be determined in each case, having regard to the terms of the resolution to be interpreted, the discussions leading to it, *the Charter provisions invoked* and, in general, all circumstances that might assist in determining the legal consequences. [emphasis added]

[91] See Delbrück (n 84) 459 [17]; Suy and Angelet (n 86) 916; DW Bowett (1994) 5 EJIL 92.

Such a construction is not so self-evident, however. It is arguable that Article 25 establishes the binding force of *all* decisions of the Council that are adopted with an intention to bind MS purportedly under a Charter provision that allows for binding action. One reason for this, apart from extrapolation from practice,[92] would be that a constitutional system cannot operate unless there is some final instance, promulgating orders or undertaking acts with which all the addressees must comply, irrespective of the lawfulness of the order or act, and for as long as the order or act is not repealed by a contrary act (*actus contrarius*).[93] As such, every action of that final authority which cannot be challenged through some established procedure continues to produce binding force *erga omnes*, regardless of its lawfulness.[94]

Again, this leads one to stumble upon the characterization of the UN legal order as a constitutional order. There are many different levels of 'constitutionalization' of a legal order, and powerful arguments both for and against the UNC establishing such an order. However, the issue quite possibly cannot be resolved through the simple transposition of domestic notions of constitutionality. The Charter was not drafted as a constitution; the effort to construe it as one *ex post facto* only exacerbates the problems. And the truth with respect to Article 25 is that it does not resolve the problem under any interpretation.[95] The question as to the legal effects of resolutions that are not in conformity with the Charter remains to be answered.

ii. *Legal consequences of non-conformity with the Charter*

The basic tenet of the approach advocating that Council decisions must be, under Article 25, 'in accordance with the Charter' in order to acquire binding force and create obligations for MS, is that resolutions adopted in excess of Council powers are invalid. In other words, *ultra vires* resolutions produce no legal effects and they cannot bind States. However, there is no special provision in the Charter regulating the legal effects of such acts,[96] Article 25 notwithstanding.

The major problem that has to be dealt with is the notion of 'invalidity' and its relationship to that of 'illegality'. Under general international law, not all illegal acts are necessarily invalid: for example a domestic statute in breach of an international obligation is not invalid, and neither is a domestic court decision that results in a breach. On the other hand, not all acts that are invalid are also necessarily illegal. In the law of treaties, for example, a treaty may be null and void on account of error, in which case there is no wrongful act on the part of any subject.[97] Further,

---

[92] See text at nn 127–9 below.   [93] See K Doehring (1997) 1 MPUNYB 93.

[94] Ibid 94–6; significantly, even the decision of a constitutional court may be such an unchallengeable action which produces binding force *ad nauseam*.

[95] cf Suy and Angelet (n 86) 917; according to Doehring (n 93) 100, the founders of the UN 'did not reflect enough on the possibilities to avoid [the] unacceptable effect' of States being bound by unlawful SCRs.

[96] cf E Lauterpacht in *Honour McNair* (1965) 99–100; Happold (n 68) 609.

[97] See Art 48 VCLT. In its commentary to Draft Art 65 on the Law of Treaties, dealing with the consequences of invalidity of a treaty, the Commission concedes that there may be cases in which

according to Lauterpacht '[n]o rule of international law forbids *governments* to perform acts ... which are incapable of producing legal effects'.[98]

In the case of SC acts, only acts that are in violation of the Charter, and at that are *ultra vires* and illegal (of which a sub-species is the *ultra vires* act),[99] could be considered also as being invalid. This is because we are not situated in the context of general international law, but rather in the context of a special system of law that lays down specific procedures to achieve a legal end while at the same time it defines the limits and purposes of powers conferred on an entity.[100] In such a case 'to say that action outside the limits expressed by the rule is a nullity seems to be no more than another way of expressing the rule itself'.[101]

This means that generally invalidity is a mere *consequence* of illegality in certain circumstances; while in others it is postulated without the invalid act being illegal at the same time.[102] In the case of SCRs, however, allegedly or potentially invalid acts will at the same time necessarily be illegal acts, as they will be in violation of the Charter.[103] It must thus be examined whether decisions that are in violation of the Charter, and at that illegal,[104] are indeed sanctioned by invalidity, and under which circumstances.

It is hardly settled in international law what a normative act being invalid signifies with respect to its legal effects.[105] The terminological confusion that accompanies the relevant discussions is great, and it is due in part to the wholesale transposition of concepts from domestic legal systems.[106] If something is 'invalid' in law, if it has no validity, it can produce no legal effects. However, at least in domestic law, not all acts that are tainted by one or the other procedural or substantive irregularity or defect are simply invalid. Some are inexistent—the irregularity is so overwhelming that the act fails even to materialize in the legal order. Others are null and void, or 'invalid' properly so called. They exist but produce no legal effect.[107] Others still

---

'neither party [is] to be considered a wrong-doer with respect to the cause of nullity', error being one of them. Special consequences are provided for such cases. See (1966) II YILC 265 [3].

[98] *Interhandel* [1959] ICJ Rep 118 (diss op) [emphasis added].

[99] A UN act is unlawful or illegal when it violates the Charter, in which case it is designated as *ultra vires*, or when it violates general international law, in which case it is *intra vires*, but may still be illegal: see Chapter 3.III above. This is evident in the following statement of Skubiszewski in his dissent in *East Timor* [1995] ICJ Rep 251 [86]: 'The Court is competent to make findings on [the] lawfulness [of resolutions of the Organization], *in particular* whether they were *intra vires*' [emphasis added].

[100] RY Jennings in *Honour McNair* (1965) 81.   [101] Ibid.

[102] cf V Gowlland-Debbas, *Collective Responses* (1990) 201.

[103] Even proponents of the aforementioned interpretative approach to Art 25 make the relevant concession: see Herdegen (n 79) 80.

[104] Legality presupposes binding law, which in the case of IOs is their constitutive instrument: see generally F Morgenstern (1976–7) 48 BYIL 241 seq.

[105] 'Normative' act is meant here as a 'juridical' act (*acte juridique*, *Rechtsakt*), ie an act that constitutes the manifestation of will of the Organization and produces legal effects, and not solely an act that establishes an obligation. See C Dominicé in R-J Dupuy (ed), *Manuel sur les organisations internationales* (1998) 442; cf J Verzijl (1935) 15 RDI 289.

[106] See P Weil (1992) 237 RdC 319; P Cahier (1972) 76 RGDIP 646.

[107] Also sometimes called 'absolute' nullity. Such acts are deprived of legal effect *ex tunc*, ie from the point of their inception, automatically.

are voidable: they exist and produce legal effect, but may be voided by a competent organ. At that point they cease to exist altogether.[108]

To some extent, the same, or similar, distinctions can theoretically be drawn in international law.[109] With respect to IOs, and in particular the UN and the actions of its principal organs, similar distinctions have indeed been advocated.[110] It has been claimed that the *ultra vires* act of a UN principal organ has no power to produce any legal effect because it is null and void.[111] It can also be claimed to be not void, but rather voidable, which means that it will produce no legal effect from the point onwards when it is voided by a competent organ;[112] up until that point, however, it will be operating and producing its intended legal effect. Finally, it is contended that the *ultra vires* or otherwise illegal act is always valid and produces legal effect for lack of an instance of review.[113]

It is beyond the scope of this study to produce a theory of nullity and its legal effect in the context of international institutional law, much less so in the context of general international law. In fact it can be claimed that this is simply impossible, as there are *theories* of nullity in international law, based on specific provisions within partial legal systems or specialized areas of the law, but no general *theory* of nullity.[114] Focusing, however, on the legal effects of acts allegedly in violation of the Charter, it still seems quite difficult to come up with any coherent results.[115]

For one, the ICJ has never found an act of a principal organ to be in violation of the Charter, and it may be doubted if it will ever do so in practice.[116] Still, in the only cases where it found acts by organs of other organizations in the UN system to be outside the scope or in violation of their constitutive instruments, it did nothing to clarify the legal effect of these acts—particularly since it was not really asked to.[117] The Court could be seen as having connected the conformity

---

[108] Also sometimes called 'relative' nullity. Such acts are deprived of legal effect *ex nunc*, ie after they have been invalidated.

[109] See Jennings (n 100) 66–7 and *passim*. cf P Guggenheim (1949) 74 RdC 213; JA Frowein in *EPIL*, vol 3 (1997) 743–4; Morange (n 62) 901 seq.

[110] See eg the discussion in the (then) IMCO in Lauterpacht (n 96) 102–6, where all possible legal effects of an act not in conformity with the constitutive instrument were advocated, with an amalgam of legal effects of different kinds of invalid acts being finally adopted by the Organization.

[111] See eg *Expenses* (n 27) 232 (diss op Winiarski), arguing for nullity.

[112] See specifically with respect to the Council, M Herdegen in *Festschrift Bernhardt* (1995) 118–19 and cf Akande (n 79) 334.

[113] See eg *Expenses* (n 27) 224 [9 *in fine*] (sep op Morelli).

[114] Weil (n 106) 320. cf E Osieke (1976–7) 48 BYIL 262; R Bernhardt in *Honour Skubiszewski* (1996) 602.

[115] cf Lauterpacht (n 96) 115.

[116] This may be yet another piece of evidence to the effect that the international system 'est allergique…à l'idée de ne pas faire crédit aux actes juridiques et à mettre en doute leur validité': Weil (n 106) 319.

[117] In *Nuclear Weapons in Armed Conflict* [1996] ICJ Rep 66, the Court found the request for an AO by the WHO to be outside of the scope of the WHO's functions (at 77–81 [22]–[26]), and then merely denied its jurisdiction to give the opinion (at 84 [31]). In *Constitution of the Maritime Safety Committee* [1960] ICJ Rep 150, the Court found that the Committee of the (then) IMCO was 'not constituted in accordance with the Convention for the Establishment of the Organization' (at 171) but did not elaborate on the legal effects of the finding, which were left for the organization to clarify. cf the second *Competence of the ILO* case, where the PCIJ simply found that the consideration of means of production did not fall within the competence of the ILO. There was in that case no act of

with the constitutive instrument of a decision with its validity, but not in any clear and unambiguous terms.[118]

In an attempt to try and discern whether the Court considers that there is a theory of validity of UN acts, and what the legal consequences of potential invalidity are, attention must turn to the relevant presumptions it has established. These are usually referred to interchangeably as 'presumption of validity' and 'presumption of legality'.[119] But it has been established that validity and legality are not one and the same notion. In fact, a careful reading of the ICJ jurisprudence can be seen to support this view.

In *Expenses*, the Court establishes a presumption that action 'appropriate for the fulfillment of one of the stated purposes' of the UN is *intra vires*.[120] However, this does not clarify what the legal consequences of *ultra vires* action would be. But according to the Court's next finding, an irregularity which belongs to the 'internal' plane of the Organization, though admittedly still rendering the decision *ultra vires*, and—it is submitted—illegal, does not deny it of legal effect,[121] that is, of its validity towards the MS. The Court clearly states that the *ultra vires* act is binding on the *body politic*,[122] which also means that it is binding on MS. This is further corroborated in *Namibia*, where the Court clearly points out that

A resolution of a properly constituted organ of the United Nations which is passed in accordance with that organ's rules of procedure, and *is declared by the President to have been so passed*, must be presumed to have been validly adopted.[123]

The distinction can be described as follows: acts in violation of 'internal rules' of the Organization, even rules regarding the division of powers between organs, are *ultra vires*, but still valid, as they produce binding effects. Acts that are outside the scope of the purposes of the Organization are also *ultra vires*, but the Court does not define their legal consequences. Presumably the point of the distinction is to clarify that these acts which are not covered by the purposes of the Organization will not produce any legal effects, despite having been passed in accordance with the relevant rules of procedure and having been declared to have been so passed.

which the Court was asked to define the legal effects: [1922] PCIJ Ser B No 3 at 59. However, the ICJ in *Jurisdiction of the ICAO Council* [1972] ICJ Rep 70 [45 *in fine*] stated obiter that, had the decision of the Council been outside the scope of its jurisdiction, it 'would have stood *reversed*' [emphasis added], which seems to imply voidability. Still, this is because Art 84 of the Chicago Convention establishes *compulsory* ICJ jurisdiction over relevant matters.

[118] eg in *Namibia* (n 90) 45 [89] the Court states that '[t]he question of the *validity or conformity with the Charter* of [decisions by the GA and the SC] does not form the subject of the request' [emphasis added], but it is not clear whether the two terms are used as being tantamount or alternative to each other.

[119] See eg de Wet (n 62) 58, who refers to the Court having established a presumption of legality and a presumption of validity interchangeably on the same page, and then again in fn 173. cf Lauterpacht (n 96) 117 openly using the two as interchangeable; as well as B Elberling (2005) 2 IOLR 352, who states that according to the 'presumption of *legality*...acts of UN organs are presumed valid' [emphasis added]. In *Bowett's Law of International Institutions* (6th edn, 2009) 297–302 Sands and Klein refer to 'validity' and 'legality' in general as interchangeable terms, as does J Klabbers in *An Introduction to International Institutional Law* (2nd edn, 2009) 213–20.

[120] (n 27) 168.   [121] Ibid.   [122] Ibid.

[123] *Namibia* (n 90) 22 [20] [emphasis added].

Such a reading introduces a tenuous distinction between acts *ultra vires* the organ and acts *ultra vires* the Organization.[124] In other words, it establishes a distinction between acts that are 'a bit' *ultra vires*, and others that are 'very' *ultra vires*. The former are valid and binding, the latter not so. This makes little sense and has rightly been criticized.[125] But another reading is possible. Perhaps the Court is establishing *two* presumptions: one of *validity*, that is virtually *irrebuttable*, and one of *legality*, that is *rebuttable*, if only with great difficulty.[126]

According to the presumption of validity, any act of a UN organ declared by its President or Chairperson to have been validly adopted, is valid,[127] irrespective of other considerations, such as 'internal' irregularities.[128] These irregularities may make the decision *illegal*, but it remains *valid* nonetheless.[129] The presumption is virtually *irrebuttable*,[130] save where someone would be able to show that the

---

[124] See Bernhardt (n 114) 603. The distinction is echoed (without stating any differing legal effects) by the ICTY in *Tadić* (Appeal on Jurisdiction) IT-94-1-AR72 (2 October 1995) [28].

[125] See eg Bernhardt (n 114) 603–4; E Osieke (1983) 77 AJIL 249.

[126] In fact a similar distinction has been drawn in theory, without, however, an elaboration of the differing legal consequences of 'procedural validity' and 'substantive legality': see Akande (n 79) 330–1.

[127] See eg the stress that the UN Legal Counsel lays in making sure that the GA President does not declare valid the ballots that have taken place in violation of Art 19 UNC: [2003] UNJY 526–7; the issue, however, remains the prerogative of the organ: ibid 527–8. Similarly, in going over the meaning of 'consensus' in UN practice, the Office of Legal Affairs stresses that

> the legal status [ie binding force] of a decision *is not affected by the manner in which it is reached*. Once adopted, it has the status of a legally adopted decision. ([1987] UNJY 175 [emphasis added])

cf [1986] UNJY 275: 'Once a legally binding…decision…is validly adopted, it is binding on all [MS]'.

[128] Egypt maintained that SCR 95 (1951) was adopted without having taken into account the Egyptian arguments and without receiving the votes of such States as the USSR, India, and China (which stated in the debate that they were not convinced of the merits of the resolution), implying that it could disregard the decision. The President of the Council, summarizing the debate, made it clear that most States in the Council regarded the resolution as having continuing validity and effect: *Repertory*, supp 1 vol I (1958) 259–60 [8]–[9]. Similarly in *Repertory*, supp 2 vol II (1964) 297 [10] several States expressed the view that SCRs adopted in accordance with Charter procedure are valid and binding until modified by the Council itself (with respect to SCR 91 [1951]).

[129] According to the UN Legal Counsel, even a SC that would be admittedly *illegally constituted* under Art 23 UNC would be viewed by the Office of Legal Affairs as being able of taking *valid decisions*, subject to compliance with Art 27, which would be characterized *in casu* as an implied quorum provision: [1979] UNJY 166 (cf the reiteration with respect to the ECOSOC in [1983] UNJY 183–4). When pressed by Guinea-Bissau to respond as to whether an embargo imposed by such an illegally constituted Council would be a *legal* or *illegal* action, and whether there would be a duty to obey (see UN Doc A/34/PV.118 [1979] 36), Counsel refrained from answering but conceded it was open to MS to challenge the validity of any decision of the Council the membership of which is in contradiction to the Charter (ibid 38). It may be claimed that what the Legal Counsel meant was that the decision was *valid* and producing legal effect, but that MS could still challenge its *legality*. cf E Suy in *Festschrift Schlochauer* (1981) 683; WM Reisman (1980) 74 AJIL 909–10. See finally the distinction in H Kelsen (1952) 4 ÖZöR 267. There is no need for a special procedure to determine the validity of the act of one organ by another organ: the acting organ may decide on the validity of the act itself: ibid 268.

[130] H Thierry (1980) 167 RdC 423 calls it 'une présomption *inconditionnelle*' (but ibid 424: still not '*irréfragable*') [emphasis added].

President did not declare the decision validly adopted.[131] This is because States may raise objections as to the validity of the act within the organ,[132] but the final decision is reserved to the organ itself.[133] Whereas this is so 'in the first instance',[134] given that 'another instance' will be lacking in most cases, the decision produces its intended legal effects.[135] The decision is thus binding on the MS.

According to the presumption of legality, on the other hand, *any* action within the Organization's purposes (extremely broad and virtually all-encompassing as they are) is considered to be *intra vires* and at that legal, since it is presumed to be in conformity with the Charter; but this presumption is *rebuttable*, that is, it is open to a State either to claim that the action was outside the Organization's purposes, or that it suffers from being adopted in violation of some Charter rule.[136] It has already been admitted that this is difficult to achieve, particularly for a State acting in isolation.[137] Still, it is not impossible and should it be managed, the Organization's act would be *ultra vires*, and at that illegal, but still, it is submitted, valid, as having been validly adopted and so declared.

---

[131] This approach in fact may explain why the Court has expressly denied that it 'possess[es] powers of judicial review or appeal in respect of the decisions taken by the [UN] organs concerned' in *Namibia* (n 90) 45 [89], while it still went on to consider the conformity of UN decisions with the Charter. As discussed in Chapter 4.III above, the Court does not expressly have power to annul a decision of a principal organ or declare its invalidity with binding *erga omnes* effect. As such, it cannot decide on the validity of a GA or SC decision—it must always presume it irrebuttably. Still, that does not mean that it cannot decide whether it is in compliance with the Charter. If it is not, the decision is still valid, but there is a strong argument that it is illegal. cf KH Kaikobad (1996) 17 AYIL 138–9.

Perhaps another possible rebuttal to the presumption of validity could be to show that the Organization's act is *ultra vires* the Organization, ie completely outside the scope of its virtually all-encompassing purposes. In that case the act would arguably be inexistent, marred by such a huge defect that it fails to materialize in the (UN) legal order. The possibility of something like this happening seems merely theoretical, and in that confirms the *virtually irrebuttable* nature of the presumption of validity.

[132] See Ciobanu (n 27) 62 seq, particularly 72 seq.

[133] Ibid 163 seq; cf Amerasinghe, *Principles of the Institutional Law of IOs* (2nd edn, 2005) 203–6. cf the UN Legal Counsel in [1984] UNJY 168 [4]; and in [1980] UNJY 187–8 [4]; and the Director of the WHO Legal Division in [1979] UNJY 199–200. The organ may, of course, request legal advice on the matter from the UN Legal Counsel, as eg in ibid; [1983] UNJY 171–2; [1982] UNJY 159–60.

[134] See *Expenses* (n 27) 203 (sep op Fitzmaurice).

[135] Fitzmaurice, while accepting the lack of a compulsory instance (ibid 202), finds the view of an irrebuttable presumption of validity to be 'too extreme' and does not consider that this is what the Court says in the Opinion (ibid 204). However, he does not offer any solution or guidance as to what might a 'second instance' be. Rather he denies the irrebuttable presumption on the basis that then the Organization would be able to do 'almost anything' unrestrained (ibid). But this is not a necessary consequence. In any case, this leads again to the discussion about a purported 'right' of last resort (disobedience, here in the form of non-payment) (ibid 205).

[136] In this sense, it would be valuable to recall an argument by B Conforti (1969) 63 AJIL 479–9: while rejecting the parliamentary doctrine of non-control over compliance with rules of procedure, considered as *interna corporis* in most jurisdictions, he distinguishes between minor violations of procedural rules for reasons of expedience, and those procedural rules the violation of which results in a denial of the right to participate in the organ's work, or to be heard, or to vote. Such violations constitute at the same time violations of Art 2(1) UNC and render the decision of the organ illegal (484–5). Putting this within the scheme here presented, the decision would be valid, as so declared by the president of the organ, but illegal as in violation of a Charter provision.

[137] See Chapter 5.I.2 above.

We must avoid the assumption that every action of the UN that is apparently *ultra vires* must be affected by some kind of nullity.[138] In accordance with the two (distinct) presumptions, *all* acts of the Organization are valid, if declared to be so by the deciding organ, even if they are *ultra vires*; also *all* acts of the Organization are at the same time *presumed* to be *intra vires* as long as they are within the Organization's purposes. They can be proved to be *ultra vires* in rebuttal. But this will not render them invalid, because even *ultra vires* acts produce legal effects. It will merely prove them illegal, with all the consequences that this draws. As such, the legal consequence of an *ultra vires* act is *not* its invalidity, but rather its illegality.

Even if all this is not accepted, and it is still argued that Article 25 denies validity, and thus binding force, to decisions that are in violation of the Charter, it must be pointed out that such a construction only covers presumably or potentially *invalid* acts, but does not refer at all to *illegal* acts that could not possibly be invalid.[139] It can only cover *normative* acts that are *ultra vires* the Council or the Organization.[140] These would then be denied legal effect, with the result that they would not bind States. This construction spurs the noted tendency to try to interpret/read into the Charter a whole set of primary rules of general international law, in order to find that a violation of general international law renders the decision *ultra vires* and thus invalid under Article 25.[141] Otherwise, a decision validly taken but in violation of general international law would necessarily command obedience.

This line of argument is due to the fact that most authors succumb to the 'old temptation of regarding wrongs as *per se ultra vires*' and then go on to attribute invalidity or nullity to the *ultra vires* act.[142] It has been shown that this is not necessarily so. But even if it were, some important issues remain pending. Only *normative* acts can be struck down by invalidity—not sets of facts.[143] Still, certain

---

[138] cf Jennings (n 100) 85. See also W Wengler (1954) 45-I AIDI 286, where it is stated that even if judicial review of IO acts is established, it is not necessary that a court should have the power to determine invalidity, or that the illegal act should *ipso facto* be deemed to produce no legal effect—an approach, however, with which Wengler himself does not agree. In general see S Talmon (2004) 75 BYIL 126–9, who demonstrates that the concept of nullity is drawn from the alleged general principle *ex injuria jus non oritur*, a principle which does not apply in general international law, non-opposability or non-recognition being preferred. cf Weil (n 106) 328, who notes that courts have responded to the problems posed by the lack of an overarching theory of nullity by employing the concept of non-recognition.

[139] According to Lauterpacht (n 96) 89, unlawful or illegal acts of IOs may be distinguished in accordance with whether they are acts that can be committed by States as well, in which case the traditional law of responsibility applies, or whether they are peculiar to IOs as 'artificial legal persons deriving all their powers from a conventional or statutory source and bound to act only within the limits and in accordance with the terms of the grant made to them', which are susceptible to being tainted by invalidity.

[140] Text at nn 35–6 above and Chapter 2 above; see further Section II in that chapter.

[141] Text at nn 146–50 in Chapter 3 above; cf the observations of van Asbeck (1954) 44-I AIDI 293 [8]; Bastid ibid 295 [IV].

[142] Jennings (n 100) 82, 85.

[143] FA Mann (1976–7) 48 BYIL 16. cf also Talmon (n 138) 134–5, 139–41; Weil (n 106) 314. Similarly, an obligation of 'non-recognition of legality' can only operate in cases where a factual situation also takes the form of a legal claim, otherwise it lacks 'real substance': see S Talmon in C Tomuschat and J-M Thouvenin (eds), *The Fundamental Rules of the International Legal Order* (2006) 125.

acts undertaken by State organs in implementation of SCRs may be attributable to the Organization.[144] These cannot be sanctioned by invalidity. In such cases, States could not justify subsequent disobedience of the decision as being permitted under Article 25: the decision was taken in accordance with the Charter. It is the decision's implementation that is in violation of international law.

To exemplify, one could consider that a prolonged sanctions regime results in the measures taken by States in implementation to be manifestly disproportionate. It was argued that this was in fact the case with respect to the Iraqi sanctions at the turn of the millennium.[145] The decision to impose the sanctions (say some ten years ago) is still in accordance with the Charter.[146] The acts of implementation, however, over which States have no latitude, are now in violation of general international law. States could not disobey the decision, because it was taken in accordance with the Charter—it is not *ultra vires* the Council. Still, the measures' conformity with general international law is very doubtful.[147]

Another question is what happens when an act that is illegal not under the Charter but under general international law, is challenged by a third State, a non-member of the Organization. Though nowadays this case appears more and more academic, due to the virtually global membership of the Organization, it is certainly worthy of attention, if only for reasons of doctrinal coherence. The third State could not rely on the Charter, this being *res inter alios acta*. It could not claim the invalidity of the act under Article 25. It could only assert that the act is internationally wrongful.

There is no need to look in the Charter for a 'licence' for States to 'judge for themselves' whether a decision is valid or invalid, as it is sought to be done under Article 25. In any event, such a unilateral assertion would not be determinative of the question.[148] States already have the power to determine for themselves whether an act of another subject is legal or illegal. As long as this power has not been explicitly limited through the introduction of third-party disinterested settlement, they have not abolished it.[149] And this power necessarily extends to any actions of any other subject of international law that may infringe unlawfully on their rights or legal interests.

Of course, if States, in the exercise of their right to auto-determination, find that a binding decision is in breach of international law, then they would understandably consider disobeying it. Unless Article 25 is interpreted as allowing this disobedience, by denying the illegal act any legal effects, the disobedient action

---

[144] See Chapter 2.II above.

[145] See among many others T Eitel (2000) 4 MPUNYB 66.

[146] Suppose that a decision to lift the sanctions is not possible because of the operation of the 'reverse veto': a permanent member vetoes or threatens to veto the resolution lifting the sanctions. This brings up another aspect of the insufficiency of the invalidity claim: how about omissions—eg if a State were to challenge the Council's inaction where arguably there is an obligation to act (cf Chapter 2.I.1.ii above)? Surely claiming invalidity of the omission would not make much sense.

[147] Eitel (n 145) 66.   [148] Lauterpacht (n 96) 115.

[149] Text at nn 66–7 in Chapter 5 above and examples at Section II in the same chapter. On an alleged duty to disobey under general international law, ie arguably entailed by the general duty to mitigate the harmful effects of an illegal act, see text at nn 282–5 below.

of States would itself be illegal.[150] The purpose thus of the approach that contends Article 25 to allow for disobedience, because the decision is invalid, is precisely to make sure that the defiance will not constitute an internationally wrongful act on the part of the defiant State, so that its international responsibility will not be engaged. But maybe the wrongfulness of the disobedience can be precluded, and thus international responsibility will not be engaged in any case.

3. Disobedience as a countermeasure

Judge Morelli stated in his Separate Opinion in *Expenses* that

> it is not possible to suppose that the Charter leaves it open to any State Member to claim at any time that an Assembly resolution authorizing a particular expense *has never had any legal effect whatever*, on the grounds that it was based on a wrong interpretation of the Charter or an incorrect ascertainment of situations of fact or law. It must on the contrary be supposed that the Charter confers finality on the Assembly's resolution irrespective of the reasons, whether they are correct or not, on which the resolution is based... [151]

It is hard to disagree with this statement. It is also hard to read it for what it really means. An act of the Assembly (or the Council for that matter) is always valid, even if it is illegal—it is not open to States to assign nullity to it. This does not preclude States from assigning proper legal effect to it, *and still considering it illegal*. And of course it does not preclude them from subsequently responding to the illegality.

i. *Legal consequences of valid but illegal acts of the UN*

An act can be valid *and* illegal,[152] but it cannot be *invalid* and illegal. Rather, in the latter case it would have to be invalid *because* it is illegal. As, in that case, it produces no legal effect, there is nothing left to constitute an illegality. The illegality has been 'extinguished' by denying legal effect. But an illegal act need not necessarily be invalid. The next question to be answered refers to the legal consequences of a valid but illegal act.[153]

In international law, because of the lack of compulsory jurisdiction, the sanction of illegality of a normative act will not be its invalidity,[154] except where there is special provision. Rather, the illegality will lead to the engagement of responsibility, and the emergence of the secondary obligations of cessation and

---

[150] Alvarez (n 26) 141.   [151] (n 27) 224 [9 *in fine*] [emphasis added].

[152] The ICJ can be seen as having accepted this in *Northern Cameroons* [1963] ICJ Rep 32, where it finds that

> *irrespective* whether the [GA] based its action on a *correct interpretation* of the Trusteeship Agreement, there is no doubt... that the resolution had *definitive legal effect*. [emphasis added]

[153] cf Verzijl (n 105) 289–92, who distinguishes between a delict and a juridical act. The first draws the consequences of responsibility (reparation and so forth), while the second is sanctioned by invalidity. But he clearly demonstrates how an act can be both a juridical act *and* a delict at the same time. This poses the problem of 'choosing' the appropriate set of legal consequences.

[154] Cahier (n 106) 648; cf Morange (n 62) 902.

reparation, supported by the sanction of countermeasures.[155] This is applicable also with respect to acts of IOs when there is no specific provision in the constitutive instrument and no possibility for binding and direct judicial review of the act.[156]

More specifically with respect to the UN, the necessary implication of the virtually *irrebuttable* presumption of validity is that the acts of UN organs will continue producing legal effect up until they are set aside by a competent judicial authority or revoked by the promulgating body.[157] As such it is not up to States unilaterally to declare them null and void.[158] In any case such a unilateral act would not and could not be decisive: it could neither authoritatively declare the act to have no legal effect, nor nullify it, that is, deprive it of its legal effect.

This, it should be noted, also applies to SCRs that are in violation of *jus cogens*. It has been widely claimed that such decisions are invalid, because of the application of Articles 53 and 64 VCLT: if the Charter cannot be interpreted to be in violation of *jus cogens*,[159] then a decision in breach of *jus cogens* is *ultra vires* and thus without legal effect. Otherwise, the concept of invalidity of acts contrary to *jus cogens* applies in this case as well.

However, the VCLT provides for a specific procedure with respect to determining the invalidity of treaties;[160] a procedure very conspicuously absent with respect to SCRs. The concept of invalidity or nullity of a decision contrary to *jus cogens* is thus not directly applicable in the context of the SC. But the most important argument comes from distinguishing between the concept of *jus cogens* in treaty law, which is meant to prohibit *derogations*, thus *limiting the contractual freedom of the parties*, and the notion of acts being *in violation* of *jus cogens*, which leads to different legal consequences altogether: the international responsibility of the subject that violated international law.[161]

---

[155] cf Cahier (n 106) 648; Bernhardt (n 114) 609; Morange (n 62) 903–4; G Berlia in *Honneur Scelle*, vol 2 (1950) 875.

[156] cf Cahier (n 106) 659–60, 663: 'il ne semble donc pas ici que l'illégalité d'un acte d'une Organisation internationale ait entraîne la nullité' (with respect to the way the [then] IMCO responded to the ICJ opinion that its act was not in conformity with its constituent instrument); Osieke (n 125) 242; idem (n 27) 21–3. cf Klabbers (n 119) 219. *A contrario* one may rely on the fact that the only time when the ICJ implied that an *ultra vires* act of an international organ may be voidable was obiter in *Jurisdiction of the ICAO Council* (n 117) 70 [45 *in fine*], but only because Art 84 of the Chicago Convention establishes *compulsory* jurisdiction over relevant matters. See finally Art 51 DARIO.

[157] cf HK Kaikobad, *The ICJ and Judicial Review* (2000) 41; Wengler (n 138) 286–7.

[158] cf Wengler (n 138) 286–7; as well as the observations by L Gajzago (1952) 44-I AIDI 315.

[159] See Chapter 3.II.1 above.

[160] Arts 65–8 VCLT, provisions which are 'key' and a 'necessary and even essential complement' to other provisions in the VCLT: cf H Waldock (1963) I YILC 87 [1]; Castrén, Gros, comments during the ILC debate on Art 25 in (1963) I YILC 167 [71], and 168–9 [86] and [88] respectively. These comments were made at a time when Arts 24 and 25 incorporated the elements that later were differently configured into Arts 50 and 51 (1963), 62 and 63 (1966), and 65–8 (1969). See also Talmon (n 138) 137 and cf A Tzanakopoulos, 'Article 67' in O Corten and P Klein (eds), *The Vienna Conventions on the Law of Treaties* (forthcoming 2011) [2]. cf also Art 71(1)(a) VCLT; Talmon (n 138) 135; JA Frowein (1987) 47 ZaöRV 77–8. In particular Art 66(a) VCLT establishes a centralized and compulsory third-party dispute resolution procedure with respect to the application of Arts 53 and 64. See for comment H Ruiz Fabri in *Vienne Commentaire* (2006) 2410–14 [27]–[32].

[161] The argument is succinctly made by Talmon (n 138) 133–4, and is of course supported by Arts 40–1 ARSIWA.

It has been stated that the doctrine of *ultra vires* is concerned with the 'legal validity of acts or the exercise of powers, not their legality or illegality in terms of breached obligations and the duty to make reparation'.[162] But MS are not solely in a 'vertical' relationship with the Organization; they are also in a 'horizontal' one,[163] as the Organization is itself bound by international obligations, either under its Charter or under general international law, which are owed to the MS, as well as (*in casu*) third States.[164] As such, States can determine that the Organization has violated its international obligations even through a normative act, through the promulgation of a decision.

In general, the consequences of an unlawful act may attach to the issuance of a norm (or decision, which is an individualized norm). In other words, issuing a norm may amount to an unlawful act,[165] when it is in violation (or when it amounts to erroneous individualization) of a hierarchically superior norm, such as a norm in the constitutive instrument (or of *jus cogens*, in harmony with which the constituent instrument is to be interpreted).[166] It is to be remembered here that virtually every Chapter VII SCR will amount to the issuance of a norm in one way or another. It will be a concretization of a general obligation (*Blankettverpflichtung*) and as such the application of the general obligation in a specific case (say, by imposing sanctions on a State or entity for posing a threat to the peace).[167] Otherwise, it will amount to the issuance of a norm through the novel process inaugurated with SCR 1373 (2001), which lays down obligations for all States in an abstract and general manner. Again, this can be seen as a concretization of the 'blanket' obligation not to constitute a threat to the peace, though of a different reach.[168]

The norm thus—that is to say unlawfully—issued may still be valid. Among other cases, it is valid when, in view of the lack of a procedure to overturn it, it cannot be overturned at all on the basis of the claim of its deficiency.[169] A similar situation appears with respect to an unconstitutional statute in domestic law, which remains valid if there is no constitutional review procedure to overturn it—as in Greece, for example: courts have to disregard the unconstitutional statute in a specific case but cannot overturn it, it remains valid until revoked.[170]

In view of the above, a SCR will remain valid despite its deficiency (illegality), in view of the lack of any judicial review avenue. Accordingly, *all* State reactions

---

[162] Amerasinghe (n 133) 197.   [163] cf Dominicé (n 26) 198–200.

[164] See for the SC in particular Chapter 3.III above.

[165] See H Kelsen, *Introduction to the Problems of Legal Theory* (1994) 118.

[166] See Guggenheim (n 109) 198. In that case, the decision is still valid ('valable'), but it is also illegal ('illicite') due to the erroneous individualization. See also H Kelsen (n 13) 365–6.

[167] See generally Chapter 3.II.2.ii above; DW Bowett in Fox (n 64) 79–80.

[168] cf C Denis, *Le pouvoir normatif* (2004) 13–16, 133 seq.

[169] Kelsen (n 165) 118; Guggenheim (n 109) 198, 207–8.

[170] See also Kelsen (n 165) 119; Akande (n 79) 334. This is what has been called 'diffused' control of the constitutionality of law. In Greece eg control of constitutionality by the courts is diffused, *ex post facto* and incidental. cf for further examples of norms found 'inoperative' in the specific case, rather than void or invalid, due to conflict with a higher rule, J Jaconelli (1979) 28 ICLQ 67–9. This situation is not otherwise unknown in international law: under Art 103 UNC a treaty obligation incompatible with an obligation under the Charter is to be set aside, becomes 'paralysed', but is not sanctioned by nullity: see E Roucounas (1987) 206 RdC 66; cf G Gaja (1981) 172 RdC 282.

to the act of the Council will be in violation of Article 25 UNC, which commands compliance. At that, the reactions by States will themselves be illegal (*rechtswidrig*).[171] Still, at the same time, the consequences of an international wrong are attached to the Council's valid but illegal act: it engages the responsibility of its author,[172] in this case the UN having acted through the Council.

ii. State response to the illegal act of the UN

State disobedience to binding SCRs within a legal order can only be, to paraphrase Kelsen, either a *delict* or a *sanction*.[173] There can be no *tertium quid*,[174] at least not within the purview of law. State disobedience thus can only be qualified as a countermeasure, otherwise it must be conceded to be a wrongful act engaging responsibility, claims of 'right of last resort' notwithstanding. This approach would render the discussions on the interpretation of the words 'in accordance with the…Charter' in Article 25 effectively moot: disobedience is not a 'right' under Article 25, but rather a reaction to a wrongful act.

Indeed, it may be submitted that State disobedience *can* be so qualified. For one, it is theoretically possible that States may resort to countermeasures against a responsible IO.[175] For another, disobedience violates the State's obligation to comply with a valid SCR (under Article 25), but this is in response to the Council's unlawful behaviour in *issuing* the norm/resolution. It is thus a breach in response to a breach. However, this fact is certainly not enough to qualify the reactive breach as a countermeasure. There are also other essential requirements that must be fulfilled.

a) Breach of an obligation owed to the responsible subject

An essential requirement for a reaction to be qualified (and excused) as a countermeasure is that it relate to the breach of an international obligation owed to the responsible subject.[176] If there is no wrongful act on the part of the respondent against the target, there is no possibility of precluding the wrongfulness of the act on the basis of countermeasures.[177] It must thus be shown that the obligation of MS under Article 25 UNC to 'accept and carry out' SC decisions is owed to the UN, rather than simply to all the States parties to the Charter. If this is so, disobedience breaches an obligation owed to the UN.

---

[171] Schilling (n 79) 95–6 makes this point, but carries on the syllogism to the effect that this must be denied because it would mean that the Council would be legally free. cf also K Osteneck, *Die Umsetzung von UN-Wirtschaftssanktionen* (2004) 33.

[172] Art 1 ARSIWA; Art 3 DARIO; Guggenheim (n 109) 198; Bernhardt (n 114) 609.

[173] H Kelsen, *General Theory of Law and State* (1961) 330.

[174] Unlike in the case of the use of force, which is the one Kelsen originally claimed to be necessarily either a delict or a sanction: see JL Kunz (1960) 54 AJIL 331.

[175] See Section I above.

[176] *Gabčíkovo-Nagymaros* (n 2) 55–6 [83]; ARSIWA Commentary 130 [4].

[177] An act that is unfriendly but not internationally wrongful cannot be qualified as a countermeasure, but is rather a measure of retorsion: ARSIWA Commentary 128 [3]; KJ Partsch in *EPIL*, vol 4 (2000) 232.

That the Organization has the capacity to have rights under general international law has been resolved since the very first years of its existence.[178] These must correspond to obligations of other subjects, in particular States, owed to the Organization under the same law. The question is whether the Organization has rights under its Charter, which creates a partial legal order. An admission to this effect would necessarily mean that MS must owe corresponding obligations under the Charter to the Organization.

In *Reparation* the Court clearly states that undertakings of MS towards the Organization inter alia under the UNC must be strictly observed. This is founded on the duty (read: international obligation) of States to render 'every assistance' to the Organization, an obligation under Article 2(5) UNC.[179] The Court then finds that

when an infringement occurs, the Organization should be able to call upon the responsible State to remedy its default, and, in particular, to obtain from the State reparation...[180]

This is nothing but the operation of the traditional rules of international responsibility: the Organization, being an injured subject, can invoke the responsibility of the MS breaching the duty of assistance and can demand reparation.[181] In that, the UN is 'invoking its own right, the right that the obligations due to it should be respected'.[182] Whereas in the case at hand the issue (and the statements of the Court) referred to reparation for the injury caused, it must be accepted that the Organization could also demand the cessation of the wrongful act if it is continuing, as will be the case in instances of disobedience.[183]

From the above it becomes clear that Article 2(5) UNC establishes international obligations for MS, which are owed to the Organization. It must be stressed in this connection that Article 25 can be seen as an elaboration of Article 2(5) in the particular context of the SC.[184] As such, the obligation to accept and carry out Council decisions is an international obligation owed by the MS to the Organization.

That obligations under the Charter, such as the duty to comply with the Organization's decisions, are owed by the MS to the Organization was an issue the

---

[178] *Reparation* (n 9) 179.
[179] Ibid 183; see also the S-G in *Namibia* [1970] ICJ Pleadings I at 100–1 [97], 108 [136]. But see JA Frowein and N Krisch in *Charter Commentary* (2002) 137–8 [2]–[6].
[180] *Reparation* (n 9) 183.
[181] cf Arts 42(a), 30–1 ARSIWA. See also *Reparation* (n 9) 180, where the Court confirms in unequivocal terms that the obligations owed by MS to the Organization are international obligations by stating inter alia that

It cannot be doubted that the Organization has the capacity to bring an *international* claim against one of its Members which has caused injury to it by a breach of its *international obligations towards it.* [emphasis added]

And at 184, where the Court actually cites the dictum of the PCIJ in *Chorzów Factory* (Jurisdiction) [1927] PCIJ Ser A No 9 at 21.
[182] *Reparation* (n 9) 184; S-G (n 179) 100–1 [96]–[97].
[183] For the relationship between cessation and restitution and the argument that cessation can constitute (partial) restitution see Chapter 6 above at Section I.
[184] See Delbrück (n 84) 459 [17]; Goodrich et al (n 89) 56.

Court did not deal with in *Expenses*.[185] Still, it can be argued that an obligation to pay assessed contributions is owed by the States to the Organization also on the basis that the latter can resort to sanctions against non-payment under Article 19.[186] Similarly, the obligation to comply with SC binding measures under Article 41 (and under Chapter VII in general) is backed by the potential sanction of the recalcitrant State being found to constitute a threat to the peace and having further Article 41 measures directed against it.[187]

b) Reactive breach undertaken by the injured subject

The internationally wrongful act is not only the *fait générateur* of responsibility,[188] but also the *fait générateur* of reaction.[189] The qualification of a wrongful act as a countermeasure and the subsequent preclusion of wrongfulness require the existence of a prior internationally wrongful act of the target against the reacting subject.[190] It is traditionally accepted that only the 'victim' of an internationally wrongful act can resort to countermeasures and only against the perpetrator.[191]

The next question is thus whether (and which) States are injured by an alleged violation of international law by the UN through Council action under Article 41. The possible breaches of international law in the instance are quite diverse, but it will be useful to follow the structure already used in Chapter 3, dealing first with breaches of UN obligations under the Charter and then with breaches of obligations under general international law.

(1) Obligations under the UN Charter

That the UNC establishes international obligations binding upon the Organization has already been discussed, and confirmed by both the ICJ and the ILC.[192] At the same time, it is stressed that the UN is not a contracting party to its constituent

---

[185] (n 27) 158, where the Court finds that '[t]he question put to the Court has to do with a moment logically anterior . . . to a question of a Member's obligation to pay'.

[186] Art 19 is 'one of the only two provisions [in the Charter] that *clearly stipulate* sanctions': Kelsen (n 63) 710 [emphasis added].

[187] This is made clear, eg in SCR 670 (1990) [12], where the Council warns that it will consider measures against those States evading or allowing evasion of its binding resolutions. In SCR 320 (1972) [4] the Sanctions Committee is requested by the Council to consider the type of action to be taken against Portugal and South Africa 'in view of [their] open and persistent refusal . . . to implement sanctions', after having expressly referred to Art 25 at [2]. cf also SCR 253 (1968) [11]–[12] and subsequent calls by States to extend sanctions to Portugal and South Africa for non-compliance with the Rhodesian sanctions and thus Art 25: *Repertory*, supp 4 vol I (1982) 292 [18]. Similar opinions were voiced with respect to potential measures against South Africa for the situation in Namibia: ibid 293–4 [24]–[25]. See also for proposals to impose sanctions against States generally for non-compliance with Art 25: supp 3 vol II (1971) 62 [103]–[104] and 63 [111]. See finally Osteneck (n 171) 34.

[188] See P-M Dupuy (1984) 188 RdC 9.   [189] Sicilianos (n 4) 20.

[190] *Gabčíkovo-Nagymaros* (n 2) 55–6 [83]; ARSIWA Commentary 130 [2]–[4]. cf *Naulilaa* (1928) 2 RIAA 1027 [d].

[191] See n 190 above. The *locus classicus* here is the *Cysne*, where the Arbitral Tribunal found that an 'essential' requirement for countermeasures to be justified is that they be *provoked* by a previous illegal act. As such they *are only admissible against the provoking State*: (1930) 2 RIAA 1056–7. See among many others KJ Partsch in *EPIL*, vol 4 (2000) 201; T Stein (1992) 30 AVR 46, 48.

[192] Text at nn 25–8 in Chapter 3 above.

instrument; but it is conceded in one breath that it is not a *third* party either.[193] This is beside the point—what matters is that the Charter imposes obligations on the Organization,[194] irrespective of whether one is inclined to ascribe 'contractual' or 'constitutional' character to them.[195] Even the 'prohibited' analogies to other fictional legal entities, be it States or limited liability companies, lead in any event to a similar conclusion: the entity is bound by its constitutive instrument, which establishes obligations binding upon it and corresponding rights for its creators.[196]

The Charter is, of course, an international treaty. Its breach gives rise to the right of an injured party to avail itself of the means of redress provided for in the treaty itself, or in the law of treaties in general,[197] but in any case does not exclude the right to countermeasures in response to the breach. As the ILC stated in its commentary to Draft Article 57 on the Law of Treaties,

A violation of a treaty obligation, as of any other obligation, may give rise to a right in the other party to take non-forcible reprisals, and these reprisals may properly relate to the defaulting party's rights under the treaty.[198]

The question that emerges with some eminence at this juncture is how to construe (or 'classify') the obligations of the UN (and thus the Council) under the Charter with respect to the membership of the Organization. The purpose of this exercise is none other than to determine those subjects that are entitled to invoke the Organization's responsibility as 'injured' by the breach,[199] and that should thus also possess the power to resort to countermeasures against the recalcitrant IO.[200]

---

[193] Zoller (n 62) 625. cf for the inverse proposition (that MS are not 'exactly' third parties to treaties concluded by the IO) C Laly-Chevalier, *La violation du traité* (2005) 179 seq.

[194] See M Lachs (1960–1) 1 IJIL 429; P Daillier in *Vienne Commentaire* (2006) 141 [4]. By direct analogy one may refer to the fact that the Organization derives rights from international treaties to which it is not a party, such as the Convention on UN Privileges and Immunities: otherwise it would make no sense for Art VIII, Section 30 of that Convention to provide for dispute settlement in the event of dispute between the UN and a MS. cf C Dominicé in L Boisson de Chazournes et al (eds), *IOs and International Dispute Settlement* (2002) 92.

[195] And similarly it is argued that MS are not in a contractual relationship vis-à-vis the UN, but rather in a constitutional or institutional relationship: ibid. See further Sachariew (n 8) 277, who points out that constituent instruments create a new subject, with the result that the obligations (of States) under the instrument are 'transformed' to obligations toward the organization. At the same time, it can be added, the constituent instrument imposes obligations on the created institution, which are owed to the MS.

[196] See eg the UK Companies Act 1985, according to which the constitutive instruments of companies (Memorandum and Articles of Association) are to be treated as a contract between the company and its shareholders and between the shareholders themselves.

[197] cf Art 5 VCLT. But see Zoller (n 62) 624 seq and text at nn 223–42 below.

[198] (1966) II YILC 253–4 [1]. cf Art 73 VCLT. See also B Simma and CJ Tams in *Vienne Commentaire* (2006) 2173–5 [70]–[73]; 2176 [78]; L-A Sicilianos (1993) 4 EJIL 353–4. International courts and tribunals have clearly applied the law of countermeasures when dealing with treaty breaches: see *Air Services* (1978) 18 RIAA 443 [81]–[82]; *Rainbow Warrior II* (1990) 20 UNRIAA 251–2 [75]; cf *Gabčíkovo* (n 2) 38 [47].

[199] cf L-A Sicilianos (2002) 13 EJIL 1133. On the question of entitlement to enforce see generally CJ Tams, *Enforcing Obligations* Erga Omnes (2005) 25–47.

[200] cf Arts 42, 49 ARSIWA and Commentary 117 [3].

Of course the Charter imposes a multitude of obligations that are diversely classified. It imposes obligations on MS towards other MS, such as the obligation not to use force. But it also imposes obligations on the Organization, and the question emerges as to whom these obligations are owed to, and as to who is injured by their breach. It is clear that the relevant obligations are not purely bilateral in nature:[201] they are not owed to the membership as an entity, because the 'membership' does not have international legal personality. Nor are they 'bilateralizable', namely a 'bundle' of bilateral obligations owed by the Organization to each and every different MS, the performance of which in specific circumstances is owed to a certain MS but not to others.[202] This becomes clear when one contemplates the Organization owing an obligation to act within its competence 'individually' to MS A but not to MS B, C, D, and so forth.

The obligations incumbent upon the UN under the Charter must thus be seen not as being owed to one State individually, but rather to a group of States,[203] the membership of the Organization. But their breach does not automatically and necessarily injure all the States in that group.

Multilateral obligations owed to a group of States may be qualified as 'integral' or 'interdependent' when their breach necessarily affects *every* State in the group, which can then invoke the responsibility of the responsible entity as an injured State.[204] 'Integral' or 'interdependent' obligations are obligations that, while not 'bilateralizable',[205] are in fact dominated by a strong synallagmatic nature: one party performs the obligation because the other parties do likewise.[206]

Breaches of multilateral obligations that are owed to a group of States but are not interdependent or integral may specially affect one or some particular States in the group but not others. Such obligations are the ones usually established for the promotion of extra-State interests, and are thus non-reciprocal in nature.[207] When the breach of such an obligation occurs, only the specially affected State(s) may invoke the responsibility of the responsible entity as injured State(s).[208]

UN obligations under the Charter do not, at first sight, fit comfortably in either category. To use an illustration, a violation of the obligation of the Organization, and thus the Council, to determine the existence of a threat to the peace before taking non-forcible binding measures most certainly will affect the MS that is targeted by the measure. This will be the 'specially affected State'. It seems that this State should be considered injured by the violation, while the others would simply be able to invoke as 'States other than the injured State'.[209] Otherwise, for example when the target of the measures is not a MS, but either a non-MS or another entity, there will be no 'specially affected State'.

---

[201] cf Arts 42(a) ARSIWA; 42(a) DARIO.

[202] See ARSIWA Commentary 118 [6], [8], and fn 672.

[203] cf ibid 118–19 [11].   [204] See Arts 42(b)(ii) ARSIWA; 42(b)(ii) DARIO.

[205] That means to say 'not reducible to a simple bundle of bilateral obligations'.

[206] Sicilianos (n 199) 1134.   [207] Ibid.

[208] See Arts 42(b)(i) ARSIWA; 42(b)(i) DARIO. Still, the other States in the relevant group will be able to invoke as 'States other than the injured State'.

[209] For which see Arts 48(1)(a) ARSIWA; 48(1) DARIO.

Most examples relating to 'integral' or 'interdependent' obligations on the other hand relate to disarmament treaties and similar instruments where 'each party's performance is effectively conditioned upon and requires the performance of each of the others'.[210] UN obligations under the Charter hardly fit this description. Still, there is no denying that a violation by the UN of its obligations under the Charter would 'radically change the position of every [MS] with respect to the further performance of its obligations' under the Charter,[211] and would 'undermine the whole régime of the treaty'.[212] The synallagmatic–reciprocal element is evident in that the MS have endowed the Organization with powers, particularly the power to make binding decisions, in exchange for limits to its powers stipulated or implied in the constituent instrument.

For example, the wrongful determination of the existence of a threat to the peace or the imposition of disproportionate sanctions may, as a matter of fact, be directed only against one MS; but as a matter of law, the wrongful determination constitutes a violation towards all MS of the Organization,[213] no less so because it obliges them to carry out the relevant decision. In view of the important role that subsequent practice and acquiescence play in the interpretation of constituent instruments, particularly the UNC, authors go a long way in endowing States with the full range of measures effectively to restrain the improper extension of powers of the Organization or their abuse.[214]

This is because a violation by the Organization of its Charter has far-reaching effects on all MS: it may effectively endow the Organization with new powers, or extend existing ones, including by relaxing their constitutional limitations.[215] It is not irrelevant that most constitutional crises in the UN have been occasioned by attempts of UN organs to expand their powers, sometimes at the expense of other organs.[216] The measures available to members in response cannot be limited to purely political pressures within the Organization's organs.[217] In this sense it can be argued that the regime of obligations imposed on the Organization by its Charter is 'non-dissociable'.[218] Or, to put it another way, it can be argued that a breach of the Charter leads to an extension of UN powers, thereby necessarily further limiting the sovereignty of MS, and as such rendering them all 'specially affected' by the breach.[219]

For these reasons, a violation of UN obligations under the Charter should be considered, it is submitted, as injuring all MS, irrespective of the fact that these UN obligations do not fit neatly within the category either of 'integral' or 'interdependent' obligations, or of other *erga omnes partes* obligations. A further argument in support of this position can be drawn from the work of the IDI on

---

[210] ARSIWA Commentary 119 [13].   [211] cf Art 60(2)(c) VCLT.

[212] cf (1966) II YILC 255 [8].   [213] cf Sachariew (n 8) 281.

[214] See DW Bowett (1970) 64 ASILProc 50–1 and cf Klabbers (n 119) 227–8.

[215] See N Angelet in *Honour Suy* (1998) 279. cf D Sarooshi, *IOs and their Exercise of Sovereign Powers* (2005) 60–1 with respect to the EC, 116 generally.

[216] D Ciobanu (1972) 55 RivistaDI 427.

[217] Such as preliminary objections to jurisdiction, for which see generally Ciobanu (n 27) 66, 169 and *passim*.

[218] cf G Perrin in *Honour Skubiszewski* (1996) 245–7.   [219] cf Tams (n 199) 46.

judicial recourse against IO decisions. Article 3 of Resolution II proposed by the Rapporteur would provide that the judgment of an international tribunal on the question of the legality of a decision of the organization should have the force of *res judicata* towards *all* members of the organization that have the capacity to attack the decision, even if they did not do so and did not take part in the proceedings.[220] As such, the decision would have *erga omnes (partes)* force. Although the Resolution was not finally adopted in that form,[221] many members of the IDI explicitly agreed with this particular point.[222] They denoted thereby that the obligations of the organization under its constituent instrument must be seen as being owed simultaneously to all members, and as being breached simultaneously as against all members.

Consequently, all MS will have the power to take countermeasures against the Organization, in particular the countermeasure of disobedience, which targets directly the Organization through non-compliance with an obligation owed to it.

One question remains, however, and relates to the troubled relationship between countermeasures and a possible 'treaty law reaction', namely that of termination or suspension of a treaty for material breach (also known as the principle *inadimplenti non est adimplendum* or [when raised as a defence] the *exceptio non adimpleti contractus*). This is codified in Article 60 VCLT, which in principle reflects customary international law.[223] Even though the VCLT does not as such apply to the UN Charter,[224] it codifies rules that have the capacity to apply to constituent instruments of international organizations.[225]

Scholarship has been divided as to whether the treaty reaction of suspension or termination on account of material breach is distinct and independent from the law of countermeasures or whether it merely forms a *species* of the *genus* countermeasures.[226] If the two are distinct reactions, as the ILC thinks,[227] then perhaps the disobedience of States to wrongful SC measures is not to be qualified as a countermeasure, but as a partial suspension of their obligations under Articles 25 and 2(5) UNC in accordance with the general international law of treaties as reflected in Article 60 VCLT.[228]

---

[220] Wengler (n 138) 269–70 (proposed art), 285 (commentary).

[221] See (1957) 47-II AIDI 476–9, 488–91.

[222] See eg (1954) 45-I AIDI 297 (Bastid); 301 (Hambro); 309 (Salvioli).

[223] *Namibia* (n 88) 46–7 [94]–[95]; *Gabčíkovo* (n 2) 62 [99]; see generally Simma and Tams (n 198) 2137–40 [6]–[10].

[224] Art 4 VCLT; cf ME Villiger, *Commentary on the 1969 VCLT* (2009) 112–13 [6]–[8]. *Contra*, curiously, Zoller (n 62) 614.

[225] cf Art 5 VCLT with the 'without prejudice' clause in Art 4 VCLT. Art 5 can be seen as reflecting customary law: Villiger (n 224) 120–1 [10].

[226] See Sicilianos (n 198) 341–2 and 359; cf Simma and Tams (n 198) 2135–7 [4]; and generally R Pisillo Mazzeschi in M Spinedi and B Simma (eds), *UN Codification of State Responsibility* (1987) 89–91.

[227] ARSIWA Commentary 128–9 [4] though without much in the way of elaboration.

[228] Since the treaty is multilateral, and since a unanimous agreement between all UN MS is a virtual impossibility, only the question of suspension, rather than that of termination, comes into play here, in accordance with Art 60(2): cf (a) with (b) and (c).

In general, the requirements for resorting to suspension, in whole or in part, of a multilateral treaty are similar to those for taking countermeasures.[229] The procedural requirements for bringing about the (partial)[230] suspension of a treaty (as opposed to merely invoking material breach as a ground for suspension), a major potential difference between the treaty reaction and countermeasures, do not apply in the instance, as Articles 65–8 VCLT do not constitute customary international law.[231] The principle of proportionality, which is applicable to countermeasures,[232] is also applicable to the treaty reaction.[233] There still remains one major difference: suspension under treaty law is only allowed for 'material' breach, while countermeasures can be taken in response to any breach.[234]

This is not the major problem, however. One could imagine that any breach by the Organization, through the SC, of its obligations under the Charter, such as that of determining the existence of a threat to the peace before resorting to Article 41 measures, or of conforming to the requirements of proportionality in taking non-forcible action to maintain or restore international peace,[235] would constitute a material breach of the UNC. The relevant provisions are arguably 'essential for the treaty's object and purpose',[236] namely the maintenance of international peace and security.[237]

The major problem, rather, is that the reaction of (partial) suspension, while arguably taken by the injured subject (if one accepts that the UNC establishes a form of interdependent or integral obligations or its violation by the Organization renders all MS 'specially affected')[238] will not be directed against the defaulting subject, as required by the rule codified in Article 60 VCLT, but rather against all MS. If one accepts that a UNC breach by the Organization renders all MS 'specially affected', these can respond but can only direct their response to the defaulting subject,[239] which in this case is the Organization. To the extent, however, that the obligations under Articles 25 and 2(5) UNC are not owed *solely* (ie 'bilateralizably') to the Organization, but to all other MS as well, the reaction would also affect all these other MS, and as such would be unlawful and unjustifiable under the rule codified in Article 60 VCLT.

In the case of interdependent or integral obligations, suspension on account of material breach by the injured subject may also affect (or: will necessarily, because of the nature of the obligations, affect) all other parties.[240] If one accepts that the

---

[229] See also Sicilianos (n 198) 343.

[230] On the availability of partial suspension when acting under Art 60 see Art 44(2) VCLT and cf Simma and Tams (n 198) 2166 [56]. Partial suspension may even refer to specific provisions, leaving all other obligations under the treaty intact: Villiger (n 224) 740–1 [10].

[231] See Tzanakopoulos (n 160) [4]–[6] with further references.

[232] See Art 51 ARSIWA and text at n 250 below.

[233] See Simma and Tams (n 198) 2169–70 [64]–[65].

[234] See ibid 2173 [70].   [235] See Chapter 3.I above.

[236] Art 60(3)(b) VCLT; see further Simma and Tams (n 198) 2142–7 [14]–[23]; Villiger (n 224) 742–3 [15]–[16]; MM Gomaa, *Suspension or Termination of Treaties on Grounds of Breach* (1996) 28–35.

[237] cf Art 1(1) UNC.   [238] See nn 203–22 above. cf Zoller (n 62) 623.

[239] Art 60(2)(b) VCLT.

[240] Art 60(2)(c) VCLT. See also Simma and Tams (n 198) 2154–5 [38]; Villiger (n 224) 745–6 [21].

UNC obligations are a form of such interdependent or integral obligations, then the suspension of the obligations under Articles 25 and 2(5) UNC would be allowed, even if these are owed to all other MS. Still, the breach of these obligations as they are owed to the Organization, which is not a party to its constituent instrument, would not be justified.

This means that the rule codified in Article 60 VCLT cannot justify disobedience, as this targets the Organization, by suspending the obligation of obedience primarily owed to it.[241] But the consideration of the treaty reaction of suspension on account of material breach is still useful, and for a number of reasons. First of all, it further bolsters the need to qualify obligations under the UNC, as far as they relate to the operation of the UN, as interdependent or integral. Further, since it can operate in parallel with countermeasures rather than being exclusive,[242] it does not preclude the qualification (and thus justification) of disobedience as a countermeasure. Rather, it complements this justification by allowing another justification for the breach of obligations under Articles 25 and 2(5) UNC to the extent that these are (also) owed to the other MS: a MS disobeying a Council resolution allegedly in violation of the UNC can justify its breach of Articles 25 and 2(5) UNC as a countermeasure against the Organization, and as a partial suspension on grounds of material breach against all (other) UN MS.

(2) Obligations under general international law

The Organization may, when acting through the Council under Article 41 UNC, breach obligations incumbent upon it not only under the Charter, but also under general international law.[243] These breaches may range from obligations under peremptory norms to obligations of the *jus dispositivum*,[244] from which, however, no derogation was intended by or allowed to the acting organ. It is, of course, impossible to classify all these obligations of the UN, and it would not advance the argument in any way.

It should suffice to state that the standard analysis with respect to the classification of obligations under general international law would apply in this case as well. In the context of the present discussion, the obligations that will come into play will be obligations under peremptory norms or customary obligations for the protection of fundamental human rights. These obligations are owed *erga omnes*,[245] that is, to the 'international community as a whole'.

As such, only a State that is specially affected by the breach of the Organization (ie the target of measures), irrespective of whether it is a member or a non-member, could invoke the responsibility of the Organization as an injured State and employ countermeasures. All other States, or all States if there is no specially affected State, though affected in their legal interests, would constitute 'States other than the

---

[241] cf Zoller (n 62) 624–6.
[242] Clearly Villiger (n 224) 748 [26]. cf C Dominicé (1999) 10 EJIL 362.
[243] See Chapter 3.II above.   [244] Ibid.
[245] cf *Barcelona Traction* [1970] ICJ Rep 32 [33]–[34]; ARSIWA Commentary 110–12 [2]–[7], 127 [8]–[10]; Art 1 of the Resolution of the IDI on 'The Protection of Human Rights and the Principle of Non-Intervention in the Internal Affairs of States' in (1990) 63-II AIDI 341.

injured State' and would not be prejudiced in resorting to 'lawful measures'.[246] The question remains as to whether 'States other than the injured State' that are also MS may resort to the countermeasure of disobedience in response to a breach of general international law.[247]

c) Proportionality and other requirements

Countermeasures, and disobedience as a particular countermeasure, can thus be lawfully taken against the Organization, as long as some additional requirements are also fulfilled. Most of these requirements, such as the substantive requirement of the provisional character and reversibility of the countermeasure, and procedural requirements of prior offers to negotiate and notice, in reality form aspects of the principle of proportionality.

Because the primary (though not the only)[248] purpose of countermeasures is to secure the performance of the secondary obligations of cessation and reparation, countermeasures must be provisional in character and thus reversible.[249] This connects to the requirement that countermeasures must be proportional to the injury suffered;[250] an irreversible countermeasure will usually indicate a punitive purpose and will as such be disproportionate save in the odd circumstance.[251] The test is thus, in the final analysis, that of proportionality. Although whether a particular measure against the UN is proportional in this sense can only be determined depending on the particular facts, disobedience will in most cases be the only available remedy to States, as is clearly illustrated by the habitual incantation of its *ultima ratio* designation. As such it will be in most cases a proportional response.

Certain procedural requirements are indicated by the ILC as necessary before resorting to countermeasures: these are a call upon the responsible subject to comply with its secondary obligations,[252] and a notification of the decision to take countermeasures along with an offer to negotiate.[253] Notwithstanding the fact that notification has been criticized as not being required under customary law,[254] it is noteworthy that all these procedural requirements were fulfilled in one of the most prominent cases of disobedience of UN sanctions to date: the (then) OAU disobedience in the Lockerbie case.[255]

In particular, for years after the adoption of sanctions by the SC in Resolution 748 (1992), the OAU, along with the Non-Aligned Movement, the OIC, and the Arab League, had been engaged in negotiations with the Council and its

---

[246] cf Arts 48, 54 ARSIWA; 48, 56 DARIO.   [247] See Section IV below.

[248] According to Zemanek (n 6) 35, no countermeasure fulfils only one function: coercive, protective, reparative, and even punitive elements are mixed both in the consideration of the author and in the perception of the recipient.

[249] Art 49(3) ARSIWA and Commentary 130–1 [7], [9]. cf Art 50(3) DARIO.

[250] Art 51 ARSIWA and Commentary 135 [6]. cf Art 53 DARIO.

[251] cf L-A Sicilianos (2005) 38 RBDI 467; generally idem (n 4) 50–6.

[252] cf Arts 52(1)(a) ARSIWA; 54(1)(a) DARIO.

[253] cf Arts 52(1)(b) ARSIWA; 54(1)(b) DARIO.

[254] Sicilianos (n 251) 479; cf Laly-Chevalier (n 193) 561.

[255] All 53 of the OAU MS were also UN MS. Similar considerations apply with respect to the OIC MS disobedience of the SC-imposed arms embargo on Bosnia: see text at nn 72–3 above.

permanent members, particularly the US and the UK as the most vehement (and in time the only) supporters of sanctions against Libya. After repeated calls to the Council to lift the sanctions in view of Libya's acceptance of a number of different proposals for the trial of the suspected Lockerbie bombers,[256] the OAU Council of Ministers claimed that the sanctions against Libya were 'unjust' and that the threat of additional sanctions was 'in violation' of the UNC and international law.[257] The Ministers called for the lifting of sanctions (and in that for the performance of the secondary obligation of cessation and possibly of 'juridical restitution') and thus implicitly threatened disobedience for the first time in 1995.[258] Further appeals for the lifting of sanctions in the same vein followed.[259]

In 1998, the OAU Assembly of Heads of State and Government called upon the Council to suspend the sanctions on Libya,[260] in order to comply with its secondary obligations. It then notified the Council that it '[d]ecides not to comply any longer with Security Council Resolutions 748 (1992) and 883 (1993) on sanctions, with effect from September 1998'.[261] The reason for this was that the SCRs 'violate Article 27 paragraph 3, Article 33 and Article 36 paragraph 3 of the United Nations Charter'.[262] Irrespective of whether the claim of violation of the particular provisions is well founded, it becomes apparent that the MS of the OAU, acting collectively through the Organization, complied with all procedural requirements for taking countermeasures. At the same time, the 'measured' nature of the response, particularly in view of the repeated calls for reconsideration,[263] furnishes a strong argument for the proportionality of the measure.

d) Possible objections

Among the possible objections, the most prominent one is that States do not refuse to comply with binding resolutions on legal but rather on political grounds.[264]

---

[256] For an extensive overview of the relevant facts see Kalala (n 29) 550 seq. See also AHG/Decl.2 (XXXIII) (2–4 June 1997) [4].

[257] See CM/Res 1566 (LXI) (n 69) at 8th preamb and [2] respectively.

[258] Ibid [6].   [259] AHG/Decl.2 (XXXIII) (n 256) [6]–[7].

[260] AHG/Dec.127 (XXXIV) (n 70) [1].   [261] Ibid [2].

[262] Ibid. An implied claim, which was expressly stated by Libya in the Council (S/PV.3864 [1998] 6), was that there had been no threat to the peace to allow for action under Chapter VII. Imbued in this is also a claim that the Council is 'not competent' to finally decide a legal dispute (ibid at 11). Further, Libya claimed that the sanctions were punitive in nature and thus in violation of human rights obligations under the UDHR, ICCPR, and ICESCR (ibid at 8). Most aspects of these claims were—more or less—echoed by other States and IOs, which also called for the lifting of sanctions: ibid at 17 (China); 20 (Kenya); 21 (Bahrain); 35–6 (Arab League); 36–8 (OAU); 38–9 (OIC); 40–2 (Mali, also on behalf of the Group of African States); 43–4 (Malta); 45–6 (Algeria); 46–7 (Indonesia); 47–8 (Syria); 48–9 (UAE); 50 (Kuwait); 51 (Yemen); 52 (Jordan); 53–4 (Egypt); 55–6 (Ghana); 56–7 (DPRK); 57–9 (Iraq); 59 (Mauritania); 59–61 (Pakistan); 61 (Zimbabwe); 62 (Namibia); 62–3 (Morocco); 64 (Tunisia); 65 (Guinea-Bissau); 65–6 (Sudan); 67 (Nigeria); 68–9 (India); 70 (Tanzania); 70–1 (Cuba); 72 (Oman); 73 (Iran); 74–5 (Malaysia); 75 (Colombia); 76–7 (Lebanon); 77–8 (Lao).

[263] So Kalala (n 29) 571, who, however, considers the aspect of 'legitimacy'.

[264] cf Ciobanu (n 27) 11, where it is implied that the USSR was 'reluctant to share the financial burden' of ONUC and UNEF primarily because it did not perceive the operations to be in its national interest.

That may very well be; however, the challenge to binding decisions is mounted on legal grounds,[265] and this is the controlling fact. Irrespective of the underlying political motives of the challenge, it is the couching of the challenge in legal terms, and in particular as the response to an illegal act, that characterizes it and allows it to be qualified as a countermeasure. In the final analysis, legal challenges (and legal acts in general) are always motivated by political considerations to some extent.[266] No one can be (or need be) presumed to act out of a purely un-self-interested desire to uphold the (rule of) law.

It may be significant in this connection that States or other subjects reacting against the UN have not *expressly* claimed to be resorting to countermeasures, despite couching their refusal to comply in legal (among other) terms. Still, it is a general feature of practice that States reacting to a violation of international law will 'only reluctantly' officially qualify their reaction as a countermeasure or 'reprisal', as it was called in the past.[267] This may be due to the negative connotations of the words 'reprisal' and 'retaliation',[268] which also led to the adoption in practice and by the ILC of the more neutral term 'countermeasure',[269] but in any case it connotes that a State may justify its action as a countermeasure in substance,[270] without, however, officially proclaiming it to qualify as belonging to that legal category.

An example of this practice can be seen in *JAT v Belgium*,[271] a case before the Brussels Court of Appeal. In that case JAT contested the Belgian measure of implementation of Council Regulation (EC) 1901/98,[272] adopted in pursuance to Common Position 98/426/CFSP concerning a flight ban on Yugoslav carriers

---

[265] The OIC declared the arms embargo on Bosnia 'illegal' as impeding the inherent right of self-defence under Art 51 UNC in a number of instances: eg Res No 6/22-P (n 72) [7]; Res No 6/23-P (n 72) [14]. The OAU claimed the Libyan sanctions to be in breach of the Charter: n 262 above. As is well known, the USSR (and France) challenged the *vires* of the GA decision on the apportionment of the budget. This led eventually to a request for an AO being addressed to the ICJ, which culminated in *Expenses* (n 27). Whether the USSR (or France) were motivated by political considerations primarily, rather than by a compelling urge to uphold UN law is irrelevant in this connection; their challenge was on legal grounds.

[266] cf the ICJ in *Nuclear Weapons* [1996] ICJ Rep 234 [13], to the effect that 'the political nature of the motives which may be said to have inspired the request... are of no relevance in the establishment of [the Court's] jurisdiction to give... an opinion'. Also in *Border and Transborder Armed Actions* [1988] ICJ Rep 91 [52], the Court found that, its judgment being a legal pronouncement, 'it cannot concern itself with the political motivation which may lead a State... to choose judicial settlement'. It is hard to see why the political motives underlying any action based on legal claims should have a bearing on its legal qualification or its legal effects.

[267] See P Malanczuk (1985) 45 ZaöRV 297. C Tomuschat (1973) 33 ZaöRV 186–7, describes measures taken by States that legally qualify as countermeasures even though not officially qualified as such.

[268] P Malanczuk (1983) 43 ZaöRV 724.

[269] See E Zoller, *Peacetime Unilateral Remedies* (1984) xv–xvii on the point and for a short history of how the term became established through its adoption by arbitral tribunals, the ICJ, and the ILC; cf J-C Venezia (1960) 64 RGDIP 466.

[270] eg when it states that a certain measure has been or is to be taken in response to an act by another subject. In that, the notification requirement can be seen as fulfilled.

[271] (10 June 1999) in [1999] Journal des tribunaux 693.

[272] 7 September 1998 [1998] OJ L 248.

between the FRY and the EC.[273] JAT claimed that the measure was in violation of the bilateral air services agreement between Belgium and Yugoslavia of 24 September 1957 and the 1944 Chicago Convention. The Court of Appeal held that the 'embargo measure' adopted by the EC and implemented by Belgium was a countermeasure, and as such the breach of the aforementioned treaties was justified.[274] Neither the EU/EC nor Belgium had officially referred to a 'countermeasure' prior to this case reaching the Belgian courts.[275]

A clear example in the context of disobedience as a countermeasure is furnished again by the OAU reaction to the Libyan sanctions. Nowhere did the MS of the OAU claimed to be taking countermeasures against the UN. However, the fact that they called for lifting of the sanctions—that is, for the cessation of the wrongful act—while also claiming that the sanctions decisions were in violation of the Charter, and notifying their intention to disobey,[276] cannot be passed over without comment. It bears more than a passing resemblance to an impeccable process of applying countermeasures.

4. Interim conclusion

Treating disobedience or resistance as a sanction, to the extent that countermeasures are, *lato sensu*, the sanctions of the international legal system,[277] is not necessarily a peculiarity of international law and its decentralized nature. Even highly centralized domestic legal orders provide for a positive right of resistance,[278] which is considered the *only sanction* of the constitutional order in extreme circumstances of internal state of necessity,[279] usually a civil war.[280] That the instances where the relevant provision can be invoked in domestic law are extremely rare[281] does not add much to the discussion; principled disobedience to SC decisions is not the most common occurrence in international law either. It just may (need to) surface more frequently in a decentralized system than in a system where the application of law is guaranteed by compulsory jurisdiction.

A final remark in this connection is necessary. One may question whether UN MS have merely the faculty of disobeying the Security Council and justifying this disobedience as a countermeasure, or whether they may, in certain circumstances, be under a duty to do so. Note that the Greek Constitution, for example, qualifies

---

[273] 29 June 1998 [1998] OJ L 190/3.

[274] See further P d'Argent (2003) 36 RBDI 588–9, 622–4.

[275] The Regulation (n 272) speaks of 'additional' or 'further measures', whereas the Common Position (n 273) speaks of 'restrictive' and 'further measures'.

[276] Text at nn 255–63 above.

[277] There is significant theoretical divergence on this point, as many authors will admit as 'sanctions' only those reactions to illegality that are based on centralized determination rather than auto-determination: see generally Leben (n 3) 9; Sicilianos (n 4) 2 seq; G Abi-Saab in *Honour Skubiszewski* (1996) 61. Still, it can be admitted that *functionally*, as the only available reactions to illegality, countermeasures are—*lato sensu*—the sanctions of the international legal order.

[278] See n 77 above.   [279] Herzog (n 77) 20–328 [6].   [280] Ibid 20–329 [7].

[281] The complete overthrow (*Beseitigung*) of the constitutional order is required under Art 20(4) of the German Constitution for the right of resistance to come into play—solitary breaches are not *normally* adequate reason for reliance on the provision: ibid 20–336 [24].

resistance as a right *and a duty* in its final provision, Article 120(4). Indeed one might argue that there is a duty to disobey an unlawful SC decision, which is nothing but an aspect of the general duty to mitigate the harmful effects of an illegal act. This general duty can be seen to have found concrete expression in Article 39 ARSIWA and corresponding Article 38 DARIO.[282]

The argument could run thus that, if the UNC does not grant MS a licence to disobey,[283] general international law does, on the basis of this 'duty to mitigate'. Every MS act in implementation of a wrongful decision of the SC can be seen as a contribution to the injury, and as such would be proscribed under the duty to mitigate. There would thus be an obligation, rather than a mere faculty, to disobey, and consequently there would be no need to justify the reaction as a countermeasure. However, as the ILC itself has noted, '[a]lthough often expressed as a "duty to mitigate", this is not an international obligation which itself gives rise to responsibility'.[284] That is, the duty to mitigate does not entail a true obligation (and thus also licence) to disobey, but rather the general guideline that '[e]ven the wholly innocent victim of wrongful conduct is expected to act reasonably when confronted by the injury'.[285]

On the basis of these considerations, it can be confirmed that disobedience of a binding SC decision remains unlawful as contrary to Article 25 UNC. It cannot be justified under a generic 'duty to mitigate' in general international law. As the ICJ confirmed in *Gabčíkovo*, the duty to mitigate 'could not... justify an otherwise wrongful act',[286] even if it may be relevant for the calculation of damages.[287] The only possible justification for the reaction of disobedience is that it is a wrongful act in response to the Council's wrongful conduct, and thus a countermeasure.

It may be readily submitted that in the context of an IO such as the UN, and given the Council's powers to impose obligations, one is faced with a vertical, rather than with a horizontal, structure. It is in the framework provided by such a horizontal structure that the principles of State responsibility, including countermeasures, were developed. As such it is only normal to question whether these traditional rules of responsibility are adequate and appropriate to be applied in a horizontal setting. A constitutional analogy seems inviting and relatively easy. Still one must be cautious of such hasty transpositions. In the final analysis, responsibility principles apply in vertical structures as well; and international responsibility is nothing like (or should not be seen as being like) domestic concepts of responsibility. It is neither civil, nor criminal: it is *sui generis*.[288] And it is also the most basic part of public international law on account of its quasi-constitutional role.[289]

---

[282] See UN Doc A/64/10 (2009) 122 [3], noting that Art 38 DARIO is 'without prejudice' to any obligation to mitigate the injury that the injured party may have under international law.

[283] As explained in Section II.2.ii above.

[284] ARSIWA Commentary 93 [11].   [285] Ibid.   [286] (n 2) 55 [80].

[287] A point confirmed by the fact that both Arts 39 ARSIWA and 38 DARIO specifically limit the scope of 'contribution to the injury' to the assessment of the form and extent of reparation: see further ARSIWA Commentary 110 [2].

[288] Sicilianos (n 251) 458.

[289] I Brownlie in M Fitzmaurice and D Sarooshi (eds), *Issues of State Responsibility* (2004) 12.

III. Other Countermeasures

The countermeasure of disobedience can be employed as a reaction to a valid but illegal normative act of the Council, such as an Article 41 resolution imposing certain binding obligations on States. However, this countermeasure cannot really be employed against operational activity that is attributable to the UN, as discussed in Chapter 2, in violation of international obligations of the Organization, elaborated in Chapter 3. Operational activities do not command obedience, as they are mere facts. There are, however, certain countermeasures that can be employed in such cases as well as against normative action.

1. Withholding of assessed contributions

Taking unilateral financial measures against an IO, either generally or with respect to assessed contributions of a particular State, has been considered as a measure for restraining the exercise of powers conferred by States to the organization.[290] It has been claimed to constitute 'the only way that a minority of [MS] can ensure that the principle of legality is upheld in the context of [IOs]', particularly in view of the lack of authoritative judicial determination of legality of the acts of the organization;[291] again a measure of last resort.[292]

In the UN context, the withholding of MS contributions has been a relatively frequent measure resorted to by States against the Organization.[293] Ever since the UNEF and ONUC debacle, where the USSR and France refused to pay their assessed contributions claiming the relevant action to be *ultra vires*, there has been 'some controversy as to whether States are under an unqualified obligation' to pay such assessed contributions, 'or whether there are circumstances under which [they could] legally withhold [them]', with most writers favouring the lack of a right to withhold payment.[294] It is submitted that there is no conflict between the two possibilities presented above in the alternative. The obligation to pay is unqualified,[295] since there is an *irrebuttable* presumption of validity, but States can still withhold contributions without incurring international responsibility.

It was claimed earlier that when the Court found the UNEF and ONUC expenses to qualify as 'expenses of the Organization', it presumed the legality of the relevant decisions. This would mean that it was still open for States to deny payment of assessed contributions if they considered the decision illegal, though they would now be faced with a very strong presumption of legality of the decision. In fact this is what happened in practice, since the USSR and France, along with

---

[290] See Sarooshi (n 215) 111 seq, 117.   [291] Ibid 112. cf Klabbers (n 119) 227–8.
[292] F Francioni (2000) 11 EJIL 59.   [293] Ibid 48–9.
[294] cf Amerasinghe in Dupuy (n 105) 331–2. In the same words Sands and Klein (n 119) 583. cf Zoller (n 62) 632 who considers the denial of payment an 'inherent right' of UN MS (after having rejected all possible justifications of the reaction under the VCLT).
[295] Also in view of the sanction provided for in Art 19 UNC.

other States, continued to deny payment even after *Expenses*.[296] This denial was based on continued claims of illegality.[297]

The denial to pay could only be justified as a countermeasure, given the decisions' continued validity and thus binding force. For such a qualification, the refusal of payment should rest on a claim of violation of the Charter or other international law,[298] while all other requirements for the lawful taking of countermeasures should also be respected. The GA decision in 1965 not to insist on the application of sanctions under Article 19 against those members withholding contributions in connection with UNEF and ONUC[299] could be construed as an acceptance of the reaction,[300] and at the same time as cessation in practice of the wrongful conduct, thereby confirming the lawfulness of the countermeasure.

In the first instance, the countermeasure of withholding contributions seems of no avail in most of the cases where States decide to react against a wrongful measure of the Council under Article 41:[301] the imposition by the Council of such measures does not usually involve any additional finance to be granted to the Organization, but rather potentially involves additional finance within the domestic legal orders of the implementing States. Still, even under this conception it is significant, for example with respect to the financing of ad hoc tribunals or other subsidiary organs created by the Council under Article 41, if these are not to be financed by voluntary contributions.

Considered as a sub-species of the general countermeasure of disobedience, however, the relevant countermeasure can serve even as a reaction to wrongful measures that do not impose financial burdens.[302] It can be employed to respond to any violation of the Charter or international law by the Organization, and in particular its SC.[303] In the final analysis, countermeasures need not be reciprocal; they need only be proportional.

2. Assistance to the targeted subject or entity

Article 2(5) UNC provides that '[a]ll Members...shall refrain from giving assistance to any State against which the [UN] is taking preventive or enforcement action.' States are thus under an obligation to omit any assistance to a State targeted by Article 41 measures in a way which would be inconsistent with the purpose of Council action.[304] Since Council measures are increasingly directly targeting

---

[296] *Repertory*, supp 3 vol I (1972) 396 [8]; cf Amerasinghe (n 294) 331.

[297] *Repertory*, supp 3 vol I (1972) 376 [33], 377 [41], 379–80 [58]–[60]; supp 4 vol I (1982) 218 [40].

[298] See also Sarooshi (n 215) 113; Francioni (n 292) 54.

[299] *Repertory*, supp 3 vol I (1972) 397 [13]–[15], 398 [26].

[300] cf D Ciobanu (1972) 55 RivistaDI 71.   [301] cf Bowett (n 214) 51.

[302] cf Klabbers (n 119) 227–8. In the parlance of civil disobedience, this would be indirect rather than direct disobedience, as it involves the violation of another rule than the one protested.

[303] cf Sarooshi (n 215) 114.

[304] Frowein and Krisch (n 179) 139 [8]. See also A Mahiou in *Charte Commentaire* (2005) 471–3.

private individuals and entities other than States, there is, by analogy, an obligation to refrain from assisting those entities.[305]

Clearly, thus, provision of assistance in any form with a view to alleviating the consequences of Council measures would constitute a breach of the obligation under Article 2(5).[306] It could, however, be considered justified as a countermeasure in response, for example, to the breach by the Council of fundamental human rights obligations, obligations incumbent upon it under general international law.[307] Again, this form of countermeasure can be seen as a sub-species of disobedience, as the obligation under Article 2(5) is meant to bolster the obligation to comply with Council decisions under Article 25.[308] But at the same time it can be employed to alleviate the factual situation on the ground, which may be in violation of international law. As implied in the OAU declarations and decisions,[309] African States took measures to alleviate the situation caused by the Council-imposed sanctions against Libya. This was because they considered the sanctions to be in violation of the Charter,[310] and also to be causing disproportionate damage to the Libyan population (as well as to neighbouring States).[311] The OIC MS found the Bosnian arms embargo to be illegal, and called upon all UN MS to assist the Bosnians, even by sending weapons.[312]

A similar situation may occur when States, in exercising their power of auto-interpretation of binding Council decisions imposing asset freezes on individuals, decide to exclude certain categories of payments, as they have done, or when they render assistance to listed individuals through non-application of the sanctions.[313] If such actions are considered to be in violation of the Council measures, then it is open to States to claim that the breach is a countermeasure responding to the violation of a fundamental human right.

---

[305] Frowein and Krisch (n 179) 139 [8].

[306] Indeed the Council 'censures in particular those States which have persisted in trading with the illegal régime [of Southern Rhodesia]..., and which have given [it] active assistance', but finds this to be a violation of Art 25: SCR 253 (1968) [12].

[307] See eg the position of the (then) OAU with respect to the Libyan sanctions: in AHG/Decl.2 (XXXIII) (n 256) [8] the Assembly of the Heads of State and Government 'appreciate the support given by the African States, individually and collectively to [Libya] with a view to mitigating the negative impact of the embargo'. See also CM/Res.1566 (LXI) (n 69) [3].

cf also the Canadian Federal Court in *Abdelrazik* (4 June 2009) 2009 FC 580: it interpreted the travel ban and asset freeze under SCR 1822 (2008) as not impeding Canada from assisting a listed Canadian to return home (at [122]–[128] and [162]–[165]). Canada was ordered to render assistance to the listed individual (including some financial assistance) and facilitate his return.

[308] See n 306 above.   [309] See n 307 above.

[310] See AHG/Dec.127 (XXXIV) (n 70) [2].

[311] See CM/Res.1566 (LXI) (n 69) at 8th preamb; AHG/Decl.2 (XXXIII) (n 256) [3]; AHG/Dec.127 (XXXIV) (n 70) at 6th preamb.

[312] Text at nn 72–3 above. Some MS did ostensibly follow up on this: cf LF Damrosch (1997) 269 RdC 125.

[313] See eg the position taken by the Swedish authorities with respect to SCR 1267 (1999) and its associated sanctions regime: text at nn 45–6 in Chapter 5 above, and the position taken by English and Canadian courts in *Othman* and *Abdelrazik* respectively: see text at nn 60–1 in Chapter 5, and n 307 above.

3. Action in domestic courts

It was argued extensively above,[314] that the determination of UN responsibility may take place through State or regional IOs' judicial organs. It was even claimed that domestic courts may be seen as imposing a countermeasure when they refuse to apply a rule of international law on the basis that the State towards which the rule is to be applied has equally failed to comply with it.[315] This is the principle of reciprocity, which in fact cannot be distinguished from countermeasures in this connection. There is no distinction between 'reciprocity' and 'countermeasures' as distinct forms of non-forcible self-help,[316] as is evidenced by the decision of the ILC to drop the distinction[317] in favour of a unitary concept in ARSIWA.[318] As such, reciprocity is rather a *species* of the *genus* 'countermeasures'.

Domestic courts can thus be seen as applying a countermeasure when they determine that another subject of international law has perpetrated an internationally wrongful act and they respond to that breach.[319] This response will sometimes not be limited simply to reciprocal non-application of a treaty against another State, as described above; it may involve other measures as well, such as for example the denial of sovereign immunity.[320] A domestic court may respond to a breach even against IOs. In *Ms Siedler v WEU*,[321] the Brussels Labour Court of Appeal found the WEU's internal procedures for the settlement of administrative disputes to be in breach of the general principle of prohibition of denial of justice, and consequently denied it immunity from domestic jurisdiction.[322]

---

[314] See Chapter 5 above at Subsections 2 and 3.

[315] cf B Simma in *EPIL*, vol 4 (2000) 32.

[316] Malanczuk (n 267) 315. *Contra* Zoller (n 269) 15, who qualifies reciprocity as an 'autonomous legal concept'.

[317] cf W Riphagen (1985) II(1) YILC 10–11: proposed Arts 8 and 9 respectively.

[318] See ARSIWA Commentary 129 [5].

[319] cf Weil (n 106) 313, according to whom national courts are 'one of the most effective sanctions mechanisms of international law', particularly eg in the application of conventional rules on the avoidance of double taxation. See also L Gradoni in WJM van Genugten et al (eds), *Criminal Jurisdiction* (2009) 149–52.

[320] One could eg conceptualize the denial of the sovereign immunity of Germany by the Italian courts in *Ferrini* (IT 2004) ILDC 19 (Corte di Cassazione) as a countermeasure in response to Germany's breach of international law. The Corte di Cassazione did not, of course, rely on such reasoning. It remains to be seen whether a relevant defence will be pleaded (even if in the alternative) in the proceedings brought by Germany against Italy in this connection: ICJ Press Release No 2008/44, 23 December 2008. It should be noted that the US Supreme Court eg has considered the terrorism exception in FSIA (28 USC §1605[a][7]—now repealed) to have been intended a 'sanction', 'to punish and deter undesirable conduct': see *Republic of Iraq v Beaty* 556 US ___ (2009); 129 S Ct 2183 (2009); (US 2009) ILDC 1360 [A2].

[321] (BE 2003) ILDC 53; [2004] Journal des tribunaux 617.

[322] See d'Argent (n 274) 613. The Brussels Court of Appeal extended this line of reasoning in a case against the ACP in its decision of 4 March 2003 *Lutchmaya v General Secretariat of the ACP Group* [2003] Journal des tribunaux 684; (BE 2003) ILDC 1363, to deny the ACP immunity from execution on the basis that the right to a fair trial includes the execution of decisions as an integral part. See d'Argent (n 274) 613–14. For discussion of both cases see ibid 614–16 as well as commentary by C Ryngaert in (BE 2003) ILDC 1363.

The decision of the Brussels court can be meaningfully interpreted as a countermeasure.[323] It does not involve a denial of immunity on the basis of non-application of an immunity instrument, or of international law domestically, or on the basis of any other similar reason.[324] Neither does it restrict the scope of immunity along the lines of *acta jure imperii—acta jure gestionis*.[325] Rather, it denies immunity on the basis of the breach of a rule of general international law, as understood by the Brussels court.

In another case, a domestic court blocked a UNICEF account, in direct violation of the State's international obligations under the Convention on UN Privileges and Immunities and the relevant agreement between UNICEF and the State concerned, ostensibly because UNICEF did not seem intent on compensating for loss of life caused by a UNICEF-operated vehicle, in violation of its obligations under Article VIII, Section 29 of the Convention. The Legal Counsel, in addressing the Permanent Representative of that State '*regrets* the delay which has arisen in settling this case' and notes that 'UNICEF has decided to settle this claim on the basis of the award given' by the domestic courts, the Organization 'thus *fulfilling its responsibilities* [under the 1946 Convention to make provisions for appropriate modes of settlement of private law disputes]'.[326] The UN Legal Counsel can be seen as treating the court decision as a countermeasure in response to UNICEF's violation of the 1946 Convention. The court reaction further seems to have prompted UNICEF to deal with the outstanding claim.

Similarly, decisions by domestic courts to strike down domestic measures implementing binding SCRs under Article 41, such as those contemplated in Chapter 5, would bind (and thus force) the State's executive not to apply the relevant measures. At the very least, this would be the case until new domestic implementation acts are adopted—which does not preclude that they would again be judicially tested.[327] This is precisely the practical outcome of the ECJ annulling the EC act implementing SCRs with respect to Kadi and Al Barakaat; and of the CFI annulling the EC act implementing SCRs with respect to Othman: the effect of the annulment is that EC MS are in breach of their obligations under Article 25 UNC, until a new EC implementing act is put in place or until they adopt their own implementing acts.[328] The outcome is similar with respect to the UK Supreme

---

[323] The reactive breach being the violation of the State's obligation to accord immunity—cf n 320 above and (in the UN context) the position of the UN Legal Counsel in [1993] UNJY 382–3.

[324] See exhaustively A Reinisch, *IOs before National Courts* (2000) 177–85.

[325] See ibid 185–214. cf *Mme Sawas c Royaume d'Arabie Saoudite* [2008] Journal des tribunaux 494–5; (BE 2007) ILDC 1146, where the Brussels Labour Tribunal denied immunity to Saudi Arabia on the basis that employment of administrative (as opposed to diplomatic) personnel in the Saudi embassy constituted an act *jure gestionis*, rather than *jure imperii*.

[326] [1992] UNJY 473–4 [emphasis added].

[327] This is in fact what has happened with respect to Mr Kadi: after having the domestic measures implementing the 1267 sanctions regime against him annulled by the ECJ in C-402/05P *Kadi* [2008] ECR I-6351, the EC re-subjected Kadi to the restrictive regime, only for Kadi to bring a new case against his listing before the CFI: T-85/09 *Kadi v Commission*, action brought on 26 February 2009: [2009] OJ C 90/37. The CFI (renamed 'General Court of the EU') decided again in Kadi's favour, annulling the new listing, on 30 September 2010.

[328] cf T Tridimas and JA Gutierrez-Fons (2008–9) 32 FILJ 704. The maintenance of the effects of the annulled Regulation that the ECJ ordered in *Kadi* (n 327) at [3] of the *dispositif* was not allowed

Court's decision to annul UK Orders in Council implementing the 1267 sanctions regime with respect to specific individuals.[329] It is accepted that the application of international law by a national court aims sometimes at constraining the activities of the national court's executive.[330] This is one of those cases, even if the courts claimed to be applying exclusively domestic law. Similarly, in the rare instances of direct challenges to SCRs, a decision by the national court to disregard the resolution would in and of itself constitute a breach that the State could only remedy through appeals, if available.[331]

At first sight, such action by domestic courts is not easily qualified as a countermeasure.[332] Domestic courts, as organs of the State, certainly have the capacity to and do perpetrate breaches of international obligations, which are of course attributable to their home States and engage those States' international responsibility.[333] If a domestic court disregards a domestic implementing measure or a SCR, as it has been suggested that it can and should,[334] this will mean that the State is in violation of Article 25 UNC, thereby perpetrating an internationally wrongful act. The breach perpetrated by the court can be justified by claiming that the SCR is itself in breach of the Organization's obligations under the Charter or general international law. Still, this internationally wrongful act could not qualify as a countermeasure without the cooperation of the executive organs, if not for any other reason, then for lack of a call on the responsible subject to comply with its secondary obligations, notification, and offer to negotiate.[335]

---

when the CFI recently annulled the same Regulation with respect to Othman: T-318/01 [2009] ECR II-1627 [95]–[99]. The EC MS are immediately in breach of the relevant SCR in this latter case.

[329] *HM Treasury v Mohammed Jabar Ahmed and Others (FC); HM Treasury v Mohammed al-Ghabra (FC); R (Hani El Sayed Sabaei Youssef) v HM Treasury* [2010] UKSC 2. Here as well a suspension of execution is given, much like in *Kadi* (n 327) above: [2010] UKSC 2 at [83]–[84] (Lord Hope, with whom Lord Walker and Lady Hale agreed). For brief comment see A Tzanakopoulos [2010] EJIL: Talk!, 23 February.

[330] cf E Benvenisti (1993) 4 EJIL 159.

[331] In *Milošević v The Netherlands* (Interlocutory Injunction) KG 01/975 (2001) 48 NILR 357, the President of The Hague District Court was asked to order the Netherlands to release Milošević. The court found that it had no jurisdiction to make such an order, by relying on the fact that the ICTY had already confirmed the legality of its establishment: ibid 360–1 [3]. However, this serves to highlight that an eventual order of release would have put the Netherlands in direct violation of its international obligations both under SCR 827 (1993) and the bilateral UN–Netherlands agreement: cf ibid 361 [3.5]–[3.6]. Further, the US Attorney-General has sued in federal courts to enjoin state authorities that put the US in violation of its treaty obligations: see *US v County of Arlington* 669 F 2d 925 (4th Cir 1982); in *Tachiona v US* 386 F 3d 205 at 212 (2d Cir 2004), the US Court of Appeal accepted that the US Government had the requisite legal interest to appeal a decision from a lower court which effectively put the US in breach of its international obligations; cf J Quigley (2002) 27 YJIL 440.

[332] This is perhaps why some authors tend to ascribe to them simply a factual power to generate a pull 'against voluntary compliance': see S Wheatley (2006) 17 EJIL 544. Others still maintain that national courts have a 'right' to review under Art 25 UNC: E de Wet and A Nollkaemper (2002) 45 GYIL 185–7.

[333] cf *Immunity from Legal Process* [1999] ICJ Rep 88 [63]. See generally C Eustathiadès, *La responsabilité internationale de l'État pour les actes des organes judiciaires* (1936); H Urbanek (1958–9) 9 ÖZöR 213.

[334] See eg A Orakhelashvili (2008) 102 AJIL 343. This, it is claimed ibid, may in fact be 'the only available remedy for the breach of international law' by the Council—yet again an *ultima ratio*, and again a measure that can be seen as a sub-species of disobedience. cf also de Wet and Nollkaemper (n 332) 185, speaking of the 'last option'.

[335] cf Arts 52(1)(a)–(b) ARSIWA; 54(1)(a)–(b) DARIO.

However, it seems exaggerated to insist on such technicalities if any calls for compliance and offers to negotiate are futile or impossible in the circumstances.[336] That relevant calls and offers to the Council will in most cases meet this fate is demonstrated in the Libyan example, where many years of efforts by the OAU and other regional organizations yielded little results—eventually leading to flat-out disobedience. Even the ILC has accepted this in principle, allowing for 'urgent countermeasures' irrespective of the obligation to notify and to offer negotiation.[337]

Although the circumstances that the Commission had in mind are admittedly not the ones contemplated here,[338] it is not beyond reason to imagine an analogous application.[339] As Doehring has stated, notification can be dispensed with when there is only one means for the exercise of countermeasures.[340] If the domestic court decision will force disobedience, as explained above, it becomes apparent that disobedience in all its different forms is virtually the only countermeasure available to MS.

4. Breach of obligations under general international law

Any other non-performance of obligations under general international law owed to the Organization could qualify as a countermeasure, and is potentially available to any State, member or non-member, and for any breach of obligations by the Organization either under the Charter (only for members) or under general international law (for members and non-members).

This is of course so, provided that the non-performance cannot relate to those international obligations which are excepted from countermeasures, such as the obligation not to use force, obligations for the protection of fundamental human rights, obligations of humanitarian character prohibiting reprisals, the obligation to respect the inviolability agents, premises, archives, and so forth, and obligations under applicable dispute settlement procedures.[341]

It would not be possible to discuss every such reactive breach which can be contemplated. This would have to be considered ad hoc and on the basis of the

---

[336] Malanczuk (n 268) 726.

[337] cf Arts 52(2) ARSIWA; 54(2) DARIO. An example of such 'urgency' is evident in the decision of the English High Court in *R (Othman) v Secretary of State for Work and Pensions* [2001] EWHC Admin 1022 [56]–[57], [60]–[61], where Mr Justice Collins uses the urgency of the situation where an individual's life or health is at risk due to the sanctions regime to justify making exceptions from the regime without requesting the assent of the Sanctions Committee.

[338] See ARSIWA Commentary 136 [6].

[339] E Benvenisti (1999–2000) 98 MichLR 193 argues that legislatures are less capable than executives of monitoring other States' violations of international law and this explains their relative inertia: these violations are 'key tools' for justifying one's own breach, both to the international community and to international tribunals. Domestic courts, however, are in fact capable of monitoring other States' compliance and this may provide further justification for their invocation of a breach and subsequent reaction.

[340] (n 23) 50–1. cf Orakhelashvili (n 334) 343, speaking of 'the only available remedy'.

[341] See Arts 50 ARSIWA; 52 DARIO.

available information. The statement, however, aims at completing the picture, before considering the position of any 'States other than the injured State'.

IV. 'Lawful' Measures by States 'Other than the Injured State'

If it is accepted that violations of the obligations of the UN under the Charter result in all MS of the Organization being injured, then the countermeasure of disobedience is virtually always available in response. However, when the Organization breaches obligations under general international law through Council action, the circle of injured States is unlikely to be as large. While the precise determination of the injured State cannot be made *in abstracto*, but rather depends on the particular primary obligation breached and its classification, it is safe to assume that the most conspicuous breaches in such circumstances will be violations of obligations under peremptory norms (though not necessarily amounting to serious breaches[342] in most cases) or of other obligations *erga omnes*.[343]

In such cases, the targeted State may be qualified as an injured State. Still, the obligations will be owed to 'the international community as a whole', which necessarily brings up the question on the position of States that are not individually injured. Even more so since, in accordance with the practice of the Council as it has evolved over recent years, the target may be no State whatsoever, but rather private individuals and legal entities.[344] In such cases no State may be individually injured by the breach.

The question of the right of States not individually injured by an internationally wrongful act to resort to countermeasures 'in the general interest' against the responsible subject has received a significant amount of attention in legal literature,[345] and has also plagued the ILC for its fair share of years, with many different solutions being proposed and adopted until their culmination in the 2001 ARSIWA.[346] In accordance with ARSIWA provisions, which are mirrored in DARIO, all States can invoke the responsibility of the UN for the violation of an *erga omnes* obligation,[347] and seek cessation, assurances and guarantees

---

[342] ie 'gross or systematic violations': Art 40(2) ARSIWA and Commentary 113 [7]–[8]. cf S Kadelbach in Tomuschat and Thouvenin (n 143) 25–6.

[343] See Chapter 3.II.1–2 above.

[344] See eg SCRs 1267 (1999); 1373 (2001) among many others.

[345] From the works exclusively devoted to the issue, only indicatively may one mention C Hillgruber in Tomuschat and Thouvenin (n 143) 265; M Dawidowicz (2006) 77 BYIL 333; G Gaja in *Memory Schachter* (2005) 31; D Alland (2002) 13 EJIL 1221; M Koskenniemi (2001) 72 BYIL 337; Frowein (n 8) 345; K Hailbronner (1992) 30 AVR 2; Stein (n 191) 38; Frowein (n 160) 67; M Akehurst (1970) 44 BYIL 1. See extensively also Tams (n 199) 198–251.

[346] Under the 1996 Articles all States were to be considered as injured by an 'international crime', and could thus resort to countermeasures—however, the Commission avoided stating this *expressis verbis*; it is inferred by implication: see Arts 40(3), 47, 51–3 in (1996) II(2) YILC 62–4. Under the 2000 Articles, the States 'other than the injured State' could take countermeasures: see Art 54 in (2000) II(2) YILC 70–1. Finally, in the discussion of DARIO, the Commission revisited the issue with suggestions being made to 'go a step further' than 2001 and provide for collective countermeasures instead of allowing 'lawful measures': UN Doc A/63/10 (2008) 261 [161].

[347] cf Arts 48(1)(b) ARSIWA; 48(1)–(2) DARIO.

of non-repetition, if appropriate, and even the performance of the obligation of reparation in the interest of the injured subject or the beneficiaries of the obligation breached.[348]

However, it has not been settled whether States entitled to invoke UN responsibility under these provisions may also resort to countermeasures to enforce compliance with the relevant secondary obligations. In a provision which serves as a saving clause[349] and which has attracted many—almost poetic at times—characterizations,[350] the Commission states that the Articles do not prejudice the right of States other than the injured State which may invoke the responsibility of a subject to resort to 'lawful' measures.[351]

It would not be possible to treat the issue exhaustively in this connection, nor would it be helpful to regurgitate the well-known debate. Suffice it to mention that the basic issue revolves around the question who is going to 'sanction' or react against breaches of obligations that are considered 'fundamental' or 'owed *erga omnes*' or 'arising under peremptory norms'.[352] Should it be solely the international community through institutionalized means?[353] Or rather, in view of the utopian allure of this suggestion, the individual States acting in a decentralized manner, perhaps with minimum coordination?[354] To state the question in terms of the traditional French theoretical framework, should one adhere to an 'institutional model' or rather to a traditional 'relational model'?[355] If the first option may seem utopian, the alternative entails an inherent risk of abuse—as does any decentralized reaction, and theorists have positioned themselves at all possible points along the spectrum.[356]

Be that as it may, the aforementioned question is, at least in the setting of countermeasures by not individually injured States against the Organization, almost moot. There are no established institutionalized means in international law for the compulsory determination of breach and the enforcement of international obligations. Even if one were to consider—over strong objections—the UN and its SC acting under Chapter VII as such an institutionalized means of law enforcement in the name of the 'international community',[357] this is of little help when it comes to enforcing the law against the UN itself.

---

[348] cf Arts 48(2) ARSIWA; 48(4) DARIO.

[349] See ARSIWA Commentary 139 [7].

[350] Sicilianos (n 199) 1142 finds the relevant Art 54 to be of 'an ambivalence worthy of the Pythian oracle', while Dawidowicz (n 345) 347 speaks of an 'agnostic' provision. Most precisely Tams (n 199) 200 finds that the ILC 'decided not to decide'.

[351] cf Arts 54 ARSIWA; 56 DARIO.

[352] See for an overview Dawidowicz (n 345) 342 seq.

[353] cf [1972] UNJY 194–5.   [354] cf eg Hillgruber (n 345) 272.

[355] See generally R-J Dupuy, *Le droit international* (2004) part one ('le droit de la société relationnelle') in contradistinction to part two ('le droit de la société institutionnelle') and specifically Sicilianos (n 251) 487–90.

[356] cf generally with respect to the oscillation between these two positions and the inherent bipolarity of (international) law M Koskenniemi, *From Apology to Utopia* (2005) *passim*.

[357] It has been argued that Council sanctions are always a reaction to illegality: to the violation of the obligation not to constitute a threat to the peace. But not every violation of law will constitute such a threat and thus be sanctioned by the Council. See further Chapter 3.II.2.ii above. Not even the UN itself understands the Council to be an organ of law enforcement. The following incident is

An argument could be made that, even if 'third' or 'non-directly injured' State countermeasures are impermissible in international law, they are exceptionally permissible when the problem of objective third-party determination has been resolved. Akehurst, for example, has argued that third-State countermeasures are admissible when they aim at enforcing a judicial decision. In such a case, he contends,

the danger of abuse by biased third States, which is the main reason for denying [them] the general right to take reprisals, is virtually eliminated by the fact that the original cause of the dispute has been dealt with by the judgment of an *impartial tribunal*.[358]

If there is no reason to doubt the impartiality of such tribunals as the ECJ or the BVerfG and the UK Supreme Court, then it would seem at least plausible that third-State countermeasures against the UN are admissible when a domestic— impartial—court has found, even if indirectly, SC Chapter VII measures to be in violation of the law. International law questions, or any law questions for that matter, would still, in such a case, be decided by a court, albeit a domestic court, and not exclusively through political processes.[359]

A definitive answer cannot be given, at least in the present state of development of international law with respect to decentralized reactions against IOs. However, it is worth summing up the thesis: all MS can, as injured States, resort to the countermeasure of disobedience or other countermeasures against the Organization if SC action under Article 41 is in breach of an obligation under the UNC. Further, if the obligation breached is an obligation under general international law, the injured States can resort to the countermeasure of disobedience and other countermeasures, if they are MS of the Organization, or other countermeasures if they are third States. In the case of violation of obligations under peremptory norms of international law or other obligations *erga omnes*, it cannot be excluded that States other than the injured State(s) will resort to the countermeasure of disobedience or other countermeasures, thereby establishing in practice the availability of countermeasures against the UN 'in the general interest'.[360]

---

instructive: in reply to a letter informing the UN that the export of freon gas to Iraq would constitute a violation of relevant international treaties, and requesting that the S-G, as the depositary, bring this to the attention of the SC, the Legal Counsel replied that

In any case...I am of the view that the episode reported by you *does not fall within the competence of the Security Council* and should not be brought to its attention. ([1994] UNJY 501 [emphasis added])

[358] Akehurst (n 345) 15–16 [emphasis added]. cf Tams (n 199) 87–9.
[359] cf A Nollkaemper (2007) 101 AJIL 762.
[360] For significant practice in countermeasures 'in the general interest' which is not limited to Western States or to a few instances see Tams (n 199) 90–1, 208 seq; Sicilianos (n 251) 494–8. On EC practice and the aforementioned *JAT* case (n 271) see E Paasivirta and A Rosas in E Cannizzaro (ed), *The EU as an Actor in International Relations* (2002) 213–15. But see also Hillgruber (n 345) 283–7 for another take; and finally ARSIWA Commentary 137–9 [3]–[6].

General Conclusion

Writing about the newborn United Nations at the beginning of the 1950s, Lissitzyn observed that its weakness 'largely protects its members from abuse of power'.[1] 'If the organization is to gain strength', he continued, 'the authority to give binding interpretations of the Charter, at least in matters directly affecting the rights and duties of states, must be lodged somewhere, preferably in a judicial organ.'[2] This was because 'an organization whose various organs *and members* all have the power to interpret the basic constitutional instrument without definite legal effect on the other organs and members can hardly be viable'.[3] These statements largely capture the problem with which this study grappled, and they also indicate the solution, as well as—it is submitted—the direction in which events are leading the UN.

No doubt the Security Council has been vested with enormous power, even if (almost) only normative power, under Chapter VII of the UN Charter. By now it is a cliché that most studies dealing with the Council attribute the exercise of this power to the end of the Cold War. As with most clichés, this one also has its grain of truth. Throughout this study the aim has been to understand the UN as an actor in international law, subjected to rules, and bearing responsibility for their violation.

Reading a paper before the Grotius Society in 1924, Josef Kunz, in summarizing Kelsen's theory, stated that

Jurisprudence as the science of law, working only with juridical methods, is only able to understand the State by understanding it *as law*. The State, as a powerful monster, is quite out of the reach of jurisprudence.[4]

Much the same can be said of the SC, and of the UN, the Organization of which it is a principal organ. Conceiving the Council as a powerful anthropomorphic creature is hardly the proper ambit of jurisprudence. The Council is rather better conceived as a sub-system of rules, as the organ of an IO created in accordance with a system of rules, and delimited by the application of a system of rules.

The Security Council has come of age; it acts in a wide field and significantly affects international life, in particular through the imposition of binding non-forcible measures. In so doing, it has been shown that the Council may violate international law and thus engage the international responsibility of the UN. There is, however, no possibility of authoritative determination of the engagement of UN responsibility for Council action under Article 41, even if that engagement can intelligibly be argued to have occurred in theory. Still, in the decentralized legal

---

[1] OJ Lissitzyn, *The ICJ* (1951) 96.   [2] Ibid 96–7.
[3] Ibid 96.   [4] JL Kunz (1925) 10 GST 121.

system that is the international legal system, the lack of authoritative determination does not exhaust the discussion, even if it demonstrates the weakness (for some) or the peculiarity (for others) of the set-up. States themselves may proceed to determine the engagement of UN responsibility. To do this, they have to overcome both legal and practical obstacles: the presumption of legality of UN (and SC) action; and their relative weakness—when acting alone—against the membership of the Organization.

States may thus proceed—and have in fact done so, in an interpretation of the practice—to determine the engagement of UN responsibility and react collectively, within other (regional) IOs. They have done so in order to counter their relative weakness when acting as units; and they have relied on legal argument to overcome the presumption of legality. Alternatively, States may be prompted or even forced to react by their own domestic courts (to which one should count regional international courts with binding authority over States). The court decision may offer a good argument for claiming UN responsibility, or may not allow any other way of compliance with the court decision *but* claiming UN responsibility, lest the State concede that it is simply breaking the law.

Following up on their auto-determination of the UN's responsibility, States have proceeded to react, in particular by disobeying the Council's binding commands. In fact, disobedience has always been championed as the 'last resort' of States faced with illegal Council non-forcible action under Chapter VII. However, the qualification 'last resort' does not have much in the way of substantive legal content. The question that presents itself with some force is that of the legal qualification of the *ultima ratio* of disobedience.

Disobedience is in the first instance illegal, as it constitutes a breach of the obligation of MS to comply with SC decisions (Article 25 UNC) and to support the UN's enforcement action by not rendering assistance to targets of such enforcement (Article 2[5] UNC). However, such a breach is justified under international law: it is undertaken by States injured by the Organization's action in response to the breach on the part of the Organization of its obligations under international law. Other cognate countermeasures are also available, even to non-MS for violations of general international law.

The threat of massive disobedience—which has now found legal justification—is a potent tool for inducing compliance of a powerful organ with international law. Within a month of the OAU decision to disobey the Libyan sanctions, a seven-year deadlock was miraculously resolved and the sanctions were suspended. The constant threat of massive disobedience of SCRs 1267 seq, forced on a number of States by their own domestic courts, has provoked a number of changes in the UN blacklisting procedures, including granting humanitarian exemptions and the introduction of a focal point for individuals to petition the Council directly for de-listing. The threat of massive disobedience has started to materialize as is evident in cases such as *Kadi* (ECJ), *Othman* (CFI), *Abdelrazik* (Canadian Federal Court), *A, K, M, Q and G* and *Hay* (High Court, Court of Appeal and UK Supreme Court) and many others still pending. This clearly led the Council to drop the focal point and establish an 'Office of the Ombudsperson' to assist the 1267 Sanctions Committee with de-listing requests in SCR 1904 (2009), but further developments should be expected.

All this, of course, is still inadequate in terms of ensuring full compliance of the Council and the UN with their international legal obligations. However, it bears testimony to the fact that decentralized pressure applied by States through the threat or exercise of disobedience, justified as a countermeasure against the Organization, serves increasingly to push the Council towards compliance. If not for anything else, for fear of being relegated to irrelevance for the second time in its 'life': this time not because the internal power struggles render it incompetent to act, but because the consensus within it (however procured) has led the Council to infringe rights—both of States, and of individuals—that have resulted from long-running struggles.

Beyond this study, one may start contemplating the value of decentralized reactions in bringing about partial centralization in particular areas of international law. That the decentralized application of 'sanctions' is an inherently destabilizing process for implementing the law is beyond doubt. Yet, it is not destabilizing enough to threaten the existence of the entire system. In particular areas, and when decentralization presents itself as a potentially significant obstacle to the functioning of the (partial) sub-system, corrective action seems to be taken by the actors in the system almost automatically, in an effort perhaps of self-preservation. In that way, it may be the actual use of decentralized reactions to an ever-augmenting degree that forces partial centralization.

Bibliography

Abi-Saab, G, '"Interprétation" et "Auto-Interprétation"—Quelques réflexions sur leur rôle dans la formation et la résolution du différend international' in U Beyerlin et al (eds), *Recht zwischen Umbruch und Bewahrung—Festschrift für Rudolf Bernhardt* (Springer, Berlin 1995) 9

—— 'De la sanction en droit international—Essai de clarification' in J Makarczyk (ed), *Theory of International Law at the Threshold of the 21st Century—Essays in Honour of Krzysztof Skubiszewski* (Kluwer, The Hague 1996) 61

—— 'Wither the Judicial Function? Concluding Remarks' in L Boisson de Chazournes et al (eds), *International Organizations and International Dispute Settlement—Trends and Prospects* (Transnational Publishers, Ardsley 2002) 241

—— 'The Proper Role of International Law in Combating Terrorism' in A Bianchi (ed), *Enforcing International Law Norms Against Terrorism* (Hart, Oxford 2004) xiii

Ago, R, 'Le délit international' (1939) 68 RdC 419

—— '"Binding" Advisory Opinions of the International Court of Justice' (1991) 85 AJIL 439

Akande, D, 'The International Court of Justice and the Security Council: Is there Room for Judicial Control of Decisions of the Political Organs of the United Nations?' (1997) 46 ICLQ 309

Akehurst, M, 'Reprisals by Third States' (1970) 44 BYIL 1

—— 'The Hierarchy of the Sources of International Law' (1974–5) 47 BYIL 273

—— 'Equity and General Principles of Law' (1976) 25 ICLQ 801

Alland, D, 'Countermeasures of General Interest' (2002) 13 EJIL 1221

Alvarez, JE, 'Theoretical Perspectives on Judicial Review by the World Court' (1995) 89 ASILProc 85

—— 'Judging the Security Council' (1996) 90 AJIL 1

—— 'The Security Council's War on Terrorism: Problems and Policy Options' in E de Wet and A Nollkaemper (eds), *Review of the Security Council by Member States* (Intersentia, Antwerp 2003) 119

—— *International Organizations as Law-makers* (OUP, Oxford 2005)

Ambos, K, 'Judicial Accountability of Perpetrators of Human Rights Violations and the Role of Victims' (2000) 6 International Peacekeeping 67

Amerasinghe, cf, 'Détournement de pouvoir in International Administrative Law' (1984) 44 ZaöRV 439

—— 'Interpretation of Texts in Open International Organizations' (1994) 65 BYIL 175

—— 'Financing' in R-J Dupuy (ed), *Manuel sur les organisations internationales* (2nd edn, Nijhoff, Dordrecht 1998) 313

—— *Principles of the Institutional Law of International Organizations* (2nd edn, CUP, Cambridge 2005)

Amorim, C, 'Effectiveness and Legitimacy of the United Nations Security Council: A Tribute to Tono Eitel' in JA Frowein et al (eds), *Verhandeln für den Frieden—Liber Amicorum Tono Eitel* (Springer, Berlin 2003) 5

Amr, MSM, *The Role of the International Court of Justice as the Principal Judicial Organ of the United Nations* (Kluwer, The Hague 2003)

Amrallah, B, 'The International Responsibility of the United Nations for Activities Carried Out by UN Peace-Keeping Forces' (1976) 32 REDI 57

Anderson, D, 'Negotiation and Dispute Settlement' in MD Evans (ed), *Remedies in International Law: The Institutional Dilemma* (Hart, Oxford 1998) 111

Angelet, N, 'Protest against Security Council Decisions' in K Wellens (ed), *International Law: Theory and Practice—Essays in Honour of Eric Suy* (Nijhoff, The Hague 1998) 277

—— 'Le droit des relations diplomatiques et consulaires dans la pratique récente du Conseil de sécurité' (1999) 32 RBDI 149

Arangio-Ruiz, G, 'State Fault and the Forms and Degrees of International Responsibility: Questions of Attribution and Relevance' in *Le droit international au service de la paix, de la justice et du développement—Mélanges Michel Virally* (Pedone, Paris 1991) 25

—— 'The ICJ Statute, The Charter and Forms of Legality Review of Security Council Decisions' in L Vohrah et al (eds), *Man's Inhumanity to Man—Essays in International Law in Honour of Antonio Cassese* (Kluwer, The Hague 2003) 41

Aston, JD, 'Die Bekämpfung abstrakter Gefahren für den Weltfrieden durch legislative Maßnahmen des Sicherheitsrats—Resolution 1373 (2001) im Kontext' (2002) 62 ZaöRV 257

Aust, A, 'The Role of Human Rights in Limiting the Enforcement Powers of the Security Council: A Practitioner's View' in E de Wet and A Nollkaemper (eds), *Review of the Security Council by Member States* (Intersentia, Antwerp 2003) 31

Barber, NW, 'Against a Written Constitution' (2008) Public Law 11

Basdevant, J, 'Règles générales du droit de la paix' (1936) 58 RdC 475

Bastid, S, 'De quelques problèmes juridiques posés par le développement des organisations internationales' in DS Constantopoulos et al (eds), *Grundprobleme des internationalen Rechts—Festschrift für Jean Spiropoulos* (Schimmelbusch and Co, Bonn 1957) 35

Bedau, HA, 'On Civil Disobedience' (1961) 58 Journal of Philosophy 653

—— 'Introduction' in idem (ed), *Civil Disobedience in Focus* (Routledge, London 1991) 1

Bedjaoui, M, 'Du contrôle de légalité des actes du Conseil de sécurité' in *Nouveaux itinéraires en droit—Hommage à François Rigaux* (Bruylant, Brussels 1993) 69

—— *The New World Order and the Security Council: Testing the Legality of its Acts* (Nijhoff, Dordrecht 1994)

—— 'Un contrôle de la légalité des actes du Conseil de sécurité est-il possible?' in Société française pour le droit international (ed), *Le Chapitre VII de la Charte des Nations Unies—Colloque de Rennes* (Pedone, Paris 1995) 255

Bennouna, M, 'Le règlement des différends peut-il limiter le « droit » de se faire justice à soi-même?' (1994) 5 EJIL 61

——'L'embargo dans la pratique des Nations Unies: radioscopie d'un moyen de pression' in E Yakpo and T Boumedra (eds), Liber Amicorum *Judge Mohammed Bedjaoui* (Kluwer, The Hague 1999) 555

Benvenisti, E, 'Judicial Misgivings Regarding the Application of International Law: An Analysis of Attitudes of National Courts' (1993) 4 EJIL 159

—— 'Exit and Voice in the Age of Globalization' (1999–2000) 98 MichLR 167

Berlia, G, 'De la responsabilité internationale de l'État' in *La technique et les principes du droit public: Études en l'honneur de Georges Scelle*, vol 2 (LGDJ, Paris 1950) 875

Berman, F, 'The Relationship between the International Criminal Court and the Security Council' in HAM von Hebel et al (eds), *Reflections on the International Criminal Court—Essays in Honour of Adriaan Bos* (TMC Asser, The Hague 1999) 173

Bermann, GA, '*Marbury v Madison* and European Union "Constitutional" Review' (2004) 36 GWILR 557

Bernhardt, R, 'Die gerichtliche Durchsetzung völkerrechtlicher Verpflichtungen' (1987) 47 ZaöRV 17

——'*Ultra vires* Activities of International Organizations' in J Makarczyk (ed), *Theory of International Law at the Threshold of the 21st Century—Essays in Honour of Krzysztof Skubiszewski* (Kluwer, The Hague 1996) 599

—— 'Article 103' in B Simma (ed), *The UN Charter: A Commentary* (2nd edn, OUP, Oxford 2002) 1292

Bianchi, A, 'Assessing the Effectiveness of the UN Security Council's Anti-Terrorism Measures: The Quest for Legitimacy and Cohesion' (2006) 17 EJIL 881

—— 'The Act of State: The State of the Act—Judicial Interpretation and Human Rights Enforcement' in MG Cohen (ed), *Promoting Justice, Human Rights and Conflict Resolution through International Law—Liber Amicorum Lucius Caflisch* (Nijhoff, Leiden 2007) 129

—— 'Human Rights and the Magic of *Jus Cogens*' (2008) 19 EJIL 491

Bindschedler, RL, 'Zum Problem der Grundnorm' in FA Freiherr von der Heydte et al (eds), *Völkerrecht und rechtliches Weltbild—Festschrift für Alfred Verdross* (Springer, Vienna 1960) 67

Bleckmann, A, 'Gedanken zur Repressalie—Ein Versuch der Anwendung der Interessenjurisprudenz auf das Völkergewohnheitsrecht' in I von Münch (ed), *Staatsrecht—Völkerrecht—Europarecht: Festschrift für Hans-Jürgen Schlochauer* (Walter de Gruyter, Berlin 1981) 193

Boisson de Chazournes, L, *Les contre-mesures dans les relations internationales économiques* (Pedone, Paris 1992)

—— 'Economic Countermeasures in an Interdependent World' in CA Bradley (ed), 'The Costs and Benefits of Economic Sanctions' (1995) 89 ASILProc 337

—— 'Advisory Opinions and the Furtherance of the Common Interest of Humankind' in eadem et al (eds), *International Organizations and International Dispute Settlement—Trends and Prospects* (Transnational Publishers, Ardsley 2002) 105

—— 'La procédure consultative de la Cour internationale de Justice et la promotion de la règle de droit: remarques sur les conditions d'accès et de participation' in P-M Dupuy et al (eds), *Völkerrecht als Weltordnung: Festschrift für Christian Tomuschat* (NP Engel, Kehl 2006) 479

Bore Eveno, V, 'Le contrôle juridictionnel des résolutions du Conseil de sécurité : vers un constitutionnalisme international?' (2006) 110 RGDIP 827

Bothe, M, 'Les limites des pouvoirs du Conseil de sécurité' in R-J Dupuy (ed), *Le développement du rôle du Conseil de sécurité: Peace-keeping and Peace-building* (Nijhoff, Dordrecht 1993) 67

—— 'Bundesverfassungsgericht und Außenpolitik—Auch ein Beitrag zur juristischen Zeitgeschichte' in U Beyerlin et al (eds), *Recht zwischen Umbruch und Bewahrung—Festschrhift für Rudolf Bernhardt* (Springer, Berlin 1995) 755

Bowett, DW, 'The Impact of the UN Structure, Including that of the Specialized Agencies, on the Law of International Organization' (1970) 64 ASILProc 48

——'The Impact of Security Council Decisions on Dispute Settlement Procedures' (1994) 5 EJIL 89

—— 'Judicial and Political Functions of the Security Council and the International Court of Justice' in H Fox (ed), *The Changing Constitution of the United Nations* (BIICL, London 1997) 73

Breutz, I, *Der Protest im Völkerrecht* (Duncker und Humblot, Berlin 1997)

Brewer-Carías, AR, *Judicial Review in Comparative Law* (CUP, Cambridge 1989)

Brierly, JL, 'Sanctions' (1931) 17 GST 67

—— 'The Basis of Obligation in International Law' in H Lauterpacht and CHM Waldock (eds), *The Basis of Obligation in International Law and Other Papers* (Clarendon, Oxford 1958)

Brölmann, C, 'A Flat Earth? International Organizations in the System of International Law' (2001) 70 NJIL 319

Broude, T and Shany, Y, 'Introduction' in T Broude and Y Shany (eds), *The Shifting Allocation of Authority in International Law: Considering Sovereignty, Supremacy and Subsidiarity—Essays in Honour of Professor Ruth Lapidoth* (Hart, Oxford 2008) 1

Brownlie, I, 'The United Nations as a Form of Government' in JES Fawcett and R Higgins (eds), *International Organization: Law in Movement—Essays in Honour of John McMahon* (OUP, London 1974) 26

——*State Responsibility—Part I* (Clarendon Press, London 1983)

—— 'State Responsibility: The Problem of Delegation' in K Ginther (ed), *Völkerrecht zwischen normativem Anspruch und politischer Realität—Festschrift für Karl Zemanek* (Duncker und Humblot, Berlin 1994) 299

—— 'The Decisions of Political Organs of the United Nations and the Rule of Law' in RSJ Macdonald (ed), *Essays in Honour of Wang Tieya* (Nijhoff, Dordrect 1994) 91

—— 'Remedies in the International Court of Justice' in AV Lowe and M Fitzmaurice (eds), *Fifty Years of the International Court of Justice—Essays in Honour of Sir Robert Jennings* (Grotius, Cambridge 1996) 557

—— 'State Responsibility and the International Court of Justice' in M Fitzmaurice and D Sarooshi (eds), *Issues of State Responsibility before International Judicial Institutions* (Hart, Oxford 2004) 11

Brunnée, J, 'International Legal Accountability through the Lens of the Law of State Responsibility' (2005) 36 NYIL 21

Bulterman, M, 'Fundamental Rights and the United Nations Financial Sanction Regime: The *Kadi* and *Yusuf* Judgments of the Court of First Instance of the European Communities' (2006) 19 LJIL 753

Burci, GL, *Legal Aspects of UN Economic Sanctions* (2000) available at <http://www.law.cam.ac.uk/rcil/Burci.doc>

Butkiewicz, E, 'The Premises of International Responsibility of Inter-Governmental Organizations' (1981–2) 11 PYIL 117

Caflisch, L, 'Is the International Court Entitled to Review Security Council Resolutions Adopted under Chapter VII of the United Nations Charter?' in N Al-Nauimi and R Meese (eds), *International Legal Issues Arising under the United Nations Decade of International Law* (Nijhoff, The Hague 1995) 633

Cahier, P, 'Les caractéristiques de la nullité en droit international et tout particulièrement dans la Convention de Vienne de 1969 sur le droit des traités' (1972) 76 RGDIP 645

Cameron, I, 'UN Targeted Sanctions, Legal Safeguards and the European Convention on Human Rights' (2003) 72 NJIL 159

Cannizzaro, E, 'A Machiavellian Moment? The UN Security Council and the Rule of Law' (2006) 3 IOLR 189

Canor, I, '"Can Two Walk Together Except They Be Agreed?" The Relationship between International Law and European Law: The Incorporation of United Nations Sanctions against Yugoslavia into European Community Law through the Perspective of the European Court of Justice' (1998) 35 CMLRev 137

Capotorti, F, 'L'extinction et la suspension des traités' (1971) 134 RdC 417

Cappelletti, M, *Judicial Review in the Contemporary World* (Bobbs-Merril, Indianapolis 1971)

—— 'The "Mighty Problem" of Judicial Review and the Contribution of Comparative Analysis' (1980) 53 SoCalLR 409

—— *The Judicial Process in Comparative Perspective* (Clarendon, Oxford 1989)

Chaumont, CM, 'La signification du principe de spécialité des organisations internationales' in *Mélanges offerts à Henri Rolin—Problèmes de droit des gens* (Pedone, Paris 1964) 55

Chesterman, S, *Who Needs Rules? The Prospects of a Rules-based International System* (2005) available at <http://www.iilj.org/research/ documents/panel_2_report.pdf>

—— 'Globalization Rules: Accountability, Power and the Prospects for Global Administrative Law' (2008) 14 Global Governance 39

—— and Jordan, DA, *The Security Council as World Executive? The Implementation and Enforcement of Rules by the Security Council* (2006) available at <http://www.iilj.org/ research/ documents/panel_4_report.pdf>

Chomsky, N, 'On the Limits of Civil Disobedience' in idem, *For Reasons of State* (Fontana/ Collins, n/a 1973) 74

Ciampi, A, 'L'Union Européenne et le respect des droits de l'homme dans la mise en œuvre des sanctions devant la Cour européenne des droits de l'homme' (2006) 110 RGDIP 85

Ciobanu, D, 'Objections to Acts Performed *ultra vires* by the Political Organs of the United Nations' (1972) 55 RivistaDI 420

—— 'The Scope of Article 19 of the UN Charter' (1972) 55 RivistaDI 48

—— *Preliminary Objections—Related to the Jurisdiction of the United Nations Political Organs* (Nijhoff, The Hague 1975)

Coffin, WS and Leibman, MI, *Civil Disobedience: Aid or Hindrance to Justice?* (American Enterprise Institute for Public Policy Research, Washington 1972)

Cohen-Jonathan, G, 'Article 39' in J-P Cot and A Pellet (eds), *La Charte des Nations Unies: Commentaire article par article* (Economica, Paris 1985) 645

Collier, JG and Lowe, AV, *The Settlement of Disputes in International Law—Institutions and Procedures* (OUP, Oxford 1999)

Combacau, J, *Le pouvoir de sanction de l'ONU: étude théorique de la coercition non militaire* (Pedone, Paris 1974)

—— 'Sanctions' in R Bernhardt (ed), *Encyclopedia of Public International Law*, vol 4 (Elsevier, Amsterdam 2000) 311

Condorelli, L, 'L'imputation à l'État d'un fait internationalement illicite : solutions classiques et nouvelles tendances' (1984) 189 RdC 9

—— and Dipla, H, 'Solutions traditionnelles et nouvelles tendances en matière d'attribution à l'État d'un fait internationalement illicite dans la Convention de 1982 sur le droit de la mer' in *Le droit international a l'heure de sa codification—Études en l'honneur de Roberto Ago*, vol III (Giuffrè, Milan 1987) 65

Conforti, B, 'The Legal Effect of Non-Compliance with Rules of Procedure in the UN General Assembly and Security Council' (1969) 63 AJIL 479

—— 'Le pouvoir discrétionnaire du Conseil de sécurité en matière de constatation d'une menace contre la paix, d'une rupture de la paix ou d'un acte d'agression' in R-J Dupuy (ed), *Le développement du rôle du Conseil de sécurité: Peace-keeping and Peace-building* (Nijhoff, Dordrecht 1993) 51

—— 'Notes sur la pratique récente du Conseil de sécurité' (1996) 43 RYDI 123

—— *The Law and Practice of the United Nations* (3rd edn, Nijhoff, Leiden 2005)

—— 'Unité et fragmentation du droit international: « Glissez, mortels, n'appuyez pas ! »' (2007) 111 RGDIP 5

Cortright, D and Lopez, GA, 'Reforming Sanctions' in DM Malone (ed), *The UN Security Council: From the Cold War to the 21st Century* (Lynne Rienner, London 2004) 167

Couvreur, P, 'Développements récentes concernant l'accès des organisations intergouvernementales à la procédure contentieuse devant la Cour internationale de justice' in E Yakpo and T Boumedra (eds), Liber Amicorum *Judge Mohammed Bedjaoui* (Kluwer, The Hague 1999) 293

Craig, P, 'The Locus and Accountability of the Executive in the European Union' in P Craig and A Tomkins (eds), *The Executive and Public Law: Power and Accountability in Comparative Perspective* (OUP, Oxford 2006) 315

—— and Tomkins, A, 'Introduction' in P Craig and A Tomkins (eds), *The Executive and Public Law: Power and Accountability in Comparative Perspective* (OUP, Oxford 2006) 1

Cramér, P, 'Recent Swedish Experiences with Targeted UN Sanctions: The Erosion of Trust in the Security Council' in E de Wet and A Nollkaemper (eds), *Review of the Security Council by Member States* (Intersentia, Antwerp 2003) 85

Craven, M, 'Humanitarianism and the Quest for Smarter Sanctions' (2002) 13 EJIL 43

Crawford, J, 'Counter-measures as Interim Measures' (1994) 5 EJIL 65

—— 'The General Assembly, the International Court and Self-Determination' in AV Lowe and M Fitzmaurice (eds), *Fifty Years of the International Court of Justice—Essays in Honour of Sir Robert Jennings* (Grotius, Cambridge 1996) 585

—— 'The Charter of the United Nations as a Constitution' in H Fox (ed), *The Changing Constitution of the United Nations* (BIICL, London 1997) 3

—— 'The International Court of Justice, Judicial Administration and the Rule of Law' in DW Bowett et al (eds), *The International Court of Justice—Process, Practice and Procedure* (BIICL, London 1997) 112

—— '*Marbury v Madison* at the International Level' (2004) 36 GWILR 505

—— 'Multilateral Rights and Obligations in International Law' (2006) 319 RdC 325

Cryer, R, 'Sudan, Resolution 1593, and International Criminal Justice' (2006) 19 LJIL 195

—— and White, ND, 'The Security Council and the International Criminal Court: Who's Feeling Threatened?' (2002) 8 YIPO 143

Curtin, D and Nollkaemper, A, 'Conceptualizing Accountability in International and European Law' (2005) 36 NYIL 3

Daillier, P, 'Article 5—Convention de 1969' in O Corten and P Klein (eds), *Les Conventions de Vienne sur le droit des traités—Commentaire article par article* (Bruylant, Brussels 2006) 137

Damrosch, LF, 'Enforcing International Law through Non-Forcible Measures' (1997) 269 RdC 9

Davidsson, E, 'Legal Boundaries to UN Sanctions' (2003) 7 IJHR 1

Dawidowicz, M, 'Public Law Enforcement without Public Law Safeguards? An Analysis of State Practice on Third-Party Countermeasures and their Relationship to the UN Security Council' (2006) 77 BYIL 333

d'Argent, P, 'Jurisprudence belge relative au droit international public (1993–2003)' (2003) 36 RBDI 575

—— 'Compliance, Cessation, Reparation and Restitution in the Wall Advisory Opinion' in P-M Dupuy et al (eds), *Völkerrecht als Weltordnung: Festschrift für Christian Tomuschat* (NP Engel, Kehl 2006) 463

d'Aspremont, J and Brölmann, C, 'Challenging International Criminal Tribunals before Domestic Courts' in A Reinisch (ed), *Challenging Acts of International Organizations before National Courts* (OUP, Oxford 2010) 111

de Brichambaut, MP, 'The Role of the United Nations Security Council in the International Legal System' in M Byers (ed), *The Role of Law in International Politics—Essays in International Relations and International Law* (OUP, Oxford 2000) 269

de Visscher, P, 'Observations sur le fondement et la mise en œuvre du principe de la responsabilité de l'organisation des Nations Unies' (1963) 40 RDIDC 165

—— 'Rapport préliminaire' (1971) 54-I AIDI 1

de Wet, E, 'Human Rights Limitations to Economic Enforcement Measures Under Article 41 of the United Nations Charter and the Iraqi Sanctions Regime' (2001) 14 LJIL 277

—— 'The Role of Human Rights in Limiting the Enforcement Power of the Security Council: A Principled View' in eadem and A Nollkaemper (eds), *Review of the Security Council by Member States* (Intersentia, Antwerp 2003) 7

—— *The Chapter VII Powers of the United Nations Security Council* (Hart, Oxford 2004)

—— 'The Security Council as a Law Maker: The Adoption of (Quasi)-Judicial Decisions' in R Wolfrum and V Röben (eds), *Developments of International Law in Treaty Making* (Springer, Berlin 2005) 183

—— 'The International Constitutional Order' (2006) 55 ICLQ 51

—— and Nollkaemper, A, 'Review of Security Council Decisions by National Courts' (2002) 45 GYIL 166

Degni-Segui, R, 'Article 24' in J-P Cot and A Pellet (eds), *La Charte des Nations Unies: Commentaire article par article* (Economica, Paris 1985) 451

Delbrück, J, 'Proportionality' in R Bernhardt (ed), *Encyclopedia of Public International Law*, vol 3 (Elsevier, Amsterdam 1997) 1140

—— 'Article 25' in B Simma (ed), *The UN Charter: A Commentary* (2nd edn, OUP, Oxford 2002) 452

della Cananea, G, 'Legittimazione e *Accountability* nell'Organizzazione Mondiale del Commercio' (2003) 53 RTDP 731

—— 'The Growth of the Italian Executive' in P Craig and A Tomkins (eds), *The Executive and Public Law: Power and Accountability in Comparative Perspective* (OUP, Oxford 2006) 243

Deman, C, 'La cessation de l'acte illicite' (1990) 23 RBDI 476

Denis, C, *Le pouvoir normatif du Conseil de sécurité des Nations Unies: portée et limites* (Bruylant, Brussels 2004)

Dietze, G, 'Judicial Review in Europe' (1956–7) 55 MichLR 539

Doehring, K, 'Die Selbstdurchsetzung völkerrechtlicher Verpflichtungen—Einige Einzelprobleme der Repressalie' (1987) 47 ZaöRV 44

—— 'Unlawful Resolutions of the Security Council and their Legal Consequences' (1997) 1 MP UNYB 91

Dominicé, C, 'La satisfaction en droit des gens' in B Dutoit and E Grisel (eds), *Mélanges Georges Perrin* (Payot, Lausanne 1984) 91

—— 'La personnalité juridique dans le système du droit de gens' in J Makarczyk (ed), *Theory of International Law at the Threshold of the 21st Century—Essays in Honour of Krzysztof Skubiszewski* (Kluwer, The Hague 1996) 147

—— 'Le Conseil de sécurité et le droit international' (1996) 43 RYDI 197

—— 'Valeur et autorité des actes des organisations internationales' in R-J Dupuy (ed), *Manuel sur les organisations internationales* (2nd edn, Nijhoff, Dordrecht 1998) 441

—— 'The International Responsibility of States for Breach of Multilateral Obligations' (1999) 10 EJIL 353

Dominicé, C, 'Request of Advisory Opinions in Contentious Cases?' in L Boisson de Chazournes et al (eds), *International Organizations and International Dispute Settlement—Trends and Prospects* (Transnational Publishers, Ardsley 2002) 91

—— 'La responsabilité internationale des Nations Unies' in J-P Cot, A Pellet, and M Forteau (eds), *La Charte des Nations Unies—Commentaire article par article* (3rd edn, Economica, Paris 2005) 141

—— 'The International Responsibility of the United Nations for Injuries Resulting from Non-military Enforcement Measures' in M Ragazzi (ed), *International Responsibility Today: Essays in Memory of Oscar Schachter* (Nijhoff, Leiden 2005) 363

Dupuy, R-J, 'Le fait générateur de la responsabilité internationale des États' (1984) 188 RdC 9

—— 'Débats' in Société française pour le droit international (ed), *Les organisations internationales contemporaine: crise, mutation, développement—Colloque de Strasbourg* (Pedone, Paris 1988) 211

—— *Le droit international* (12th edn, PUF, Paris 2004)

Dupuy, P-M, 'Sécurité collective et organisation de la paix' (1993) 97 RGDIP 617

—— 'Sécurité collective et construction de la paix dans la pratique contemporaine du Conseil de sécurité' in U Beyerlin et al (eds), *Recht zwischen Umbruch und Bewahrung—Festschrift für Rudolf Bernhardt* (Springer, Berlin 1995) 41

—— 'The Constitutional Dimension of the Charter of the United Nations Revisited' (1997) 1 MP UNYB 1

Dworkin, R, *Taking Rights Seriously* (new impression [corrected] with appendix Duckworth, London 1978)

Eagleton, C, 'International Organization and the Law of Responsibility' (1950) 76 RdC 323

Économidès, C, 'Recours à la force par des États membres des Nations Unies et/ou par des organisations régionales sur habilitation en vertu du Chapitre VII de la Charte des Nations Unies' (2005) 58 RHDI 325

Eissen, M-A, 'The Principle of Proportionality in the Case-Law of the European Court of Human Rights' in RSJ Macdonald et al (eds), *The European System for the Protection of Human Rights* (Nijhoff, Dordrecht 1993) 125

Eitel, T, 'The UN Security Council and its Future Contribution in the Field of International Law—What May We Expect?' (2000) 4 MP UNYB 53

Elaraby, N, 'Some Reflections on the Role of the Security Council and the Prohibition of the Use of Force in International Relations: Article 2(4) Revisited in Light of Recent Developments' in JA Frowein et al (eds), *Verhandeln für den Frieden—Liber Amicorum Tono Eitel* (Springer, Berlin 2003) 41

Elberling, B, 'The *Ultra Vires* Character of Legislative Action by the Security Council' (2005) 2 IOLR 337

—— 'The Next Step in History-Writing through Criminal Law: Exactly How Tailor-Made is the Special Tribunal for Lebanon' (2008) 21 LJIL 529

Elias, TO, *New Horizons in International Law* (2nd rev edn [by FM Ssekandi], Nijhoff, Dordrecht 1992)

Eustathiadès, C, *La responsabilité internationale de l'État pour les actes des organes judiciaires et le problème du déni de justice en droit international*, vol 1 (Pedone, Paris 1936)

Falcón y Tella, MJ, 'Legal Justification for Civil Disobedience?' (2002) 13 FYIL 19

—— *Civil Disobedience* (Nijhoff, Leiden 2004)

Farrall, JM, *United Nations Sanctions and the Rule of Law* (CUP, Cambridge 2007)

Fasoli, E, 'Declaratory Judgments and Official Apologies as Forms of Reparation for the Non-Material Damage Suffered by the State: the Djibouti-France Case' (2008) 7 LPICT 177

Fassbender, B, 'The United Nations Charter as Constitution of the International Community' (1998) 36 CJTL 529

—— *UN Security Council Reform and the Right of Veto—A Constitutional Perspective* (Kluwer, The Hague 1998)

—— '*Quis judicabit?* The Security Council, Its Powers and Its Legal Control' (2000) 11 EJIL 219

—— *The United Nations Charter as the Constitution of the International Community* (Nijhoff, Leiden 2009)

Fawcett, JES, 'Détournement de pouvoir by International Organizations' (1957) 33 BYIL 311

Fiedler, W, 'Gegenmaßnahmen' in W Fiedler, E Klein, and AK Schnyder, *Berichte der Deutschen Gesellschaft für Völkerrecht: Gegenmaßnahmen*, vol 37 (cf Müller, Heidelberg 1998) 9

Fitzmaurice, GG, 'The Law and Procedure of the International Court of Justice: International Organizations and Tribunals' (1952) 29 BYIL 1

—— *The Law and Procedure of the International Court of Justice* (Grotius, Cambridge 1986)

Flogaïtis, S, 'Judicial Review of Legislative Acts in Greece' in CM Zoethout et al (eds), *Control in Constitutional Law* (Nijhoff, Dordrecht 1993) 145

Foot, P, 'The Great Lockerbie Whitewash 1989–2001' in J Pilger (ed), *Tell Me No Lies—Investigative Journalism and its Triumphs* (Vintage, London 2005) 214

Fox, H, 'The International Court of Justice's Treatment of Acts of the State and in Particular the Attribution of Acts of Individuals to the State' in N Ando et al (eds), Liber Amicorum *Judge Shigeru Oda*, vol I (Kluwer, The Hague 2002) 147

Francioni, F, 'Multilateralism à la Carte: The Limits to Unilateral Withholdings of Assessed Contributions to the UN Budget' (2000) 11 EJIL 43

Franck, TM, 'Legitimacy in the International System' (1988) 82 AJIL 705

—— 'The "Powers of Appreciation": Who is the Ultimate Guardian of UN Legality?' (1992) 86 AJIL 519

—— 'The Security Council and "Threats to the Peace": Some Remarks on Remarkable Recent Developments' in R-J Dupuy (ed), *Le développement du rôle du Conseil de sécurité: Peace-keeping and Peace-building* (Nijhoff, Dordrecht 1993) 83

—— 'The Political and the Judicial Empires: Must there be Conflict over Conflict-Resolution?' in N Al-Nauimi and R Meese (eds), *International Legal Issues Arising under the United Nations Decade of International Law* (Nijhoff, The Hague 1995) 621

—— 'The United Nations as Guarantor of International Peace and Security: Past, Present and Future' in C Tomuschat (ed), *The United Nations at Age Fifty: A Legal Perspective* (Kluwer, The Hague 1995) 25

—— 'Is the UN Charter a Constitution?' in JA Frowein et al (eds), *Verhandeln für den Frieden*—Liber Amicorum *Tono Eitel* (Springer, Berlin 2003) 95

Frederking, B, *The United States and the Security Council—Collective Security since the Cold War* (Routledge, London 2007)

Fremuth, M and Griebel, J, 'On the Security Council as a Legislator: A Blessing or a Curse for the International Community?' (2007) 76 NJIL 339

Fritsche, C, 'Security Council Resolution 1422: Peacekeeping and the International Criminal Court' in JA Frowein et al (eds), *Verhandeln für den Frieden*—Liber Amicorum *Tono Eitel* (Springer, Berlin 2003) 107

Frowein, JA, 'Die Verpflichtungen erga omnes im Völkerrecht und ihre Durchsetzung' in R Bernhardt (ed), *Völkerrecht als Rechtsordnung, Internationale Gerichtsbarkeit, Menschenrechte: Festschrift für Hermann Mosler* (Springer, Berlin 1983) 241

—— 'Collective Enforcement of International Obligations' (1987) 47 ZaöRV 67

—— 'Reactions by Not Directly Affected States to Breaches of Public International Law' (1994) 248 RdC 345

—— 'Vorbemerkung zu Artikeln 8–11' in idem and W Peukert (eds), *EMRK-Kommentar* (2nd edn, NP Engel, Kehl 1996) 32

—— 'Nullity in International Law' in R Bernhardt (ed), *Encyclopedia of Public International Law*, vol 3 (Elsevier, Amsterdam 1997) 743

—— 'Issues of Legitimacy around the United Nations Security Council' in idem et al (eds), *Verhandeln für den Frieden—Liber Amicorum Tono Eitel* (Springer, Berlin 2003) 121

—— 'The UN Anti-Terrorism Administration and the Rule of Law' in P-M Dupuy et al (eds), *Völkerrecht als Weltordnung: Festschrift für Christian Tomuschat* (NP Engel, Kehl 2006) 785

—— and Krisch, N, 'Article 2(5)' in B Simma (ed), *The UN Charter: A Commentary* (2nd edn, OUP, Oxford 2002) 136

—— and — 'Article 39' in B Simma (ed), *The UN Charter: A Commentary* (2nd edn, OUP, Oxford 2002) 717

—— and — 'Article 41' in B Simma (ed), *The UN Charter: A Commentary* (2nd edn, OUP, Oxford 2002) 735

—— and — 'Introduction to Chapter VII' in B Simma (ed), *The UN Charter: A Commentary* (2nd edn, OUP, Oxford 2002) 701

Furukawa, T, 'Le double rôle de la Cour international de justice à l'égard des organisations internationales' in *Mélanges offerts a Paul Reuter—Le droit international: unité et diversité* (Pedone, Paris 1981) 293

Gaillard, E, and Pingel-Lenuzza, I, 'International Organizations and Immunity from Jurisdiction: To Respect or To Bypass' (2002) 51 ICLQ 1

Gaja, G, '*Jus Cogens* beyond the Vienna Convention' (1981) 172 RdC 271

—— 'A "New" Vienna Convention on Treaties between States and International Organizations or between International Organizations: A Critical Commentary' (1987) 58 BYIL 253

—— 'Some Reflections on the European Community's International Responsibility' in HG Schermers et al (eds), *Non-Contractual Liability of the European Communities* (Nijhoff, Dordrecht 1988) 169

—— 'Réflexions sur le rôle du Conseil de sécurité dans le nouvel ordre mondial' (1993) 97 RGDIP 297

—— 'Do States have an Obligation to Ensure Compliance with Obligations Erga Omnes by Other States?' in M Ragazzi (ed), *International Responsibility Today: Essays in Memory of Oscar Schachter* (Nijhoff, Leiden 2005) 31

—— 'The Review by the European Court of Human Rights of Member States' Acts Implementing European Union Law: "Solange" Yet Again?' in P-M Dupuy et al (eds), *Völkerrecht als Weltordnung: Festschrift für Christian Tomuschat* (NP Engel, Kehl 2006) 517

García-Amador, FV, 'La responsabilité internationale de l'État: La responsabilité des organisations internationales' (1956) 34 RDISDP 146

Gardam, JG, 'Proportionality and Force in International Law' (1993) 87 AJIL 391

Gasser, H-P, 'Comments' in HHG Post (ed), *International Economic Law and Armed Conflict* (Nijhoff, Dordrecht 1994) 175

—— 'Collective Economic Sanctions and International Humanitarian Law—An Enforcement Measure under the United Nations Charter and the Right of Civilians to Immunity: An Unavoidable Clash of Policy Goals?' (1996) 56 ZaöRV 871

Gazzini, T, 'The Normative Element Inherent in Economic Collective Enforcement Measures' in LP Forlati and L-A Sicilianos (eds), *Les sanctions économiques en droit international* (Nijhoff, Leiden 2004) 279

Gill, TD, 'Legal and Some Political Limitations on the Power of the UN Security Council to Exercise its Enforcement Powers under Chapter VII of the Charter' (1995) 26 NYIL 33

Ginther, K, *Die völkerrechtliche Verantwortlichkeit internationaler Organisationen gegenüber Drittstaaten* (Springer, Vienna 1969)

Gomaa, MM, *Suspension or Termination of Treaties on Grounds of Breach* (Nijhoff, The Hague 1996)

Goodrich, LM, Hambro, E, and Simmons, AP, *Charter of the United Nations: Commentary and Documents* (3rd edn, Columbia University Press, New York 1969)

Goodwin-Gill, GS, 'State Responsibility and the "Good Faith" Obligation in International Law' in M Fitzmaurice and D Sarooshi (eds), *Issues of State Responsibility before International Judicial Institutions* (Hart, Oxford 2004) 75

Gowlland-Debbas, V, *Collective Responses to Illegal Acts in International Law—United Nations Action in the Question of Southern Rhodesia* (Nijhoff, Dordrecht 1990)

—— 'Security Council Enforcement Action and Issues of State Responsibility' (1994) 43 ICLQ 55

—— 'The Relationship between the International Court of Justice and the Security Council in the Light of the *Lockerbie* Case' (1994) 88 AJIL 643

—— 'The Functions of the United Nations Security Council in the International Legal System' in M Byers (ed), *The Role of Law in International Politics—Essays in International Relations and International Law* (OUP, Oxford 2000) 277

—— 'Introduction' in eadem (ed), *United Nations Sanctions and International Law* (Kluwer, The Hague 2001) 2

—— 'The Domestic Implementation of UN Sanctions' in E de Wet and A Nollkaemper (eds), *Review of the Security Council by Member States* (Intersentia, Antwerp 2003) 63

—— 'Implementing Sanctions Resolutions in Domestic Law' in eadem (ed), *National Implementation of United Nations Sanctions—A Comparative Study* (Nijhoff, Leiden 2004) 33

Gowlland Gualtieri, A, 'The Environmental Accountability of the World Bank to Non-State Actors: Insights from the Inspection Panel' (2001) 72 BYIL 714

Gradoni, L, 'Making Sense of "Solanging" in International Law: The *Kadi* Case before the EC Court of First Instance' in WJM van Genugten et al (eds), *Criminal Jurisdiction 100 Years After the 1907 Hague Peace Conference* (TMC Asser, The Hague 2009) 139

Graefrath, B, 'Responsibility and Damages Caused: Relationship between Responsibility and Damages' (1984) 185 RdC 9

—— 'Jugoslawientribunal—Präzedenzfall trotz fragwürdiger Rechtsgrundlage' (1993) 47 NJ 433

—— 'Leave to the Court What Belongs to the Court: the Libyan Case' (1993) 4 EJIL 184

—— 'International Crimes and Collective Security' in K Wellens (ed), *International Law: Theory and Practice—Essays in Honour of Eric Suy* (Nijhoff, The Hague 1998) 237

Grant, RW and Keohane, RO, 'Accountability and Abuses of Power in World Politics' (2005) 99 APSR 29

Gray, CD, *Judicial Remedies in International Law* (Clarendon, Oxford 1990)
—— 'The Choice between Restitution and Compensation' (1999) 10 EJIL 413
Greenawalt, K, *Conflicts of Law and Morality* (OUP, New York 1989)
Griller, S, 'International Law, Human Rights and the European Community's Autonomous Legal Order: Notes on the ECJ Decision in *Kadi*' (2008) 4 EuConst 528
Gros, A, 'Le problème du recours juridictionnel contre les décisions d'organismes internationaux' in *La technique et les principes du droit public: Études en l'honneur de Georges Scelle*, vol 1 (LGDJ, Paris 1950) 267
—— 'The Problem of Redress Against the Decisions of International Organizations' (1950) 36 GST 30
Gröschner, R, 'Artikel 20 IV (Widerstandsrecht)' in H Dreier (ed), *Grundgesetz—Kommentar*, vol 2 (Mohr Siebeck, Tübingen 1998) 210
Gross, L, 'The International Court of Justice and the United Nations' (1967) 120 RdC 313
—— 'States as Organs of International Law and the Problem of Autointerpretation' in idem, *Selected Essays on International Law and Organization* (Nijhoff, Dordrecht 1993) 167
Guggenheim, P, 'La validité et la nullité des actes juridiques internationaux' (1949) 74 RdC 191
Guillaume, G, 'Terrorism and International Law' (2004) 53 ICLQ 537
Hafner, G, 'Accountability of International Organizations' in WE Holder (ed), 'Can International Organizations be Controlled? Accountability and Responsibility' (2003) 97 ASILProc 236
—— 'Accountability of International Organizations—A Critical View' in RSJ Macdonald and DM Johnston (eds), *Towards World Constitutionalism: Issues in the Legal Ordering of the World Community* (Nijhoff, Leiden 2005) 585
Hailbronner, K, 'Sanctions and Third Parties and the Concept of International Public Order' (1992) 30 AVR 2
Halberstam, D and Stein, E, 'The United Nations, the European Union, and the King of Sweden: Economic Sanctions and Individual Rights in a Plural World Order' (2009) 46 CMLRev 13
Haltern, U, 'Gemeinschaftsgrundrechte und Antiterrormaßnahmen der UNO' (2007) 62 JZ 537
Hambro, E, 'Quelques problèmes touchant à la Cour internationale de justice' (1962) 15 RHDI 1
Happold, M, 'Security Council Resolution 1373 and the Constitution of the United Nations' (2003) 16 LJIL 593
Harlow, C, *Accountability in the European Union* (OUP, Oxford 2002)
Hegde, VG, 'Indian Courts and International Law' (2010) 23 LJIL 53
Heliskoski, J, *Mixed Agreements as a Technique for Organizing the International Relations of the European Community and its Member States* (Kluwer, The Hague 2001)
Henckaerts, J-M, 'The Conduct of Hostilities: Target Selection, Proportionality and Precautionary Measures under International Humanitarian Law' in M Hector and M Jellema (eds), *Protecting Civilians in 21st Century Warfare* (WLP, Nijmegen 2001) 11
Herdegen, M, 'Der Sicherheitsrat und die autoritative Konkretisierung des VII. Kapitels der UN-Charta' in U Beyerlin et al (eds), *Recht zwischen Umbruch und Bewahrung—Festschrift für Rudolf Bernhardt* (Springer, Berlin 1995) 103
—— 'Review of the Security Council by National Courts: A Constitutional Perspective' in E de Wet and A Nollkaemper (eds), *Review of the Security Council by Member States* (Intersentia, Antwerp 2003) 77

—— 'The "Constitutionalization" of the UN Security System' (1994) 27 VJTL 135

van den Herik, L and Schrijver, N, 'Eroding the Primacy of the UN System of Collective Security: The Judgment of the European Court of Justice in the Cases of Kadi and Al Barakaat' (2008) 5 IOLR 329

Herzog, R, 'Artikel 20' in T Maunz and G Dürig (eds), *Grundgesetz Kommentar*, vol 3 (CH Beck, Munich 2007)

Hexner, EP, 'Teleological Interpretation of Basic Instruments of Public International Organizations' in S Engel (ed), *Law, State, and International Legal Order—Essays in Honor of Hans Kelsen* (University of Tennessee Press, Knoxville 1964) 119

Higgins, R, *The Development of International Law through the Political Organs of the United Nations* (OUP, London 1963)

—— 'The Place of International Law in the Settlement of Disputes by the Security Council' (1970) 64 AJIL 1

—— 'The United Nations and Lawmaking: The Political Organs' (1970) 64 ASILProc 37

—— 'The Advisory Opinion on Namibia: Which UN Resolutions Are Binding under Article 25 of the Charter?' (1972) 21 ICLQ 270

——*Problems and Process: International Law and How we Use it* (Clarendon, Oxford 1994)

—— 'The Legal Consequences for Member States of the Non-Fulfillment by International Organizations of their Obligations Toward Third Parties: Preliminary Exposé' (1995) 66-I AIDI 251

—— 'A Comment on the Current Health of Advisory Opinions' in AV Lowe and M Fitzmaurice (eds), *Fifty Years of the International Court of Justice—Essays in Honour of Sir Robert Jennings* (Grotius, Cambridge 1996) 587

—— 'The UN Security Council and the Individual State' in H Fox (ed), *The Changing Constitution of the United Nations* (BIICL, London 1997) 43

—— 'Remedies and the International Court of Justice: An Introduction' in MD Evans (ed), *Remedies in International Law: The Institutional Dilemma* (Hart, Oxford 1998) 1

Hinojosa Martínez, LM, 'The Legislative Role of the Security Council in its Fight Against Terrorism: Legal, Political and Practical Limits' (2008) 57 ICLQ 333

Hinsley, FH, *Power and the Pursuit of Peace: Theory and Practice in the History of Relations between States* (CUP, Cambridge 1963)

Hirsch, M, *The Responsibility of International Organizations Toward Third Parties—Some Basic Principles* (Nijhoff, Dordrecht 1995)

—— 'The Responsibility of Members of International Organizations: An Analysis of Alternative Regimes' (2005) 6(2) GVICL 8

Hofmann, R, 'Die Rechtskontrolle von Organen der Staatengemeinschaft' in R Hofmann, A Reinisch, T Pfeiffer, S Oeter, and A Stadler, *Berichte der Deutschen Gesellschaft für Völkerrecht: Die Rechtskontrolle von Organen der Staatengemeinschaft; Vielfalt der Gerichte—Einheit des Prozessrechts?*, vol 42 (cf Müller, Heidelberg 2007) 1

Holder, WE, 'International Organizations: Accountability and Responsibility' in idem (ed), 'Can International Organizations be Controlled? Accountability and Responsibility' (2003) 97 ASILProc 231

Honoré, T, 'The Right to Rebel' (1988) 8 OJLS 34

International Law Association, 'Final Report on the Accountability of International Organisations' in *Report of the Seventy-first Conference—Berlin* (London 2004) 164

Jaconelli, J, 'Constitutional Review and Section 2(4) of the European Communities Act 1972' (1979) 28 ICLQ 65

Jaqué, J-P, 'Rapport général: le constat' in Société française pour le droit international (ed), *Les organisations internationales contemporaines: crise, mutation, développement— Colloque de Strasbourg* (Pedone, Paris 1988) 3

Jayawickrama, N, 'India' in D Sloss (ed), *The Role of Domestic Courts in Treaty Enforcement—A Comparative Study* (CUP, Cambridge 2009) 243

Jenks, CW, 'The Status of International Organizations in Relation to the International Court of Justice' (1946) 32 GST 1

—— 'The Conflict of Law-Making Treaties' (1953) 30 BYIL 401

—— *The Prospects of International Adjudication* (Stevens and Sons, London 1964)

Jennings, RY, 'Nullity and Effectiveness in International Law' in *Cambridge Essays in International Law—Essays in Honour of Lord McNair* (Stevens and Sons, London 1965) 64

—— 'Report' in Max Planck Institute for Comparative Public Law and International Law (ed), *Judicial Settlement of International Disputes—An International Symposium* (Springer, Berlin 1974) 35

—— 'The Judicial Enforcement of International Obligations' (1987) 47 ZaöRV 3

—— 'The International Court of Justice after Fifty Years' (1995) 89 AJIL 493

—— 'The Role of the International Court of Justice' (1997) 68 BYIL 1

Johnson, K, 'Civil Disobedience as Consent' (1979) 12 ARSP-Beiheft (Neue Folge) 33

Johnson, LD, 'Views from Practice' in NM Blokker and HG Schermers (eds), *Proliferation of International Organizations: Legal Issues* (Kluwer, The Hague 2001) 471

Johnstone, I, 'Security Council Deliberations: The Power of the Better Argument' (2003) 14 EJIL 437

Joyner, CC, 'United Nations Sanctions After Iraq: Looking Back to See Ahead' (2003) 4 ChicJIL 329

Joyner, DH, 'Non-Proliferation Law and the United Nations System: Resolution 1540 and the Limits of the Power of the Security Council' (2007) 20 LJIL 489

Kadelbach, S, '*Jus Cogens*, Obligations *Erga Omnes* and other Rules—The Identification of Fundamental Norms' in C Tomuschat and J-M Thouvenin (eds), *The Fundamental Rules of the International Legal Order* (Nijhoff, Leiden 2006) 21

—— and Kleinlein, T, 'International Law—A Constitution for Mankind? An Attempt at a Re-appraisal with an Analysis of Constitutional Principles' (2007) 50 GYIL 303

Kaikobad, KH, 'The Court, the Council and Interim Protection: A Commentary on the *Lockerbie* Order of 14 April 1992' (1996) 17 AYIL 87

—— *The International Court of Justice and Judicial Review— A Study of the Court's Powers with Respect to Judgments of the ILO and UN Administrative Tribunals* (Kluwer, The Hague 2000)

Kalala, T, 'La décision de l'OUA de ne plus respecter les sanctions décrétées par l'ONU contre la Libye: Désobéissance civile des États africains à l'égard de l'ONU' (1999) 32 RBDI 545

Kapteyn, PJG, 'The Role of the ECJ in Implementing Security Council Resolutions' in E de Wet and A Nollkaemper (eds), *Review of the Security Council by Member States* (Intersentia, Antwerp 2003) 57

Karl, W, 'Protest' in R Bernhardt (ed), *Encyclopedia of Public International Law*, vol 3 (Elsevier, Amsterdam 1997) 1157

Keith, KJ, *The Extent of the Advisory Jurisdiction of the International Court of Justice* (Sijthoff, Leyden 1971)

Keller, H and Fischer, A, 'The UN Anti-terror Sanctions Regime under Pressure' (2009) 9 HRLR 257

Kelsen, H, *Allgemeine Staatslehre* (Springer, Berlin 1925)

—— *Reine Rechtslehre—Einleitung in die rechtswissenschaftliche Problematik* (Franz Deuticke, Leipzig/Vienna 1934)

—— *The Legal Process and International Order* (Constable and Co, London 1935)

—— 'Sanctions in International Law under the Charter of the United Nations' (1946) 31 IowaLR 499

—— *The Law of the United Nations: A Critical Analysis of its Fundamental Problems* (Praeger, New York 1950)

—— *Principles of International Law* (Rinehart, New York 1952)

—— 'Was ist ein Rechtsakt?' (1952) 4 ÖZöR 263

—— 'Die Einheit von Völkerrecht und staatlichem Recht' (1958) 19 ZaöRV 234

—— *Reine Rechtslehre—Mit einem Anhang: Das Problem der Gerechtigkeit* (2nd edn, Franz Deuticke, Vienna 1960)

—— 'Vom Geltungsgrund des Rechts' in FA Freiherr von der Heydte et al (eds), *Völkerrecht und rechtliches Weltbild—Festschrift für Alfred Verdross* (Springer, Vienna 1960) 157

—— *General Theory of Law and State* (Russell and Russell, New York 1961)

—— *Allgemeine Theorie der Normen* (Manz, Vienna 1979)

—— *Introduction to the Problems of Legal Theory* (trans by BL and SL Paulson, Clarendon, Oxford 1994)

Kennedy, D, *Of War and Law* (Princeton University Press, Princeton 2006)

Keohane, RO, 'The Concept of Accountability in World Politics and the Use of Force' (2003) 24 MichJIL 1121

Kewenig, WA, 'Die Anwendung wirtschaftlicher Zwangsmaßnahmen im Völkerrecht' in WA Kewenig and A Heini, *Berichte der Deutschen Gesellschaft für Völkerrecht: Die Anwendung wirtschaftlicher Zwangsmaßnahmen im Völkerrecht und im Internationalen Privatrecht*, vol 22 (cf Müller, Heidelberg 1982) 7

Kirgis, FL, 'The Security Council's First Fifty Year' (1995) 89 AJIL 506

—— 'Restitution as a Remedy in US Courts for Violations of International Law' (2001) 95 AJIL 341

Klabbers, J, 'Straddling Law and Politics: Judicial Review in International Law' in RSJ Macdonald and DM Johnston (eds), *Towards World Constitutionalism: Issues in the Legal Ordering of the World Community* (Nijhoff, Leiden 2005) 809

—— 'Kadi Justice at the Security Council?' (2007) 4 IOLR 293

—— *An Introduction to International Institutional Law* (2nd edn, CUP, Cambridge 2009)

Klein, E, 'Paralleles Tätigwerden von Sicherheitsrat und Internationalem Gerichtshof bei friedensgefährdenden Streitigkeiten' in R Bernhardt (ed), *Völkerrecht als Rechtsordnung, Internationale Gerichtsbarkeit, Menschenrechte: Festschrift für Hermann Mosler* (Springer, Berlin 1983) 467

—— 'Sanctions by International Organizations and Economic Communities' (1992) 30 AVR 101

Klein, F, 'Artikel 20' in B Schmidt-Bleibtreu and F Klein, *Kommentar zum Grundgesetz für die Bundesrepublik Deutschland* (5th edn, Luchterhand, Neuwied 1980) 387

Klein, P, *La responsabilité des organisations internationales dans les ordres juridiques internes et en droit des gens* (Bruylant, Brussels 1998)

Köck, HF, 'UN-Satzung und allgemeines Völkerrecht—Zum exemplarischen Charakter von Art 103 SVN' in K Ginther (ed), *Völkerrecht zwischen normativem Anspruch und politischer Realität—Festschrift für Karl Zemanek* (Duncker und Humblot, Berlin 1994) 69

Kokott, J, 'Souveräne Gleichheit und Demokratie im Völkerrecht' (2004) 64 ZaöRV 517

Kolb, R, 'Note sur l'émergence d'une maxime de l'utilisation du moyen le moins fort (« *civiliter uti* ») en droit international public' (2006) 39 RBDI 599

—— 'Le contrôle de Résolutions contraignantes du Conseil de sécurité des Nations Unies sous l'angle du respect du jus cogens' (2008) 18 RSDIE 401

Kooijmans, P, 'Provisional Measures of the UN Security Council' in E Denters and N Schrijver (eds), *Reflections on International Law from the Low Countries in Honour of Paul de Waart* (Nijhoff, The Hague 1998) 289

Koschorreck, W, 'Article 17' in B Simma (ed), *The UN Charter: A Commentary* (2nd edn, OUP, Oxford 2002) 332

Koskenniemi, M, 'The Police in the Temple—Order, Justice and the UN: A Dialectical View' (1995) 6 EJIL 325

—— 'Solidarity Measures: State Responsibility as a New International Order?' (2001) 72 BYIL 337

—— *From Apology to Utopia—The Structure of International Legal Argument* (CUP, Cambridge 2005)

Kreczko, AJ, 'The Unilateral Termination of UN Sanctions Against Southern Rhodesia by the United Kingdom' (1980) 21 VaJIL 97

Krisch, N, 'The Pluralism of Global Administrative Law' (2006) 17 EJIL 247

Krökel, M, *Die Bindungswirkung von Resolutionen des Sicherheitsrates der Vereinten Nationen gegenüber Mitgliedstaaten* (Duncker und Humblot, Berlin 1977)

Kuijper, PJ and Paasivirta, E, 'Further Exploring International Responsibility: The European Community and the ILC's Project on the Responsibility of International Organizations' (2004) 1 IOLR 111

Kunz, JL, 'On the Theoretical Basis of the Law of Nations' (1924) 10 GST 115

—— 'Sanctions in International Law' (1960) 54 AJIL 324

Lachs, M, 'The Law In and Of the United Nations' (1960–1) 1 IJIL 429

—— 'Le rôle des organisations internationales dans la formation du droit international' in *Mélanges offerts à Henri Rolin—Problèmes de droit des gens* (Pedone, Paris 1964) 157

Ladwig, B, 'Regelverletzungen im demokratischen Rechtsstaat—Begriffliche und normative Bemerkungen zu Protest, zivilem Ungehorsam und Widerstand' in K Roth and B Ladwig, *Recht auf Widerstand?—Ideengeschichtliche und philosophische Perspektiven* (Universitätsverlag Potsdam, Potsdam 2006) 55

Lagerwall, A, 'Article 64—Convention de 1969' in O Corten and P Klein (eds), *Les Conventions de Vienne sur le droit des traités—Commentaire article par article* (Bruylant, Brussels 2006) 2299

Laker, T, *Ziviler Ungehorsam: Geschichte—Begriff—Rechtfertigung* (Nomos, Baden-Baden 1986)

Laly-Chevalier, C, *La violation du traité* (Bruylant, Brussels 2005)

Lamb, S, 'Legal Limits to United Nations Security Council Powers' in GS Goodwin-Gill and S Talmon (eds), *The Reality of International Law—Essays in Honour of Ian Brownlie* (Clarendon, Oxford 1999) 361

Lapidoth, R, 'Some Reflections on the Law and Practice Concerning the Imposition of Sanctions by the Security Council' (1992) 30 AVR 114

Lauterpacht, E, *Aspects of the Administration of International Justice* (Grotius, Cambridge 1991)

—— 'Judicial Review of the Acts of International Organizations' in L Boisson de Chazournes and P Sands (eds), *International Law, the International Court of Justice and Nuclear Weapons* (CUP, Cambridge 1999) 92

Lauterpacht, H, 'De l'interprétation des traités' (1950) 43-I AIDI 366

—— *The Development of International Law by the International Court* (Stevens and Sons, London 1958)

—— 'The Legal Effects of Illegal Acts of International Organizations' in *Cambridge Essays in International Law—Essays in Honour of Lord McNair* (Stevens and Sons, London 1965) 88

Lavalle, R, 'A Novel, if Awkward, Exercise in International Law-Making: Security Council Resolution 1540 (2004)' (2004) 51 NILR 411

Lavranos, N, 'The Interface between European and National Procedural Law: UN Sanctions and Judicial Review' in idem and D Obradovic (eds), *Interface between EU Law and National Law* (Europa Law Publishing, Groningen 2007) 349

—— 'UN Sanctions and Judicial Review' (2007) 76 NJIL 1

Leben, C, 'Les contre-mesures inter-étatiques et les réactions à l'illicite dans la société internationale' (1982) 28 AFDI 9

Lissitzyn, OJ, *The International Court of Justice—Its Role in the Maintenance of International Peace and Security* (Carnegie Endowment for International Peace, New York 1951)

Lowe, AV, 'Can the European Community Bind the Member-States on Questions of Customary International Law?' in M Koskenniemi (ed), *International Law Aspects of the European Union* (Nijhoff, The Hague 1998) 149

—— 'The Politics of Law-Making: Are the Method and Character of Norm Creation Changing?' in M Byers (ed), *The Role of Law in International Politics—Essays in International Relations and International Law* (OUP, Oxford 2000) 207

—— 'Responsibility for the Conduct of Other States' (2002) 101 JJIL 1

—— *International Law* (OUP, Oxford 2007)

Lysen, G, 'Targeted UN Sanctions: Application of Legal Sources and Procedural Matters' (2003) 72 NJIL 291

Macdonald, RSJ, 'The International Community as a Legal Community' in idem and DM Johnston (eds), *Towards World Constitutionalism: Issues in the Legal Ordering of the World Community* (Nijhoff, Leiden 2005) 853

Macdonald, T and Macdonald, K, 'Non-Electoral Accountability in Global Politics: Strengthening Democratic Control within the Global Garment Industry' (2006) 17 EJIL 89

Mahiou, A, 'Article 2, paragraphe 5' in J-P Cot, A Pellet, and M Forteau (eds), *La Charte des Nations Unies—Commentaire article par article* (3rd edn, Economica, Paris 2005) 467

Malanczuk, P, 'Countermeasures and Self-Defence as Circumstances Precluding Wrongfulness in the International Law Commission's Draft Articles on State Responsibility' (1983) 43 ZaöRV 705

—— 'Zur Repressalie im Entwurf der International Law Commission zur Staatenverantwortlichkeit' (1985) 45 ZaöRV 293

—— 'Reconsidering the Relationship between the ICJ and the Security Council' in WP Heere (ed), *International Law and The Hague's 750th Anniversary* (TMC Asser, The Hague 1999) 87

Malintoppi, A, 'De la notion d'organisation en droit international' in *Recueil d'études de droit international en hommage à Paul Guggenheim* (Tribune, Geneva 1968) 825

Mani, VS, 'Centripetal and Centrifugal Tendencies in the International System: Some Reflections' in RSJ Macdonald and DM Johnston (eds), *Towards World Constitutionalism: Issues in the Legal Ordering of the World Community* (Nijhoff, Leiden 2005) 241

Mann, FA, 'The Consequences of an International Wrong in International and National Law' (1976–7) 48 BYIL 1

Marko, J, 'Challenging the Authority of the UN High Representative before the Constitutional Court of Bosnia and Herzegovina' in E de Wet and A Nollkaemper (eds), *Review of the Security Council by Member States* (Intersentia, Antwerp 2003) 113

Marschik, A, 'Legislative Powers of the Security Council' in RSJ Macdonald and DM Johnston (eds), *Towards World Constitutionalism: Issues in the Legal Ordering of the World Community* (Nijhoff, Leiden 2005) 457

Martenczuk, B, 'The Security Council, the International Court and Judicial Review: What Lessons from Lockerbie?' (1999) 10 EJIL 517

McGoldrick, D, 'State Responsibility and the International Covenant on Civil and Political Rights' in M Fitzmaurice and D Sarooshi (eds), *Issues of State Responsibility before International Judicial Institutions* (Hart, Oxford 2004) 161

McWhinney, E, 'The International Court as Emerging Constitutional Court and the Co-ordinate UN Institutions (Especially the Security Council): Implications of the *Aerial Incident at Lockerbie*' (1992) 30 CYIL 261

—— 'Judicial Wisdom, and the World Court as Special Constitutional Court' in U Beyerlin et al (eds), *Recht zwischen Umbruch und Bewahrung—Festschrift für Rudolf Bernhardt* (Springer, Berlin 1995) 705

Mégret, F, 'A Special Tribunal for Lebanon: The UN Security Council and the Emancipation of International Criminal Justice' (2008) 21 LJIL 485

Mendelson, MH, 'State Acts and Omissions as Explicit or Implicit Claims' in *Le droit international au service de la paix, de la justice et du développement—Mélanges Michel Virally* (Pedone, Paris 1991) 373

—— and Hulton, SC, 'The Iraq-Kuwait Boundary' (1993) 64 BYIL 135

Meng, W, 'Internationale Organisationen im völkerrechtlichen Deliktsrecht' (1985) 45 ZaöRV 324

Meron, T, *Human Rights and Humanitarian Norms as Customary Law* (Clarendon, Oxford 1989)

Messineo, F, 'The House of Lords in *Al-Jedda* and Public International Law: Attribution of Conduct to UN-Authorized Forces and the Power of the Security Council to Displace Human Rights' (2009) 56 NILR 35

Milanović, M, 'An Odd Couple—Domestic Crimes and International Responsibility in the Special Tribunal for Lebanon' (2007) 5 JICJ 1139

—— and Papić, T, 'As Bad As It Gets: The European Court of Human Rights's *Behrami and Saramati* Decision and General International Law' (2009) 58 ICLQ 267

Mindaoudou, DA, 'Le droit de résistance dans les constitutions africaines: un droit illusoire à vocation décorative?' (1995) 7 RADIC 417

Monaco, R, 'Le contrôle dans les organisations internationales' in E Brüel et al (eds), *Internationalrechtliche und Staatsrechtliche Abhandlungen—Festschrift für Walter Schätzel* (Hermes, Düsseldorf 1960) 329

Morange, G, 'Nullité et inexistence en droit international public' in *La technique et les principes du droit public: Études en l'honneur de Georges Scelle*, vol 2 (LGDJ, Paris 1950) 895

Morgenstern, F, 'Legality in International Organizations' (1976–7) 48 BYIL 241

—— *Legal Problems of International Organizations* (Grotius, Cambridge 1986)

Mosler, H, 'Introduction—Problems and Tasks of International Judicial and Arbitral Settlement of Disputes Fifty Years after the Founding of the World Court' in Max Planck Institute for Comparative Public Law and International Law (ed), *Judicial Settlement of International Disputes—An International Symposium* (Springer, Berlin 1974) 3

—— 'The International Society as a Legal Community' (1974) 140 RdC 1

—— 'Supra-National Judicial Decisions and National Courts' (1980–1) 4 HICLR 425

Murphy, WF, 'An Ordering of Constitutional Values' (1980) 53 SoCalLR 703

Niemeyer, HG, *Einstweilige Verfügungen des Weltgerichtshofs, ihr Wesen und ihre Grenzen* (Robert Noske, Leipzig 1932)

Nollkaemper, A, 'Internationally Wrongful Acts in Domestic Courts' (2007) 101 AJIL 760

—— 'The Netherlands' in D Sloss (ed), *The Role of Domestic Courts in Treaty Enforcement—A Comparative Study* (CUP, Cambridge 2009) 326

Nolte, G, 'The Limits of the Security Council's Powers and its Functions in the International Legal System—Some Reflections' in M Byers (ed), *The Role of Law in International Politics—Essays in International Relations and International Law* (OUP, Oxford 2000) 315

O'Connell, ME, 'Debating the Law of Sanctions' (2002) 13 EJIL 63

Oeter, S, 'The International Legal Order and its Judicial Function: Is there an International Community—Despite the Fragmentation of Judicial Dispute Settlement?' in P-M Dupuy et al (eds), *Völkerrecht als Weltordnung: Festschrift für Christian Tomuschat* (NP Engel, Kehl 2006) 583

Oette, L, 'A Decade of Sanctions against Iraq: Never Again! The End of Unlimited Sanctions in the Recent Practice of the UN Security Council' (2002) 13 EJIL 93

Oosthuizen, GH, 'Playing the Devil's Advocate: The United Nations Security Council is Unbound by Law' (1999) 12 LJIL 549

Orakhelashvili, A, 'The Impact of Peremptory Norms on the Interpretation and Application of United Nations Security Council Resolutions' (2005) 16 EJIL 59

—— *Peremptory Norms in International Law* (OUP, Oxford 2006)

—— 'The Acts of the Security Council: Meaning and Standards of Review' (2007) 11 MP UNYB 143

—— '*R (on the application of Al-Jedda) (FC) v Secretary of State for Defence*' (2008) 102 AJIL 337

Osieke, E, '*Ultra Vires* Acts in International Organizations—The Experience of the International Labour Organization' (1976–7) 48 BYIL 259

—— 'Unconstitutional Acts in International Organizations: The Law and Practice of the ICAO' (1979) 28 ICLQ 1

—— 'The Legal Validity of *Ultra Vires* Decisions of International Organizations' (1983) 77 AJIL 239

Osteneck, K, *Die Umsetzung von UN-Wirtschaftssanktionen durch die Europäische Gemeinschaft* (Springer, Berlin 2004)

Paasivirta, E and Kuijper, PJ, 'Does One Size Fit All?: The European Community and the Responsibility of International Organizations' (2005) 36 NYIL 169

—— and Rosas, A, 'Sanctions, Countermeasures and Related Actions in the External Relations of the European Union: a Search for Legal Frameworks' in E Cannizzaro (ed), *The European Union as an Actor in International Relations* (Kluwer, The Hague 2002) 207

Pallis, M, 'The Operation of UNHCR's Accountability Mechanisms' (2005) 37 NYUJILP 869

Papastavridis, E, 'Interpretation of Security Council Resolutions under Chapter VII in the Aftermath of the Iraqi Crisis' (2007) 56 ICLQ 83

Parameswaran, K, 'Der Rechtsstatus des Kosovo im Lichte der aktuellen Entwicklungen' (2008) 46 AVR 172

Partsch, KJ, 'Reprisals' in R Bernhardt (ed), *Encyclopedia of Public International Law*, vol 4 (Elsevier, Amsterdam 2000) 200

—— 'Retorsion' in R Bernhardt (ed), *Encyclopedia of Public International Law*, vol 4 (Elsevier, Amsterdam 2000) 232

Paulus, AL, 'Germany' in D Sloss (ed), *The Role of Domestic Courts in Treaty Enforcement—A Comparative Study* (CUP, Cambridge 2009) 209

Paulus, AL and Müller, J, 'Security Council Resolution 1718 on North Korea's Nuclear Test' (2006) 10 ASIL Insights (3 Nov) available at <http://www.asil.org/insights.cfm>

Pauwelyn, J, 'Enforcement and Countermeasures in the WTO: Rules Are Rules—Towards a More Collective Approach' (2000) 94 AJIL 335

—— *Conflict of Norms in Public International Law—How WTO Law Relates to other Rules of International Law* (CUP, Cambridge 2003)

Payandeh, M, 'Rechtskontrolle des UN-Sicherheitsrates durch staatliche und überstaatliche Gerichte' (2006) 66 ZaöRV 41

Pellet, A, 'Rapport introductif: Peut-on et doit-on contrôler les actions du Conseil de sécurité?' in Société française pour le droit international (ed), *Le Chapitre VII de la Charte des Nations Unies—Colloque de Rennes* (Pedone, Paris 1995) 221

—— 'L'imputabilité d'éventuels actes illicites – Responsabilité de l'OTAN ou des États membres' in C Tomuschat (ed), *Kosovo and the International Community—A Legal Assessment* (Kluwer, The Hague 2002) 193

Pérez Gonzalez, M, 'Les organisations internationales et le droit de la responsabilité' (1988) 92 RGDIP 63

Perrin, G, 'La détermination de l'État lésé: les régimes dissociables et les régimes indissociables' in J Makarczyk (ed), *Theory of International Law at the Threshold of the 21st Century—Essays in Honour of Krzysztof Skubiszewski* (Kluwer, The Hague 1996) 243

Petersmann, E-U, 'How to Reform the UN System? Constitutionalism, International Law, and International Organizations' (1997) 10 LJIL 442

Pfander, JE, 'Government Accountability in Europe: A Comparative Assessment' (2003) 35 GWILR 611

Pfluger, F, *Die einseitigen Rechtsgeschäfte im Völkerrecht* (FG Wil, n/a 1936)

Pisillo Mazzeschi, R, 'Termination and Suspension of Treaties for Breach in the ILC Works on State Responsibility' in M Spinedi and B Simma (eds), *United Nations Codification of State Responsibility* (Oceana, New York 1987) 57

Politakis, GP, 'UN-Mandated Naval Operations and the Notion of Pacific Blockade: Comments on Some Recent Developments' (1994) 6 RADIC 173

Politis, N, 'Le problème des limitations de la souveraineté et la théorie de l'abus des droits dans les rapports internationaux' (1925) 6 RdC 5

—— 'Le régime des représailles en temps de paix' (1934) 38 AIDI 1

Puner, NW, 'Civil Disobedience: An Analysis and Rationale' (1968) NYULR 651

Quigley, J, '*LaGrand:* A Challenge to the US Judiciary' (2002) 27 YJIL 435

Ratner, SR, 'Democracy and Accountability: the Criss-Crossing Paths of Two Emerging Norms' in GH Fox and BR Roth (eds), *Democratic Governance and International Law* (CUP, Cambridge 2000) 449

—— 'The Security Council and International Law' in DM Malone (ed), *The UN Security Council: From the Cold War to the 21st Century* (Lynne Rienner, London 2004) 591

Rawls, J, *A Theory of Justice* (rev edn, OUP, Oxford 1991)

Reinisch, A, *International Organizations before National Courts* (CUP, Cambridge 2000)

—— 'Developing Human Rights and Humanitarian Law Accountability of the Security Council for the Imposition of Economic Sanctions' (2001) 95 AJIL 851

—— 'Governance without Accountability?' (2001) 44 GYIL 275

—— 'Securing the Accountability of International Organizations' (2001) 7 Global Governance 131

——'Verfahrensrechtliche Aspekte der Rechtskontrolle von Organen der Staatengemeinschaft' in R Hofmann, A Reinisch, T Pfeiffer, S Oeter, and A Stadler, *Berichte der Deutschen Gesellschaft für Völkerrecht: Die Rechtskontrolle von Organen der*

Staatengemeinschaft; Vielfalt der Gerichte—Einheit des Prozessrechts?, vol 42 (cf Müller, Heidelberg 2007) 43

—— 'Introduction' in idem (ed), *Challenging Acts of International Organizations before National Courts* (OUP, Oxford 2010) 1

Reisman, WM, 'The Case of the Nonpermanent Vacancy' (1980) 74 AJIL 907

—— 'The Constitutional Crisis in the United Nations' (1993) 87 AJIL 83

—— 'Peacemaking' (1993) 18 YJIL 415

—— and Stevick, DL, 'The Applicability of International Law Standards to United Nations Economic Sanctions Programmes' (1998) 9 EJIL 86

Rensmann, T, 'The Constitution as a Normative Order of Values: The Influence of International Human Rights Law on the Evolution of Modern Constitutionalism' in P-M Dupuy et al (eds), *Völkerrecht als Weltordnung: Festschrift für Christian Tomuschat* (NP Engel, Kehl 2006) 259

Ress, G, 'The Interpretation of the Charter' in B Simma (ed), *The UN Charter: A Commentary* (2nd edn, OUP, Oxford 2002) 13

Rideau, J, *Juridictions internationales et contrôle du respect des traités constitutifs des organisations internationales* (LGDJ, Paris 1969)

Ritter, J-P, 'La protection diplomatique à l'égard d'une organisation internationale' (1962) 8 AFDI 427

Romano, CPR, 'International Organizations and the International Judicial Process: An Overview' in L Boisson de Chazournes et al (eds), *International Organizations and International Dispute Settlement—Trends and Prospects* (Transnational Publishers, Ardsley 2002) 3

Rosand, E, 'The Security Council as "Global Legislator": *Ultra Vires* or Ultra Innovative?' (2005) 28 FILJ 542

Roth, K, 'Geschichte des Widerstandsdenkens—Ein ideengeschichtlicher Überblick' in idem and B Ladwig, *Recht auf Widerstand?—Ideengeschichtliche und philosophische Perspektiven* (Universitätsverlag Potsdam, Potsdam 2006) 7

Roucounas, E, 'Engagements parallèles et contradictoires' (1987) 206 RdC 9

Ruiz Fabri, H, 'Article 66—Convention de 1969' in O Corten and P Klein (eds), *Les Conventions de Vienne sur le droit des traités—Commentaire article par article* (Bruylant, Brussels 2006) 2391

—— 'Article 66—Convention de 1986' in O Corten and P Klein (eds), *Les Conventions de Vienne sur le droit des traités—Commentaire article par article* (Bruylant, Brussels 2006) 2429

Sachariew, K, 'State Responsibility for Multilateral Treaty Violations: Identifying the "Injured State" and its Legal Status' (1988) 35 NILR 273

Sachs, M, 'Artikel 20' in idem (ed), *Grundgesetz Kommentar* (2nd edn, CH Beck, Munich 1999) 743

Sadurska, R and Chinkin, CM, 'The Collapse of the International Tin Council: A Case of State Responsibility?' (1990) 30 VaJIL 845

Salmon, JJA, 'Les Accords Spaak-U Thant du 20 février 1965' (1965) 11 AFDI 468

Sands, P and Klein, P, *Bowett's Law of International Institutions* (6th edn, Sweet & Maxwell/Thomson Reuters, London 2009)

Sano, H-O, 'Good Governance, Accountability and Human Rights' in idem and G Alfredsson (eds), *Human Rights and Good Governance: Building Bridges* (Nijhoff, The Hague 2002) 123

Sari, A, 'Jurisdiction and Responsibility in Peace Support Operations: The *Behrami* and *Saramati* Cases' (2008) 8 HRLR 151

Sarooshi, D, 'The Legal Framework Governing United Nations Subsidiary Organs' (1996) 47 BYIL 413

—— *The United Nations and the Development of Collective Security—The Delegation by the UN Security Council of its Chapter VII Powers* (Clarendon, Oxford 1999)

—— 'The United Nations Collective Security System and the Establishment of Peace' (2000) 53 CLP 621

—— 'Aspects of the Relationship between the International Criminal Court and the United Nations' (2001) 32 NYIL 27

—— 'The Peace and Justice Paradox: The International Criminal Court and the UN Security Council' in D McGoldrick, P Rowe, and E Donnelly (eds), *The Permanent International Criminal Court—Legal and Policy Issues* (Hart, Oxford 2004) 95

—— *International Organizations and their Exercise of Sovereign Powers* (OUP, Oxford 2005)

—— 'The Role of Domestic Public Law Analogies in the Law of International Organizations' (2008) 5 IOLR 237

Sato, T, 'The Legitimacy of Security Council Activities under Chapter VII of the UN Charter since the End of the Cold War' in J-M Coicaud and V Heiskanen (eds), *The Legitimacy of International Organizations* (United Nations University Press, Tokyo 2001) 309

Savarese, E, 'Issues of Attribution to States of Private Acts: Between the Concept of *de facto* Organs and Complicity' (2005) 15 IYIL 111

Scelle, G, *Précis de droit des gens: Principes et systématique*, vol 1 (Sirey, Paris 1932)

Schachter, O, 'Interpretation of the Charter in the Political Organs of the United Nations' in S Engel (ed), *Law, State, and International Legal Order—Essays in Honor of Hans Kelsen* (University of Tennessee Press, Knoxville 1964) 269

—— 'The Quasi-Judicial Role of the Security Council and the General Assembly' (1964) 58 AJIL 959

—— 'International Law in Theory and Practice' (1982) 178 RdC 1

—— 'Self-Help in International Law: US Action in the Iranian Hostages Crisis' (1984) 37 JIA 231

—— *International Law in Theory and Practice* (Nijhoff, Dordrecht 1991)

—— 'The UN Legal Order: An Overview' in CC Joyner (ed), *The United Nations and International Law* (CUP, Cambridge 1997) 3

Scheinin, M, 'State Responsibility, Good Governance and Indivisible Human Rights' in H-O Sano and G Alfredsson (eds), *Human Rights and Good Governance: Building Bridges* (Nijhoff, The Hague 2002)

Scheuner, U, 'Die Rechtsetzungsbefugnis internationaler Gemeinschaften' in FA Freiherr von der Heydte et al (eds), *Völkerrecht und rechtliches Weltbild—Festschrift für Alfred Verdross* (Springer, Vienna 1960) 229

Schilling, T, 'Die "neue Weltordnung" und die Souveränität der Mitglieder der Vereinten Nationen' (1995) 33 AVR 67

—— 'Der Schutz der Menschenrechte gegen Beschlüsse des Sicherheitsrats – Möglichkeiten und Grenzen' (2004) 64 ZaöRV 343

Schlemmer-Schulte, S, 'The World Bank, its Operations, and its Inspection Panel' (1999) 45 RiW 175

—— 'The World Bank Inspection Panel: A Model for other International Organizations?' in NM Blokker and HG Schermers (eds), *Proliferation of International Organizations: Legal Issues* (Kluwer, The Hague 2001) 483

Schlochauer, HJ, *Der Rechtsschutz gegenüber der Tätigkeit internationaler und übernationaler Behörden* (Klostermann, Frankfurt 1952)

Schmalenbach, K, 'International Organizations or Institutions, Legal Remedies against Acts of Organs' in R Wolfrum (ed), *Max Planck Encyclopedia of Public International Law* (OUP, Oxford) available at <http://www.mpepil.com>

Schmidt-Aßmann, E and Möllers, C, 'The Scope and Accountability of Executive Power in Germany' in P Craig and A Tomkins (eds), *The Executive and Public Law: Power and Accountability in Comparative Perspective* (OUP, Oxford 2006) 268

Schreuer, CH, 'The Relevance of United Nations Decisions in Domestic Litigation' (1978) 27 ICLQ 1

Schrijver, N, 'The Future of the Charter of the United Nations' (2006) 10 MP UNYB 1

Schweigman, D, *The Authority of the Security Council under Chapter VII of the UN Charter: Legal Limits and the Role of the International Court of Justice* (Kluwer, The Hague 2001)

Seidl-Hohenveldern, I, 'Die völkerrechtliche Haftung für Handlungen internationaler Organisationen im Verhältnis zu Nichtmitgliedstaaten' (1961) 11 ÖZöR 497

—— 'Access of International Organizations to the International Court of Justice' in AS Muller et al (eds), *The International Court of Justice—Its Future Role after Fifty Years* (Nijhoff, The Hague 1997) 189

Seyersted, F, 'United Nations Forces—Some Legal Problems' (1961) 37 BYIL 351

—— 'Settlement of Internal Disputes of Intergovernmental Organizations by Internal and External Courts' (1964) 24 ZaöRV 1

Shahabuddeen, M, 'Municipal Law Reasoning in International Law' in AV Lowe and M Fitzmaurice (eds), *Fifty Years of the International Court of Justice—Essays in Honour of Sir Robert Jennings* (Grotius, Cambridge 1996) 90

Shany, Y, *National Courts as International Actors: Jurisdictional Implications* (2008–9) available at <http://www.ssrn.com>

Sicilianos, L-A, *Les réactions décentralisées à l'illicite: Des contre-mesures à la légitime défense* (LGDJ, Paris 1990)

—— 'The Relationship between Reprisals and Denunciation or Suspension of a Treaty' (1993) 4 EJIL 341

—— 'L'autorisation par le Conseil de sécurité de recourir à la force: une tentative d'évaluation' (2002) 106 RGDIP 5

—— 'The Classification of Obligations and the Multilateral Dimension of the Relations of International Responsibility' (2002) 13 EJIL 1127

—— 'Sanctions institutionnelles et contre-mesures: tendances récentes' in LP Forlati and L-A Sicilianos (eds), *Les sanctions économiques en droit international* (Nijhoff, Leiden 2004) 3

—— 'La codification des contre-mesures par la Commission du droit international' (2005) 38 RBDI 447

Simma, B, 'From Bilateralism to Community Interest in International Law' (1994) 250 RdC 217

—— 'Reciprocity' in R Bernhardt (ed), *Encyclopedia of Public International Law*, vol 4 (Elsevier, Amsterdam 2000) 30

—— and Pulkowski, D, 'Of Planets and the Universe: Self-contained Regimes in International Law' (2006) 17 EJIL 483

—— and Tams, CJ, 'Article 60—Convention de 1969' in O Corten and P Klein (eds), *Les Conventions de Vienne sur le droit des traités—Commentaire article par article* (Bruylant, Brussels 2006) 2131

Singer, P, 'Civil Disobedience as a Plea for Reconsideration' in HA Bedau (ed), *Civil Disobedience in Focus* (Routledge, London 1991) 122

Skubiszewski, K, 'Remarks on the Interpretation of the United Nations Charter' in R Bernhardt (ed), *Völkerrecht als Rechtsordnung, Internationale Gerichtsbarkeit, Menschenrechte: Festschrift für Hermann Mosler* (Springer, Berlin 1983) 891

Skubiszewski, K, 'The International Court of Justice and the Security Council' in AV Lowe and M Fitzmaurice (eds), *Fifty Years of the International Court of Justice—Essays in Honour of Sir Robert Jennings* (Grotius, Cambridge 1996) 606

Slaughter, A-M, 'The Accountability of Government Networks' (2001) 8 IJGLS 347

van Sliedregt, E, 'The European Arrest Warrant: Between Trust, Democracy and the Rule of Law—Introduction: The European Arrest Warrant: Extradition in Transition' (2007) 3 EuConst 244

Sorel, J-M, 'L'élargissement de la notion de menace contre la paix' in Société française pour le droit international (ed), *Le Chapitre VII de la Charte des Nations Unies—Colloque de Rennes* (Pedone, Paris 1995) 3

—— 'Les arrêts de la CIJ du 27 février 1998 sur les exceptions préliminaires dans les affaires dites de Lockerbie: et le suspense demeure...' (1998) 102 RGDIP 685

Spiropoulos, J, 'Les Nations Unies et le maintien de la Paix' (1948) 1 RHDI 258

Starke, JG, 'Imputability in International Delinquencies' (1938) 19 BYIL 104

Stavropoulos, CA, 'The Practice of Voluntary Abstentions by Permanent Members of the Security Council under Article 27, Paragraph 3, of the Charter of the United Nations' (1967) 61 AJIL 737

Stein, T, 'Die regionale Durchsetzung völkerrechtlicher Verpflichtungen—Europa' (1987) 47 ZaöRV 95

—— 'International Measures against Terrorism and Sanctions by and against Third States' (1992) 30 AVR 38

—— 'Kosovo and the International Community—The Attribution of Possible Internationally Wrongful Acts: Responsibility of NATO or of its Member States?' in C Tomuschat (ed), *Kosovo and the International Community—A Legal Assessment* (Kluwer, The Hague 2002) 181

Steinberger, H, 'The International Court of Justice' in Max Planck Institute for Comparative Public Law and International Law (ed), *Judicial Settlement of International Disputes* (Springer, Berlin 1974) 193

Sunkin, M, 'Judicial Review' in P Cane and J Conaghan (eds), *The New Oxford Companion to Law* (OUP, Oxford 2008) 653

Suy, E, 'Some Legal Questions concerning the Security Council' in I von Münch (ed), *Staatsrecht—Völkerrecht—Europarecht: Festschrift für Hans-Jürgen Schlochauer* (Walter de Gruyter, Berlin 1981) 677

—— 'Article 25' in J-P Cot and A Pellet (eds), *La Charte des Nations Unies: Commentaire article par article* (Economica, Paris 1985) 475

—— 'The Role of the United Nations General Assembly' in H Fox (ed), *The Changing Constitution of the United Nations* (BIICL, London 1997) 55

—— 'Article 53—Convention de 1969' in O Corten and P Klein (eds), *Les Conventions de Vienne sur le droit des traités—Commentaire article par article* (Bruylant, Brussels 2006) 1905

—— and Angelet, N, 'Article 25' in J-P Cot, A Pellet, and M Forteau (eds), *La Charte des Nations Unies—Commentaire article par article* (3rd edn, Economica, Paris 2005) 909

Suzuki, E and Nanwani, S, 'Responsibility of International Organizations: The Accountability Mechanisms of Multilateral Development Banks' (2006) 27 MichJIL 177

Swindells, F, 'UN Sanctions in Haiti: A Contradiction under Articles 41 and 55 of the UN Charter' (1997) 20 FILJ 1878

Szasz, PC, 'Granting International Organizations *Ius Standi* in the International Court of Justice' in AS Muller et al (eds), *The International Court of Justice—Its Future Role after Fifty Years* (Nijhoff, The Hague 1997) 169

Sztucki, J, 'International Organizations as Parties to Contentious Proceedings before the International Court of Justice ?' in AS Muller et al (eds), *The International Court of Justice—Its Future Role after Fifty Years* (Nijhoff, The Hague 1997) 141

Szurek, S, 'La Charte des Nations Unies—Constitution mondiale?' in J-P Cot, A Pellet, and M Forteau (eds), *La Charte des Nations Unies—Commentaire article par article* (3rd edn, Economica, Paris 2005) 29

Talmon, S, 'The Statements by the President of the Security Council' (2003) 2 CJIL 419

—— 'The Constitutive versus the Declaratory Theory of Recognition: *Tertium Non Datur*?' (2004) 75 BYIL 101

—— 'Responsibility of International Organizations: Does the European Community Require Special Treatment?' in M Ragazzi (ed), *International Responsibility Today: Essays in Memory of Oscar Schachter* (Nijhoff, Leiden 2005) 405

—— 'The Security Council as World Legislator' (2005) 99 AJIL 175

—— *Kollektive Nichtanerkennung illegaler Staaten—Grundlagen und Rechtsfolgen einer international koordinierten Sanktion, dargestellt am Beispiel der Türkischen Republik Nord-Zypern* (Mohr Siebeck, Tübingen 2006)

—— 'The Duty Not to "Recognize as Lawful" a Situation Created by the Illegal Use of Force or Other Serious Breaches of a *Jus Cogens* Obligation: An Obligation without Real Substance?' in C Tomuschat and J-M Thouvenin (eds), *The Fundamental Rules of the International Legal Order* (Nijhoff, Leiden 2006) 99

—— 'A Plurality of Responsible Actors: International Responsibility for Acts of the Coalition Provisional Authority in Iraq' in P Shiner and A Williams (eds), *The Iraq War and International Law* (Hart, Oxford 2008) 185

—— 'Security Council Treaty Action' (2009) 62 RHDI 65

—— 'The Responsibility of outside Powers for the Acts of Secessionist Entities' (2009) 58 ICLQ 493

Tammes, AJP, 'Decisions of International Organs as a Source of International Law' (1958) 94 RdC 265

Tams, CJ, 'Consular Assistance: Rights, Remedies and Responsibility: Comments on the ICJ's Judgment in the *LaGrand* Case' (2002) 13 EJIL 1257

—— 'Recognizing Guarantees and Assurances of Non-Repetition: *LaGrand* and the Law of State Responsibility' (2002) 27 YJIL 441

—— *Enforcing Obligations Erga Omnes in International Law* (CUP, Cambridge 2005)

—— 'Enforcement' in G Ulfstein et al (eds), *Making Treaties Work—Human Rights, Environment and Arms Control* (CUP, Cambridge 2007) 391

Thallinger, G, 'Sense and Sensibility of the Human Rights Obligations of the United Nations Security Council' (2007) 67 ZaöRV 1015

Thierry, H, 'Les résolutions des organes internationaux dans la jurisprudence de la Cour internationale de justice' (1980) 167 RdC 385

Thirlway, H, 'The Law and Procedure of the International Court of Justice 1960–1989 (Part Three)' (1991) 62 BYIL 1

Tomkins, A, 'The Struggle to Delimit Executive Power in Britain' in P Craig and A Tomkins (eds), *The Executive and Public Law: Power and Accountability in Comparative Perspective* (OUP, Oxford 2006) 16

Tomuschat, C, 'Repressalie und Retorsion—Zu einigen Aspekten ihrer innerstaatlichen Durchführung' (1973) 33 ZaöRV 179

—— 'International Courts and Tribunals with Regionally Restricted and/or Specialized Jurisdiction' in Max Planck Institute for Comparative Public Law and International Law (ed), *Judicial Settlement of International Disputes—An International Symposium* (Springer, Berlin 1974) 285

—— 'Ein Internationaler Gerichtshof als Element einer Weltfriedensordnung' (1994) 49 Europa Archiv 61

—— 'Die internationale Gemeinschaft' (1995) 33 AVR 1

—— 'The International Responsibility of the European Union' in E Cannizzaro (ed), *The European Union as an Actor in International Relations* (Kluwer, The Hague 2002) 177

—— 'Article 36' in A Zimmermann et al (eds), *The Statute of the International Court of Justice—A Commentary* (OUP, Oxford 2006) 589

—— 'Comment on Cases T-306/01 and T-315/01' (2006) 43 CMLRev 537

Tridimas, T and Gutierrez-Fons, JA, 'EU Law, International Law and Economic Sanctions Against Terrorism: The Judiciary in Distress?' (2008–9) 32 FILJ 660

Tsoutsos, A, 'Le principe de la légalité dans l'ordre juridique international' (1954) 7 RHDI 35

—— 'Judicial Supervision of International Legality' (1963) 16 RHDI 267

Tzanakopoulos, A, 'Attribution of Conduct to International Organizations in Peacekeeping Operations' [2009] EJIL: Talk! (10 March) available at <http://www.ejiltalk.org>

—— 'Chapter VII Measures (UN Charter) (with regard to International Tribunals)' in A Cassese (ed), *The Oxford Companion to International Criminal Justice* (OUP, Oxford 2009) 260

—— 'The UK Supreme Court Quashes Domestic Measures Implementing UN Sanctions' [2010] EJIL: Talk! (23 February) available at <http://www.ejiltalk.org>

—— 'Domestic Court Reactions to UN Security Council Sanctions' in A Reinisch (ed), *Challenging Acts of International Organizations before National Courts* (OUP, Oxford 2010) 54

—— 'United Nations Sanctions in Domestic Courts: From Interpretation to Defiance in *Abdelrazik v Canada*' (2010) 8 JICJ 249

—— 'Article 67' in O Corten and P Klein (eds), *The Vienna Conventions on the Law of Treaties—A Commentary* (OUP, Oxford forthcoming 2011) available at <http://www.ssrn.com>

—— 'Human Rights and UN Security Council Measures' in E de Wet and J Vidmar (eds), *Norm Conflicts and Hierarchy in Public International Law: The Place of Human Rights* (forthcoming 2011) available at <http://www.ssrn.com>

—— 'Judicial Dialogue in Multi-level Governance: the Impact of the *Solange* Argument' in OK Fauchald and A Nollkaemper (eds), *Unity or Fragmentation of International Law: the Role of International and National Tribunals* (Hart, Oxford forthcoming 2011) available at <http://www.ssrn.com>

Ueki, T, 'Responsibility of International Organizations and the Role of the International Court of Justice' in N Ando et al (eds), Liber Amicorum *Judge Shigeru Oda*, vol 1 (Kluwer, The Hague 2002) 237

Uerpmann, R, 'Grenzen zentraler Rechtsdurchsetzung im Rahmen der Vereinten Nationen' (1995) 33 AVR 107

Urbanek, H, 'Das völkerrechtsverletzende nationale Urteil' (1958–9) 9 ÖZöR 213

—— 'Die Unrechtsfolgen bei einem völkerrechtsverletzenden nationalen Urteil; seine Behandlung durch internationale Gerichte' (1961) 11 ÖZöR 70

Valticos, N, 'L'expansion du droit international et le Conseil de sécurité—A la pénible recherche du maintien de la paix' (1996) 43 RYDI 409

Vázquez, CM, 'Judicial Review in the United States and in the WTO: Some Similarities and Differences' (2004) 36 GWILR 587

Venezia, J-C, 'La notion de représailles en droit international public' (1960) 64 RGDIP 465

Verdross, A, 'Jus Dispositivum and Jus Cogens in International Law' (1966) 60 AJIL 55

—— 'Le principe de la non intervention dans les affaires relevant de la compétence nationale d'un État et l'article 2(7) de la Charte des Nations Unies' in *Mélanges offerts à Charles Rousseau—La communauté internationale* (Pedone, Paris 1974) 267

—— and Simma, B, *Universelles Völkerrecht: Theorie und Praxis* (3rd edn, Duncker und Humblot, Berlin 1984)

Verzjil, J, 'La validité et la nullité des actes juridiques internationaux' (1935) 15 RDI 284

Villiger, ME, *Commentary on the 1969 Vienna Convention on the Law of Treaties* (Nijhoff, Leiden 2009)

Virally, M, 'La notion de fonction dans la théorie de l'organisation internationale' in *Mélanges offerts à Charles Rousseau—La communauté internationale* (Pedone, Paris 1974) 277

Voeffray, F, 'Le Conseil de sécurité de l'ONU: gouvernement mondial, législateur ou juge ? Quelques réflexions sur les dangers de dérives' in MG Cohen (ed), *Promoting Justice, Human Rights and Conflict Resolution through International Law—Liber Amicorum Lucius Caflisch* (Nijhoff, Leiden 2007) 1195

Waldock, CHM, 'General Course on Public International Law' (1962) 106 RdC 1

Watson, GR, 'Constitutionalism, Judicial Review, and the World Court' (1993) 34 HILJ 1

Watts, A, 'The International Rule of Law' (1993) 36 GYIL 15

—— 'The International Court of Justice: Efficiency of Procedures and Working Methods—Report of the Study Group Established by the British Institute of International and Comparative Law as a Contribution to the UN Decade of International Law' in DW Bowett et al (eds), *The International Court of Justice—Process, Practice and Procedure* (BIICL, London 1997) 27

Weeramantry, CG, 'The Function of the International Court of Justice in the Development of International Law' (1997) 10 LJIL 309

Weil, P, 'Le droit international en quête de son identité—Cours général de droit international public' (1992) 237 RdC 9

Weiler, JHH, 'The Geology of International Law: Governance, Democracy and Legitimacy' (2004) 64 ZaöRV 547

Wellens, K, 'ILA Committee on Accountability of International Organizations' (1999) 1 ILF 107

—— 'The Primary Model Rules of Accountability of International Organizations: The Principles and Rules Governing their Conduct or the Yardsticks for their Accountability' in NM Blokker and HG Schermers (eds), *Proliferation of International Organizations: Legal Issues* (Kluwer, The Hague 2001) 433

—— *Remedies against International Organizations* (CUP, Cambridge 2002)

—— 'Fragmentation of International Law—Establishing an Accountability Regime for International Organizations: The Role of the Judiciary in Closing the Gap' (2004) 25 MichJIL 1159

Wengler, W, 'Der Begriff des Völkerrechtssubjektes im Lichte der politischen Gegenwart' (1951–3) 51 Die Friedens-Warte 113

Wengler, W, 'Recours judiciaire à instituer contre les décisions d'organes internationaux: Rapport et projet de Résolutions' (1952) 44-I AIDI 224

—— 'Recours judiciaire à instituer contre les décisions d'organes internationaux: Projet revisé de Résolutions avec commentaire' (1954) 45-I AIDI 265

—— 'Recours judiciaire à instituer contre les décisions d'organes internationaux: Matériel d'illustration au projet de Résolutions' (1957) 47-I AIDI 5

Wessel, RA, 'The *Kadi* Case: Towards a More Substantive Hierarchy in International Law?' (2008) 5 IOLR 323

Wheatley, S, 'The Security Council, Democratic Legitimacy and Regime Change in Iraq' (2006) 17 EJIL 531

White, ND, 'The World Court, the WHO and the UN System' in NM Blokker and HG Schermers (eds), *Proliferation of International Organizations: Legal Issues* (Kluwer, The Hague 2001) 85

—— 'Book Review of Erika de Wet *The Chapter VII Powers of the United Nations Security Council*' (2004) 75 BYIL 380

—— 'The Applicability of Economic and Social Rights to the UN Security Council' in MA Baderin and R McCorquodale (eds), *Economic, Social and Cultural Rights in Action* (OUP, Oxford 2007) 89

—— and Abass, A, 'Countermeasures and Sanctions' in MD Evans (ed), *International Law* (2nd edn, OUP, Oxford 2006) 509

Wickremasinghe, C and Verdirame, G, 'Responsibility and Liability for Violations of Human Rights in the Course of UN Field Operations' in C Scott (ed), *Torture as Tort—Comparative Perspectives on the Development of Transnational Human Rights Litigation* (Hart, Oxford 2001) 465

Williams, D, 'Courts and Globalization' (2004) 11 IJGLS 57

Wolfrum, R, 'Article 1' in B Simma (ed), *The UN Charter: A Commentary* (2nd edn, OUP, Oxford 2002) 39

Wood, MC, 'The Interpretation of Security Council Resolutions' (1998) 2 MP UNYB 73

Woods, N, 'Making the IMF and the World Bank More Accountable' (2001) 77 International Affairs 83

—— and Narlikar, A, 'Governance and the Limits of Accountability: the WTO, the IMF, and the World Bank' (2001) 53 ISSL 569

Yee, S, 'The Responsibility of States Members of an International Organization for its Conduct as a Result of Membership or Their Normal Conduct Associated with Membership' in M Ragazzi (ed), *International Responsibility Today: Essays in Memory of Oscar Schachter* (Nijhoff, Leiden 2005) 435

Zacklin, R, 'Responsabilité des organisations internationales' in Société française pour le droit international (ed), *La responsabilité dans le système international—Colloque du Mans* (Pedone, Paris 1991)

Zemanek, K, 'The Unilateral Enforcement of International Obligations' (1987) 47 ZaöRV 32

—— 'Is the Security Council the Sole Judge of its Own Legality?' in E Yakpo and T Boumedra (eds), Liber Amicorum *Judge Mohammed Bedjaoui* (Kluwer, The Hague 1999) 629

—— 'New Trends in the Enforcement of *erga omnes* Obligations' (2000) 4 MP UNYB 1

Ziegler, K, 'Strengthening the Rule of Law, but Fragmenting International Law: The *Kadi* Decision of the ECJ from the Perspective of Human Rights' (2009) 9 HRLR 288

Zimmermann, A, '"Acting under Chapter VII (…)"—Resolution 1422 and Possible Limits of the Powers of the Security Council' in JA Frowein et al (eds), *Verhandeln für den Frieden*—Liber Amicorum *Tono Eitel* (Springer, Berlin 2003) 253

Zoethout, CM, 'Reflections on Constitutionalism in the Netherlands' in eadem et al (eds), *Control in Constitutional Law* (Nijhoff, Dordrecht 1993) 153

Zoller, E, *Peacetime Unilateral Remedies: An Analysis of Countermeasures* (Transnational Publishers, Dobbs Ferry 1984)

—— 'The "Corporate Will" of the United Nations and the Rights of the Minority' (1987) 81 AJIL 610

Zwanenburg, M, *Accountability of Peace Support Operations* (Nijhoff, Leiden 2005)

Index

NB: for page references to cases and other primary authorities, please consult the relevant tables at the beginning of this volume.